DIVIDED
WE STAND

DIVIDED WE STAND

American Jews, Israel, and the Peace Process

OFIRA SELIKTAR

Westport, Connecticut
London

Library of Congress Cataloging-in-Publication Data

Seliktar, Ofira.
    Divided we stand : American Jews, Israel, and the peace process / Ofira Seliktar.
      p. cm.
    Includes bibliographical references (p.) and index.
    ISBN 0–275–97408–1 (alk. paper)
      1. Jews—United States—Attitudes toward Israel. 2. Arab-Israeli
conflict—1993—Peace—Foreign public opinion, American. 3. Israel—Foreign public
opinion, American. 4. Jews—United States—Politics and government—20th century. 5.
Public opinion—Jews. 6. Public opinion—United States. 7. Israel and the diaspora. I.
Title.
E184.J5 S42   2002
956.05'3—dc21   2001057731

British Library Cataloguing in Publication Data is available.

Library of Congress Catalog Card Number: 2001057731
ISBN: 0–275–97408–1

First published in 2002

Praeger Publishers, 88 Post Road West, Westport, CT 06881
An imprint of Greenwood Publishing Group, Inc.
www.praeger.com

Printed in the United States of America

The paper used in this book complies with the
Permanent Paper Standard issued by the National
Information Standards Organization (Z39.48–1984).

10 9 8 7 6 5 4 3 2 1

To My Sons, Yaron and Dror

Contents

Abbreviations

ACLU	American Civil Liberties Union
ACRI	Association for Civil Rights in Israel
ADL	Anti-Defamation League
AFSI	Americans for a Safe Israel
AIPAC	American Israel Public Affairs Committee
AJC	American Jewish Committee
AJCongress	American Jewish Congress
AJPS	American Jewish Population Survey
APN	Americans for Peace Now
ARZA	Association of Reform Zionists of America
AWACS	Airborne Warning and Control System
CAMERA	Committee for Accuracy in Middle East Reporting in America
CCAR	Central Conference of American Rabbis
CDI	Center for Defense Information
CDM	Coalition for Democratic Majority
CIA	Central Intelligence Agency
CIPAC	Christian Israel Public Action Campaign
CJF	Council of Jewish Federations
CLAL	National Jewish Center for Learning and Leadership
CLIP	Collegiate Leadership Internship Program

CONAME	Committee on New Alternatives in the Middle East
CNFMP	Coalition for a New Foreign and Military Policy
DOP	Declaration of Principles
ECE	Experiment in Congregational Education
FLAME	Facts and Logic About the Middle East
GNP	gross national product
IDF	Israel Defense Forces
IFCJ	International Fellowship of Christians and Jews
IMRA	Independent Media Review & Analysis
IPF	Israel Policy Forum
IPS	Institute for Policy Studies
IRIS	Information Regarding Israel's Security
JCPA	Jewish Council for Public Affairs
JDL	Jewish Defense League
JINSA	Jewish Institute for National Security Affairs
JPL	Jewish Peace Lobby
MCPL	Members of Congress for Peace through Law
MEMRI	Middle East Media Research Institute
MEPFA	Middle East Peace Facilitation Act
MFN	most favored nation
MFO	Multinational Force and Observers
MK	member of Knesset
MOU	Memorandum of Understanding
NATO	North Atlantic Treaty Organization
NCC	National Council of Churches
NCRAC	National Community Relations Advisory Council
NIF	New Israel Fund
NJA	New Jewish Agenda
NJC	National Jewish Coalition (now Republican Jewish Coalition)
NJCRAC	National Jewish Community Relations Advisory Council
NJPS	National Jewish Population Survey
NSAJ	National Survey of American Jews
NSC	National Security Council-Israel
ONAD	Overseas Needs Assessment and Distribution Committee
PA	Palestinian Authority
PACs	political action committees
PAM	Peace Accord Monitoring

PEF/IEF	Palestine Endowment Fund/Israel Endowment Fund
PEJE	Partnership for Excellence in Jewish Education
PLO	Palestine Liberation Organization
PN	Peace Now
RDF	Rapid Deployment Force
SOIL	Save Our Israeli Homeland
STAR	Synagogue Transformation and Renewal
UAHC	Union of American Hebrew Congregations
UIA	United Israel Appeal
UJA	United Jewish Appeal
UJC	United Jewish Communities
VAT	Victims of Arab Terror International
WCI	Word Committee for Israel
WJC	World Jewish Congress
WZC	World Zionist Congress
WZO	World Zionist Organization
ZOA	Zionist Organization of America

Introduction: American Jewish Identity, the Perceptions of the State of Israel, and the Peace Process

This book seeks to analyze the impact of the peace process on the American Jewish community and its relations with Israel. For some three decades after the establishment of the state of Israel it was customary to argue that American Jewry had almost unanimously supported its foreign policy. In fact, a corollary observation held that support for Israel had become the only issue that could reliably unite the community and overcome numerous internal differences. More recently, observers have noted that not only had this reflexive support vanished, but also the community had become deeply divided with regard to Israel. As one observer put it, "far from unifying American Jews, Israel divides them on both political and religious ground."[1]

In order to understand why the peace process has turned into an agent of polarization, a discussion of the complex relations between the American Jewish Diaspora and Israel is in order. It is argued that this relationship is driven by the changing identity needs of American Jews, which affect the perception of Israel and its foreign policy. A groundbreaking study on diasporas, defined as "ethnic minority groups of migrant origins residing and acting in host countries" concluded that the interactions of such groups with their "homelands" or "countries of origin" is mediated by the perceived attitudes of the host societies toward the ethnic groups. A good starting point for the analysis of this triadic relationship is the examination of the motivation of the ethnic group for maintaining relations with its homeland. Indeed, such an approach is most pertinent in regard to American Jews for whom Israel is more than a homeland in the straightforward theoretical sense of the model.[2]

Scholars have long argued that because of their highly mobile existence in the Diaspora, Jews had created a religious culture based on time. Elazur described it as "shared temporal rhythm rather than rootedness in a common land." To fill their yearning for space, the land of Israel "reminded a vitally important territory for them," one "to which they expected to be restored to at the appropriate time."[3] Despite the creation of the state of Israel, the vast majority of American Jews elected to stay in the United States, making it necessary to redefine their connection to the spatial dimension. Such a modification was especially necessary because, by the beginning of the twentieth century, the vast majority of the community was secularized and liberal. Out of the need to accommodate such disparate elements of identity, the perceptions of Israel as both a symbol of Jewish ethnoreligious particularism and secularized universalism had emerged.

Investing Israel with dual symbolism solved another problem for American Jews, which, as any other ethnic minority, needed to reconcile its attachment and activity on behalf of the "homeland" with norms and practices of the host society. Envisioning Israel as the only liberal and Western-type democracy in the Middle East enabled the community to claim total congruence with domestic and foreign policy goals of the United States. According to the Diaspora study, "undesirable conflicts" with the norms of a host country can lead to feelings of cognitive dissonance and allegations of dual loyalty.[4] Equally important, the self-image projected by Israel as a progressive country poised to become a "light to the gentiles" had fitted neatly with the perceptions of American Jews. To the extent that the Middle East conflict was incorporated into such perceptions, it tended to reinforce American Jewish expectations of Israel. An embattled homeland fighting wars of self-defense against an overwhelming Arab enemy bent on its destruction provided the necessary moral clarity to sustain the attachment. Even better, the security of the Jewish state became a source of mobilization and unity of the Diaspora on behalf of the homeland. As one historian put it, "if a home country is attacked and is fighting a war perceived as defensive, the Diaspora community is likely to 'rally around the flag.' "[5] Starting with the collection of funds, communal mobilization came to include pressure on the U.S. government to assist Israel and a vigorous advocacy and public relations effort to explain Israeli foreign policy needs. Soon after, "working on behalf of Israel became a principle expression of Jewishness" in a community whose growing secularization and assimilation left precious few expressions of commonality.[6]

The perceived congruence in the triadic relationship between American Jews, Israel, and the United States reached a peak after the Six Day War. Alarmed by the demographic attrition, the community searched for a new formula for Jewish identity for its secularized members, which lead to the development of a civil religion whose focal point was Israel. The underlying hope was that, by revitalizing attenuated Jewish identity, the "Israeli connection" would reverse the twin evils of Jewish demography, high rates of assimilation, and a decline in voluntary endogamy. The widespread perception of Israel's heroic performance during the war had also dovetailed nicely with the newly acquired ethnic pride of American Jews, a reflection of the general transition to an ethnically based multicultural ethos that replaced the founding melting pot ideology. Clinching the triadic fit was the high rating Israel received in the wake of the 1967 war from the host population and a growing conviction that Israel served as an American strategic asset in the Middle East.

That such rare congruence could not last long became evident soon after the Yom Kippur War. The realization that Israel could not evolve into a transferable source of Jewish identity for many in the community, and especially the younger generation, triggered a new debate about how best to fight demographic attrition. While the liberal and secularized segment of American Jewry advocated a return to a prophetic-universalist Jewish identity, the ethnonationalists continued to base their identity on a total identification with the state of Israel. Adding to the mix was a resurgent Judaism derived from the tenets of orthodoxy.

The split in the Jewish community coincided with the victory of the hard-line Likud party whose vision of Greater Israel had dramatically changed Israel's handling of the peace process. The morally complex problems of fighting an offensive war in Lebanon and the treatment of the Palestinian population had polarized American Jews. Whereas the "prophecists-universalists" judged Israel through the prism of Western values of human rights and conflict resolution, the nationalists defined their Judaism through a number of litmus tests, such as the retention of the West Bank, the Golan Heights, and the indivisibility of Jerusalem. For the majority of the Orthodox who subscribed to the tenets of religious Zionism, the retention of territories, referred to by their Hebrew names of Judea and Samaria, was a necessary step in the process of Redemption.

Further complicating matters were the changes in American attitudes toward the Middle East peace process. The Likud policy provoked sharp criticism known to trigger cognitive dissonance in an ethnic minority, and the frequent conflicts between American administrations and successive Likud governments threatened the more liberal secularists with the specter of double loyalty. This segment of the community was also most reluctant to enter into an alliance with the conservative Republicans and evangelical Christians who replaced liberal Democrats as the segment of the American electorate most supportive of Israel. In fact, the debate about whether American Jews should help bolster the congressional strength of the conservatives for the sake of Israel became as divisive as the perceptions of Israel's handling of the peace process.

The Oslo accord and the subsequent efforts of the Labor governments to negotiate a final end to the Arab-Israeli conflict had resulted in a new reconfiguration of the triadic relationship. Mirroring the bitter cleavages in Israel, American Jewry split into warring camps of Oslo proponents and opponents at a time when the secularized segment of the community embarked upon yet another redefinition of Jewish identity in which Israel became noticeably more marginal. The indifference and collapse of communal consensus gave those deeply committed to the competing visions of Israel a free hand in appealing directly to kindred sentiments in American foreign policy. As these complex and mutually reinforcing divisions in the three foci of the triad play out, Israel may turn into a permanent symbol of communal disunity.

In spite of its obvious advantages, tracking the ever-changing triadic relation is not easy since it involves an interactive analysis of real-time events in Israeli and American foreign policy, identity driven attitudinal factors, and the more amorphous ideational changes. To capture the latter two this work will use a combination of survey data and the increasingly popular methodology of communal discourse analysis. As formalized by Giandomenico Majone, such analysis focuses on the writings of academics, journalists, and polemicists in the community. The discursive community approach is derived heavily from public writings, public interviews and even paid advertising which various group in the community use to influence each other, to gain legitimacy or influence policy.[7]

The organization of this book reflects the theoretical outline developed above. The eight chapters provide chronological-thematic discussion of the relations between the identity needs of American Jews, the perception of Israel and the peace process, and the inputs of American foreign policy. The concluding chapter analyzes the patterns formed because of this interaction and assesses the future.

DIVIDED
WE STAND

1

Warming Up to the Jewish State

Prior to Word War II, American Jews showed little enthusiasm for the idea of Jewish statehood in Palestine. Reflecting broad historical trends, only the small Zionist minority advocated Jewish sovereignty. To the large Reform denomination preoccupied with acculturation into American society, a Jewish state represented regression to a "primitive" ethnic past and a threat of double loyalty. A small but vocal anti-Zionist group warned about the grave dangers to Judaism should Jews succeed in establishing a state of their own. Orthodox Jews were vehemently opposed to what they perceived as the secular way in which the incipient state was founded.

However, the Holocaust changed the terms of the debate. Confronted by the enormous suffering of their European brethren and faced with the problem of displaced persons, the majority of American Jews embraced the idea of a Jewish state. The newly found popularity of Zionism was reflected in the fact that a large number of Jews in the United States became involved in political support for Zionist causes. There was widespread rejoicing when Israel was established in 1948. Despite these seemingly sincere feelings, American Jews were slow to warm up to the new state. As indicated in the introductory chapter, the relations between the Diaspora and the "home" state were filtered through a complex triadic relationship at the center of which stood the identity needs of American Jews. Newly upwardly mobile and eager to integrate into the wider society, the community had to balance the task of their newly found Americanism with the tribal pull of the "ancestral-state."

THE RUSH TO THE SUBURBS AND JEWISH IDENTITY:
THE INTEGRATIONIST IMPERATIVE

Traditional Judaism has been described as an amalgam of religious and eth-nocultural elements, sometimes referred to as "tribal markers." In addition to following a body of theological prescripts, Jews have also defined themselves as a "people," whose boundary was delineated by common ancestry, a shared history, and common cultural heritage. While successfully sustaining the com-munity through history, this amalgam had begun to unravel under the impact of modernity. In a switch to what was seen as the more "respectable" religious definition, the German Reform Movement in the nineteenth century was the first to discard the more tribal aspects of Jewish identity. In the United States, where German Reformers made a strong impact, this trend was temporarily reversed when millions of East European Jews arrived at the turn of the century. Their traditional Jewish identity, a blend of religion and ethnicity, was preserved through intense social interaction in the ghettoes of large American cities.

However, these bonds were challenged when, after the end of World War II, the American-born children of the immigrants profited from a dramatic rise in socioeconomic status. In what amounted to a second mass migration, they moved to the suburbs, where numerous synagogues and a multitude of com-munal organizations soon sprouted. So vigorous was the effort of creating a Jewish infrastructure that academic and lay observers at the time saw in this new "Golden Ghetto" an assurance of Jewish continuity for generations to come. A number of early surveys supported the hope that Jews, in spite of their geo-graphical dispersion, would continue the pattern of close and intense personal contacts that had ensured Jewish survival in the past. In one study, respondents reported that, by and large, they tend to associate with each other; while pleasant, contacts with gentile neighbors and coworkers were superficial. There was also little indication of intermarriage and other forms of ethnic disaffiliation.[1]

To the more theoretically oriented scholars, such behavior indicated that Jews felt a strong sense of "belonginess" to the community and that they accepted this tie as a positive and meaningful element in their identity.[2] More important, analyzed in terms of identity structure, American Jews seemed to be equally at ease in relating to the religious and peoplehood or tribal components of their identity. This alleged balance was said to translate into a delicately defined equilibrium between the integrationist and survivalist imperatives. In the lan-guage of minority psychology, the former is shorthand for the group's desire to shed its particularistic characteristics and absorb the value system of the host society. The latter denotes the equally compelling urge to retain the traditional heritage.

In spite of the early optimism that American Jewry would be able to perform such an exquisite balancing act, signs that assimilation may win out soon began to appear. A study of Jewish adolescents found that there was a decline in ritual observance, a rise in skepticism, and a marked antipathy toward ethnoreligious particularism, the hallmark of traditional Judaism. The respondents rejected the concept of "Chosen People" and other elements of group distinctiveness in favor of egalitarianism and democracy. Marshall Sklare's famous 1958 Lakeville study of an affluent Jewish suburb near Chicago was even more revealing. Sklare found that the religious rituals that were most commonly retained by the Jews he interviewed required relatively little effort, did not demand isolation or a unique lifestyle, and only marginally impinged on social and economic mobility of the individual. For instance, attending a Passover dinner or lighting candles on Hanukkah were very popular, but observing Sabbath and dietary laws were marginal. More telling, the divine and miraculous elements of the holidays were discarded in favor of a universalistic-secular focus on man's "unquenchable desire for freedom." In a sign of religious skepticism some respondents claimed that belief in God should be "supplemented by ethics." Sklare viewed such a reinterpretation of traditional tenets as more in harmony with "secular components" of American life, leading him and other observers to claim that suburban Judaism was essentially a "social synagogue" phenomenon known as a "shul with a pool."[3]

A highly popular book by Will Herberg, *Protestant, Catholic, Jew*, gave a sociological "seal of approval" to the notion that postwar Jewish identity should be defined in religious terms alone. Herberg, a fixture on the synagogue lecture circuit, argued that Judaism, as refined by midcentury American sensibilities, is part of a religious triad that reflects the dominant religious values of the United States, along with the Protestant and Catholic faiths. Some critics such as Melvin I. Urofsky chastised Herberg for purging Judaism of its ethnic-tribal characteristics. Eugene Borowitz wrote that Jews turned their survival skills to "comport themselves so that might be undistinguishable from genuine, Protestant Americans." But Herberg's vision of a "sanitized" Jewish identity endured because, as Edward Shapiro pointed out, the survivalists' fear that "Jewish suburbanization would result in assimilation" was overshadowed by the desire for "normalization" accompanied by a large dose of denial that a conflict between the two existed.[4]

It was left to Charles Liebman to explain that this denial was part of the ambivalence built into American Jewish identity. In his groundbreaking book *The Ambivalent American Jew*, Liebman argued that a majority of Jews "were torn" between the "desire for acceptance" by the host society and the desire "for group identity and survival as a distinct community." Liebman and others listed several manifestations of this ambivalence. As part of their conviction that Jews should be treated as "though Jewishness does not exist," American Jews were highly pleased when told "that they don't look Jewish or behave Jewishly." At the same time they were "scandalized" by intermarriage and other forms of societal inclusiveness. The insistence that Jewishness should not be used as a criterion by the larger society, clashed with an "outrage" over the fact that the State Department discriminated against Jews in its hiring policies.[5]

Reluctant to make a choice between the integrationist-survivalist alternatives, suburban Jews found it hard to legitimate institutions of ethnic or national ex-clusiveness. Hence, there was a rush to embrace the more socially acceptable notion of religious identity, but even here Liebman found a strong effort to "universalize" the creed and give it an Enlightenment patina. At its core was a belief in the capacity of the human intellect to create a progressive cosmopolitan society with a strong commitment to social welfare. Indeed, some early 1950's surveys showed that respondents defined a "good Jew" in terms of support for humanitarian causes. Such universalizing was especially attractive to those who searched for compatibility between Judaism and Americanism. Numerous ob-servers commented on the "proclivity to universalize the Jewish message and present it in an ecumenical American idiom." As Auorbach noted, it was tempt-ing to assume that "the Hebrew Bible was a preliminary draft of the American constitution [sic], that the Hebrew prophets were founding fathers of American liberalism."[6]

This ambivalent Jewish American identity had important implications for the relations between the community and the newly created state of Israel. In fact, Jewish sovereignty presented American Jews bent on pursuing the integrationist imperative with a considerable dilemma.

THE MEANING OF ISRAEL: THE MYTH AND REALITY OF THE JEWISH STATE

The voluminous literature on the meaning of Israel for American Jews attests to the complexity of the issue. There is little doubt that, in its essence, the relationship has been construed around the tribal or peoplehood component of identity. For most American Jews the establishment of the state after the trauma of the Holocaust was a manifestation of the continuity of the Jewish people across time and space. As Urofsky put it, "it was a partial recompose" for the Holocaust, a meaning giving event to what was an utterly cosmological catas-trophe." Israel's birth amidst what was seen as a valiant war of independence was also significant. It was perceived as an answer to the historical lack of power and passivity epitomized by the yellow star and the horror of the exter-mination camps. "The new Jew, the Israeli born and raised in freedom . . . would be the hero to whom American Jews could proudly point out," restoring their dignity and self-assurance. The new Israeli Jew was "far removed from the ghetto-victim stereotype of the past." This imagery indicated that support for Israel and preoccupation with the Holocaust stemmed from the common root of the "beleaguered nature of Jewish existence."[7]

Closely related to the symbolic aspects of peoplehood was the very real fact that the new state provided a haven for Jewish refugees from Eastern Europe, the Middle East, and elsewhere. Well before 1948, American Jews, secure in their adopted homeland, demonstrated a philanthropic interest in creating a ref-uge in Palestine. After the Holocaust, this sentiment was enhanced greatly by the realization that all Jews could face a harsh contingency someday, somewhere. Betraying this self-interest, the new reasoning was that there must be a Jewish homeland, "at least for everybody else and, God forbid, us too." The concept of Israel-as-refuge was strongly manifested in American Jewish distaste for Israeli immigrants to the United States. One study found that the latter were treated with a "mixture of suspicion, coolness, and even condemnations" since they seemed to detract from the almost "sacred status" of Israel as a refuge.[8]

Even without the legacy of the Holocaust, a Jewish state would have appealed to the ethnic-national part of the Jewish identity. It normalized the status of Jews in America and put them on an equal footing with Irish, Italian, or Polish immigrants. Cardin wrote that "Israel gave us stature and status" and Dershowitz commented that since 1948 Jews were treated as "truly first class citizens in a non-Jewish state." This normalization went beyond the nostalgia for a home, a "heim," or an "ancestral" place to visit in lieu of czarist Russia or anti-Semitic Poland, as some sociologists have claimed. Ontologically, it transformed the Jewish condition and gave meaning to what the philosopher Emil Fackenheim called the "unauthentic position of the Jews."[9]

Despite its obvious advantages, the Jewish state generated a certain amount of psychological unease in a community that defined its identity largely in religious-integrationist terms. Scholars have pointed out that in order to cope with such contradictions American Jews had to idealize and universalize the Israeli experience. Jonathan Sarna, a leading authority on American Judaism, asserted that Israel was perceived as a "model state" where the American ideal of democracy of social justice and of liberty reign. He added that, for the most part, these images "spoke to the needs of American Jews and reflected their ideas and fantasies rather than contemporary realities . . . of Israel." Early Jewish guidebooks invited tourists to experience their own "Wild West of the 1880s" or the growing pain of young America freeing itself "from British law," adding that barely after a decade Israel displayed "its Yankee ways."[10]

A number of observers noted that by envisioning Israel as "an ideological extenuation of American liberalism in the Middle East," Jews could equate Zionism with "good Americanism." Significantly, Israel was favored mostly as an embattled democracy; "the Jewish state flickered only dimly as a source of indifference or unease." So strong was this need that American Jews came to see Jewish nationalism "as destined to the realization of a set of enlightened universalistic values." This "mission ideology" helped to bring the "Zionist vision of Israel into significant accord with the ethos of American people. In the words of one liturgical text, "praying for the peace of Jerusalem is the same as praying for the unity of all humanity and peace throughout the world."[11] The urge to Americanize and universalize Israel was also reflected in the root metaphors constructed by the community to depict the Jewish state. One study listed the most prevalent metaphors as "haven," "pioneers," "democracy," "westernized," and "asset to America." Steven M. Cohen, a leading expert on American Jewish public opinion, identified additional images like "industrious," "vibrant," "progressive," and "idealistic." Help for Israel was equated with loyalty to America and a fight for democracy "in the feudal Middle East."[12]

Perhaps most telling was the immense popularity of *Exodus*, a book by Leon Uris depicting the heroic yet civilized struggle for Israel's independence. The movie version of the novel in which the conveniently blond, blue-eyed Paul Newman played the lead role of Ari Ben Canaan, assumed an iconic status in the community. Even though critics argued that Ben Cannan "stands in roughly the same relation to [the] reality of Israel as Scarlett O'Hara, Rhett Buttler to the American Civil War," such constructs were important to American Jewry. They provided comfort, reassurance and, above all, the rationalization needed to protect the community from choosing between the values of integration and tribal attachment.[13]

Maintaining an idealized image of Israel also relieved the U.S. Diaspora from seeking factual knowledge about its reality. Indeed, early polls indicated high levels of affective attachment, but only limited cognitive understanding of the state. A 1945 national Roper poll of Jews and a 1948 survey of Baltimore Jews found overwhelming support for the establishment of the state and a concern for its survival and success. Baltimore Jews had also supported all forms of assistance to the new state, including American aid. However, the Lakeville study found no correlation between emotional attachment and intellectual knowledge of the sample. Beyond generalities, few were well-informed on the specifics of the situation in Palestine, including the names of such prominent military organizations as the Haganah. The Lakeville study showed a similar pattern. Some 90 percent of the respondents claimed they would feel a sense of loss if Israel was destroyed and a majority supported political and economic aid. But few demonstrated any cognitive interest in Israeli politics or society beyond an increase in the use of Israeli-made ornaments and souvenirs for home decorations. Only 8 percent attempted to study Hebrew, and the same percentage reported listening to radio and television programs about Israel; a miniscule 2 percent said they attended lectures or study groups pertaining to Israel.[14]

The same affective-cognitive disparity manifested itself in a study of over 1,100 adolescents from the B'nai B'rith Youth Organization conducted in 1959. Some 76 percent felt that Israel is the "most wonderful event" in Jewish history, and 84 percent indicated a considerable "degree of unhappiness" over the possibility that Israel may be destroyed. Yet the vast majority of the teenagers were poorly informed about Israel and showed no desire to learn more about the cultural riches of the new state. Such results were particularly disappointing to those who felt that Israel would become a cultural center for Diaspora Jewry in the sense envisioned by Ahad Ha'am (a Jewish philosopher who envisioned the Jewish state as a cultural center for Jews). Urofsky noted that, thought analysts searched "pathetically," it became clear that, apart from "surface artifacts of Israeli life" few American Jews were willing to "base their lives on Israeli standards." Needless to say, almost no one was eager to fulfill the Zionist tenet of aliya (immigration). The Baltimore study respondents indicated that they had no desire to leave America, which they considered home. In the Lakeville survey only 1 percent of the sample agreed that American Jews should immigrate to Israel or encourage their children to do so; in the B'nai B'rith study less than 1 percent felt the same way.[15]

There were some who decried what Cohen called the "undifferentiated, uniform, and stereotype images of Israelis." A participant in a *Commentary* symposium on Jewish identity complained about "our obsession" with the Jew "armed, blond and blue eyed," investing him, as it was, with "some of the attributes of our tormentors." Others argued that, far from being a model state, Israel is affected with "racial bigotry," "political machination," "excess of nationalism," and "cultural fundamentalism." Taking this argument one step further, one panelist wrote that Israel "represents many incompatible values" and called on the Jewish state to "sacrifice its national interest" for the sake of "world peace and social justice."[16]

Yet it was David Ben-Gurion who presented the most serious challenge to the affective-behavioral dissonance of the community. Evoking the classic Zionist tenet that Jewish life in the Diaspora is necessarily inferior and prone to the dangers of assimilation, Ben-Gurion castigated American Jews for their failure to immigrate to Israel. The Israeli prime minister accused American Jews of practicing "armchair Zionism" and called upon Zionist leaders to provide an example by making aliya. This and other frictions presented enough of a reality to prompt the U.S. Diaspora to develop more effective institutions for relating to the Jewish state. Such an endeavor was not easy since the new community failed to coalesce around a single vision of Zionism, making it a "house divided."[17]

INSTITUTIONALIZING THE ISRAELI CONCERNS: THE CONFERENCE OF PRESIDENTS AND THE AMERICAN ISRAEL PUBLIC AFFAIRS COMMITTEE

Interest group theory emphasizes the importance of group cohesion in influencing the political process. Such cohesion allows leaders to speak for the group and gives legitimacy to its goals. However, reflecting historical fissures in U.S. Jewry, attempts to unite on the issue of Palestine/Israel fell short of the theoretical expectations. The American Jewish Conference convened in 1943 to debate the role of American Jews in the postwar period; it opened amid tension over the prospects of a sovereign Jewish state in Palestine. The American Jewish Committee (AJC), reflecting the Reform view of universalistic Judaism, was apprehensive about double loyalty. AJC representatives walked out of the conference, charging the Zionists with failure to keep the issue of Palestine off the agenda. The American Council for Judaism, which was vehemently opposed to a Jewish state in Palestine, supported the AJC's position.

The issue of Holocaust survivors in Europe further inflamed the rift. The AJC worked hard to relax U.S. immigration laws as a way of solving the Jewish refuge problem, but the Zionists argued that the survivors were entitled to a state in Palestine. Exasperated, the AJC and the council implied that the Zionists, in their zeal to establish a Jewish state, sabotaged all alternative plans to find a haven for the displaced persons and even coerced them to choose Palestine. The foundation of Israel in 1948 rendered most of these disputes academic, but consensus had eluded the numerous Jewish organizations that were called to develop pro-Israeli policies. The National Community Relations Advisory Council (NCRAC), which was established in 1944 as an umbrella organization of the local federations (it was renamed NJCRAC in 1971 when the term Jewish was added), avoided potential division by focusing on domestic issues. Up to the midfifties Israel was either not mentioned in its Joint Program Plan or was referred to in vague platitudes.[18]

In the absence of a working consensus, the community found it difficult to handle the urgent need to institutionalize philanthropic aid to Israel. In 1950, leaders of the Council of Jewish Federations (CJF)went to Israel to set up a framework for charitable contributions, including the establishment of Israel Bonds. Because of American tax laws, most of the funds were raised by the United Jewish Appeal (UJA) and funneled to the United Israel Appeal (UIA), which funded the Jewish Agency. The politicized nature of the agency irritated some American Jewish groups, which questioned the allocation of funds. The Zionist Organization of America (ZOA) was unhappy with the fact that Ben-Gurion's Mapai ("Labor") party received more money than the right-wing General Zionist party. The Mizrachi Organization of America and Agudat Israel, two Orthodox groups, protested that the agency helped finance the secular-socialist educational system in Israel.[19]

The problem of redefining Zionism was even more vexing. Borowitz explained that Ben-Gurion's call to make aliya made most American Jews anxious. Not only was their discrepancy between attitude and behavior exposed, but it also raised the specter of double loyalty. The problem became so acute that Jacob Blaustein, the president of the AJC, negotiated an agreement with the Israeli prime minister in 1951 whereby Israel and American Jews promised not to interfere in each other's affairs. In spite of agreement, Israeli leaders went on to demand that American Zionists act upon their convictions and immigrate. At the World Zionist Congress in 1951 Ben-Gurion, declared that American Zionism was "bankrupt." Ten years later he shocked American Jewry by declaring that there can be no meaningful cultural, or even religious, life in the Diaspora. Interestingly, the plea for aliya went beyond Zionist ideology and was rooted in Israeli's desperate efforts to attract Western Jews. The new state hoped to balance the absorption of thousands of refugees from Arab countries with better-educated American Jews. As one high-ranking Israeli official admitted: "I would give you ten Arab Jews for one American Jew." American Jews, long sensitive to accusations that their commitment to Israel was largely verbal, charged Ben-Gurion with interference that violated the Blaustein accord. The president of

Mizrachi went so far as to urge Ben-Gurion to stop the "cold war against American Zionists."[20]

Finding the right balance in the relationship was also necessary because of the bitterness generated when different factions in the community attempted to influence the political system in Israel. The battle came to a head when some pro-Labor organizations accused the ZOA of trying to defeat the Mapai coalition, eliciting a countercharge that the U.S. Labor camp exceeded the boundaries of proper involvement in Israeli politics. In spite of heated debates, the American Zionist Council could not define what constituted a "proper interest" in Israeli affairs. This failure gave later legitimacy to the efforts of different groups to influence the peace process and even shape the Jewish state. Perhaps the greatest impediment to unity stemmed from the fact that, in trying to influence American foreign policy toward Israel, the community spoke with many voices. Particularly worrisome to many American Jews was the staunchly anti-Zionist American Council for Judaism, whose executive director Elmer Berger developed close ties with the Eisenhower administration. To counter this influence and facilitate communication with the administration, which was seen as hostile to Israeli interests, presidents of sixteen organizations decided in 1954 to meet informally to coordinate policies on Israel. This impromptu arrangement proved itself inadequate when the community tried to dissuade President Dwight D. Eisenhower and his secretary of state, John Foster Dulles, from pressuring Israel in the aftermath of the Sinai Campaign of 1956. The community was particularly dismayed when Dulles met in February 1957 with a delegation of mostly non-Zionist leaders. In 1959, the Conference of Presidents of Major Jewish Organizations, also known as the Presidents Conference, was formally constituted, adopting, among others, the majority rule of decision making. To assure a wide representation, the Conference agreed to accept only major organizations that had a national following.[21]

The question of representation was a crucial one. The U.S. Diaspora had never achieved the status of the European Jewish *adah*, a coherent polity ruled by a central body. With permeable and fluid boundaries, a voluntaristic tradition, and disparate ideological interests, the question of who is a legitimate representative of American Jewry was not easily answered. Moreover, in order to increase its effectiveness, the Conference tried to present a unified front by denying that significant differences over Israel existed. Such tactics frustrated members, who made their opinions known in Washington. According to former Israeli Foreign Minister Abba Eban, in its initial stage the Conference "simply became one more voice they [the administration] had to listen to."[22]

Still, the Conference had a number of advantages that contributed to its gradual ascendance over competing groups. Since Washington subsequently embraced it as the semiofficial representative of the American Jewish community on matters relating to Israel, access to the executive branch became easier. The Conference was also helped by the creation of an official congressional Jewish lobby. Founded in 1954 as the American Zionist Council on Public Affairs, it was renamed the American Israel Public Affairs Committee (AIPAC) in 1959. AIPAC's base in Washington and its considerable expertise made it highly effective in lobbying on behalf of Israel, thus amplifying the efforts of the Presidents Conference.[23]

UJA's heavy reliance on the Israeli driven "crisis mobilization" to raise money, added prestige to the Conference. The strategy originated in 1948 when UJA almost quadrupled its annual intake, a pattern that spurred other "emergency" drives for Israel. Although about half of the contributions went to domestic use, UJA leadership felt that overseas crises "moved givers the most and loomed as far more critical than a hospital or community center." Equally important, the psychological reward system offered by a sovereign state far surpassed anything that a private charity could provide. As Liebman put it, "What can Harvard University or the Metropolitan Museum . . . do to compete with a luncheon given by Golda Meir?" Another observer argued that representing Israel's interests had thrust some Jews into a "dizzying political stratosphere." It was not lost on observers of the Jewish American scene that those organizations that embraced the cause of Israel "rocketed to communal prominence," leaving others behind. The AJC's hesitant embrace of Israeli advocacy is a case in point; it eventually jointed the Presidents Conference because of the apparent fear of being marginalized.[24]

While the Presidents Conference and AIPAC were formed to represent a broad spectrum of Israeli foreign policy concerns in the United States, it soon became obvious that the Arab-Israeli struggle posed the greatest challenge to the community. On both the institutional and individual level, American Jewry came to realize that relating to the state of Israel could not be separated from the realities of the Middle East conflict.

PERCEPTIONS AND MISPERCEPTIONS OF THE ARAB-ISRAELI CONFLICT: ARABS AS THE "NEW-OLD" ENEMY

International relation theory indicates that a complex web of factors underpins perceptions of an enemy. Robert Jervis contended that such images are fed by events embedded in the collective history of a society, events that are experienced firsthand by individuals, as well as generalized beliefs about the nature of international reality. Once acquired, such perceptions form a powerful mechanism for interpreting information about the conflict. Moreover, to maintain cognitive consistency, images of the enemy are hardened, creating "a strong tendency for people to see what they expect to see and to assimilate incoming information to pre-existing images." Not surprisingly, misperceptions abound when a conflict is perceived as intense and central to the actors.[25]

American Jewish attitudes toward the Arab-Israeli conflict were driven by a number of highly interactive factors. Perhaps the most important one was linked to the view of Palestine as the haven for Jewish refugees from Europe. It is common to assert that in the thirties and forties American Jews were oblivious to the Palestinian problem, a perception that changed little after 1948. Because of this essentially humanitarian conceptualization of the problem, the community found it hard to understand the overwhelming enmity of the Arab countries toward Jewish sovereignty. The refusal of the Arab states to recognize Israel after 1948 and their often-proclaimed goal of destroying the "Zionist entity" solidified the perception that Arabs were to blame for the war. The failure of successive international efforts launched in the 1950s to solve the Arab-Israeli conflict had only enhanced the image of Arab intransigence and menace. The specter of imminent catastrophe was so embedded in the collective conscious-ness of the community that in questionnaires designed to measure closeness to Israel, the respondents were routinely asked how they would feel "if the Arab states should succeed in carrying out their threat to destroy Israel." Polls taken in the 1940s and 1950s confirm that a majority of American Jews held the Arab governments responsible for perpetuating the conflict. In the 1948 Baltimore survey 94 percent of the respondents asserted that Palestine was the most im-portant trouble spot in the world, and 62 percent wanted the U.S. government to help the Jews fight for their state. In 1953 and 1955 nearly 70 percent of American Jews viewed the Arabs as the catalysts for the Middle East struggle.[26]

Underlying this view of unrelenting Arab enmity was a core belief that Israel became the new and collective target of the old scourge of Jewish existence—anti-Semitism. Though, objectively speaking, Christian anti-Semitism was quite different from the Arab reaction to Israel, centuries of psychological condition-ing made it difficult for American Jews to make this distinction. The Arab habit of couching anti-Israeli sentiments in classic anti-Semitic language and the sym-bolism of some of their actions legitimized these anxieties. Probably most of-fensive was the ban imposed on American Jewish travel to, or transit through, Arab countries. A number of leading experts commented on the perceptual cor-relation between gentile-Christian hostility and Arab hostility. Cohen noted that "for American Jews, caring about Israel is tied to worrying about the 'goyim.' " Bernard Susser and Liebman added that worrying about Israel is "rooted in the traditional adversity-centered view of Jewish life."[27]

Making this linkage even more potent was the shadow of the Holocaust. The disparity of power in the Middle East and the threat of physical annihilation that Israel seemingly faced at the hands of its neighbors worked to magnify these fears. Not surprisingly, in its first decades of existence, Israel was routinely depicted as David, threatened by the Arab Goliath and the image of a "needy, embattled, dependent" Jewish state was a communal staple. Spurred by the guilt over their inability to help the victims of the European Holocaust, American Jews declared their resolve to "prevent another Holocaust." Some of the re-spondents in the Sklare's survey even declared that the "possibility of a second holocaust presents us with an opportunity to cleanse the record of the 1930s and 40s." As with all emotionally laden perceptions, the empirical question of whether another Holocaust was imminent in the Middle East was overshadowed by a powerful triadic imagery whereby Israel came to be perceived as the victim, the Arabs as the perpetrators, and the American Jews as the rescuers.[28]

War realities in the Middle East and popular depictions of the Arab-Israeli conflict reinforced the view of the Arabs as aggressive and barbaric. Critics have often blamed Uris's *Exodus* for perpetuating the stereotypes of Arabs as savage and cowardly and pointed out that, by contrast, the novel portrayed the Jews as highly moral, reluctant warriors. But others contended that Uris's "construction of the Arab character" was tailor-made for the morally black and white picture of the Middle East conflict in which American Jews wished to believe. Indeed, Arthur Hertzberg asserted that Uris's clichéd depiction of Israelis as "totally noble" and of Arabs as the "Middle East equivalent of the murderous Indians of Hollywood Westerns" reflected an American Jewish reluctance to deal with the moral ambiguities of power and war. He castigated the community for failing to embrace the more nuanced Israeli novel *Khirbat Khiza*, "which spoke with pain about Jews with machine guns lording it over Arabs."[29]

The need to preserve a morally acceptable perception of the Arab-Israeli conflict had extended to the treatment of the Palestinians. As noted, American Jews had little understanding of the intricacies of the population configuration in Palestine, a fact that did not change radically after the 1948 war. Urofsky explained that "the plight of the Palestinian Arab refugees caused little concern in the American Jewish community" because of its preoccupation with saving Jewish refugees. Since American Jews "opened their hearts and their purses" for their kin, there was an expectation that the Arab governments would do the same for their brethren. As for the origin of the refugee problem, Urofsky, like most of the community, accepted the official Israeli version that the Palestinians left voluntarily at the urging of their leaders, adding that the "Israeli leaders did their best to convince their Arab neighbors not to run away." American Jews were also eager to point out that, unlike the warm welcome accorded to Jewish refugees from Arab countries, the Palestinians were, by and large, isolated in refugee camps where "hatred and lust for vengeance festered and grew."[30]

While the moral imperative in the perception of the Arab-Israeli conflict was uppermost, instrumental considerations also mandated a relatively black and white picture of Israel's security. None was more important than fund-raising activities which, as noted, were structured around Israel's embattled image. As one Jewish functionary argued "the stark reality was that Arabs could loose ten wars, but Israel could not loose one."[31] Although local Jewish federations were often upset because overseas needs cut into their share of the contributions—an issue that came to a head during the contentious UJA conference in 1949—it was also widely recognized that Israel's security crises helped fill the communal coffers.

Critics would later charge that using Israel to raise all the communal funds was exploitative and showed a lack of confidence on the part of the American Jewish leadership in their ability to raise money directly for domestic use. However, the UJA was mindful of the 20 percent drop in contributions in 1949, which was attributed to the "relaxation of the crisis mentality" after the triumph of Israel's independence. It was also noted that one of the most successful fund-raising tools was the "Israel mission," structured around security needs of the new state. Participants were given "confidential" briefings on security, or taken to a military base or another strategic location in order to emphasize the continuing threat. As for the stay-home donors, "speakers at fund-raising events would remind audiences of Nasser's vow 'to drive Jews into the sea.' " Nor was it lost on UJA that, as a result of the Sinai Campaign, fund-raising improved again, due largely to the Special Survival Fund and the Emergency Rescue Fund. With so much at stake, the Middle East conflict-driven "crisis campaign had become a staple of UJA operations."[32]

Not all Jews accepted the mainstream version of the Arab-Israeli conflict. Most eager to "unmask" the reality of the Middle East struggle was the American Council for Judaism whose leaders—Berger and Arthur M. Lilienthal—felt very strongly that the creation of a Jewish state had shortchanged the Palestinians. In 1949, the council helped to establish the Holy Land Emergency Liaison Program to fight for the rights of the refugees. Both leaders blamed Israel for precipitating the conflict, a theme that Lilienthal propagated in his numerous books, including his 1953 anti-Zionist manifesto, *What Price Israel?*. I.F. Stone, a left-leaning Jewish American journalist who had earned considerable fame by covering the underground passage of Holocaust survivors to Palestine, added his charge that Jewish sovereignty disfranchised the Palestinians. In his book *Underground to Palestine*, Stone proposed a binational state that would recognize the equal presence of Jews and Arabs. Although such luminaries as philosopher Martin Buber and Judah Magnes, the Jewish American president of the Hebrew University, had advocated binationalism in the past, Stone's proposal proved highly unpopular. As one observer noted, it aborted what "might have been a hero [reception] on the synagogue lecture circuit."[33]

Nahum Goldmann, a leading figure in the Zionist movement, and some of his close associates, including Philip Klutznick, the then-president of B'nai B'rith, offered a more muted dissent from the mainstream perception of the Middle East struggle. Goldmann, who played a key role in securing U.S. support for the 1947 UN partition resolution, was less eager than other Zionist leaders to see immediate Jewish sovereignty. He urged a delay in hope of reaching an understanding with the Arabs. After the 1948 war, Goldmann wrote about the "shock and terrible blow to Arab pride" that the defeat inflicted and implied that this trauma promoted the Arabs to heal their "psychological wound" by dreaming of "victory and revenge." Goldmann was also pessimistic about Ben-Gurion's capacity for bringing peace, holding him to be "organically incapable of compromise" and driven by a "will for power."[34]

While the Jewish community was not entirely happy with Goldmann's position, his mild dissent did not threaten the consensual view of the Arab-Israeli conflict in the same way as the more radical vision of the American Council for Judaism. Most upsetting to organized Jewry was the fact that the council sought to shape American foreign policy in the Middle East. Berger developed a close friendship with Henry A. Byroade, assistant secretary of state for Near Eastern Affairs in the Eisenhower administration. Berger was credited for Byroade's very public scolding of Israel for not "integrating sufficiently in the Middle East" and for the later hints that American interests were not served by the Jewish state. Given the fact that the commitment of American Jews to Israel was tempered by their need to demonstrate good American citizenship, the whiff of dissonance created by the council was alarming. The Lakeville study showed that respondents felt comfortable in supporting Israel because of the perceived overlap between American and Israeli goals, a notion that was carefully cultivated by Israeli spokesmen. Such dissonance was especially testing to a community that was only beginning to find its ways in the complexities of Washington's foreign policy.[35]

CONSONANCE AND DISSONANCE: AMERICAN JEWS AND U.S. FOREIGN POLICY IN THE MIDDLE EAST

Commenting on the success of the Zionist movement in America, one observer declared that "American recognition of the State of Israel signified the successful" translation of the Zionist policy into U.S. foreign policy.[36] While both friends and opponents of Israel have often expressed similar views, the reality was more complicated. Opinion polls show that after the Holocaust general public support for a Jewish state increased dramatically. However, a small but influential force in the foreign policy community remained skeptical and even hostile. At its core were State Department officials who were concerned by Arab reaction and mainline Protestant denominations that had large missionary interests in the Middle East. Although President Harry S. Truman overrode the objections of the so-called "Arabists" in his administration and recognized Israel, much of American foreign policy toward the new state remained ambiguous.

These ambiguities had increased during the Eisenhower administration. Faced with a deepening Cold War, the administration expressed anxiety about possible Arab defection into the Soviet camp. The tension between Israel and its Arab neighbors regarding water, the status of Jerusalem, and border security was seen in Washington as complicating its already delicate balancing act in the Middle East. In 1953, Secretary of State Dulles informed Israel that it would risk American aid because of the Bnot Ya'akov water diversion project on the Jordan River. The State Department was further angered when Israel moved its Foreign Ministry to West Jerusalem and invited the United States to move its embassy to the capital. Israeli raids across the borders in retaliation for Arab terrorist attacks were even more irritating to the administration. When, in October 1953, a special Israel Defense Forces (IDF) unit attacked the Jordanian village of Kibya, killing more than fifty civilians, the State Department described the raid as "shocking" and announced the formal suspension of aid.

This development stunned the community, not in the least because of the dreaded prospect of double loyalty. On the one hand, American Jews felt obligated to defend Israel, whose toll from terrorism rose to some four hundred dead and more than eight hundred wounded, and whose fragile economy was in dire need of foreign capital. On the other hand, taking on a popular president and a war hero could undermine the perception that Jewish loyalties were not in alliance with American interests. Caught between two powerful imperatives, the community showed little consensus. Predictably, the right-leaning ZOA and the Zionists-Revisionists of America were first to condemn the administration, followed somewhat more hesitantly by the AJC, the National Council of Jewish Women, and finally Hadassah. The more liberal American Jewish Congress (AJCongress), whose president Joachim Prinz disliked Ben-Gurion, did not get involved, whereas the American Council for Judaism eagerly denounced Israel.

In the end, the timid and divided community did little to sway the administration, which restored aid only after Israel agreed to abandon the water diversion project. Still, the Jewish community learned three important lessons from this first high-profile venture into foreign policy lobbying. First, the crisis prompted the consolidation of Israeli advocacy in the form of the Presidents Conference and AIPAC. In one of its first acts, AIPAC's forerunner, the American Zionist Council of Public Affairs, had to cope with the public relations fallout from the Kibya raid. Second, steps to cultivate Congress as a counterweight to the administration were broadened, whereby AIPAC became the official congressional lobby. Third, and most important, there was a vigorous effort to turn the alleged commonality of foreign policy interests between Israel and the United States into a reality.[37]

Given the anti-Israeli sentiments of the American foreign policy establishment, this was a tall order. During the early fifties, Washington had hoped to establish a closer relationship with Egypt, whose President Gamal Abdul Nasser had had initial support in some Central Intelligence Agency (CIA) and military circles. However, when Nasser, angered by the denial of a loan to build the Aswan High Dam, chose an alliance with the Soviet Union, the threat of radical nationalism in the Middle East changed the equation. Still, the administration reacted with anger when Israel joined Great Britain and France in an attack on Egypt following the expropriation of the Suez Canal in 1956. With public opinion decrying Israel's use of force, the Sinai Campaign became a major problem for the American Jewish community. Polls indicate that Jewish opinion during that war was clearly at odds with official American policy. Some three-quarters of the respondents blamed the Arabs for the war, as opposed to 7 percent who blamed Israel. In 1957, only 2 percent blamed Israel and 83 percent blamed the Arabs. The dissonance reached new heights when President Eisenhower forced Israel's withdrawal from the Sinai Peninsula, occupied during the war. As one historian noted, American Jews "learned a lesson that an open rupture between Israel and America is . . . harmful to Jewish interests."[38]

In spite of this setback, work on reconciling American and Israeli interests in the Middle East continued apace. The task was made easier by the rapid spread of Soviet influence in the region, which prompted the administration to issue the Eisenhower Doctrine that vowed a defense against communism. American Jewish advocates could point out that Israel was a Western bulwark against "Nasserism backed by Communism." Israel Goldstein, an outgoing president of the AJCongress, criticized the State Department for its illusion about Nasser. Significantly, the American foreign policy community gradually embraced the same notion. A 1958 National Security Council memorandum noted that support for Israel would be a "logical corollary" of opposition to "radical Arab nationalism." Israel, with support from Washington, concluded a pact with Turkey, Iran, and Ethiopia, three pro-Western countries in the region and helped American interests in black Africa, South Africa, and Rhodesia.[39]

By the time John F. Kennedy arrived in the White House in 1961, the essentials of "special relations" between the United States and Israel were sketched out. Kennedy, whose close victory over Richard Nixon indebted him to the Jewish constituency, was willing to acknowledge publicly American friendship with Israel. But, like his predecessors in the White House, the president had to balance American Jewish concerns with larger foreign policy interests, putting Israel on notice that its policies had created strains "for the United States in the Middle East." Applying his own brand of political activism to the region, Kennedy also hoped to tackle the "perennials" of the Arab-Israeli conflict: the water issues, the Palestinian refugee problem, Israeli retaliatory raids, and the arms race.[40] In the end, Kennedy's balancing act left the Jewish community uneasy about the president's true intentions. The administration called on Israel to settle the refugee problem and joined the UN condemnation of a 1962 raid on Syria. Yet it also agreed, albeit secretly, to sell Hawk missiles to counteract the advanced Soviet planes acquired by the Arab states. The White House also let it be known that it had distanced itself from the American Council for Judaism, an important gesture to the increasingly pro-Zionist community. When Kennedy was assassinated in 1963, American Jews mourned him as a true friend, but they were unsure about the future of the "special relations."

Whatever the achievements in forging a better climate in Washington, managing the strains in the U.S.–Israeli relations took a toll on the community. Although American Jews publicly defended Israel, the quarrel between dovish leaders like Goldmann and Prinz and Ben-Gurion became louder. The hard-line ZOA attacked Prinz for his alleged "anti-Zionist" sentiments, prompting a *Life* magazine story about the "crisis of Zionism." Closely related to these problems were signs of a growing disenchantment with Israel and its role in American Jewish life. Nathan Glazer, a leading sociologist, pointed out that after 1948 there was an "expression of ebullient feelings," but in specific terms, "Israel has meant almost nothing for American Judaism." Another commentator felt that Zionism and Israel had lost their relevance and warned about "symptoms of estrangement" and "apathy" among the younger generation. Prinz declared "Zionism—for all practical purposes" dead.[41]

In 1960, James P. Warburg, a prominent American Jewish leader, attacked many of the policies of Israel, especially the treatment of Arab refugees. He questioned the wisdom of UJA contributions to a "foreign government which openly engages in propaganda attempting to influence the policy of the government of the United States." Jacob Petuchowski, in his widely debated book *Zion Reconsidered*, summed up much of this anti-Israeli sentiment. He argued that Zionism was not instrumental to Jewish survival and called the obsession with the needs of the Jewish state "counterproductive." Urofsky added that in the early sixties, the "earlier eagerness to glorify and imbibe everything Israeli passed as American Jews came to see not only Israel's very real accomplishment but some flaws as well."[42] These and other commentators urged a more mature and realistic appraisal of the links between U.S. Jews and Israel. However, the Six Day War was destined to change American Jewish–Israeli relations in ways that few could fathom.

2

The Six Day War and the Emergence of "Sacred Unity"

Less than two decades after American Jews embraced the integrationist imperative, the religious-universalistic definition of Judaism began to lose its luster. Anxiety about the demographic shrinkage of the community and the rise of cultural pluralism in America made an ethnic, peoplehood-based identity look more attractive. Israel, fresh from the victorious Six-Day War, provided the center of a new ethnically based civil Jewish religion. At its height, many expected this "sacred unity" between Israel and the American Diaspora to stem assimilation and cure other communal problems. However, the 1973 war and the vagaries of the peace process tarnished the image of Israel, leading to doubts about its centrality in Jewish identity.

THE NEW QUEST FOR JEWISH IDENTITY: FROM INTEGRATIONISM TO SURVIVALISM

By the early sixties the American Jewish experiment in integrationism looked like a success. Statistical surveys and anecdotal evidence indicate that within one decade Jews became geographically mobile, economically secure, and socially acceptable. Almost half of Jewish families had an annual income of between $7,000 and $15,000, a figure attained only by 25 percent of gentiles. The original gambit on Judaism as a religious identity seemed to be paying off as well. Redefined as an ethical tradition easily reconcilable with the American ethos, it freed the Jews from a demanding and exclusionist lifestyle. In the language of social psychology, "the extent to which Jews were like other Jews" had greatly decreased, and the extent to which they became like all other men "had greatly increased."[1]

Ironically, the very success of integrationism triggered a nagging anxiety over the survival of the community. The early optimism that Jews could retain their distinctive identity was replaced with a muted unease that occasionally boiled over into open criticism of the alleged emptiness of the "social synagogue." To the sociologically attuned observers a number of factors stood out as potential "red flags." First, voluntary endogamy of the suburban Jews declined in the early sixties, giving way to increased rates of intermarriage. According to some estimates, intermarriage rates stood at 25 to 30 percent, well above the 10 percent in the 1950s. The second sign of modernity was the rising divorce rate among Jewish families. This further exacerbated the problem of low fertility rates and attributed to the higher educational level and professional aspiration of the younger generation.[2]

The Israelis, ever-eager to demonstrate the tenuous character of Jewish life in the Diaspora, were the first to raise the alarm. In 1962, an Israeli official published a report that predicted the disappearance of the Jewish community within a generation. *Look* magazine elaborated on the issue in a 1963 cover story on the "Vanishing American Jew." Some American Jewish analysts concurred with the view that the community was doomed to shrink. Charles Zibbel warned about the demographic costs of the geographical dispersion. More significantly, John Slawson, the head of the AJC and a strong supporter of intergrationism, was having second thoughts. Writing in early 1967, he bemoaned the weak and confused Jewish identity and listed the signs of "pathology," such as increasing rates of intermarriage and the indifference or even "apostasy" of young Jews. Speaking around the same time, the former Supreme Court Justice Arthur Goldberg blamed Jews for emulating the Christians too closely and warned about the "danger of losing our identity as Jews."[3]

Demographic doomsday anxiety was not new. The noted historian Simon Rawidowicz observed that Jews are an "ever-dying people," a community always in fear that theirs would be the last generation to survive. However, the alarm raised in the early sixties had a special urgency. Commentators pointed out that, for the first time in history, American Jews enjoyed freedom and tolerance. With a decline in traditional forms of anti-Semitism and the openness of the host society, assimilation became tempting. Some even conceded that Ben-Gurion, who predicted that freedom would provide the *mitat n'shika*, the "kiss of death" for the Diaspora, might have been right. The notion that Jews were headed toward oblivion by assimilation was particularly vexing in light of the tremendous losses of the Holocaust. The philosopher Emil Fackenheim made famous his 614th commandment of "not handling a posthumous victory to Hitler." That Jews may play into the hand of their historical persecutors by voluntarily disappearing into the host society was, as one observer put it, "nothing short of terrifying" to the committed members of the community and their leaders. With so much at stake, it was only a question of time before the Jewish community abandoned integrationism in favor of what Jonathon S. Woocher called the "sacred survival" imperative.[4]

While articulating the new communal goal was relatively easy, finding ways to bolster Jewish identity proved more difficult. At the most fundamental level, the problem was rooted in a deep disagreement over how to define an authentic Jewish identity. To begin with, the religious-universalist definition of Judaism of the "social synagogue" period was predicated on a liberal and enlightened political milieu. However, the relatively harmonious concept of American liberalism in the 1950s was rapidly disappearing, a victim of the breakup of the New Deal coalition. The civil rights movement, the war in Vietnam, and the emergence of the militant New Left introduced an increasingly consonant note into the Jewish-liberal equation. As Cohen put it, the principle means by which "Jews gave meaning to their lives—namely political liberalism—had begun to loose its glamour and attractiveness." What is more, the civil and political ferment of the early sixties had challenged the melting pot ideology to which the majority of American Jews were beholden. Following the success of the black consciousness movement, group-based notions of identification became increasingly fashionable, inflaming ethnic assertiveness and particularism. The personal identity movement of the countercultural revolution with its emphasis on "roots" had also contributed to this change. To quote one scholar, "many people were seeking meaning in the 'community' "; for Jews that meant ethnic community (Raab, 1991).[5]

Those who searched for a peoplehood-based identity could draw on the writing of Mordecai M. Kaplan, the philosopher of the Reconstructionist movement. Kaplan—who was influenced by Emil Durkheim's notion of religion as a collective, rather than individual, phenomenon—argued that Judaism should focus on belonging, rather than believing. Although critics scoffed at Kaplan's notion that history and culture, not theology, defines Jewishness, the communal orientation attracted an increasing following among younger Jews. Kaplan's reinterpretation of religious practices as expressions of communal togetherness was a boon to secularized Jews who lost their belief in a personal God and His stringent commandment. Still, this more tribal definition of Jewish identity could not automatically reverse the demographic decline. Indeed, the countercultural revolution, with its bias against traditional family life, seemed to amplify some of the factors that hastened the numeric decline in the first place. But those who tried to resurrect the historical-tribal tradition, were not sure that an ethnic revival based on the receding Yiddish cultural roots would appeal to the second- and third-generation Jews. Above all, a Kaplan-style communalism would not have reached the fully secular Jews, who retained a modicum of Jewish identity, but were divorced from both Jewish religion and tradition.[6]

With the Jewish census expected to show the adverse trends scheduled for 1970, the debate among the advocates of different approaches became feverish. Nevertheless, few could predict that the Six Day War of 1967 would provide a stunning solution to the identity needs of American Jews. Commenting on Israel's role as *deus ex machina*, one scholar wrote that "everything that could be done was tried but the hemorrhaging continued. Israel provided a way out."[7]

THE SPOILS OF VICTORY: ISRAEL AS THE NEW JEWISH RELIGION IN AMERICA

A large body of writings attests to the impact of the Six Day War on American Jews. Both anecdotal evidence and rigorous research indicate that the response to Israel's sense of mortal danger before June 6, 1967 and its surprising victory was widespread and deeply felt. There is a virtual consensus that American Jews turned their often ambivalent and conflicted feelings about the Jewish states into a love affair. Norman Podhoretz, a leading commentator, referred to it as an epiphany: "those who were already Zionists were born again, and those who had resisted or remained indifferent now experienced what might be described as baptism by proxy fire." The experience of Thomas Friedman, recalled in his book *From Beirut to Jerusalem*, is illustrative in this respect. Jerold S. Auerbach commented that Friedman, a "three-day-a-year Jew," who believed in a "Judaism without land," was "converted" to a fervent Israel advocate. Alan Dershowitz noted that more than a few of his acquaintances "on the road to assimilation" were transformed by the "epochal" events of June 1967. Their support for Israel "turned them back to the synagogue" and other "Jewish pursuits." The noted author Marie Syrkin explained that "Israel is a source of affirmative Jewish awareness" and an antidote to assumption so overwhelming that religion "cannot undo it." Others referred to Israel as becoming a "naches machine," a Yiddish expression denoting pride and pleasure.[8]

In terms of communal needs, the June war played into a number of often-contradictory identity factors. From the American Jewish perspective, there were powerful parallels between the Holocaust and the existential threat to Israel. One survey found that 87 percent of the sample were reminded of the Holocaust when contemplating Israel's fate at the hands of the Arabs. In a repeat poll, one Lakeville respondent was emphatic that Israel's struggle should not end with a "march to the ovens." Milton Himmelfarb, a research director of the AJC, wrote: "Jews had a sudden realization that genocide . . . and a desire to murder Jews" were not a thing of the past, but were real and present." Given the fact that Israel was seen as a redemptive counterbalance to the Holocaust, a new calamity would have been morally and psychologically unbearable. Such sentiments were undoubtedly enhanced by the publication, in April 1968, of Arthur D. Morse's *Why Millions Died: A Chronicle of American Apathy*. The cottage industry that Morse's book spawned amplified Jewish American guilt over the European tragedy. An Israeli defeat would have again signaled the indifference of the community to its overseas brethren, enhancing what one observer termed a "deep and abiding sense of guilt" for its passivity during the Holocaust.[9]

While the Holocaust-induced anxiety was running deep, the remarkable victory was feeding the hero image of Israel. Few were immune to the visuals that inundated the media. The "strong, handsome Israeli solider" swimming in the Suez Canal, featured on the cover of the June issue of *Life* magazine, and the group of paratroopers at the Western Wall were particularly popular. For those Jews who were still bothered by the ghetto-victim stereotype of the Diaspora, such images provided a much-needed antidote. Jacqueline Levine, a longtime leader of the AJCongress, summed up much of this sentiment when she declared that "Israel made us all stand a little taller in 1967." Moshe Dayan, the dashing Israeli defense minister widely credited with the victory, became a much ad-mired figure in the Jewish community. One critic wrote that American Jews could vicariously identify with the "sun-bronzed rugged fearless Ari Ben-Canaan" contrasted with the image of cowardice associated the Diaspora." An-other commented that to the idealized view of Israel "where happy kibbutzniks danced around campfires at night after draining the swamps and making the desert bloom" were added images of "Israeli generals who combined Napoleon's strategic genius, General George Patton's determination, and Audie Murphy's personal courage."[10]

Making Israel the focus of Jewish identity was a logical choice for a com-munity in search of a new self-definition. The spontaneous, emotional, and al-most universal response of American Jews left no doubt that the ethnic-tribal sentiments written off in the fifties were very much alive. Scholars have noted that, in recalling the war effort, individual Jews and Jewish publications would often use the term "we," as in "how splendidly 'we' have fought" or "how many Arabs did *we* kill". (emphasis added). A rabbi described his congregation over-taken by vicarious heroism: "I, the shoe salesman, killed an Arab, I, the heart specialist, captured the tank." As Kurt Levin, a leading social psychologist pos-tulated, such a proprietary use of the term "we" denotes interdependence of fate, a key ingredient in ethnic identity.[11]

The "reethnization" of the community around Israel had a number of advan-tages. Most importantly, Israel became the lynchpin in the evolving "civil relig-ion" of American Jews. It became the center of Jewish aspirations and an extraordinary resource for a revitalized Jewish consciousness. By working for Israel, Jews could reestablish the ethnic-communal bonds that had worn thin in the process of assimilation. So much so that for large segments of American Jewry the Jewish state replaced the synagogue and the Torah as the symbol of Judaism. Irving Greenberg contended that the most widely observed mitzvah was a contribution to the UJA and Israel Bonds. Some sociologists argued that nonsupport for Israel was judged to be a more severe form of deviance than intermarriage, a stricture that was applied most readily to leaders. As one com-mentator put it, "An American Jewish 'leader' could be married to a gentile, he could be a stranger to the synagogue, but if he became a public critic of Israel, he would soon become a former Jewish leader." The Jerusalem Program adopted by the World Zionist Organization in 1968 reaffirmed the centrality of Israel in Jewish life. Among others, the program aimed at preserving Jewish identity through fostering Hebrew education and other contacts with Israel. To this end, there was an increase in the number of Hebrew classes offered by synagogues and Jewish centers, and trips to Israel became a popular form of "pilgrimage."[12]

The fact that American Jews perceived Israel as both victorious and vulnerable added to its appeal. It was already argued that, even before the Six Day War, Israel's security served as the rationale for the "mobilization model" of Judaism. After 1967, even more of the communal effort was diverted toward care and sustenance of the Jewish state. Contribution to Jewish causes increased dramatically after the war—from $136 million to $317—and the share that went to Israel reached 65 percent. There was also an increase in behavioral indices of pro-Israeli sentiments like visits to Israel and aliya. Albert Chernin, the long-time executive of NJCRAC, declared that in the field of communal relations, "our first priority is Israel," a stunning admission that "the political effort to shore up Israel superseded all other concerns."[13]

Testifying to the strength of the Israeli appeal, the anti-Zionists, triggered by the near disintegration of the American Council for Judaism, all but vanished from the scene. The hitherto lukewarm Reform movement decided to hold its 1968 conference of the World Union of Progressive Judaism in Jerusalem. A 1970 survey found that 82 percent of Reform adults and 67 percent of Reform youth found it either "essential" or "desirable" to support Israel. Ranked with other imperatives of a "good Jew," support for Israel went up from fourteenth place in 1957 to fifth in 1970. In what was perhaps the most poignant commentary, Iphigene Ochs Sulzberger, the heiress to the *New York Times* and its long standing anti-Zionist line, visited Israel in 1971 where she was warmly greeted by Golda Meir.[14]

What facilitated this wholesale embrace of Israel was the redefinition of Zionism. The old adage of Ben-Gurion that Zionism equals aliya, was replaced by a more convenient formula. The new Zionist was "one who views Israel as his or her personal center and cultural center and for whom Israel plays a central role in personal life and identity." The relatively light burden of "Israelism-as-Zionism" led some to dub it "armchair Zionism," but it attracted numerous new followers, including many Jewish veterans of the civil rights movement and the Vietnam war protests. Quite significantly, testimonies of an instant "Zionist conversion," à la Friedman, appeared in the personal biographies of many of the future leaders of the Jewish community. "Israeliness" was especially attractive to secular and unaffiliated Jews who failed to connect to the community through the more traditional religious context. Although, as Liebman wryly noted, focusing on Israel as a center of Jewishness was a "religious sentiment" with no equivalent in Western theology, its appeal to Jewish secularists and atheists was undeniable. Even the normally critical Hertzberg declared that the Six Day War "has united those with deep Jewish commitments . . . and touched those "who previously seemed untouched by them."[15]

Whatever their degree of religiosity, many Jews were taken by the newly boosted religious, Bible-and-land vision of Judaism. Unlike the synagogue-based rabbinical variety, the Six Day miracle enabled even secular Jews to partake in a great redemptive theodicy. The land of Israel was "miraculously restored" by the IDF, as predicted in the book of Deuteronomy: "with a mighty hand and an outstretched arm, with great terror, signs, and wonders." In this sense Israel became a transcendent object to American Jews, not unlike a "secular priest." On the other hand of the religious spectrum, such sacrilization of Zionism attracted the Orthodox Jews and enhanced their commitment to Israel. Thus for the first time since 1948, virtually the entire community was united in one cause. The fact that Israel became the lowest common denominator for all Jews was enthusiastically welcomed. Steven M. Cohen, an astute observer, wrote that Israel appealed to the universalists and particularists, to the liberals and the conservatives. Thus, the "sacred unity" epitomized by the motto "we are one" promised to usher a new Jewish renaissance.[16]

"SACRED UNITY": THE MECHANICS OF THE NEW CIVIL RELIGION

The hope for Jewish revival was most timely. The National Jewish Population Study, published in 1971, revealed what many had suspected for some time: the rate of intermarriage had risen from 7 percent in the 1950s to 31 percent by the end of the sixties. This and other data would later lead Elihu Bergman to publish a highly alarmist prediction that the American Jewry are destined to almost vanish within a century. In order to avert such an outcome, almost every Jewish organization, regardless of its *raison d'être*, adopted some type of an "Israel vision." In addition to philanthropy and political activism, there were vigorous celebrations of Israel's Independence Day and other Israel-centered events. The popularity of Hebrew classes and Israeli folk dancing had increased dramatically. Millions attended Zionist banquets and lectures by Abba Eban, Meir, and other fluent English speakers from Israel. The visits to Israel, known as "missions," became practically *de rigueur* for leadership and were encouraged for the rank and file. Through these visits participants were said to "express their commitment to Israel and bring meaning to their lives as Jews in America."[17]

Whether such experience could translate into personal choices that would keep Jews within the fold ultimately depended on how well Israel could serve as a "source of personal meaning." Earl Raab noted that Israel "was the indispensable well spring" and the catalyst for the increased "network of connections" among American Jews. Yet, in spite of the genuine and deeply emotional initial reaction to the Six Day War, empirical data indicate that the influence of Israel on the belief system of the American Jews was not lasting. Upon his return to Lakeville, Sklare did not find much impact in terms of change in identity and behavior. A 1994 conference on the influence of the Six Day War on Diaspora Jewry found that the war "accelerated some trends and briefly retarded the unfolding of others, but ultimately did not fundamentally transform the Jewish communities." This and other studies have pointed out that, in order to create a real change in the identity-behavior nexus, Israel would have to be embedded in the essential and constant part of the core identity of American Jews. But, as Cohen claimed, pro-Israelism was situational, bubbling up or simmering down in response to threat; Gideon Shimoni called it "circumstantial centrality." What is more, there was no dramatic improvement in the level of understanding and knowledge about Israel. With minor changes, the early pattern of high emotional engagement and low cognition underlaid the "sacred unity" relation.[18]

Such a peculiar combination of closeness and distance attracted critical scrutiny. In fact, many thoughtful observers voiced doubts about the real impact of Israel on the private lives of American Jews. The noted scholar Jacob Neusner was among the first to warn that pro-Israelism cannot solve the identity crisis of the community. Daniel J. Elazar coined the term "Israelolotry" to denote his contention that American Jews turned to worshiping Israel rather than the God of Israel. Immanuel Jacobovits, the chief rabbi of Britain, bemoaned that, for many Jews, Israel became "a vicarious haven of their residual Jewishness, conveniently replacing the "personal discipline of Jewish life." Eugene Borowitz was equally sure that "we cannot function as Jews by trying to live a vicarious Israeli existence on American soil." David Vital, a member of a 1978 AJC task force, created to study Israeli–American Jewish interaction, objected to the report's optimistic tone. Liebman wrote that that the "honeymoon" was temporary and that the relations were "bound to sour." Others, citing some preliminary empirical data, cautioned that the jury was still out on whether Israel would truly compel American Jews to make a commitment to a Jewish lifestyle.[19]

While such sentiments would prove prescient, in the decade following the Six Day War there was a widespread perception that Israel was indeed the "sacred priest" of the secularized American Jewry community. A major factor in nourishing this image was the shift toward public, as opposed to private, Judaism. Sociologists of religion have argued that in modern societies people tend to live in a "plurality of words," with often sharp dichotomies between the public and private realms. It was in the public realm that commitment to Israel manifested itself the most, making Israel-centered Judaism a truly civic religion of American Jews. So much so that it turned around the nineteenth-century Enlightenment injunction of "Be a Jew in your home and a human being outside." With so much focus on public manifestations of civic Judaism—philanthropic contributions and political activism—it was easy to overlook that, at the private level, Jews were absolved from following the tenets of their faith. David Clayman, a high-ranking AJCongress official, noted that "fundraising was the key. You worshiped at the altar of Israel by contributing. Jewish observance was raising money, not going to the synagogue." Neusner called it "checkbook Judaism," adding that the "holy life" moved from the private domain to a public organizational forum.[20]

Israel's popularity would have probably peaked earlier had it not been for the October war of 1973. The Yom Kippur War, which saw Israel overwhelmed by a successful Arab attack, electrified the community. Whatever reservations individual Jews might have had about the "sacred union," they were put aside in

order to deal with Israel's dire situation. The UJA pledged an emergency do-
nation of $100 million and planned to raise an additional $750 million during
1973. The generosity and sacrifice of many Jews was so great that it led one
observer to write: "they gave, and gave again and gave still more." A 1974–75
Harris survey found that 87 percent of the respondents agreed with the statement
that American Jews "have a special obligation to support Israel with funds and
other aid."[21]

The less-than-stellar performance of the IDF, coupled with the massive American help during the war, convinced the community to redouble its advocacy
efforts on behalf of Israel. Going beyond financial support, lobbying and educational campaigns created an ever-wider network of commitment among organizations. Starting in 1973, there was a growing belief that Israel's security
and survival depended on American Jews, and, ultimately, on the United States.
Convinced that Israel became a virtual client state of America, the community
added to its civic religion the duty of lobbying to secure U.S. military and
economic aid. A 1975 Harris poll revealed that 96 percent of American Jews
supported the U.S. decision to send military supplies to Israel; only 2 percent
opposed such aid. By 1997, only one quarter of respondents of a survey of
federation members believed that Israel could defend itself without American
help.[22]

Concerns closer to home also motivated such vigorous engagement in civic
Judaism on behalf of Israel. The oil embargo that followed the October war and
the ensuing gasoline shortage created widespread public resentment. Fearing a
backlash against American Jews, the November 1973 General Assembly of the
Council of Jewish Federations (CJF) decided to launch an emergency public
relations campaign on behalf of Israel. According to one federation official,
"there was anxiety, almost panic in the community." The $3 million fund created
by the assembly was used to explain and defend Israel's foreign policy positions.
These efforts intensified greatly after the United Nations passed a resolution
accusing Zionism of racism in 1975. More important, anti-Israeli sentiments—
coupled with the decline in traditional forms of anti-Semitism—led to a redefinition of the meaning of anti-Semitism. A 1974 Anti-Defamation League
(ADL) report set the tone. It described the new anti-Semitism as "callous indifference to Jewish concerns, a failure to appreciate the most profound apprehen-
sions of the Jewish people and a blandness and apathy in dealing with
anti-Jewish behavior, particularly when directed at the State of Israel." Nathan
Perlmutter, the ADL director, explained that today's "anti-Semitism is anti-
Zionism" and blamed "oil dependency" and the "thirst for recycled petrodollars"
for anti-Israeli sentiments."[23]

Redefining anti-Semitism was also helpful in combating the growing New
Left critique of Israel. In 1967, the Students for a Democratic Society adopted
a militant anti-Israeli resolution, followed by the National Convention on New
Politics—a broad alliance of New Left groups—which voted to condemn Israel
for its "imperialist Zionists war." Publications of the Students Non-Violent Co-

ordinating Committee carried virulent attacks on Israel and once featured a Star of David with a dollar sign superimposed on it. The Black Panthers were often on record denouncing Israel's "colonialism" and "imperialism." Even without the accompanying drumbeat against American imperialism in Southeast Asia, such claims were bound to make the Jewish community extremely uncomfortable. While individual Jews resigned in great number from New Left groups, the Jewish defense organizations launched a comprehensive attack. The ADL's Perlmutter accused the "apologists" for the New Left of indifference to Israel's fate and of spreading anti-Semitic rhetoric.[24]

American Jews were equally rattled by the stand of liberal Christian churches which, in spite of decades of ecumenical dialogue, failed to speak out on Israel's behalf in the anxious days before the June war. Inviting comparisons with the indifference of the Catholic Church to the Holocaust, the National Council of Churches (NCC) topped its silence with a subsequent declaration against "territorial expansion" by armed forces. The NCC became a leading advocate for Palestinian refugees and, in 1974, called on the American government to establish relations with the Palestinian Liberation Organization (PLO). The American Friends Service Committee took a similar position in its highly publicized 1970 report "Search for Peace in the Middle East." Faced with what was perceived as a bitter betrayal, the ADL denounced the liberal churches, and the AJC, a leader in the ecumenical dialogue, expressed extreme disappointment. Less diplomatically, the Jewish press accused the liberal Christians of anti-Semitism.[25]

These and other developments spurred the community into an increasingly vigorous engagement in the peace process. At its heart was the notion that criticism of Israel's foreign policy is detrimental to the security of the Jewish state and should be vigorously combated. As two leading experts, Lipset and Raab, put it, "defensiveness of American Jews about Israel has been profoundly heightened by the recognition . . . that Israel's survival depends on support of American Jews."[26]

FIGHTING THE "GOOD FIGHT": AMERICAN JEWISH PERCEPTIONS OF THE ARAB-ISRAELI CONFLICT

Arab actions preceding the Six Day War helped Israel to gain the moral high ground in the United States. Opinion polls indicated that, by a wide margin, Americans viewed the Arabs as aggressors, a perception enhanced by Egypt's violation of international law and the eviction of the United Nation peacekeepers. To American Jews, President Nasser's belligerence was nothing short of an effort to complete the Final Solution, a perception reflected in the postwar surveys. When a Harris poll asked "Who do you think has more right on their side, the Arabs or Israel?" 99 percent of the respondents said that Israel has more right on its side. The same percentage of respondents also expressed sympathy for Israel.[27] Arab refusal to consider the Israeli peace offer of July 1967, epitomized in the famous three "no's" of the Khartoum conference—no peace, no negotiations, no recognition—further reinforced the image of Arab intransigence. By contrast, Israel's status as the only true peace-loving country in the Middle East soared.

Arab collusion with the Soviet Union, which was suspect of playing a major role in instigating the war, strengthened the unprecedented wave of support for the beleaguered Jewish state. Whatever communist sympathies American Jews harbored in the thirties and forties had long evaporated in the face of Soviet domestic anti-Semitism and its increasingly strident anti-Israeli tone. After the June war, the entire communist bloc severed diplomatic relations with Israel and launched a virulent anti-Israeli campaign in the UN. By portraying the Six Day War as a major struggle in the Cold War, American Jews could argue that helping Israel benefited American foreign policy. As already indicated, being able to square support for Israel with American national interest was important to a community keenly aware of the perils of cognitive dissonance. Theodore Draper's article in *Commentary* argued that Israel deserved to be helped because it was a victim of Soviet aggression, a theme adopted by activists who lobbied the Johnson administration and Congress for additional military and financial aid.[28]

Helping to paint a black and white view of the Middle East reality was the growing influence of a disparate coalition of Jewish neoconservatives, right-wing Zionists, and Orthodox Jews, often referred to as the "New Jews." The leftist critique of Israel had enraged Jewish neoconservatives, already upset by what they perceived to be the bankruptcy of liberalism, black militancy, and the aggressiveness of the Soviet Union. Led by Podhoretz, the editor of *Commentary*, Irving Kristol from Public Interest, and Martin Peretz from the New Republic, neoconservatives took a hard-line position toward the Arabs and their Soviet patrons. Peretz, whose break with the New Left in the wake of the war was highly dramatic, used his magazine to establish a reputation as one of the most militant defenders of Israel. Helped by the intellectual heft of *Commentary*, the movement built a case for the view that the Soviet Union is a global menace bound to destabilize the Middle East and destroy Israel. As if to prove this argument right, in 1970 Moscow decided to ship large quantities of advanced airplanes and missile systems to Egypt, which were reportedly manned by Russians.[29]

Long considered a marginal force in the American Jewish community, right-wing Zionists were the successors of the American Revisionist Zionism. Peter Bergson, a leader of the Irgun—a right-wing underground organization in Palestine—and the playwright and propagandist Ben Hecht, spearheaded it in the 1940s. The 1967 war gave the right-wing Zionists a new lease of life, not the least because Menachem Begin, the revisionist leader and a former leader of the Irgun, was invited to serve in the National Unity Government, formed on the eve of the war. The ZOA, the oldest Zionist group in America, which incorporated many revisionist themes, denounced Labor-Zionism for its willingness to partition the land of Israel. Like the neoconservatives, Jacques Torczyner, the president of the ZOA, supported a hawkish American foreign policy that could protect Israel.[30]

Even more surprising was the foreign policy awakening of the Orthodox community, which, as noted, was at best tepid about Israel. Accounting for this turnaround was the growing popularity of a Zionist reinterpretation of the notion of redemption. Initiated by Rabbi Abraham Kook, the chief rabbi of Palestine, and continued by his son Rabbi Zvi Yehuda, the new theology viewed the creation of a secular Israel as *hathalat ha-geula*, "the dawn of redemption." The nationalist-religious movement, which originated in Rabbi Kook's Merkaz Harav yeshiva in Jerusalem, viewed the seemingly miraculous victory in 1967 as a further step in the redemptive process. Many of Kook's disciples established the *Gush Emunim*, "Bloc of the Faithful," movement, dedicated to settling the newly acquired territories, planting the first outpost in Hebron in 1968. While religious-Zionists were a minority, their view that the land of Israel was sacred and nonnegotiable became a virtual dogma in the Orthodox camp. The Union of Rabbis for the People and Land of Israel was one of the many Orthodox organizations that were created to lobby for a hard-line Israeli foreign policy.[31]

As always, the ideological positions staked out by the Jewish community were amplified by the institutional imperative. In the wake of the war, the two major Israel defense organizations—Presidents Conference and AIPAC—were catapulted to unprecedented prominence in the national and international arena. While the Conference became the undisputed spokesman for Israel in the community, lobbying for the vastly increased needs of Israel was assigned to AIPAC. Other organizations followed suit. NJCRAC formed an Israel Task Force and underwrote a national bureau of pro-Israel speakers and the CJF urged Jewish community groups to make Israel a major priority on their agendas. AJC allocated up to 50 percent of its budget to Israel-related activities, followed by ADL with 30 percent, and the AJCongress with 14 percent. Propelled by the organizational momentum and imbued with a sense of historical mission, virtually all organized Jewish groups were eager to emphasize the existential nature of the Arab-Israeli conflict. As one scholar put it, with so much buildup every issue was portrayed as a "life-and-death" struggle. Another critic noted that the organized community adopted a Hobbesian philosophy of "do not trust anyone."[32]

Among the most crucial issues on the communal agenda was the need to respond to the American peace initiatives. Both the Johnson administration and Richard Nixon, who came to power in 1969, tried to use Israel's overwhelming victory to trade territory for peace. The UN Resolution 242, adopted in November 1967 provided the rudiments of such an agreement. In December, William Rogers, Nixon's secretary of state, announced a peace initiative. It called for Israel's withdrawal from most of the occupied territories, an Israeli-Jordanian condominium in Old Jerusalem, and the right of Palestinian refugees to choose between reparation and resettlement. The government of Meir vehemently rejected the Rogers Plan, arguing that it would lead to Israel's destruction. On

January 25 and 26, 1970, AIPAC sent some fourteen hundred Jewish activists to Congress to lobby against the proposal.[33]

Responding to the Palestinian problem was another important task. As already noted, before 1967 most American Jews viewed the issue as part of a humanitarian problem. The occupation of the West Bank and the Gaza Strip created a new awareness of Palestinian nationhood, prompting one commentator to worry that "the administration and policing of large areas populated by Arabs were bound to create nightmarish problems."[34]

However, the terrorist tactics adopted by the PLO and a host of even more radical organizations, prevented any buildup of sympathy for the Palestinians. An Arab study of what was termed "Palestinian revolutionary violence" between July 1968 and November 1979 listed scores of plane hijackings; bomb attacks on Israeli, American, and European airports and travel officers; kidnappings; and bloody attacks on civilian targets in Israel. Among the more conspicuous were the hijackings of Western airplanes to Jordan, the murder of the Israeli Olympic team in Munich, the bombing of a Swissair plane en route to Tel Aviv, the attack on a Russian train carrying Jewish immigrants, and the Entebbe hijacking. Some of these attacks, which resulted in thousands of casualties, were directed against the United States and other countries that were considered supportive of Israel.[35] The Palestinian Covenant that called for the liberation of the entire territory of Palestine left little doubt that Israel's right to exist was totally rejected.

With so much negative publicity it was relatively easy for the Jewish community to support the official Israeli position that stipulated that as long as the Palestinians refuse to recognize Israel and renounce terrorism, there should be no negations. Details of the covenant were widely disseminated in the Jewish community, a process helped by a book published by a former head of the Mossad, Yehoshafat Harkabi (*Arab Attitudes toward Israel*). Still, most American Jews felt that Israel was not inherently expansionistic and, given the right circumstances, it would relinquish the territories. This time around, American Jewish attitudes were close to the population at large. A series of opinion polls found that between June 1967 and January 1979, some 40 to 56 percent of Americans supported the Israeli position in the conflict, as opposed to the 4 to 14 percent who took the Arab side. A 1975 Yankelovich poll revealed that, by a vast plurality, Americans considered the PLO to be a "terrorist organization" and "anti-U.S." When asked about sympathy, a 1975 Harris poll found that 33 percent of the sample sided with the Israelis and only 14 percent with the Palestinians. A similar poll in 1976 saw sympathy for Israel increase to 40 percent and for the Palestinians decrease to 10 percent. As one historian observed, for most of this period Jews and gentiles alike subscribed to the distinction made by Henry Steele Commager between Jewish nationalism as "benign" and devoted to peace and Arab nationalism as committed to "chauvinism, militarism, and territorial and cultural imperialism."[36]

Also high on the communal agenda was securing financial assistance for Israel. It was already noted that the Jewish response to Israeli financial need in 1967 was compassionate and generous, a development that was duplicated after the Yom Kippur War. However, even the most optimistic fund-raisers understood that Israel's financial needs would exceed the capacity of the community, as after 1973 the country's direct and indirect defense expenditure nearly doubled to 36 percent of the gross national product (GNP). To fill the gap, AIPAC decided to lobby Congress to increase its military aid to Israel. Between 1967 and 1971 American military assistance averaged some $40 million a year, increasing to an annual average of $400 in the next three years. In 1974–75 the United States contributed some $1.5 annually, a sum that represented 42 percent of Israel's defense expenditure.[37]

The organized community had applied itself with equal vigor to assuring American supply of military hardware. Given the fact that historically American administrations were reluctant to sell arms to Israel, this was an uphill battle, but one that had a very high level of support among rank and file. Polls taken in February 1971 and January 1975 revealed that an average of 95 percent of American Jews wanted the United States to send military equipment to Israel, and more than half supported dispatching American troops to the Middle East.[38] In an early test of the Jewish resolve, AIPAC persuaded a number of congressmen to press the Johnson administration to sell 50 Phantom F-4 jets to Israel. In April 1968 Representative Bertram L. Podell (D–N.Y.) had introduced a "sense of House resolution" for the sale supported by 100 members. In June 1968, Senator Stuart Symington (D–Mo.), in whose state the Phantoms were built, was also mobilized, prompting President Lyndon B. Johnson to announce the sale in December. In 1973 Senator Clifford Case (R–N.J.) introduced legislation to transfer to Israel Phantom jets and other military equipment to replace losses incurred in the Yom Kippur War. Case and other sympathetic legislators were also behind the large increase in American financial assistance for Israel.

While a success, the battle over the Phantoms illustrated the difficulty of advancing Israel's interests in the Arab-Israeli conflict. The Johnson administration was convinced that American national interest mandated a balanced approach to the Middle East. The White House was also reluctant to become the principle supplier of arms to Israel, a message that Paul Warnke, the assistant secretary of defense, conveyed to Israeli officials.[39] Underpinning this reluctance was the traditional State Department belief that supporting Israel would hurt U.S. relations with the Arabs and drive them even more speedily into the Soviet camp. To change such deeply entrenched perceptions there was a need to demonstrate that defending Israel served American security in the Middle East and beyond. As developed by the community, the new line of argument pushed the idea that rather than a case of charity, Israel represented a strategic asset in the Middle East.

BEYOND CHARITY: AMERICAN JEWS AND THE
DOCTRINE OF ISRAEL AS A STRATEGIC ASSET

Critics have long argued that the concept of Israel as a strategic asset was forced on a reluctant American foreign policy establishment by a well-oiled Jewish lobby. In this view, the Campaign Finance Act of 1974, which led to the creation of political action committees (PACs), had greatly amplified the influence of the Jewish lobby in Washington. In the 1980 election there were seven pro-Israeli PACs, raising to seventy-five six years later. Even though the Jewish lobby increased its power and influence in the 1970s, the emergent notion of Israel as a strategic asset was part of a more complex struggle over the shaping of American foreign policy.[40]

By the midsixties the foreign policy consensus forged in the 1950s around the policy of containing communism had begun to unravel. The New Left, which established its credentials during the anti-Vietnam protest, rejected what was described as American realpolitik of militarism and imperialism in favor of a new foreign policy paradigm. At the core of the new creed, known as New Internationalism, was a belief in such "moralpolitik" issues as world peace, concern for Third World countries, and human rights. With much of U.S. policy discredited by the war in Vietnam, the New Internationalist successfully challenged the view that the Soviet Union posed a threat to American national interests. The increasingly popular revisionist-academic literature blamed Washington's aggression and militarism for triggering the Cold War, while arguing that the Soviet Union is essentially peace loving and nonexpansionist. What is more, the New Internationalists asserted that it was not Soviet meddling, but indigenous struggle for liberation and equality that fueled regional conflicts. To imbue American foreign policy with moral principles, the New Left demanded a substantial reduction in defense budgets, a switch from a globalist to a regionalist view of international conflicts, and a commitment to the anticolonial struggle of Third World countries.[41]

To change the foreign policy paradigm, the New Politics group and the Conference of Concerned Democrats, a brainchild of veteran anti-Vietnam and civil rights activists that crystallized in 1967, decided to penetrate the Democratic party. The New Politics movement orchestrated the "dump Johnson" campaign and supported Eugene McCarthy for the Democratic nomination in 1968. When Hubert Humphrey, the candidate of the traditional liberal Democrats, lost the election to Nixon, the New Politics activists settled on George McGovern as their standard-bearer. McGovern, an ardent New Internationalist, was gravely concerned that America was "on the wrong side of history," and advocated a better relation with the Soviet Union, Cuba, and other revolutionary regimes. New Internationalism was strengthened by the congressional influx of anti-Vietnam activists and leftist advocates, who founded the Members of Congress for Peace through Law (MCPL), a caucus dedicated to progressive foreign policy. The MCPL was aided by the Coalition for a New Foreign and Military

Policy (CNFMP), an umbrella group of leftist lobbies that advocated American disarmament and aid to "progressive" Third World countries. The Institute for Policy Studies (IPS), a radical leftist think tank founded by Marcus G. Raskin and Richard Barnet in 1963, popularized these themes through a highly successful outreach program on Capitol Hill and in the media. The IPS-sponsored Militarism and Disarmament Project and its affiliate, the Center for Defense Information (CDI), offered a detailed rebuttal of the view that the Soviet Union posed a danger to American national interests. The New Internationalists demanded that the United States cease to supply military aid to its traditional allies and castigated Israel as an outpost of American imperialism in the Middle East.[42]

When Nixon narrowly defeated Humphrey in 1968, it fell to Henry Kissinger, his national security adviser, to fashion a response to the increasingly popular New Internationalist themes. While emphasizing realpolitik and the need for credible deterrence, the Nixon administration signaled that the rigid bipolar world of containment was obsolete. The new policy of détente envisaged a peaceful coexistence with Moscow and a curtailment of American involvement in Third World conflicts. The Nixon doctrine of 1969 called on American regional allies to shoulder the burden of defense against communism, but made no effort to designate Israel as Washington's regional "influential" in the Middle East.

In fact, the ongoing Arab-Israeli conflict exposed the contractions in the détente policy. On the one hand, Nixon and Kissinger came to appreciate Israel's value as a regional security asset. Such a view was influenced by intelligence reports in 1970 that confirmed active Soviet involvement in the war of attrition waged by Israel and Egypt across the Suez Canal. Washington's misgivings that the Soviet Union was exploiting the conflict in order to dominate the Middle East were further confirmed when the Syrians, with the apparent blessing of Moscow, decided to intervene in the civil war between King Hussein of Jordan and the Palestinian guerrillas in September 1970. When Israel partially mobilized the IDF to stop the Syrian invasion into Jordan, the White House, which was spared from a costly effort to save the monarchy, decided to anoint Israel as its strategic asset. Without totally discarding the moral imperative, Kissinger could now argue that, by backing Israel, Washington was in a better position to weaken the Soviet influence in the Middle East. In 1971, the administration swiftly approved Israel's request for additional Phantom jets and other military equipment, and made subsequent arms-transfers routine.[43]

On the other hand, the policy of détente mandated developing a closer relation between Washington and Moscow. The Roger initiative was designed to solve the conflict and, at the same time, secure Soviet cooperation in the Middle East. Running on a separate track were American proposals for a Big Two and a Big Four meeting, to which Russia was invited in order to help mediate the Arab-Israeli conflict. When, in September 1970, Anwar Sadat succeeded Nasser as president, the administration sensed that the chances for a settlement in the region increased. The Yom Kippur War further confirmed for Washington that the problem needed to be resolved not only for the sake of regional stability in the Middle East, but also in order to save the larger American design of détente. Building upon the cease-fire agreement, Kissinger embarked upon his step-by-step diplomacy with hopes of achieving a more durable solution.

However, the administration's realpolitik-based détente policy and Israel's role as a strategic ally encountered considerable domestic opposition. Spurred by the bombing of Cambodia, the New Left bitterly attacked the Nixon-Kissinger team for its alleged aggression toward the Soviet Union and its progressive regimes the globe over. McGovern, who secured the Democratic nomination for the 1972 presidential election, was running on a platform of anti-militarism and anti-imperialism. He reiterated the view that the Soviet Union does not pose a threat to American national security and urged his fellowmen to "abandon their paranoia about Moscow." To ease the military buildup, the candidate vowed to make deep cuts in nuclear and conventional weapons. McGovern was an early advocate of including the Palestinians in the peace negotiations, a stand shared by Senator William Fulbright (D-Ark), the powerful chairman of the Foreign Relations Committee, who also urged an independent Palestinian state. Although McGovern lost by a landslide to Nixon, a left-leaning Congress and the mounting Watergate problems of the administration sustained the influence of the New Left.[44]

It fell to a group of conservative Democrats led by Henry Jackson and neo-conservatives such as Podhoretz to challenge the McGovernites and other New Internationalists. In 1973 Jackson, Daniel Patrick Moynihan, Jeane Kirkpatrick, and other hawkish Democrats created the Coalition for Democratic Majority (CDM), which accused the New Left of "appeasing" Moscow and endangering the national security of the United States. In his memoir, Podhoretz argued that McGovern wanted to turn the United States into an active sponsor of revolutionary regimes in the Third World. Emphasizing his credentials as a proud Zionist, Podhoretz pointed to the "inextricable connection between the survival of Israel and American military strength." Murray Friedman, an AJC official, who contended that a strong American military was the best guarantee for Israel's security, made much the same argument. Moynihan used Podhoretz's slogan of "strong America-secure Israel" in his successful run against Bella Abzug and Ramsey Clark—two of the most radical New Internationalists—for the New York senatorial nomination in 1976.[45]

To propagate further the idea that Israel is a strategic ally in a region threatened by Soviet expansionism, a number of neoconservative Jews founded the Jewish Institute for National Security Affairs (JINSA) in 1976. JINSA newsletters and publications depicted the radical Arab states as tools of Moscow's domination in the Middle East and exposed the links of the PLO to revolutionary movements in Latin American and elsewhere. Among the activists involved with JINSA was Richard Perle, an aide to Senator Jackson, and Stephen D. Bryen, who worked for both Senator Case and the CDM. Some of the JINSA supporters would later become associated with the Committee on Present Danger, a neoconservative foreign policy group that helped to articulate the foreign policy vision of Ronald Reagan.[46]

Perle and Bryen were instrumental in challenging the centerpiece of the administration détente policy, namely an effort to extend most favored nation (MFN) trade status to Moscow. Kissinger asserted that the normalization of trade relations would compel the Soviet Union to moderate its international behavior and hoped to enlist Moscow's help in his difficult negotiations with North Vietnam. However, Jewish activists and their sympathizers in Congress decided to link the trade issue to an increase in Jewish immigration from the Soviet Union. Senator Jackson, who addressed the National Council for Soviet Jewry in 1972, promised to take up the fight against the administration. For Jackson, Moynihan and others in the CDM, the issue of Jewish immigration was a "god send" on two counts. First, they hoped to slow the momentum toward normalization with the Soviet Union. One observer noted the senator's "desire to obstruct, if not to prevent, the implementation of détente, because, in his view the Soviet Union was a threat to the free world." Another was more blunt: "Jackson is more anti-Soviet than he is pro-Soviet Jews. He's a cold warrior. He is going to milk the Jewish bloc for everything it's got." Second, and equally important, the CDM group planned to force presidential candidate McGovern, who was sensitive to charges of double standards on human rights, to embrace the Jewish immigration advocacy. Indeed, at a rally for Soviet Jews in August 1972 the reluctant McGovern announced that "Soviet Jews should not be forgotten when talking about peace and economic agreement." He later promised the Presidents Conference to fight against the MFN legislation for Russia.[47]

Some American Jews, unwilling to offend Nixon, a certified friend of Israel, were not happy about Jackson's effort to link the MFN status to Jewish immigration. There were also those who feared that the Jackson crusade would undermine the efforts to ease superpower tensions, a liberal cause that had many champions in the community. What is more, the government of Meir, which was quite reluctant to get involved in a fight between Nixon and Congress, counseled against the amendment. However, Jackson and the Jewish neoconservatives twisted the community's arm by mobilizing the National Council for Soviet Jewry and Jewish grass-root support. In spite of Nixon's contention that the amendment, co-sponsored in the House by Charles Vanik, was a threat to détente and global peace, it was passed by a congressional coalition of traditional liberal Democrats and conservative Republicans who distrusted détente. A reluctant Gerald Ford, who replaced Nixon in 1974, signed the amendment into law on January 3, 1975.

Conventional wisdom has it that the Jackson-Vanick amendment represented a watershed in the relations between the organized Jewish community and the American government. To both critics and admirers, it looked like "Jewish activists had taken on the Nixon administration and the Kremlin and won." However, some argued that neoconservatives used the community to undermine both the New Internationalists and détente. Whatever the case, Kissinger, upon becoming secretary of state in the Ford administration, was quick to discover the new Jewish clout. When the secretary, angered by Israel's refusal to reciprocate Egyptian concessions, persuaded Ford to call for an "reassessment" of U.S.– Israel policy, a euphemism for suspending arms sales, the reaction was swift and decisive. Within a few weeks, in May 1975, AIPAC organized a letter signed by seventy-six U.S. senators who scolded the administration for endangering Israel, which was described as a crucial bulwark against Soviet influence in the Middle East. In yet another sign of defiance of the Ford administration, and in spite of Israeli reluctance, the Jewish lobby undertook a successful effort to pass legislation targeting the Arab boycott of Israel.[48]

While the Jackson-Vanick amendment undoubtedly represented the "coming of age" of the Jewish community, the string of legislative achievements came at a cost. Behind the impressive façade of communal solidarity in action, the issue of Israel and the conduct of the peace process were creating tensions between the right and the left. As the debate heated up, the fervent hope that Israel would be able to bind American Jews with the glue of "transcendental" meaning was dashed.

HOLDING THE FORT: COMMUNAL CONSENSUS AND ITS CHALLENGERS

For reasons discussed elsewhere, it was imperative for the community to develop and sustain a consensus on the peace process. Largely inspired by the Labor formula of land-for-peace, the official orthodoxy spelled out positions on the occupied territories, PLO and the Palestinians, the status of Jerusalem, and the pace of negotiations with the Arab countries. American Jews were called upon to support the Israeli view that progress should be pegged to Arab willingness to compromise. Jerusalem was to have remained the united capital of Israel and the territories were to be held until the Palestinians gave up terrorism and recognized Israel. Negotiation with what was described as "terrorists" were considered beyond the pale because it would legitimize the PLO and send a signal that "terrorism pays." As already noted, by staking out these positions, the organized community could count on the support of an overwhelmingly number of American Jews.

However, the democratic majority that backed the consensus did not impress the small but growing number of critics. The first to react was the radical Jewish left. Accordingly to one account, by the early seventies there were over one hundred radical Jewish groups. Among the better known were the Committee on New Alternatives in the Middle East (CONAME), Jewish Radical Committee, International Committee of the Left for Peace in the Middle East, Coordinating Committee of Jewish Intellectuals, Students Against Middle East Involvement, Search for Justice and Equality in Palestine, Middle East Research and Information Project, Organization for Peace and Justice in the Middle East, the Jewish Peace Fellowship, Radical Zionist Alliance, the Ad Hoc Committee on the Liberation of Palestine and Israel and the IPS.[49]

With varying degrees of vigor these groups attacked Israel for forming an imperialist alliance with the United States and its "colonial" subjugation of the Palestinians. For many, including the veteran critic I.F. Stone, the Israeli policy and the American Jewish support of it amounted to an immoral display of "tribal" self-interest in violation of the higher prophetic ethics of universal justice. For others, beholden to the New Left creed of Third Worldism, a "moral crusade for the displaced Palestinians" was a convenient avenue of protest against the United States. In spite of its stridency, the radical critique did little to perturb the Jewish establishment. Jewish spokesmen could point to the fact that these groups were marginal and harbored such known critics of Israel as Noam Chomsky from CONAME, or Raskin and Barnet from IPS. Others accused the radical movement, which failed to denounce the Palestinian atrocities, of hypocrisy and inconsistency. Historian Walter Laqueur argued that "the present stance of the Jewish radical is a halfway house, morally and intellectually inconsistent, and thus untenable in the long run."[50]

Harder to tackle was the challenge posed by the Breira group, founded in 1973 as the Project of Concern in Israeli-Diaspora relations. The name, meaning "Alternative" in Hebrew, was chosen to denote an alternative approach to the Arab-Israeli conflict. Although some of Breira activists such as the IPS-affiliated Arthur Wascow hailed from the radical Zionist camp, others were more mainline figures. Among them were Balfour Brickner of the Union of American Hebrew Congregations (UAHC), Rabbi David Wolf Silverman of the Jewish Theological Seminary, and Rabbi Max Ticktin, the associate director of the national B'nai B'rith Hillel Foundation. Irving Howe, Nathan Glazer, and other Jewish luminaries declared their sympathy, but did not officially join.

Breira called for the establishing of a Palestinian state in the occupied territories and a comprehensive peace with the Arab countries based on territorial concessions. In addition to expressing such taboos, the moral implication of Breira advocacy was even more chilling to the mainstream. One historian noted that the message here was no "longer what happened to Israel but what happened to the Palestinians." The group's magazine *Interchange*, congressional testimony, mailings, and paid advertisements attracted the attention of major American newspapers, leading to headlines that emphasized a growing willingness of American Jews to publicly criticize Israel. Breira's work with Israeli peace activists and its meetings with Palestinian representatives created equally sensational news, with some articles suggesting a Jewish "civil war." According to one account the impact of Breira alarmed the Israeli government, which urged the organized community to suppress the dissent.[51]

Sensing a threat to the consensus, loyalist organizations reacted with outrage. The ZOA accused Breira of being a spokesman for the PLO and the "mythical Palestinians." Union of Orthodox Jewish Congregations of America condemned Breira for its criticism of Israel. A Hadassah newsletter called it a "cheerleader for defeatism" and an AIPAC publication denounced it for "undermining U.S. support for Israel." Others accused Breira of being a front for the PLO, demanding that it should rename itself "Jews for Fatah." An article in one of the Jewish newspapers charged that the "Hillel Foundations have developed into incubators for Breira's perspectives," which deceitfully lure young Jews to act "as funnels" for its pro-PLO information to the masses of unknowing students. Breira was denied membership in local Jewish bodies and individual members, many of them Hillel campus rabbis, came under intense pressure to quit the organization in order to save their jobs. The campaign against Breira forced the group to disband shortly after its first and only national conference in 1977.[52]

Lost in the storm over Breira was the incipient challenge posed to the communal consensus by the militant right wing. Leading the way was the Jewish Defense League (JDL) founded in 1968 by Rabbi Meir Kahane, Bertram Zweibon and Morton Dolinsky. The JDL, which copied the violent dissent practiced by the Black Panthers, moved quickly to stake out a radical position on the issues of Jewish immigration from the Soviet Union and the Arab-Israeli conflict. JDL activists attacked Soviet and Arab targets in the United States and engaged in protest against the Jewish left, including meetings of Breira. Operating under the slogan "Never Again" JDL supported the Greater Land of Israel, a policy which, in its view, mandated the expulsion of Palestinians from the territories. To bolster its claims, the JDL distributed a book, *Battleground: Facts and Fantasy in Palestine*, penned by Shmuel Katz, the propaganda chief of the Irgun and a close associate of Begin. Katz contended that the Palestinians were recent arrivals to the land of Israel and did not deserve self-determination.[53]

Katz, who became a leader in the Land of Israel Movement, a maximalist Israeli organization, helped to create in 1971 the Americans for a Safe Israel (AFSI). AFSI's self-described goal was to persuade American Jews to reject the land-for-peace formula of Labor in favor of the peace-for-peace model favored by the Israeli right wing. AFSI, which initially functioned as a think tank, generated a large amount of material devoted to establishing Israel's legitimacy in the West Bank, Gaza, and the Sinai Desert. One of AFSI's cofounders, the sociologist Rael Jean Isaac published a number of exposés, on Breira and the IPS. AFSI gained a higher profile in the Jewish community when a number of mainstream organizations such as AIPAC and NJCRAC decided to distribute its pamphlets, along with Katz's *Battleground*.[54]

Suppressing challenges to the official position on the Arab-Israeli conflict created a crisis of legitimacy for the organized community. On balance, the treatment of Breira hurt the most. Doubts about Israel's wisdom of handling the peace process were not limited to the radical left. Writing in early 1973, Leonard Fein asserted that a "growing number of American Jews are becoming somewhat restive," leading to a quest for a "more mature understanding of Israel." Howe and other intellectuals signed advertisements protesting Israel's settlement policies, and prominent leaders like Philip Klutznik and Nahum Goldmann hinted at their unhappiness. Rabbi Jacobovits lamented the loss of Jewish values as manifested by the refusal to "speak out on the problem of Arab refugees." The journalist Stephen Rosenfeld critically examined the strategic and moral reasons for American support for Israel. He concluded that U.S. strategic interests demand good relations with Arabs and that Israel's moral claim was compromised by its treatment of Palestinians.[55]

Many American Jews had also expressed anxiety over combining their hawkish positions on Israel with their liberal views on Vietnam and other foreign policy issues. The strains of what A.F.K. Organski called the "schizoid stand" were never far from the surface. During a 1969 World Zionist Organization meeting, Hertzberg criticized Meir for praising Nixon's foreign policy and Borowitz denounced the "unrelenting pressure" of Israeli officials to get American Jews to vote for Nixon. Commenting on this "schizophrenia," Urofsky posited that American Jews found themselves partially paralyzed at the thought of having to support the Nixon administration, which was "entering the worst throes of the Watergate scandal."[56]

Perhaps the most damaging aspect of the Breira affair related to the issue of free discourse. For a community priding itself on individualism and a democratic tradition, the exercise in collective censorship was highly demoralizing. Critics compared it to McCarthyism, witch-hunt or a communal *herem*, or "ostracism," where Breira activists were proclaimed by most "Jewish professional and communal leaders" as 'heretics' (if not traitors)." One critic reminded his readers that Old Testament prophets spoke out against their fellow Israelites and their leaders, but had never been branded as traitors. Borowitz noted that the need to rally around Israel introduced a new "sacred cow" into the community: talking to an American audience, "you are not allowed to say anything bad about the State of Israel. It is assumed either that you are a paid agent of Mao Tse-Dung or of the American Council for Judaism or that there is something the matter with you as a Jew." Chomsky, a frequent target of communal opprobrium, complained that the "questioning of Israel policies has largely been silenced, with effective use of the moral weapons of anti-Semitism and 'Jewish self-hatred.' "[57]

Such criticism pointed to the conundrum that the Israeli-focused civil religion created for the community. Following the official line of the peace process became a part of the "good Jew" script and even mild dissent was seen as sacrilegious, because, as Liebman explained, support for Israel represented the "crucial boundary" of the Jewish community. Stifling criticism became synonymous with boundary maintenance, turning the positions on the peace process into a series of litmus tests for communal membership. Other scholars added that the requirements of boundary maintenance created a dichotomy between pro- and anti-Israeli positions. Those who were found to hold anti-Israeli positions were labeled enemies of the Jewish people and "turned upon by the organized mainstream of the Jewish community."[58]

The measures used to curtail Breira acquired a life of their own when mainline organizations became embroiled in an internal debate about the best way to protect Israel and offer a modicum of free discourse. NJCRAC and the AJC commissioned internal studies on the limits of dissent, and the Presidents Conference and the Synagogue Council of America held public hearings on the issue. Helped by Israeli officials, the Conference developed a set of basic guidelines for a modified consensus on the Arab-Israeli conflict. American Jews were advised that they could air their disagreements in private, but must publicly stand united with Israel. Towing the new line, Joachim Prinz, the vice president of the World Jewish Congress and a Breira sympathizer took to pleading for a "discreet" criticism of Israel. The community was also asked to honor Israeli democracy because, "Israelis were the only ones entitled to decide Israeli policy, since they alone bore the risks." The ban on negotiations with the PLO was reiterated, along with a demand that Palestinians give up terror and recognize the state of Israel.[59]

Although the new rules adopted in 1977 did not save Breira, some were optimistic that a more civil discourse could hold the communal fort without stifling dissent. The organized community was also confident that, by instituting voluntary restraints, the appearance, if not the reality of "sacred unity" with Israel could be preserved. These expectations were shattered when, in October 1977, the right-wing Likud party came to power in Israel.

3

Straining the "Sacred Unity": American Jews in the Era of Likud

Even before the victory of Likud, there were growing doubts about the ability of the Israel-centered civil religion to stop the demographic decline. The foreign policy vision of the Likud government created a communal split between those who stuck to an ethnonationalistic or religious definition of Judaism and those who wanted to go back to an identity based on ethical universalistic principles. The conduct of the peace process became the battleground on which the two sides waged a fierce struggle for the soul of Judaism. While the leadership of the organized community tried to preserve the semblance of "sacred unity," the deep divisions among American Jews weakened the Israel-centered civil religion.

ENCOUNTERS WITH REALITY: LIKUD AND THE VISION OF GREATER ISRAEL

In May 1977, the Israeli voters gave Menachem Begin and his Likud party a narrow victory, ending three decades of Labor rule. The election results shocked the community whose scant understanding of the Israeli political scene was severely taxed by the new political phenomenon. Leonard Fein, who was a liberal critic, admitted total surprise: "it was as if George Wallace and the crazies had won." Comfortable with the Labor leaders and steeped in the mythology of a liberal and progressive Israel, few American Jews had an understanding of the political vision of Begin. A few years before, one of them worried about the possibility of a fascist state in Israel and pointed to the "slowly climbing support" of Israel's right-wing Gahal party, the predecessor of Likud. But Rabbi

Alexander Schindler, the chairman of the Conference of Presidents, contended that Begin was not a hawk and cautioned against falling into the trap of calling politicians "hawks and doves."[1]

When Begin took office in June, Likud's commitment to the revisionist ideology of Greater Israel was made quite clear. In one of his first official acts Begin visited a Gush Emunim settlement near Nablus, where he promised that there would be more "Elon Mores." On this and other occasions the new prime minister rejected the notion of a foreign rule in Judea and Samaria and insisted that the land be called by its biblical name. Still, many American Jews dismissed the ideological undertones of Likud's policy toward the Middle East conflict. As Hertzberg noted, "the mainstream of the American Jewish community wanted to believe that Begin was really a hard bargainer, a pragmatic politician in the American mold, who was announcing these ideological propositions in order to negotiate from strength." He added that many American Jews "tried to pretend to themselves that the Likud were a bunch of tough minded businessmen . . . who asked for a maximum price and would settle eventually for something less."[2]

Behind the urge to pretend that Begin was only a tougher version of Labor was the underlying psychological unease with the new Israeli leader. A number of observers noted that Menachem Begin did not fit well into the American Jewish vision of Israel. At best, "his Polish accent" and "formal manners" were a far cry from the heroic images of the native-born *sabras*. At worst, "his ill fitting suits, Yiddish-accented English" made him look like an "Old World uncle who had suddenly reemerged from the shadow of Diaspora history," a stereotype from which American Jews were eager to disassociate themselves. Moreover, Begin, the antithesis of Ari Ben Canaan, "sharply contradicted . . . images of Israel as the land of muscular kibbutzniks . . . who wore *kova tembel* by day, danced the *hora* all night, and piloted their planes and tanks to astounding military victories early next-morning." It was not lost on the community that the press "had a field day" in commenting on the new prime minister's East European "pedigree." *Time*'s infamous comment that Begin rhymes with Fagin, the anti-Semitic stereotype from *Oliver Twist*, was a remainder of the enduring nature of anti-Semitic imagery (cited in Goldberg).[3]

As mythology gave way to reality, American Jews were compelled to take a hard look at the political culture that brought Begin to power. If Begin had no place in their version of Israel, his base of support of lower-class Jews from Arab countries, known as Second Israel, and the religious camp were even more alarming. One observer noted that for many American Jews "fixated on the image of Israel as a land settled by their European Jewish ancestors" the Sephardim "present an exotic—if not repellent—image." Indeed, some Jewish commentators implied that the Sephardim are essentially primitive, chauvinistic, and hostile to the values of liberal democracy. Milton Viorst explained that "in contrast to the ideas of democracy, secularism, liberalism and socialism" of the Ashkenazim, the "Sephardim brought to Israel the Islamic tradition of patriarchal rule." He also alleged that the Sephardim have a "black-and-white vision of politics," leading them to inject into "everyday contest for power a passion generally associated with the East rather than the West." Roberta Strauss Feuerlicht contended that the "Sephardim who have a relatively low level of education and no experience with democracy are easy prey for demagogues." She added that Sephardi mobs shout "King Begin" and attack opposition candidates. Bernard Avishai stated that the social outlook of the Sephardim "is now not very different from the one they had in Casablanca or Algiers before 1950." Fein went so far as to hint that Israel detoured from the path of Western liberalism because "the wrong people" immigrated to the Jewish state. Even the well-meaning Urofsky declared that the Sephardim would ultimately become useful citizens but "would never have the familiarity and comfort that comes naturally to those raised in sophisticated, industrialized societies."[4]

Paradoxically, the peoplehood-based identification with Israel magnified the shock of the encounter with Second Israel. The perceived bond between American Jews and the Israelis was nurtured by their common Ashkenazi heritage. When Sephardi Jews became the majority, it reduced the sense of a common culture and made it harder for some American Jews to identify with the Israelis. As Tivnan put it, "when they look at Israel, they see the face not of their European and Russian cousins but of Jews from Arab countries, the Sephardim." It was less than helpful that some Sephardim were openly rebelling against the European Jews who founded the state. Fein described a pattern of radical Sephardi protest that included signs like "Ashke-Nazi" and "Ashkenzim to Auschwitz." Increasingly, the new demography was hard for those who were nurtured on the images of *Exodus* and the kibbutzim. To those American Jews who were "obsessed with the view that Israel is the West in the East," the realities of Second Israel were less than welcome.[5]

Fearing the alienating effects of the new Israeli image, some communal leaders tried to calm down the anti-Sephardi agitation. Schindler professed guilt over the fact that American Jews see the world through Ashkenazi-WASP eyes and are too glib in generalizing about the Sephardim. Irving Greenberg, the founder of the National Jewish Center for Learning and Leadership (CLAL), a national leadership center, denounced the talk about Sephardi "primitivism, chauvinism, religious extremism" and pointed out that the coming of age of a new political group is a sign of a flourishing democracy. True to form, Norman Podhoretz castigated the left for losing their usual compassion for lower classes because of a "fear of being swamped by people whose level of cultural development seemed hopelessly primitive and whose undifferentiated hatred of the Arabs seemed nothing short of racist."[6]

American Jews were equally worried about the Orthodox camp that helped to propel Begin to victory. The community was more aware of the extent of Orthodox power in Israel because of the periodical demands of the religious parties to change the Law of Return to reflect the Orthodox view of conversion. Already in March 1972, the official organ of the Labor Zionist Alliance of the

United States complained about the demands of the Israeli orthodoxy. The heightened visibility of the Orthodox parties in the Likud coalition put a spotlight on their ambitious agenda. Soon after, in 1978, the World Zionist Organization (WZO), spurred by the American Reform and Conservative movements, passed a resolution demanding equal treatment of all branches of Judaism. While American Jews wanted Israel to be a Jewish state, it was the "ethnic Judaism light" variety that most of them had in mind. That Israel may move into the uncharted waters of theocracy was not only alarming from the perspective of the "who is a Jew" issue, but also raised fears about the Western and democratic image of the state. As Feuerlicht implied, the Orthodox camp was determined to change Israel into the Vatican of the Jewish people.[7]

It was also distressing to some in the community that both the Orthodox and the Sephardi Jews supported Begin's hard-line approach to the peace process. As already noted, the former believed in the theologically mandated vision of Greater Land of Israel. The latter were said to have harbored a deep mistrust of the Arabs. Avishai, a critic of the Likud, explained that they "arrived in Israel with a deep hatred for Arabs, which . . . reflected their own collective tragedy." Viorst added that, in line with their political culture, the Sephardim responded to the Arabs with "raw emotions" and sought to settle "scores against an old enemy." He and others pointed out that Israeli opinion polls indicated that both Orthodox and Sephardi Jews were twice as likely as the Ashkenazim to support extreme positions in favor of controlling the Arabs of the occupied territories. Edward Tivnan quoted one poll that showed more than 50 percent of Israeli teenagers, most of them Sephardi Jews, harbored nondemocratic attitudes toward non-Jews in general and to Arabs in particular.[8]

The image of a polarized Israel led by a hard-line Likud party that was empowered by a radical political culture, was bad news for a community struggling to stem the demographic decline. While few accepted Bergman's prediction that by 2076 the number of Jews would decline to 940,000, the anxiety over the future was palpable. Doubts about the ability of the Israel-centered civil religion to provide a meaningful focus of identification were growing. A 1981 survey by the CJF found that the younger generation was showing progressive signs of alienation form Israel. Woocher, who first articulated the concept of civil religion, warned that commitment to Israel was a vital symbol, but not necessarily an "irreplaceable one." He quoted a poll that indicated that only 56 percent of respondents thought that Jewish people couldn't survive without Israel, as opposed to 90 percent who thought so about the Jewish religion.[9]

Others, especially left-wing critics, argued that the hard-line peace policies of Likud made American Jews increasingly uncomfortable with the Israeli-based aspects of their identity. According to this argument, the perceived congruence between liberalism and support of Israel would be hard to sustain in face of the new political culture of the country. According to one historian, Begin's fusion of nationalism and religious orthodoxy contradicted the "secular universalist tenets that were at the core of Labor Zionism and mainstream American Judaism." In other words, "instead of the Hebrew prophets, whose jeremiads for justice made them the patron saints of Jewish liberalism in the modern era, they heard a disconcerting call for the land of Israel for the people of Israel according to the Torah of Israel." Implied in this criticism was a growing realization that "sacred unity" was conditional, depending on a continuation of Israel as a liberal and enlightened state. The new Israel of Begin felt short of being liberal and enlightened, at least by the elevated standards of American Jewry.[10]

Signs of discomfort were also emerging at the level of Israel's symbolic representation. Woocher warned that Jews supported a "mythically potent Israel . . . which acquires its powerful hold . . . by virtue of a meaning that transcends its own reality." He and others called to adjust the foundational myth of pioneering sabras, but there was no agreement on how the new reality should be presented. Melvyn H. Bloom, a fund-raiser for the UJA, recalled that in the late 1970s his team of planners disagreed on what images of Israel should be used for the upcoming campaign. While there were obvious benefits to portraying Israel as a poor Third World country, fund-raisers were reluctant to draw attention to Second Israel. According to one historian, prior to 1977 UJA was aware of the socioeconomic gap in Israel—including the problems of poverty, juvenile delinquency, prostitution, and drug addiction—but felt that such issues would discourage potential contributors. The social gaps would have been embarrassing, especially as Israel was being touted as a model state.[11]

It is against this sort of background that the organized community had to make an adjustment in its Israeli strategies. With a minirevolt against "pocket book" Judaism brewing in its ranks and a general decline in contributions, Project Renewal, which linked American donors to social welfare issues in Israel, was launched in the late 1970s. Most of the project's funds were allocated for rehabilitating the largely Sephardi slums and development towns. Given the new realities in Israel, it was hoped that Project Renewal would forge a more realistic link between the community and the "new Israelis." However, Paul Cowan, a critic of organized Jewry, argued that even after Likud's victory American Jews were reluctant to grapple with the issue of the new Israeli demography. He charged that in the absence of a real debate, the community tended to hold onto the images of Israel that "exist in our head" rather than the ones that exist in the world.[12]

In trying to mend the relations between American Jews and Begin's Israel, the organized community was also mindful of its task of defending Israel's foreign policy in the United States. This task was made more difficult because of Jimmy Carter's embrace of New Internationalism.

THE JEWISH COMMUNITY AND THE CARTER MORAL CRUSADE: THE CHALLENGE OF NEW INTERNATIONALISM

After McGovern's landslide defeat in 1972, the left wing of the Democratic party pinned its hope on a number of progressive candidates like Morris K. Udall and Frank Church. The ascendancy of Carter in the 1976 primaries was not welcome news for New Left stalwarts. Carter's "conversion" to human rights was of a recent vintage and his fidelity to the regionalist perspective untested. To make sure that the party's nominee for the president of the United States would adhere to the New Internationalist vision, the Democratic Platform Committee urged Carter to adopt cuts in military spending and implement regionalism.

Whether guided by an inner conviction or coaxed by his left-wing critics, Carter used his inauguration address in January 1977 to announce a radical change in American foreign policy. Top billings went to such moralpolitik issues as human rights, cuts in military spending, and a call for a regional perspective on conflict. Carter pronounced himself cured of the "inordinate fear of Communism" and assured his audience that a more morally just global order was imminently obtainable. To show his regionalist mettle, soon after the inauguration, the new president denounced Kissinger's philosophy of linking regional conflict to Soviet machinations and promised a reevaluation of regional conflagrations. He also delighted the New Internationalists by insisting that the United States should tackle the problem of "North-South" relations, a euphemism for embracing Third World countries.[13]

The new moral crusade upset the Jewish community. At a minimum, Carter's dedication to regionalism threatened to undermine the hard-won recognition of Israel as a U.S. strategic asset in the Middle East. American Jews became truly alarmed when, on May 19, 1977, the president issued a memorandum that pledged to make arm transfers an "exceptional foreign policy instrument." The memorandum exempted North Atlantic Treaty Organization (NATO) countries and Japan, but did not mention Israel, Iran, and other American allies. To add to the uncertainty, the administration, which decided to push for a comprehensive solution of the Arab-Israeli conflict, abandoned Kissinger's long-standing policy of a gradual approach to the peace process. The new strategy was recommended by the Brookings Institute's report "Toward Peace in the Middle East," published at the end of 1975. The article was authored by Zbigniew Brzezinski, Carter's national security adviser, and the Brookings Middle East Study Group. On February 17, 1977, the president elaborated on his peace vision by stating that, "in exchange for suitable security arrangements," Israel "should and would withdraw to the June 5, 1967 lines, with only such modifications as might be mutually acceptable." Carter was also in a hurry to implement another major recommendation of the Brooking's report, which called to grant self-determination for the Palestinian people. In a March 16 speech he declared that "there should be a homeland provided for Palestinian refugees who have suffered for many, many years."[14]

Such a dramatic change in American foreign policy distressed American Jews, the majority of whom voted for Carter. When just before his electoral defeat Prime Minister Yitzhak Rabin visited the White House in March, the testy meeting dismayed the organized community. There was little doubt that the election of Begin, who believed that the West Bank was part of the historical land of

Israel, would make matters worse. In spite of their personal unhappiness with Begin, a number of major Jewish organizations decided to support publicly the Likud government. Leading the way was Schindler, a self-described dove. Schindler revealed that, as the Conference chairman, he had little choice but to maintain the unity of the Jewish people. Immediately after Likud's victory, Schindler sent a message to all Jewish organizations declaring support for Israel's democracy and its elected government. When Schindler subsequently met the new Israeli prime minister, he favorably compared Begin's sense of responsibility for the Jewish people with Rabin's often more hostile approach to American Jews.[15]

The decision of the organized community to support the Likud government is best understood within the context of the unprecedented criticism of Begin by the American media and the political class. In addition to the perceived anti-Semitic barbs, commentators had competed with each other to expose Begin's terrorist past and decried the "extremists" in Israel. United Jewish support was important in signaling to the Carter administration that it could not capitalize upon the general unhappiness with the new Israeli government to push its Middle East peace plans. As expected, the press widely reported Schindler's endorsement of Begin, which made an impact on the White House. When Begin made his first visit to Washington he was cordially received by the White House. To further impress the political establishment, the organized community received the prime minister with warmth, if not with the usual adulation reserved for the likes of Ben-Gurion, Abba Eban, or Golda Meir.

The closing of ranks around Begin took place amid signs that the Carter administration was showing a "pro-Arab tilt." The Conference of Presidents and AIPAC were upset because Carter vetoed an Israeli request to sell its Kfir jets to Ecuador. He also refused to sell additional concussion bombs to the Israeli Air Force and was responsive to the business community's fight against the antiboycott bill. In June, Jewish activists on Capitol Hill circulated a long list of grievances, including a demand for the removal of some of Carter's Middle East experts, whom they blamed for a pro-Arab bias. The real target of their criticism was Brzezinski, whose comments on the "inherently rigid" Israeli politics and involvement in the Brookings Report opened him to charges that he was Carter's pro-Arab "Svengali." Unable or unwilling to accept Carter's genuine commitment to New Internationalism, the Jewish community blamed the Polish-born Brzezinski, who was occasionally referred to as "that Polish anti-Semite."[16]

Carter's drive to include the Soviet Union in the peace process increased the ire of the Jewish community. On October 1, 1977, the White House announced that the superpowers would cosponsor a Middle East conference in Geneva with the aim of securing the interests of all parties to the conflict. Although the declaration did not mention the rights of the Palestinians, Schindler denounced it as "an abandonment of America's historic commitment to the security and survival of Israel," adding that the community "was very upset, very unhappy."

Mark Siegel, Carter's liaison to American Jews, was left with the unenviable task of explaining the communiqué to the Jewish leaders. According to one account, some four thousand telegrams a day poured into the White House, mostly from outraged Jews. In an effort to mend bridges, Carter assured a meeting of Jewish congressmen in the White House that he would rather commit political suicide than hurt Israel.[17]

Sadat's peace initiative saved the organized community from a head-on collision with the Carter administration. During his historic visit to Israel in November, Sadat proposed to exchange the Sinai Peninsula for a peace treaty with Egypt. In spite of the initial euphoria, the negotiations bogged down over the extent of territorial concession and the Palestinian problem. Begin's offer of a limited autonomy and his government's policy of accelerating Jewish settlements in the territories enraged the administration. Reacting to an Israeli plan in January 1978 that called for "bolstering" the existing settlements in Sinai and breaking ground for six new ones, Carter and his secretary of state, Cyrus Vance described the settlement as "illegal" and an "obstacle to peace." Even Schindler—who initially assumed that Begin, faced with the requirements of statesmanship, would move to the center—was uneasy. The press and the American public opinion added to Jewish foreboding. While Sadat was universally praised, editorials attacked Begin as a "liability to Israel and American Jews."[18]

With Jewish morale at low ebb, it was the administration's decision in February to sell F-15 jet fighters to Saudi Arabia that offered the community an opportunity to mobilize around an issue that impacted Israel's security. The decision of the Conference and AIPAC to oppose the sale of arms to an Arab country was a step up from earlier and more modest efforts to secure military aid to Israel. It was designed to confront an administration that was widely rumored to have wanted to "break the back of the Jewish lobby." In March, Schindler accused Brzezinski of being "antagonistic"; the adviser complained that the chairman of the Conference called him "anti-Semitic." The strategy proved highly successful in diverting Jewish attention from Begin's settlement policies and the Palestinian issue, a development undoubtedly helped by the March 11 PLO attack on two civilian buses near Haifa that killed scores of people. The White House was again bombarded with angry messages, meetings were organized in synagogues, and the president was picketed on his trip to Los Angeles. The damage was compounded when Siegel handed in a letter of resignation that expressed "strong and personal reservations" about the wisdom and timing of the arms sale.[19]

Feeling besieged, Carter tried to placate the Jewish community. On Israel's thirtieth anniversary the president announced the formation of a Commission on the Holocaust, later renamed U.S. Holocaust Memorial Council. During a congressional hearing on the sale of the aircraft, Vance testified that the Saudis were supportive of the Egyptian peace effort. Secretary of Defense Harold Brown emphasized the Soviet threat to the desert kingdom. AIPAC, under the leadership of its combative executive director Morris Amitai, was not swayed, making the vote for the F-15 package a test of Jewish resolve. In the end Carter, who compromised on the terms of the sale, won a narrow victory in the Senate. Begin immediately denounced the vote as an attempt to impose a peace treaty on Israel, and former Prime Minister Rabin, in an effort to best his rival, called the decision the "greatest setback" for Israel in a decade.[20]

With the outcry over the Saudi arms sale growing, Carter could hardly rest on his laurels. In June 1978, facing a collapse in Iran and Soviet encroachments in Africa, he convened a group of senior Democratic leaders to seek advice. The group urged him to stay aloof from the peace negotiations, but Carter's crusade to bring peace to the Middle East got the better of him. In early July Vice President Walter Mondale invited twenty-eight Jewish leaders for a "goodwill visit" to Israel. Nevertheless, he failed to dissipate the fears that the administration was preparing to pressure Israel into negotiations. Risking further confrontation with the organized Jewish community, the president finally cajoled Begin into accepting an invitation to Camp David in September. The Camp David accord was a personal vindication for Carter. In addition to providing for a peace settlement between Israel and Egypt, the agreement laid out a framework for a transition into self-rule for the Palestinians by recognizing the "legitimate rights" of the Palestinian people. Ironically, it was the same language that got the president into hot water with the Jewish community when it appeared in the October 1977 communiqué announcing the Geneva conference.[21]

Contrary to expectations, the signing of the peace treaty between Israel and Egypt in 1979 did not mollify the community. Carter saw Camp David as an opportunity to proceed with the next stage of his peace plan, the settling of the Palestinian issue. In an August 1 speech, the president was alleged to have compared the Palestinian problem to the civil rights issue in the United States. The Jewish establishment immediately denounced Carter for bestowing the legitimacy of civil rights on the PLO. Carter was also reported to have considered giving a major speech on the Middle East, in which he planned to emphasize the divergent interests of Israel and the United States and denounce the Begin government for its intransigence. The president changed his mind only after some Jewish leaders warned him that he might risk "opening the gates of anti-Semitism in America."[22]

Still, the administration was actively looking for ways to circumvent the ban on contacts with the PLO, which Kissinger imposed in 1975 during his step-by-step diplomacy. In the forefront of this effort was Andrew Young, Carter's ambassador to the UN and an ardent proponent of refocusing American foreign policy on the Third World. On August 13 it was reported that Young had met with Zehdi Labib Terzi, the PLO observer in the UN. Two days later, after Israel complained, Young was forced to resign. The community greeted the departure of Young, the most senior African American in the administration, with joy, but the incident inflamed the already tenuous relations between Jews and blacks.[23]

Young's replacement, Donald McHenry, was equally committed to the New

Internationalist vision of good relations with Third World countries. In March 1980, McHenry voted for a UN resolution that condemned Israeli settlement policies in the occupied territories and East Jerusalem. Although Carter declared that the vote was a "misunderstanding," Vance, in a testimony before Congress, conceded that the Israeli settlements contradicted international law, and that the administration considered East Jerusalem part of the occupied territories. Soon after, Ariel Sharon, a member of Begin's cabinet, met with Jewish leaders and criticized them for not protesting more forcefully. Among others, Sharon contended that there should have been 100,000 Jews picketing the White House.[24]

In May Begin declared that "settlement of Jews in the Land of Israel is absolutely legal and accords with international law." In June Israel announced that it would seize Arab land to build settlements near Nablus, a move that was immediately condemned by the White House as a violation of international law. When, on June 30, the Knesset approved a basic law that proclaimed united Jerusalem to be the capital of Israel, the United States abstained from a UN resolution condemning the legislation. To rally the community to Israel's defense, Begin appealed directly to American Jews in a letter published in the *New York Times* on July 25. He wrote: "I believe with all my heart that Eretz Israel ['land of Israel'] belongs to the whole Jewish people and not only to those Jews who live in it." Sharon, who was already on record urging Jews to defend settlements, stated that the question of Israeli security is a "question for Jews anywhere in the world."[25]

The strategy of the Israeli government seemed to have worked. The American Jewish Council adopted a resolution that criticized Carter's stand on Israeli settlement policy, asserting that "settlements are not contrary to international law and were required for security purposes." The council further reaffirmed that "Jews have a right to live on the West Bank" and "that only Israel can decide through its democratic process what its settlement policy should be."[26] Once again, the organized community created a façade of stare-down with an unsympathetic administration. However, Carter and his allies could draw comfort from the growing shrillness of the internal American Jewish discourse over Begin's conduct of the peace process.

BEGIN'S NEW ISRAEL AND THE WARS OF THE JEWS

The hope that the demise of Breira would put an end to divisiveness in the Jewish community was put to rest by the emergence of Begin's New Israel. The elections energized both the left and the right and spawned a large number of new organizations. Breira's immediate successor was the New Jewish Agenda (NJA), which was formed in 1978 by Gerald Serotta and Albert Axelrod, two Hillel rabbis who had been associated with Breira. Some seven-hundred activists attended its founding conference in Washington, D.C., in 1980. Unlike Breira, NJA tried to mainstream its concerns by adopting the vocabulary and rituals of traditional Judaism mixed with the prophetic notions of social justice. The NJA platform criticized the Jewish community for "retreating from social action" and for becoming "extremely self-oriented." The same standards of justice were applied to the Middle East conflict, where NJA called for a "compromise through negotiations with the Palestinian people and Israel's Arab neighbors." In an effort to promote Palestinian self-determination, NJA activists initiated contacts with moderate Palestinians, while strongly denouncing Israel's settlement policies in the territories.[27]

More exclusively concerned with to the peace process was Americans for Peace Now (APN), founded in 1981 as a support group for the Israeli peace movement Peace Now (PN). Initially called American Friends of Peace Now, the new organization fought to overcome the reluctance of the American Jewish community to accept the message of the Israeli peace camp. APN also served as a conduit for specialized groups such as the student-oriented Progressive Zionist Congress. Like its fellow peace groups, APN denounced the settlement policies of the Begin government and called for direct negotiations with the Palestinians.[28]

Another outgrowth of the Breira legacy was the New Israel Fund (NIF), established in 1979 by Jonathan Cohen and his wife Eleanor Friedman, a wealthy San Francisco couple. By 1983 the NIF, which developed an impressive fundraising capability, moved to New York. Unlike Breira and NJA, which did political work in the American Jewish community, the fund strove to reshape the political culture in Israel. According to the fund's statement of purpose, "our concept of philanthropy for Israel must be broadened to include not only *tzedakah*, providing concrete needs and services, but also *tikkun*, the healing, mending and transformation of a suffering society." High on the priority list of the NIF were activities devoted to the protection of civil rights of both Jews and Arabs and reconciliation between the two peoples. Among its most prominent grantees was the Association for Civil Rights in Israel (ACRI) and Neve Shalom, a Jewish-Arab village in Israel. In an effort to change the attitudes of the Sephardim toward the peace process, the NIF funded the East Toward Peace, a Sephardi counterpart to Peace Now. Targeted philanthropy or "*tzedaka* collective" was first endorsed by Breira, which was opposed to the undifferentiated giving to the UJA.[29]

The vastly reinvigorated right matched the challenge from the left. In addition to the JDL and AFSI, a host of pro-Likud organizations, including the Likud U.S.A., were added to the rostrum. Renamed later Revisionist Zionists of America, the organization promised to discourage Palestinian statehood west of the Jordan River. Gerald Strober, a Likud sympathizer, founded the Committee of American Jews in Support of Prime Minister Begin. Borrowing a page from the leftist approach of targeted charity, right-wing and religious groups had created special funds to bolster the settlement movement in the West Bank. The Hebron Fund, established in 1982 by the Gush Emunim leader Rabbi Moshe Levinger, raised considerable amounts of money to buy Arab property in Hebron. Monroe Spen, a Florida millionaire and a Kahane supporter, helped to finance the Temple Mount Faithful, a group dedicated to rebuilding the Third Temple in Jerusalem. In 1984 Irving Moskowitz and other wealthy American Jews created the American Friends of Ateret Cohanim, which through its subsidiary, the Jerusalem Reclamation Project, acquired property in East Jerusalem. American donations to the settlers were also transferred through the Palestine Endowment Fund/Israel Endowment Fund (PEF/IEF), a tax exempted charity in New York that channeled funds to more than a thousand mostly nonpolitical organizations in Israel.[30]

Perhaps equally significant, the right-wing groups devoted a considerable amount of time to attacking the propeace organizations. AFSI's Rael Jean Isaac compared the NJA to the Verband Nationaldeutscher Juden ("Society of National German Jews"), a fringe group in Weimar, Germany that supported the emerging National Socialist Party. AFSI published a pamphlet denouncing the NIF for "providing financial muscle for a handful of Israeli extremists who, lacking the electoral constituting to radically transform the Jewish state, seek a constituency in New York and Berkeley." In the same vein, Joseph Puder criticized the NIF for trying to transform Israel into a state that, in the words of the Israeli American writer Ze'ev Chafets, would "meet the approval of the ACLU [American Civil Liberties Union], the *Nation* magazine and the Sierra Club." He also described the members of East for Peace as "Sephardic extremists" who have benefited from the NIF. Ruth R. Wisse, a leading Yiddish Scholar from Harvard, accused the propeace groups of trying to expose, pillory, and defeat the democratic government of Israel. The right-wing critics maintained that a Palestinian state would pose a mortal threat to Israel. Some took a cue from Begin, who compared Yasser Arafat to Hitler, arguing that Arafat's goal of destroying the state of Israel was tantamount to the Final Solution. Indeed, Shmuel Katz, Begin's public affairs liaison, propagated the idea that a Palestinian state would "spearhead the final solution" in his frequent appearances in the United States.[31]

The tension between the proponents and opponents of Begin's handling of the peace process was not limited to the political fringes of the Jewish community. On April 21, 1978, the *New York Times* gave coverage to a letter of support for PN. It was signed by thirty-six prominent American Jews—including Leonard Bernstein, and the Nobel laureates Saul Bellow and Kenneth Arrow—who described themselves as "life-long friends of Israel." The letter, which was organized by Fein and read at a large PN rally in Israel, criticized Begin for his lack of response to the Sadat initiative and for his settlement policies. When Likud's supporters in Israel organized a counterrally under the slogan "Secure Peace," the American Committee in Support of Prime Minister Begin gathered hundreds of signatures in favor of the Israeli prime minister.[32]

Similar exchanges followed with numbing regularity. In 1980, Cynthia Ozick denounced officials in the Carter administration who promoted relations with the PLO, which she described as "self-destructive." A number of prominent American Jewish leaders attacked Ozick, calling her position "irredentist chauvinism." Others pointed out that, like Arafat, Begin was "a man of blood," who became a conventional politician. Following on the heels of the Ozick fracas was another letter of fifty-nine prominent Jews who urged Begin to stop his newly announced settlement drive. In addition to Bellow and Bernstein, the petitioners included the respected Zionist author Marie Syrkin, Walter Laqueur and Rabbi Eugene Borowitz. In March 1980, Edgar Bronfman, the head of the World Zionist Congress (WZC) and a prominent Zionist leader, attacked Begin's settlement policies. Arthur Hertzberg, a persistent critic of the Begin government who published a large number of op-eds in major papers, earned the enmity of many in the community. Even less prominent personalities were sucked into the vortex of the wars of the Jews. The journalist Avishai recalled that, after writing that Begin's victory was rooted in the new political culture of Israel, a well-known columnist and childhood friend broke off relations with him.[33]

Going beyond heated rhetoric, "the Jewish wars" generated a flurry of actions. Goldmann, the veteran Zionist leader and a cofounder of the Conference of Presidents was among the first to act against Begin. Goldmann, who once described the idea that God ordered the Israelis to occupy the Greater Israel as "profanation," traveled in November of 1977 to Washington to urge Carter and his advisers to "break the Jewish lobby in the United States." Philip Klutznick, who defended Carter during the Camp David process, was "skewered" by some mainstream organizations. In April 1978, reacting to the perceived Israeli intransigence over negotiations with Egypt, the leaders of the AJC, the AJCongress, ADL, and NJCRAC went to Israel to remonstrate with Begin. The so-called mission of eight created a stir in the community, but Begin supporters managed to isolate the petitioners. The dovish NJCRAC was hit particularly hard; the Israeli government shunned it and by mid-1980, its Israel task force was dissolved.[34]

In January 1981 the World Jewish Congress (WJC) released a report on the "Implications of Israel-Arab Peace for World Jewry," which was influenced by Goldmann and Klutznick and incorporated much of the original critique of Breira. The report, a virtual catalog of complaints about New Israel, expressed distress over Israel's approach to peace and the Palestinian problem, the gap between the Sephardim and Ashkenazim, and the treatment of Israeli Arabs. It noted that the Jewish state was a "troubled, anxious and demoralized society" beset with major and divisive economic, social, and political problems, and wondered about Israel's ability to attract the younger generation of well-educated and acculturated American Jews. The main message was that Diaspora needed an "Israel they can admire" and that "Israel-as-is" would not do. Even more eye-catching was some of the commentary on the report. Calling Israel a "sick society," a *Moment* magazine article stated that the life of Diaspora Jewry is essentially purposeless. Since Israel has been the "purpose" of American Jewry, and "since American Jewry has now come to see that its purpose is confounded, we are in a state of crisis."[35]

Underlying this intense discourse were the deep fissures in the Jewish community that formed over the meaning of Jewish identity. As already noted, even before Likud's ascendancy there were those who doubted whether a peoplehood definition of Judaism, centered on Israel, would attract the younger generation. Lost in the outcry over Breira's approach to the Arab-Israeli conflict was its argument of *geula ba-goalh*, a notion that a meaningful Jewish existence can be achieved in the Diaspora without the help of Israel. As Breira and its ideological heirs asserted, a true Jewish identity should be construed around the prophetic tradition of social justice and *tikkun olam*, social action to mend the world. After Likud's victory, even some more mainstream organizations seemed to concur with this vision. The Association of Reform Zionists of America (ARZA) adopted in September 1978 a platform that called for the strengthening of the state of Israel based on prophetic vision of justice and peace. The ARZA resolution went on to add that "Reform can augment the Zionist vision of the just society by calling for the same kind of concern with moral and social issues in Israel that we have advanced in America." Hertzberg, referring to the liberal vision of Ben-Gurion, wondered how American Jews "could support a different country from the one its founders had intended." He asserted that Israel must remain a "moral cause, consonant with America's highest ideal and one that would do proud liberalism, which should be the true priority of American Jews.[36]

On the other hand of the divide were those who firmly believed that Jewish identity in the Diaspora should be firmly rooted in Israeli-centered nationalism. As Jacques Torczyner, the former president of the ZOA, declared, "whatever the Administration will want to do . . . the Jews in America will fight for Israel. It is the only thing we have to sustain our Jewish identity." These self-described "tribalists" scoffed at the notion that a prophetic tradition of justice would be robust enough to bind future generations of Jews to the community. They denounced the "prophecists" as either "dogmatic liberals" who "could only tolerate an Israel that mirrors their political and cultural test," or misguided reformists who believe that "men could achieve universal regeneration through political and social action." In this view, such secular messianism was a mask for the New Left or, alternatively, a sign of assimilation into the Western culture.[37]

By insisting that Jewish identity be inexorably linked to the defense of the state of Israel, the nationalists created a new benchmark for a "good Jew." Isaac posited that "the safety of Israel must be the overriding national concern of modern Jewry." Since, in their opinion, safety was safeguarded by the territorial acquisitions of the Six Day War, those who questioned Likud's maximalist policy did not share the central value of the Jewish community of "securing the survival of Israel." Arguing that the left-wing groups are outside the communal pale, ZOA and AFSI fought to block NJA, NIF, and APN from membership in local and national Jewish organizations. In one case, the ZOA prevailed upon the Jewish Community Council of Greater Washington to reject the membership petition of the NJA. However, in other localities the peace groups managed to gain membership by claiming that a refusal to deal with the issue of occupied territories and the PLO would be injurious to Israel's national security. As one peace activist put it, "it is all those who resist any compassion, any compromise, any concern for those with whom Israel must ultimately come to terms" that harm Israel.[38]

The fight over membership opened a virtual Pandora's box of charges and countercharges of dissension, disloyalty, and bad faith. The shrillness of these exchanges forced the community to consider the more fundamental issue of permissible discourse in a voluntaristic society.

THE ESOTERIC ART OF CRITICIZING ISRAEL: WHO CAN SAY WHAT, WHEN, AND WHY

Political science literature asserts that societies engage in continuous discourse as they work out normative problems that affect their existence. In a democratic polity the daily discourse is free and open to all members. There is no doubt that, as members of the larger American society, Jews have been committed to an open and vigorous exchange of ideas. However, the principle of unfettered debate faced an uphill battle in a minority community with vague and permeable borders and whose membership was voluntary and fragile. Anticipating the importance of the issue of criticism, the AJC published a position paper entitled "American Jews and Israel: Limits of Democracy and Dissent" in the fall of 1978. Earlier on, George Gruen, the Middle East expert of the AJC, published a list of pros and cons on dissent in the AJC's magazine *Forum*.[39]

Even a perfunctory analysis of the discourse on Israel reveals that being a minority weighted heavily on the minds of the participants. Many of the Jewish leaders believed that open criticism of Israel by other Jews, no matter how well intentioned, would trigger anti-Semitism. This centuries-old reflex was compounded by the decision of the ADL to redefine anti-Semitism as anti-Israelism. Playing on such fears, Begin repeatedly equated criticism of his policies with anti-Zionism and anti-Semitism. On one occasion, Begin proclaimed that "No one will frighten the large and free Jewish community of the United States. No one will succeed in deterring them with anti-Semitic propaganda."[40]

The fact that newspapers gave disproportional coverage to the Jewish critics of Israel only deepened the suspicion of those who suspected anti-Semitic motives. Although the papers argued that such coverage amounts to a "man bites dog" story meriting more prominence than the ritualistic expression of support of Israel, many Jewish critics were not convinced. Most suspicious were Jewish nationalists who compared criticism of Israel to the efforts of the Nazis and the PLO to delegitimize the Jews. In the words of Steven Cohen, "It reached the point where Ruth Wisse could write an article in *Commentary* denouncing "American Friends of Peace Now" by drawing a parallel between Nazi and PLO "Delegitimation of the Jews" and the criticism of Israeli government policies by such leading American Jewish thinkers as Rabbi Arthur Hertzberg and *Moment* magazine editor Leonard J. Fein."[41]

Closely related to such considerations was the anxiety that internal criticism would help the Arabs and other enemies of Israel to delegitimize the Jewish state so that it could be sacrificed on the altar of American interests. In his article "The Abandonment of Israel," Podhoretz painted a terrifying picture of the West ready to abandon Israel in order to pacify the "god of Arab oil." On May 21, 1978, the ZOA ran an ad in the *New York Times* accusing the Carter administration of "selling Israel for petro-dollars." Wisse asserted that Jewish critics do the bidding of Arab states that had embarked on a major campaign to delegitimize the Jewish state. Worse, such Jews ignored the connection between the "oil crisis and rising Arab influence in America and the consequent pressure on Israel."[42]

Even those who did not share such dark visions agreed that internal criticism would detract from the unified posture of the community vis-à-vis the administration. Hertzberg, who was then leaving the presidency of the AJCongress, spoke of the "terrible dilemma" that public criticism presents. Since Jews knew that "public dissent in America becomes an anti-Israel weapon," many of them kept quiet. This factor was uppermost on the minds of leaders of the organized community who were involved in lobbying the administration. It was common knowledge in Washington that the White House, encouraged by Goldmann and Klutznick, was seeking out leaders critical of Begin. Indeed, trying to drum up support for the Geneva conference, Secretary Vance organized a meeting of some fifty activists from the Presidents Conference and local federations, many of whom were sympathetic to the administration. However, Schindler managed to outmaneuver the secretary of state by persuading the invitees to stick to the official communal position. Schindler and AIPAC leaders were also convinced that Carter's decision to sell the F-15 planes to Saudi Arabia stemmed from the hope that the Jewish community, racked by internal dissent, would not muster enough opposition. Under these circumstances Jewish leaders chose to believe that that criticism of Israel would "only feed the Administration's pro-Arab sympathies; instead of publicly differing with Begin's policies, they began to circle the wagons to defend against Jimmy Carter's policies."[43]

Such dissension had important financial implications. Although contributions to the UJA had declined since the peak years of 1967 and 1973, Israel's needs still served as a major marketing device. Public bickering was perceived as harmful to the continuing generosity of the donors. Rabbi Howard Addison, the vice president of the Labor Zionist Alliance, argued that the local federations viewed Israel as a "symbol of Jewish unity and revitalization, a common platform upon which all Jews can stand." This symbol should not "be sullied nor the platform weakened by partisan political struggles," so as not to affect the "community growing ever more united and expressing that unity through ever-increasing levels of Jewish philanthropy."[44]

Viewed from the perspective of a minority, efforts to prevent cracks in the wall of Jewish unity made sense. At the same time, stifling free discourse was highly damaging because of the voluntary membership and the fragile boundaries of the community. As already argued, Jewish commitment to Israel was tinged with anxiety over dual loyalty and other factors that could trigger cognitive dissonance. Social science literature has demonstrated that reaction to such dissonance can take two forms. As Albert Hirschman noted, some people deal with their psychological predicament by practicing "voice," that is, changing the offensive reality through participation and criticism. Others choose to "exit," or leave the group, a solution that is especially attractive to marginal members. Faced with the prospect of demographic hemorrhage, some leaders argued that muzzling criticism would alienate the younger and more marginal Jews and drive them away from the community. Albert Vorspan, a senior official with the UAHC admitted that "[t]he real choice now is between speaking up and turning off." Thus, in spite of efforts by the ZOA and AFSI, the NJA, NIF and APN had been gradually, albeit grudgingly, admitted into the communal fold, promoting Isaac to complain that in spite of "Agenda's [NJA] far more savage assault on Israel," the community reacted with "surprise acquiescence."[45]

Still, communal leaders who supported criticism reserved the right to decide the "boundary issue" of who could legitimately partake in the critique of the Jewish state. In his guidelines Gruen asserted that only those who are committed to Israel should have the right to criticize; he described such commitment as based on an "intimate involvement" with the domestic, social, and political life of Israel. Elie Wiesel, the Holocaust spokesman and the moral voice of the community, declared that critics of Israel should "previously demonstrate" an attachment to Israel, which he described as being on "Israel's side when it was at risk and alone." Conversely, those "who have never loved Israel, never uttered a world on its behalf, never spoken out in its defense" have lost the right to participate in the discourse. While Gruen's and Wiesel's opinions were widely shared, the vagueness of the formula left the boundary issue open to competing interpretations. Critics tried to justify their stand by professing interest in Israel's welfare, but their right-wing opponents attacked them for being "marginal Jews," unqualified to speak out.[46]

To lessen the damage from the debate about Israel's handling of the peace process, Jewish leaders pursued two interrelated strategies. The first strategy aimed at minimizing public expression of discontent in favor of discreet private criticism. The 1977 annual report of the Presidents Conference stated that "dissent ought not and should not be made public . . . because . . . the result is to give aid and comfort to the enemy and to weaken that Jewish unity which is essential for the security of Israel." A number of American politicians, including Carter, confirmed that Jews were more likely to criticize Israel in private. Paul Findley, a longtime congressman, wrote that, in his twenty-two years on Capitol Hill, he could not recall a Jewish House representative or senator who publicly criticized Israel. Findley, who blamed the Jewish lobby for his electoral defeat, added that "Jewish members [of Congress] may voice discontent in private conversations," but never in public. Indeed, the Israeli government was quite often subject to private criticism. In early 1978, Begin commissioned a poll of 150

American Jewish leaders who, three to one, felt that Israel was not moderate enough. The results were never published and the leaders did not go on record to register their misgivings. Theodore R. Mann, who replaced Schindler as the chairman of the Conference of Presidents, revealed that in 1979 he advised Begin privately that his right-wing cabinet made it hard to maintain a "united American Jewry."[47]

Some communal leaders were ready to criticize Begin in the Israeli papers but refused to do the same in the United States. For instance, Lawrence Tisch, a major business figure and UJA donor, said in a February 1978 interview with *Ha'aretz* that "for thirty years we [American Jewish leadership] have been building for Israel the image of a peace-loving country. Begin destroyed this image in three months." When asked to repeat his comments in the United States, Tisch refused. He and other leaders explained that the Israelis have the luxury of conducting their debates in their own society and in their own language, whereas American Jews had to do it under the "glare of a Gentile press." Using the same rationale, the organized community was often hostile to Israeli leftists who took to criticizing the Begin government on the pages of the *New York Times* and *Washington Post*.[48]

The second strategy involved efforts to shape the content of the discourse. One of the major advantages that Israel had enjoyed in the public relations battles in the United States was the perception that the Arabs were intransigent. As was argued, the Arab refusal to negotiate with Israel, coupled with PLO terrorism, made it easy for American Jews to postpone a critical evaluation of the problems involved in the peace process. However, Sadat's initiative and a decision of the PLO's National Council in 1979 to adopt diplomacy as its main tool in the struggle for national liberation changed the Middle East equation. Fein was among the first to ask whether it was Israel under Begin that had became intransigent. The theme of Israel's alleged intransigence, a mainstay in the leftist critique of Israel, was adopted by more mainstream organizations, which opened their own channels of communication with the Arabs. Faced with the prospect of a major public relations debacle, the community leadership urged to conduct a "constructive debate" by, among other things, toning down the references to Israel's intransigence. Ironically, on April 12, 1978, AFSI placed a large ad in the *New York Times* depicting Holocaust victims under the heading "Six Million Jews Who Were Not Intransigence."[49]

In many respects, the effort to structure the debate on Israel's foreign policy was successful. In mid-1980 Theodore Mann, the outgoing chairman of the Conference, publicly criticized Begin for his settlement policies. But, for most leaders "it was business as usual—a Sicilian-like *omerta* on the pros and cons of current Israeli policy remained the norm." This infuriated critics who charged that the leadership of the community was not sensitive to the beliefs of the rank and file. Michael Lerner, who founded the left-wing journal *Tikkun*, declared that the American Jewish leadership does "not speak for us," adding that "[t]heir religion is the religion of blind support for Israel."[50] Going beyond the issue of

Israel's foreign policy, this and other charges touched upon the questions of legitimacy and representation in the American Jewish community.

VOX POPULI: AMERICAN JEWISH ATTITUDES TOWARD
THE PEACE PROCESS

As with the issue of criticism, the voluntary nature of the community complicated the issue of representation. Strictly speaking, the leaders of the community derived their legitimacy from the members of their organizations. But according to observers, the voices of the rank and file were often lost in what one observer described as the "arcane, byzantine, and convoluted" inner workings of the Jewish organizational world. Israel's defense organizations like the Conference of Presidents and AIPAC were especially vulnerable to charges that they were not speaking for the community.[51] Once the conduct of the peace process became contentious, both the critics of Israel and their detractors in the community were eager to prove that they represented the people.

Democratic legitimacy was also important for those who criticized the Begin government in private. During a February 1980 visit to Israel, Richard Maass, the president of the AJC, declared that Begin should not overestimate the support of American Jews just because some one hundred thousand turned out to cheer him in the United States.[52] With all sides claiming legitimacy, tracking American Jewish opinion became crucial. Starting in the early 1980s, a large number of surveys sought to provide a relatively objective view of American Jewish attitudes on a wide range of peace process issues. In addition to the commercial polls, the AJC asked Steven Cohen to direct the National Survey of American Jews (NSAJ). The initial round of the NSAJ was conducted in the fall and winter of 1981–82 and included a representative sample of some seven hundred respondents.

The data indicated that the overall feelings toward Israel were positive. In a 1981 Yankelovich poll, an overwhelming 91 percent of respondents reported a favorable feeling; the comparable 1981 NSAJ figure was 96 percent. The survey also revealed that 73 percent of the sample said that they would feel a sense of great personal loss if Israel was destroyed and 93 percent of respondents said that the "continuation of Israel as a Jewish state is important." American Jews were equally supportive of U.S. economic and military aid to Israel. Ninety-three percent of the respondents of a February 1981 Yankelovich poll approved of U.S. continuing economic and military support for Israel. A July 1980 Harris poll found that 53 percent of the sample were in favor of sending American troops, should Israel be overrun by Arab armies.[53]

American Jews gave Israel high grades for its interest in pursuing peace. The NSAJ revealed that some three-quarters of the sample felt that the overall Israeli policy toward the peace process was neither too hawkish nor too dovish. A July 1980 poll showed that 80 percent of the sample thought that Israel wanted "very much" to conduct a peace treaty with Egypt; 75 and 50 percent thought that

Israel wanted to achieve a peace agreement with Jordan and Syria respectively. Still, the NSAJ discovered that 41 percent of its respondents rejected the possibility of trading territories for peace. The hawkish element either believed that Israel has the right to retain the territories or felt that territories were more important than peace.[54]

There was more variability of opinion concerning the Palestinian issue. In a July 1980 Harris poll 90 percent of the sample stated that Israel was right in refusing to negotiate with the PLO because it is a terrorist organization. A February 1981 Yankelovich poll put this number at 62 percent and the NSAJ survey found 74 percent who supported this statement. The Harris poll revealed that 53 percent of American Jews wanted Israel to talk to the PLO if the PLO would recognize Israel and denounce terrorism. A September 1981 *Newsweek*-Gallop poll put this figure at 69 percent. In the NSAJ 66 percent of the respondents agreed that Israel should not negotiate with "a terrorist organization that wants to destroy Israel."[55]

Attitudes toward establishing a Palestinian state as a general principle were more positive. The July 1980 Harris poll found that 49 percent supported such a state and 36 percent opposed it, with 15 percent undecided. But when a question brought the PLO or the security issue into the picture, support fell precipitously. Only 6 percent were willing to support a PLO-controlled state and an additional 14 percent were ready to abide by a Palestinian state that might jeopardize Israeli security. A *Newsweek*-Gallop poll of September 1981 showed a meager 9 percent who agreed to an independent Palestinian state. The NSAJ put the number of those willing to support a PLO-led state at 28 percent. Some 64 percent felt that an independent Palestinian state would be used "as a launching pad" to endanger Israel's security. A similar number agreed with the statement in a Harris poll that Russia would use a Palestinian state to destroy Israel and the Middle East. When asked to choose between two extreme options— annexation of the territories by Israel or creation of a Palestinian state—42 percent preferred annexation. Only 28 percent thought that annexation was a greater evil and 30 percent were undecided. Further probing revealed that if the choice was between "annexation" and "peace," most of the undecided would move toward the "peace" category.[56]

Separating support for Israel and the Israeli government produced some interesting results. A September 1981 poll by *Newsweek*-Gallop found that 53 percent of the respondents felt that the policies of Begin hurt support for Israel in the United States. But clear majorities in the *Newsweek* poll and Harris poll were in agreement with Begin's policies. Only 44 percent rejected the statement that Begin's settlement policies make a peace accord almost impossible. By a large margin (66 percent to 25 percent), American Jews disagreed with the statement that Begin "seems inflexible"; 90 percent gave Begin high marks for Camp David. Sixty-nine versus 9 percent approved of the bombing of the PLO headquarters in Beirut in 1981, and only 11 percent reported that they were less sympathetic to Israel than five years ago. The right to criticize Israel featured in a number of questions. The NSAJ found that 57 percent of the sample supported the right of American Jews to criticize Israel, as opposed to 31 percent who disagreed. When asked whether Israelis should be able to exercise the same right, 70 percent of the respondents agreed. As for the hotly debated issue of Israel's morality, a majority of the respondents—52 percent—agreed that Israel should be held to higher moral standards than other countries.[57]

Stephen Cohen and others who analyzed the attitude of American Jews pointed out several inconsistencies. On the one hand, a substantial part of the community seemed to be dovish in the aggregate. Cohen, who developed a composite profile of his respondents, determined that 45 percent were doves and 30 percent were hawks. On the other hand, a sizable number of those polled expressed hard-line positions on the Palestinian issue, including the equanimity with which many accepted the annexation option. This was especially surprising given the fact that a majority of respondents thought Israel should follow a higher moral order. The "Begin factor" was equally puzzling. The Israeli leader was not personally popular, a possible reflection of his image as an Old World Jew, but a solid majority of American Jews supported his policies. Raab explained the inconsistency by pointing out that the community was not uneasy about Begin's policies per se, but was concerned with its effect on Israel's standing in America. Avishai asserted that the opinions might reflect a visceral reluctance to criticize Israel. He noted that "many American Jews live a Jewish life so attenuated, so barely strung together by vicarious political Zionism and pro-Israeli institutions, that they view dissent from official Israeli policy on the Palestinians as a breaking of cultural and institutional vessels for which there is no replacement." Whatever the reason, the popular attitudes mirrored the deep divisions described in the discourse.[58]

On balance, the nationalists such as the ZOA or AFSI could take more comfort from the results. The charge that they were a fringe radical minority was clearly belied by the substantial number of Jews who were willing to condone retention of Arab territories and the annexation of the West Bank. Such numbers were undoubtedly encouraging to the Israeli government, whose American Jewish critics often warned it about eroding popular support. While the peace advocates could point to a dovish majority, the fact that so many American Jews were against Palestinian sovereignty must have come as an unpleasant surprise. The peace activists, who chastised the communal leadership for not being representative enough, were in for even a bigger shock after the NSAJ's poll of leaders revealed that they were considerably more dovish than the rank and file. Cohen concluded that the "leaders favor territorial compromise by a margin of better than four to one, they reject the notion of permanent Israeli control of the West Bank by nearly three to one, they favor a suspension of settlement activity by better than two to one." Some observers speculated that a relatively hawkish popular mood made these leaders squeamish about criticizing Israel in public. For those who needed more proof of the sentiments of American Jews, the 1980 elections provided conclusive evidence. President Carter, who garnered 68 percent of the Jewish vote in 1976, got only 45 percent in 1980. As one observer pointed out, this was "an all-time low for a Democratic candidate, not to mention an incumbent."[59]

Given the distribution of American Jewish opinions on the peace process, the hard-line Ronald Reagan, who challenged Carter in 1979, seemed to be a better prospect for the Likud government. This was certainly the hope of the large number of Jews who, out of concern for Israeli policy, voted for him. However, as was often the case in the turbulent Arab-Israeli conflict, a sudden and dramatic event had again undermined all the calculations. When Israel found itself embroiled in the war in Lebanon, both the new administration in Washington and the American Jewish community was forced to reevaluate its attitudes toward the Begin government.

4

The War in Lebanon: Defending an Offensive War

The ascendancy of the neoconservative paradigm in American foreign policy promised to lift the Israeli–U.S. relations to a new level of cooperation and reciprocity. Unlike his predecessor, who viewed Israel as an occasionally burdensome American charity in the Middle East, President Ronald Reagan tried to incorporate the Jewish state into his global strategic vision. However, the war in Lebanon and the hard-line policies of the Likud government had repeatedly strained the relation between Jerusalem and Washington. Moreover, the war and its aftermath accelerated the division in the Jewish community and raised the specter of double loyalty, alienating many of the more secularized and marginal Jews. Although the majority of the community did not support Israel's offensive war, the right wing was galvanized to defend it. The bitter discourse among American Jews triggered the privatization of the Jewish lobby, a process that was accelerated by Likud's effort to establish an independent lobbying network in the United States.

REVERSAL OF FORTUNE: ISRAELI RELATIONS WITH THE REAGAN ADMINISTRATION

Upon gaining power in 1981, Reagan proceeded to implement his foreign policy vision. Drawing on the neoconservative critique of Carter's New Internationalism, Reagan reinstated "realpolitik," the globalist perspective, and the notion that the Soviet Union's expansionist drive is a major threat to American national interest. The president asserted that the United States should project its military might and be ready to use it if necessary, especially in tackling regional conflagrations and international terrorism. Applied to the Middle East, these principles translated into a strong support for Israel along the lines of the neoconservative *Commentary* circles. As already noted, neoconservatives considered Israel to be a surrogate for the free world threatened by an alliance of communist dictatorships and Third World terrorism. As the president put it, "Israel is the only stable democracy we can rely on in a spot where Armageddon could come . . . we need an ally in that area." Because of the administration's position that the PLO is a Soviet-backed outpost in the Middle East, the White House showed considerable sympathy for Israel's efforts to combat Palestinian terrorism.[1]

Jewish neoconservatives associated with the administration helped to formulate this pro-Israeli policy. A group of wealthy Republican Jewish donors from the National Republican Jewish Coalition, including Albert Spiegel and Max Fisher who were also involved with AIPAC and the Jewish PACs, contributed to Reagan's election campaign. Equally important was the influence of Richard Perle, Steven Bryen, and other activists from JINSA. Perle, who was appointed assistant secretary of defense for international security policy, and Bryen, who secured a lower ranking position in the Pentagon, immediately set out to promote a close strategic alliance between Israel and the United States. Another strong pro-Israel voice was Douglas J. Feith, an assistant secretary of defense. Some higher ranking officials in the administration embraced the JINSA notion that Israel was a strategic asset and a bargain to boot. Jeane Kirkpatrick, who was named the American ambassador to the UN, was part of the neoconservative circle, and Alexander M. Haig, Reagan's secretary of state, appreciated Israel's military muscle in the Middle East.[2]

Still, Israel did not fit easily into Reagan's larger design to contain Soviet subversion in the Middle East through a regional alliance of pro-Western Arab countries. To begin with, the fragile cease-fire in the civil war in Lebanon collapsed in April 1981, prompting Syria to move surface-to-air missile (SAM) antiaircraft to the Bekaa Valley and accelerating PLO's attacks on Israel's northern border. With tensions increasing on a daily basis, the administration, which assigned a low priority to the Palestinian issue, was forced to reevaluate its position and appointed a special envoy to the Middle East. While the envoy, Philip Habib, was trying to settle the conflict, Israel surprised Washington with its June attack on an Iraqi nuclear reactor near Baghdad. Although the Begin government explained that the Iraqi Osirak nuclear reactor was built to produce nuclear weapons that could endanger Israel's existence, the action was strongly criticized in the United States. The administration voted for a UN resolution that condemned Israel and suspended the delivery of four F-16 aircraft to Israel, a high-profile rebuke.

The international imbroglio apparently helped Likud to eke out a small victory over Labor in the June 30 elections. What is more, Begin included a number of well-known hard-liners in his cabinet and appointed Ariel Sharon to head the important ministry of defense. When the PLO, which accumulated considerable firepower in Lebanon, attacked northern Israel on two occasions in July, the IDF retaliated by bombing PLO's headquarters in Beirut. The attack, which caused considerable civilian casualties, generated more criticism in the United States and a further delay in the delivery of the F-16s. The round of hostilities in the Middle East promoted the media, some members of Congress, and government officials to describe Israel "as a 'prickly' and unpredictable ally." They and others criticized Begin for endangering American interests in the Middle East.[3]

In spite of questions surrounding Begin's policy, the administration proceeded with plans to integrate Israel in its overall strategy of containing Soviet influence in the Middle East. The three elements of the containment strategy called for conducting exercises of the Rapid Deployment Force (RDF) in Egypt, Oman, and other countries friendly to the United States; the delivery of sophisticated weapon systems to Saudi Arabia; and a strategic cooperation pact with Israel. It was JINSA that first advocated the concept of a strategic alliance with Israel, a move that the Pentagon began implementing through a number of joint ventures, such as developing military technology, aiding the Nicaraguan contras, training security forces in Zaire, sending arms to Iran, and sharing intelligence.

But Haig also saw a formal agreement with Israel as a way to win congressional approval for the proposed sale of AWACS (Airborne Warning and Control System) to Saudi Arabia. When the administration first proposed the sale in April, Israel and its allies in the United States opposed it on the grounds that the system would alter the balance of power in the region and pose a direct danger to its territory. However, the Begin government, anxious to remain on good terms with the Reagan administration, hesitated to challenge the popular president. There were also those in the Israeli establishment who felt that the AWACS could be dealt with at the tactical level. Ezer Weitzman, a former commander of the Israeli Air Force, declared that the "Israelis could shoot down this plane in less than a minute and a half."[4]

The extent to which the sale posed a danger to Israeli security was only one of the factors that influenced the stand of the organized Jewish community. AIPAC, which spearheaded the opposition to AWACS in Congress, was concerned that Reagan's preoccupation with the Soviet threat in the Middle East would prompt it to build up the military arsenal of moderate Arab states. The fact that oil interests and the aerospace industry lobbied for the sale reinforced the community's concern that Israel's interests would be sacrificed for economic gains. Nathan Perlmutter reiterated that the AWACS sale revealed the "real anti-Semitism in America." In his view the "real" anti-Semites were the "Semitically-neutral arms salesmen who talked of jobs, of black ink for the aerospace industry and of recycling petrodollars."[5]

Internal communal considerations also played a role. Zoe Danon Gedal, the author of a comprehensive study on the Jewish lobby, argued that AIPAC— supported by virtually all major Jewish organizations—used the AWACS fight to unify the badly split community behind what was described as an "existential threat" to Israel's security. In her view, the fact that during such crises it was easy to mobilize the community was not lost on communal leaders who used "dramatic, panicky language" to "motivate large numbers of American Jews to take action and give money." The same tactics were also useful in "discouraging members of the community who do not wish to be outside the mainstream from expressing alternative viewpoints." All in all, the AWACS fight was expected to energize American Jews who were unhappy with the Israeli government and demoralized by the deep schisms in the community. As Danon Gedal put it, "everyone across the political spectrum was able to join in this anti-AWACS struggle and the big, healthy clean fight that it provided."[6]

AIPAC failed to avert the AWACS sale, which the Congress approved in October after a personal intervention by Reagan. Still, in a move to soften the blow, the administration concluded the negotiations on a strategic agreement with Israel. On November 30, Casper Weinberger, Reagan's secretary of defense and his Israeli counterpart, Sharon, signed a Memorandum of Understanding (MOU), which listed various measures that the two countries would take to fight the Soviet threat in the Middle East. However, the White House suspended the pact after the Israeli Knesset, at the urging of Begin, annexed the Golan Heights on December 14. The "Golan Law" angered the administration, which voted with other members of the Security Council to condemn Israel and declare the annexation "null and void without any international effect." Begin retaliated by canceling the MOU altogether and noisily complaining that the United States treated Israel as a "banana republic."[7]

The rocky relations between Jerusalem and Washington, coupled with the growing tension in the Middle East, had forced Reagan to revise his optimistic view of the Arab-Israeli conflict. By early 1982, it became clear that the intractable enmity between Israel, the Palestinians and their Syrian backers would defeat any hope for an anti-Soviet alliance between moderate Arab states and Israel. Ironically, the administration, which had little appreciation for Carter's dogged efforts to solve the conflict and made virtually no effort to revive the moribund Palestinian autonomy talks, had to tackle the intricacies of the situation in a hurry. In the spring of 1982, the Israeli government notified Reagan's envoy, Philip Habib, of its intention to preempt the Palestinian buildup in Lebanon. Although the ambassador was critical, Haig and other officials were prepared to see a limited strategic action against the PLO in southern Lebanon. After Israel invaded Lebanon on June 6, President Reagan declared that the "fighting in Lebanon must stop, and Israel should bring its forces home. But this is not enough. We must work to stamp out the scourge of terrorism that in the Middle East makes war an ever-present threat."[8] The United States also blocked the UN's attempt to impose a cease-fire on Israel.

As the Israeli advanced in the direction of Beirut and the limited operation turned into a full-fledged war, the administration divided sharply over a proper response. While Haig argued that Israel should be allowed to punish the PLO, Weinberger and National Security Adviser William Clark recommended that the

Unites States halt the fighting. Israel's assault on the PLO strongholds in Beirut caused extensive damage and high civilian casualties, a fact that was duly conveyed by the extensive television coverage. On August 12, after a particularly fierce bombardment of West Beirut, Reagan pleaded with Begin to stop the war, but Israeli attacks ceased only after the PLO agreed to a withdrawal from Beirut, a move that was completed on September 1.

On the same day, the Reagan administration unveiled a new initiative to solve the Arab-Israeli conflict. Based on Labor's land-for-peace formula, the plan called for the Arab states to recognize Israel and envisaged a Palestinian entity within the framework of Jordan. There was to be a freeze on settlements and, after a period of autonomy, the territories were to be transferred to Jordan. Hope that the Reagan initiative would calm the Middle East was dashed when the Israeli government immediately rejected the plan. Begin denounced it as a sellout to the Arabs and, four days later, announced the construction of seven new settlements in the West Bank. The administration described this turn of events as "most unwelcome," and added that continual settlement activity was damaging to the peace process, raising doubt about Israel's commitment to peace.[9]

Before the administration had a chance to formulate a response to the Israeli position, the situation in Lebanon spun out of control. Unbeknownst to Americans, Sharon planned to use the invasion to restructure the troubled political system in Lebanon with the help of the Christian leader Bashir Gemayel, who was elected the president of Lebanon on August 23. Gemayel was expected to restore order, assert Christian dominance, and sign a peace treaty with Israel. However, on September 14 Gemayel was assassinated on Syrian orders; four days later the Christian Phalangists entered the Palestinian refuge camps of Sabra and Shatila and murdered some eight hundred people.[10] The indirect Israeli involvement in the massacre triggered an unprecedented wave of criticism in the United States. Reagan issued a scathing denouncement, echoed by administration officials and members of Congress. Coming on top of the extremely negative coverage of the war in Lebanon, the Sabra and Shatila disaster threatened to turn the American public against Israel. This was particularly bad news for the community, which followed the conduct of the war with growing unease and amid alarm that the fragile appearance of unity cultivated since 1977 would crumble in the face of Israel's first offensive war.

SPLITTING MORAL HAIRS: CLASHING AMERICAN JEWISH ATTITUDES TOWARD THE WAR IN LEBANON

It is difficult to overestimate the impact of the war in Lebanon on American Jews. As one observer put it, "[i]n June 1982, the fault line between hawks and doves, which had been threatening to split the American Jewry apart for a decade and a half, broke open."[11] At the more subterranean level, the war had exacerbated the simmering tensions between the tribal-nationalist and the universalist-prophetic wings of the community. To understand the deeply polarizing effect of the war, it should be recalled that at the heart of the debate between the tribalists and the prophecists was the issue of morality, community, and power. While the former considered the exercise of power in defense of communal goals morally justified, the latter were more ambiguous when faced with military might. As long as Israel was threatened by implacably hostile Arab states, both sides could agree that the defensive actions belong in the category of just wars. Indeed, when Israel announced that the incursion would be limited to destroying the PLO infrastructure in northern Lebanon, there was little outcry from the doves who accepted the notion of self-defense.

However, the occupation of Beirut and the Sabra and Shatila massacre made it clear to many American Jews that Israel crossed into the perilous territory of an offensive war. To those who cut their political teeth during the war in Vietnam, the parallels were too close for comfort. This was particularly true of the NJA, the Jewish Committee for Israeli-Palestinian Peace—a group formed in order to force Israel out of Lebanon—and other long-standing critics of Likud. Viorst wrote that Israel "has failed the limits of what armed might can achieve," adding that "[i]t relies on guns, so unfamiliar in the Jewish past." Arthur Hertzberg published a highly bitter op-ed in the *New York Times* headlined "Begin Must Go" and Klutznick renewed his crusade against the Likud government. Fein bemoaned the fact that American Jews had been disposed to "rally around the flag" when it came to Israel, adding that "the flag now is a suburb of Beirut, and that's a long way to go for a rally."[12]

Israel's perceived moral failure in Lebanon triggered more mainline reaction as well. In a major speech to the UAHC, Rabbi Schindler, now past chairman of the Presidents Conference, attacked Israel for starting a war "for the first time . . . when it was not under immediate attack." Summing up the moral discontent, one observer noted that in the eyes of many American Jews, Israel "had become a bully on the Middle East block." Bernard Avishai lamented the ascendance of an "utterly nationalistic, self-absorbed Zionism," identified with "power, Bible, defiance and settlements." The philosopher Michael Walzer observed that the "bombing and shelling of West Beirut is hard to explain, and will ultimately prove, I suspect, impossible to justify."[13]

While the universalists painted Israel as the new Goliath, the nationalists saw the war as a continuation of a David-like struggle for self-defense. The ZOA president Ivan Novick argued that Israel was struggling against the scourge of terrorism in the Middle East. JINSA contended that "Israel did the Dirty Work" in Lebanon by striking a blow against the international terrorism sponsored by the Soviet Union. Podhoretz asserted that Israel's incursion into Lebanon should be compared to the allied troops who invaded France during World War II in order to liberate it from the German conquers. The nationalists accused the Jewish liberals of being disillusioned with the power-based policies of Likud and of misrepresenting the truth about Lebanon. Greenberg explained that by standards of power, Israel's overall ethical performance was "exemplary," but it could not satisfy those who judged it by the radical standards of powerlessness.

Isaac added that Jewish liberals evaluated Israel using ideal standards that were divorced not only from the realities of the Middle East but also from traditional Jewish perspectives. He noted that, in holding Israel to perfectionist standards, such Jews "came into conflict with what is fundamental to Judaism, its national-religious attachment to the Land." Isaac castigated the "sizable contingent of Reform and Conservative rabbis" who "called themselves a modern example of Judaism prophetic tradition," for "developing its moral muscle by flagellating Israel."[14]

Auerbach posited that Israel served as a "Rorschach test" for American Jews. Once it failed to conform to their "throbbing liberal fantasies," it became the latest "God That Failed," converting the "cliché of the once heroic Israeli David, as played by Paul Newman in Exodus" to a "menacing Goliath, the deformed progeny of Ariel Sharon and Meir Kahane." Isaac went so far as to attribute the liberal critique to the "all-too-familiar pathological Jewish self-hatred." Others charged that the "liberal fundamentalism" of Israel's critics was part of a larger political culture of the New Left. According to Hilton Kramer "the lethal combination of guilt, fear . . . and sentimentality toward the Third World" that played such a crucial role in the criticism of the war in Vietnam, was virtually replicated in Lebanon. Kaplan found that the upsurge in criticism of Israel was related to the "deplorable confusion and self hatred that sickened the American body politics after Vietnam." These observers have also charged the New Left with creating a "moral inversion" whereby "Nazi crimes were attributed to the Jewish state" and the "PLO was cloaked in the mantle of anti-fascists resistance." Podhoretz linked the attack on Israel to an upsurge of global anti-Semitism.[15]

In specifying the external factors that worked to tarnish Israel's image, these and other critics have focused on the role of the media. In their view the coverage of the war by the American news organizations raised questions of accuracy and objectivity. Jewish sources had also accused the media of double standards, imbalance in treatment of sources and manipulations of footage. A report titled "The Journalists' War Against Israel" listed numerous cases of anti-Israeli bias in the coverage of the war. The Jewish right wing was especially vocal; AFSI even petitioned the Federal Communication Commission to revoke the license of the National Broadcasting Company (NBC) because its coverage of the war in Lebanon violated the fairness doctrine in broadcasting. The Committee for Accuracy in Middle East Reporting in America (CAMERA), which was founded during the war in Lebanon, had, according to some observers, subsequently turned into a zealous watchdog of the interests of the Likud government.[16]

The notion that the media was to blame for Israel's vows in Lebanon resonated with the mainstream Jewish community. Henry Siegman of the AJCongress angrily complained that the PLO was not condemned for its role in hurting Lebanese civilians. He asserted that the PLO is to blame for the high civilian toll because it positioned its military outposts in residential areas. The AJC commissioned its own detailed study of the war coverage. As Sheila Decter from the AJCongress explained, "[i]t was very difficult to sound nice and sup-portive of Israel when it was bombarding Beirut. On the other hand, we had no problem criticizing the media for showing pictures of bombed-out buildings and not making it clear that the PLO had done that over a number of years." How-ever, the massive protest in Israel following the Beirut massacre made it more difficult for American Jews to criticize the media bias. One observer noted that the Tel Aviv rally where 400,000 protested against their own government "took some of the wind out of the Jewish critics' sails, making it harder for them to occupy the moral high ground." Some top Israeli leaders such as Mordechai Gur, a former IDF chief of staff, also criticized the conduct of the war. Indeed, the war galvanized the peace movement in Israel and enhanced the legitimacy of the rapidly growing camp of Begin's critics. In addition to the well-established PN, a host of fledgling new groups took to denouncing Likud in most scathing tones.[17]

Given these developments, even the nationalists found it hard to claim that the outcry over the war in Lebanon was part of an anti-Semitic campaign against the Jewish state. But right-wing spokesmen tried to minimize the impact of the Israeli left wing by putting it in the context of the political culture in Israel. Podhoretz noted that the election of Menachem Begin gave rise to an alienated intellectual elite, which, like its American counterpart, fomented an "adversary culture." Edward N. Luttwak explained that, in spite of its ancient history, Israel has an immature political culture. As a result, the response of many Israelis is "hysterical," leading to "chronic exaggeration." He warned against accepting these exaggerations and their attendant "negative caricatures of Israeli reality" at face value.[18]

Right-wing efforts to delegitimize the Israeli critics of the war provoked a sharp response from the left wing of the community. A *Moment* commentary stated that "in Israel the culture of the West has been defeated by the numbers of the East," adding that authoritarianism could not be ruled out in the future. One commentator asserted that "the stakes for Israel are too high for it to allow its democracy, and its commitment to Western values, to be swallowed up by nationalistic yearnings." Another proclaimed that "Israel is now more 'Arab' due to its increasing population of Arabs and Jews from Arab countries." He ventured that "Israel is likely to be less democratic, more chaotic, more unpre-dictable." What worried them most was the rising popularity of Meir Kahane and his radical nationalist policies, which called for the expulsion of both the Palestinians and the Israeli Arabs. Viorst proclaimed that "Kahanism, the viru-lent new ideology . . . captured the allegiance of an alarming number of Israelis." Leon Wieseltier noted that though Kahane's party had only one seat in the Knesset, opinion polls indicated that in a new election his strength would be increased fivefold.[19]

The perceived need to protect Israel from sliding into what Wieseltier called "radical and frequently racist nationalism" promoted the left-wing camp to in-tensify their public critique. Schindler, the most prominent convert to open criticism, explained that private criticism was ineffective: "we were milked [by Begin], both for financial and moral support" but "we were treated with contempt." He and others urged the creation of a "Diaspora Parliament," which would make policy recommendations to Israel. Not incidentally, many of the Israeli peace advocates applauded the idea of American Jewish pressure on the Begin government. The Israeli writer Amos Elon was one of the many who expressed hope that the Jewish community would help pressure the Begin government to change its policies. A *Ha'aretz* journalist wrote, "you American Jews, you liberals, you lovers of democracy are supporting its destruction here by not speaking out against the government action."[20]

Calls to intervene in the Israeli political process infuriated the right wingers. The nationalists pointed out that Israel had a democratically elected government and that attacks on Begin amounted to "impugning Israeli democracy" just because Likud was elected by the votes of "North African immigrant, Soviet émigrés, and religious Jews." Many repeated the dictum of Norman Podhoretz, who asserted that if Jews chose not to make aliya they forfeit the moral right to pass public judgment on Israeli politics. Right-wing spokesmen singled out *Moment*'s editor Leonard Fein, the NJA, and the American supporters of PN for special criticism. Wisse described as "greatly alarming" the efforts of PN to "seek help from outside the country to defeat a duly elected government." She alleged that Fein vowed "from the banks of the Charles [River] to topple the Begin government." Edward Alexander accused the NJA of refusing to "respect the sovereignty of democratically elected Israeli government."[21]

The argument about the sanctity of Israeli democracy was immediately challenged by the left. Noting that democratic elections can sometimes lead to distinctively nondemocratic outcomes, critics raised the possibility that Israel could elect leaders like Sharon or even Kahane. One study quoted Shlomo Ben-Ami, a Sephardi professor at Tel Aviv University and a future senior Labor politician, who said: "Israel is a Mediterranean country" where "most of the population is not committed to democratic values." The same study related that more than 50 percent of the Israeli teenagers interviewed in a 1984 poll, most of them Sephardi Jews, harbored antidemocratic attitudes toward non-Jews and especially Arabs. Forty-seven percent wanted to reduce the rights of Israeli Arabs and 60 percent believed that Arabs of Israel "are not entitled to fully equal rights." Using this and other data, left-wing critics were quick to point out that Israel's invasion of Lebanon was a natural progression of its policies of subjugating the Palestinian population. The sociologist Nathan Glazer bemoaned that "Israel is far gone along the road of helotizing the conquered Arab population," and a *Moment* editorial talked about the "Belfastization of the West Bank." Schindler urged American Jews to make a statement on the Palestinian issue. These and other commentators warned that the occupation of the territories would result in a course of "provocation" and guarantee a "permanent conflict."[22]

Whatever the merits of these arguments, prospects for a rational discourse in the community were eroded by the progressively bitter nature of the exchange.

Alexander called the NJA "the hissing Israel haters" and referred to Fein as "veteran fomenter from within." Maier Deshell attributed the criticism of Israel to the coming of age of a leadership "of self-assertion and narcissism." The actor Richard Dreyfuss was physically assaulted after speaking at a peace rally for Israel. In November 1982, three Orthodox rabbis in Massachusetts excommunicated members of NJA and other Jews who signed an ad criticizing the invasion of Lebanon. Neusner was so upset with the pallid response of Jewish leaders to the Beirut massacre, that he called them "craven, cowardly, hypocritical"—a parade of people "lacking all moral commitment." Hertzberg described American Jews as a "one issue lobby in Washington" and wrote a scathing exposé on the "illusion of unity" in the community. Avishai charged that "Jews who strongly support Jewish defense organizations . . . have come to treat political action on behalf of Israel's diplomacy as a kind of self-evident corporate responsibility." These and other charges were formalized in the growing body of writings that lamented the "tragedy of Zionism."[23]

The spectacle of a divided community trading insults on the pages of the Jewish and general press horrified many intellectuals and communal leaders, some of whom tried to explain why Israel's image had gone from utopia to dystopia. Sarna attributed the increased criticism of Israel to a change in the mythology of the Jewish state: after Lebanon, some Jews "who were jarred out of their dream world" exchanged their "utopian myths for demonic ones." He described it as "an immature but hardly unprecedented response to disappointment," and called for developing more realistic attitudes toward Israel. Concern for realism was also behind the AJC's decision to establish in 1982 the Institute on American Jewish-Israeli Relations to "increase understanding and dialogue between the two largest, most vibrant Jewish communities in the world." Accusing the media of fomenting the split, because divisiveness among Jews was "more titillating than most wars or earthquakes," was also a popular explanation. Although there is some evidence that the media found the dispute quite tantalizing, public opinion polls indicated that the war in Lebanon had seriously polarized the Jewish community. Rabbi Greenberg from CLAL shocked many American Jews by wondering whether, by the year 2000, there would be one unified Jewish people.[24]

THE LEGACY OF LEBANON: THE GROWING CLEAVAGE IN THE AMERICAN JEWISH COMMUNITY

The NSAJ and a number of commercial polls evaluated the effects of the war in Lebanon on the attitudes of American Jews. In early September 1982 Cohen found that 49 percent of the respondents supported Israel's right to send military forces into West Beirut to expel the PLO. Twenty-seven percent agreed that "Israel should have attacked and destroyed the PLO military forces in West Beirut." Only 5 percent totally condemned Israel's drive into Lebanon. As for sympathy for Israel, 48 percent reported an increase in feelings, 48 percent did not register any change in the level of feelings, and 10 percent felt less sympathetic. A *Newsweek*-Gallup poll taken after Sabra and Shatila found that 33 percent of the sample were more sympathetic to Israel, 36 percent less sympathetic, and 31 percent reported no change in their sympathies. However, 65 percent of American Jews regarded Israel as at least partially responsible for the massacre and 78 percent felt that Begin's policies had damaged Israel.[25]

The war had also changed some of the attitudes of American Jews toward the core issues of the conflict, including negotiation with the PLO, territorial compromise, and a Palestinian state. The 1982 NSAJ sample split 31 percent for and 52 percent against territorial compromise; in the following year the split was 42 to 34 percent. As for negotiations with the Palestinians, in 1982, 66 percent thought that Israel should talk to the PLO provided it recognized Israel. In June 1983 this number went up to 70 percent. The *Newsweek*-Gallup poll found that 45 percent of its respondents were willing to consider territorial compromise. As before, the leadership sample of the NSAJ was more dovish than the rank and file. A Steven Cohen and Wacher poll of American Jewish leaders published in *Ha'aretz* on April 10, 1983, showed that 77 percent supported territorial compromise and 65 percent were willing to end Israel's control of the West Bank.[26]

Although the aggregate results did not indicate a radical change from the previous years, the socioeconomic patterns of the responses raised alarm in the community. Cohen noted that those who were more inclined to criticize Israel were younger, more educated, more liberal, more cosmopolitan, and less likely to be involved in the organized community. Analyzing these and other results, Gabriel Sheffer, an Israeli political scientist, repeated the warning that the younger generation would be less likely to support Israel in the future. Absent a specialized survey, it is only possible to speculate that the group identified by Cohen and Sheffer fit the profile of the prophecists who became disenchanted with Likud's hard-line policies. But the alienation of younger Jews from Israel had implications that went beyond the war in Lebanon, touching, as it was, on the survivalist imperative of the community. The demographic data of the early 1980s raised new concerns about the dwindling number of Jews and sparked a major controversy between those who argued that the community was assimilating and their opponents, who maintained that American Jews were not disappearing but merely transforming. Fought out in the pages of learned journals, popular publications, and public forums, the debate between the so-called assimilationists and the transformationists transfixed the community.[27]

As the demographers and the sociologists argued their case, the role of Israel as a chief agent of Jewish identify came under renewed scrutiny. Not surprisingly, the universalist critics of Israel were the first to question the utility of the Israel-centered brand of Judaism. After the Beirut massacre Schindler stated that "the question for us now is how to take people who have been using Israel as a kind of kidney machine, without which they cannot live, and teach them . . . that they have worth as Jews independent of Israel." Two months later he urged

American Jews to "affirm our [their] identity" apart from Israel. Glazer criticized the continuous preoccupation with Israel and asked what "does Jewish life mean to American Jews if so much of its is wrapped up in Israel?" Fein admitted that, in response to American Jews "needs," they came to view Israel more as a faith than a place, but the new challenge is to "reassess the classic Zionist point that the Diaspora condition is peripheral."[28]

The NSAJ provided a more objective evaluation of Israel's position as the center of American Jewish identity. Summing up the new developments, Cohen used Max Weber's thesis on the routinization of charisma to argue that Israel had "lost some of its glamour" in the "consciousness of many American Jews." He added that defending Israel is still part of the public and communal agenda, but the issue fails to fill the private concerns of American Jews, which can be better met through close family and community relations. Cohen predicted that the relationship with Israel would continue to shift with events in the Middle East and, more importantly, with the "shifting consciousness of American Jews—the constructs of images, myths, values, and symbols through which they understand themselves as American Jews." Although little understood at the time, Cohen's findings were the first indication that a switch toward a more Diaspora-oriented and privatized form of Judaism was afoot.[29]

How much of this phenomenon was attributable to the polarizing effect of Israel is difficult to estimate. In his 1982 survey, Cohen failed to establish a correlation between strong attachments to Israel and the attitudes toward the Arab-Israeli conflict. He found that about half of his doves and hawks were strongly committed, while the rest were only weakly "leaning" toward the issues involved in the conflict. However, other observers noted that the war in Lebanon had hardened the attitudes of the nationalists and universalists and contributed to the creation of two distinctive ideological camps in the American Jewish community. One historian asserted that "it is difficult to exaggerate Menachem Begin's role as symbolic catalyst for liberal Jewish disaffection with the Jewish state." Nevertheless, to those nationalists strongly committed to Israel, the Begin vision was alluring. A study of Young Leadership Conference found that the respondents were far more "hawkish than other groups and more supportive of Likud policies." Forty-eight percent of the sample wanted Israel to maintain permanent control over the territories, as opposed to the 26 percent who disagreed. Some 53 percent of the respondents rejected the notion that the Palestinians have the right to a homeland. Such numbers contrasted sharply with the general sample of Cohen, which showed the younger cohorts less engaged in the peace process.[30]

Moreover, the war in Lebanon created enough cognitive dissonance to discourage the more marginal Jews. Cohen himself admitted that many American Jews were caught between their commitment to a liberal worldview and their anxieties about the state of Israel, which required support for hard-line foreign policies. Seymour M. Lipset and Raab noted that the "strain between the liberalism of Jews and their avid support for Israel" was borne out by polls that found that large majorities of Jews are "remarkably antimilitarist," especially in their massive support for reduction of U.S. military budget. Yet the 1984 NSAJ sample approved—by 64 to 24 percent—the statement that "in order to be a reliable military supporter of Israel, the U.S. should maintain a strong military capacity." Indeed, it was this kind of cognitive dissonance that some leftist activists hoped to utilize when they attempted in the late 1970s to get American Jews out of "the bind of being doves in Vietnam and hawks on Israel."[31]

Other analysts agreed the Likud government complicated the liberalism of American Jews. Stephen Sharot and Nurit Zaidman insisted that the new Israel robbed American Jews of the perceived consonance between support for Israeli politics and their "Americanism." It was pointed out that the affinity of American Jews for liberalism was a fundamental component of their identity, superseding their identification with Israel which "waxed and waned." Since the Likud government shifted the Israeli political balance to the right, American Jews "experienced the pain of dual loyalty, not, as in the classic model, between Israel and America, but between Israel and liberalism." In identifying Israel with muscular, right-wing nationalism, "Begin activated some of their deepest concerns about their loyalty as Americans, their identity as Jews, and their credentials as liberal."[32]

Adding to the pain of having to choose between liberalism and Israel was the apprehension about dual loyalty. For most of Israel's existence, the attitudes of Jews and non-Jews toward the Arab-Israeli conflict have not differed dramatically. But unhappiness with Israel's invasion of Lebanon and the shock of the Beirut massacre changed this equation. The *Newsweek*-Gallop poll, which compared the attitudes of a national and Jewish sample, found significant differences. Whereas 36 percent of Jews reported being less sympathetic to Israel, 51 percent of non-Jews said they were less sympathetic than a year ago. Thirty-two percent of non-Jews held Israel "very much responsible for the massacre," as opposed to 11 percent of Jews. Asked about U.S. aid to Israel, 50 percent of non-Jews and only 11 percent of Jews wanted it suspended. Attitudes toward the Palestinian issue were equally lopsided. Thirty-one percent of non-Jews wanted to return the West Bank to Jordanian sovereignty and 23 percent supported the creation of an independent Palestinian state. The comparable number for Jews was 16 and 7 percent respectively. The "palatable unease" with Begin was exacerbated when the Israeli leader, disregarding the anti-Israeli sentiments, openly called on the community to defend the vision of Greater Israel against American pressure.[33]

Washington's efforts to cope with the aftermath of the war in Lebanon exposed the American Jews to further problems of double loyalty. When the Israelis withdrew to southern Lebanon in September 1983, President Reagan dispatched marines to enforce the fragile cease-fire. Such an action was strongly welcomed by American Jews, who had traditionally supported a pro-Israeli American military intervention by a ratio well exceeding 70 percent. However, the American public approved of Reagan's decision by a small margin of 48 to

42 percent. Following the attack on the marine barracks in Beirut on October 23, the support for American military presence dwindled to a meager 17 percent. American Jews were also at odds with the general sentiments in the country after the hijacking of the TWA airplane in June 1985. More than half of the American sample thought that Israel should release Shiite prisoners in exchange for the TWA hostages. More ominously for the Jews, more than 30 percent of respondents in a series of the WP-ABC surveys in June felt that the United States "should reduce its ties to Israel in order to lessen the acts of terrorism against us in the Middle East." Even if these numbers were not dramatic, the discrepancy between Jewish and non-Jewish attitudes were large enough to put the more liberal and marginally attached Jews on edge. According to Mitchell Geoffrey Bard, such Jews were most likely to worry about the negative opinions of gentiles. Raab described such behavior as a "failure of nerves," a tendency to exaggerate the "negative reaction of other Jews and other Americans in certain times of crisis."[34]

Whatever the sources of cognitive dissonance, the Pollard affair, which came three years after the war in Lebanon, had given pause even to the most committed members of the community. Jonathan Pollard, who worked for U.S. navy intelligence, was arrested for espionage on behalf of Israel and sentenced to life imprisonment in 1987. To escape the charge of dual loyalty, most of American leaderships hastened to condemn Pollard and the Israeli government. Morris B. Abram, the chairman of the Presidents Conference, called the espionage "inexcusable" and approved the life sentence. ADL's Perlmutter criticized Israel's "stupidity" and Tom Dine of AIPAC declared that Israel did not come to terms with the fact that "a criminal act . . . and treason against my government was committed." Fueling Jewish anxiety was the reaction of Congress, where some of the most pro-Israeli legislators accused the Likud government of arrogance and creating a cloud over the "axiom of Israel's moral worthiness." The debate reached a boiling point after the Israeli political scientist Shlomo Avineri published an open letter to American Jews on March 10, 1987. Using blunt language, Avineri accused them of anxiety and cowardice allegedly bred by their *galut* ("Diaspora") existence. Responding in kind, Stuart Eizenstat, chairman of the Institute on American Jewish-Israeli Relation of the AJC, berated Avineri for failing to "understand the concerns of a Jewish minority," and for using the Pollard affair "to denigrate the authenticity of Jewish life in America." He and other critics of Avineri, including Thomas Mann of the AJCongress, made it clear that the majority of American Jews would not compromise their loyalty in order to protect such broadly defined security interest.[35]

In the end it was left to the nationalists to defend Pollard and Israel's handling of the affair. The ZOA maintained that Pollard received a disproportionately harsh sentence and accused the organized community of not doing more to help the spy, a stand that was supported by AFSI. They viewed Pollard as a hero who tried to defend Israel's security in a treacherous Middle East. Rabbi Avi Weiss wrote that Pollard bothered American Jewish critics because of their "self absorbed concern with the effect of Pollard's action on their own careers." A subsequent 1991 poll reflected the polarized attitudes of the community on the issue. Only 29 percent of the respondents said that Pollard's sentence was too harsh and only 22 percent maintained that American Jewish organizations ought to campaign to reduce the sentence.[36]

While the war in Lebanon and the Pollard affair served as a dramatic reminder of the cognitive dissonance that American Jews were likely to incur while defending Israel's interests, there were subtler but equally wrenching costs. Historically, it was the Democrats, the liberals, and the trade unions that formed the backbone of support for Israel in the American electorate. By the early 1980s the composition of this "supportive public" had changed considerably. Following the Reagan realignment, it was mostly conservative Republicans who approved of the activist policies of the Likud government, including the war in Lebanon. Seventy percent of those who identified themselves as Republicans, conservatives, and Reagan's supporters preferred Israel as opposed to the PLO. In geographic terms, Israel enjoyed greater popularity in the South, Midwest, and rural parts of the United States.[37]

When Republicans took control of the Senate and improved their standing in the House of Representatives, conservative legislators assumed the chairmanship of a number of committees and subcommittees vital for Israel. It quickly became clear that in order to protect Israel's good standing with Congress, the organized community would need to abandon its traditional support for liberal legislators and help to elect conservative ones. One commentator urged Jews to get over their "natural instinct" to rally to the liberal side and make sure that the Senate contains as "many [conservative] supporters of Israel as possible." However, this strategy upset many Jewish liberals. Writing in the *New Republic*, Robert Kuttner blasted the "unholy alliance" lubricated by money flowing from the Jewish PACs to right-wing Republicans. Hertzberg criticized Jewish PACs for "supporting candidates solely on the basis of their attitudes toward Israel" and predicted an anti-Semitic backlash.[38]

Even harder to swallow was the budding alliance between the right wing of the community and evangelical Christians. It was already noted that, starting in 1967, mainline Protestant churches took an increasingly pro-Palestinian stand in the Arab-Israeli conflict. In 1980 the NCC adopted a resolution that urged mutual recognition of PLO and Israel. In 1981 four hundred liberal clergymen called on the United States to reduce aid to Israel until the human rights of the Palestinians were recognized, a step that outraged the Jewish community. According to Perlmutter, the NCC endangered the interests of Israel and American Jews by demanding to include the PLO in the peace process.[39]

Such a stand contrasted dramatically with the Christian Zionist sentiments of the evangelicals who, like the Merkaz Harav circles, viewed the retention of the occupied territories as part of a prophetic process unfolding in the Middle East. Ed McAteer, who established in 1979 the Religious Roundtable to advance the Christian agenda, was a supporter of the Temple Mount Faithful. McAteer, who organized the Prayer Breakfast in Honor of Israel during the annual meeting of the National Religious Broadcasters, had a model of the Third Temple displayed in the hall. Douglas Krieger, an evangelical entrepreneur and a Middle East adviser to McAteer, was coorganizer with oil millionaire Terry Risenhoover and Stanley Goldfoot, a key Israeli supporter of the Temple to the evangelicals, of the Jerusalem Temple Foundation. The two Americans had also set up an affiliate Temple Mount Foundation in Los Angeles. According to reports, the Goldfoot group, which also included Spen, had raised millions of dollars to help establish the Temple, buy Arab land in the territories, and help Ateret Cohanim to purchase property in East Jerusalem. During the invasion of Lebanon the CBN station of Pat Robertson, a leading figure in the Christian Roundtable, offered daily commentaries that interpreted the unfolding events according to end-time biblical prophecy.[40]

The political usefulness of Christian eschatology was not lost on Begin, who presented Jerry Falwell, a prominent member of the Christian Roundtable, with the Jabotinsky Award. A number of conservative American Jewish leaders seemed to agree. In December 1980 they argued in the American Jewish press that "there is far greater potential commonality of interests among Jews and the Moral Majority." Jacques Torczyner, a past president of the ZOA, declared that "we have . . . come to a conclusion that the right-wing reactionaries are the natural allies of Zionism and not the liberals." Perlmutter asserted that "we feel more comfortable today with Reverend Bailey Smith, the leader of the Southern Baptist Convection." In 1983 Rabbi Yechiel Eckstein founded the International Fellowship of Christian and Jews (IFCJ), which, among others, hosted an annual "Solidarity with Israel" program featuring speakers such as Robertson and Jerry Falwell. Gerald Strober, the Likud activist who organized the Committee for Begin, coordinated the Jewish community outreach to the evangelicals.[41]

While the neoconservatives and Orthodox Jews welcomed the relations with the Christian Right, the liberals rebelled against such an alliance. In a resolution passed in 1981, the AJCongress strongly rejected cooperation with the evangelical right. Schindler called it "madness" and "suicide" and urged "not to honor those whose works are anathema to everything for which we stand." Many liberals were resentful of the fact that the evangelicals colluded with Jewish PACs to defeat proabortion, prowelfare liberal candidates who were critical of Begin's policies. The case of Jesse Helms, the conservative senator from North Carolina, was particularly striking. Helms, who narrowly defeated the liberal former governor Jim Hunt in the bitterly contested 1984 election, received help from conservative Jews like the failed financier Ivan Boesky. Robert Jacobs, a New York real estate developer with strong ties to Peter Goldman, then head of AFSI, and to JDL's Kahane, was another important contributor. In another celebrated case, Mark Siljander, a Michigan Republican and an evangelical Christian, campaigned against the Jewish liberal incumbent by urging voters to send another "Christian to Congress."[42]

What ruffled many liberal feathers was the fact that the Jewish PACs and individual donors, eager to ensure an Israel-friendly Congress, inadvertently helped to "Christianize" America. As Fein put it, "for every ounce of protection we theoretically gain for Israel, we will lose a pound of protection for pluralism." Taking a broader philosophical perspective, Kristol described this development as "the Jewish dilemma." He also chastised the American Jews for constantly striving to be more Jewish, but objecting to the wishes of American Christians to "become more Christian." Another neoconservative stated that "Israel's political fortune should not be tied to the health of liberalism." However, after the 1984 election a group of prominent liberal Jews tried to challenge the AIPAC–supported single-issue PACs by creating Multi-Issue PACs (MIPACs), where support for Israel was a "threshold issue—necessary but not sufficient." These and other critics pointed out that Jewish money has moved well to the right of the voting sentiments of American Jews. MIPACs created more controversy, with AIPAC proponents charging that the "issue of survival of Israel" takes precedent over domestic concerns. Still, putting Israel's survival first exacted a heavy emotional price among the rank and file. A subsequent ADL poll revealed that Jews had regularly rated Christian fundamentalists as a group most inimical to them. Nine-tenths of liberals, three-quarters of moderates, and two-thirds of conservatives in the survey were alarmed by the role of evangelicals in American politics.[43]

Although the divisions did not paralyze the organizational community, it made it more difficult to articulate a clear position on the peace process.

SPEAKING FOR ISRAEL IN A FRAGMENTED COMMUNITY: THE CHALLENGE OF THE PRESIDENTS CONFERENCE AND AIPAC

In looking at the structure of the Israeli-related discourse of American Jews it is important to note that by the early 1980s there were some three hundred independent national Jewish organizations, some two hundred local federations and about five thousand synagogues. One historian described them as a "large and somewhat ragged crowd of organizations and societies and institutions," some of whom are in "direct competition with each other."[44] The divisiveness over the war in Lebanon and Israeli settlements in the West Bank had made the work of the Israel defense organizations particularly difficult.

The Conference of Presidents, which was nominally accountable to its constituent members, was affected the most. The problems stemmed from the position of the Conference, which was also shared by AIPAC, that Jewish defense organizations should support the elected government of Israel. As Kenneth Bialkin, the chairman of the Conference, noted before the 1984 election in Israel, "If the [Labor] wins . . . we will support them, if the Likud wins and pursues a strong line in the West Bank, we will get behind them." During the early Begin years, the Conference sponsored pro-Israeli rallies and placed advertisements in newspapers. After the invasion, Howard Squadron, then chairman of the Conference, called on the United States to support Israeli policy. In an effort to create the appearance of unity, the Conference helped to coordinate a *New York Times* advertisement signed by 131 leaders of Jewish organizations and other prominent American Jews that equated the action with eradicating terrorism.[45]

However, the Conference was forced to alter its stand when the Sabra and Shatila massacre created an outcry in the community. According to Schindler, the Conference held an emergency meeting with the Israeli ambassador to Washington, Moshe Arens. After Arens tried to defend Israel's entry into West Beirut and blamed anti-Semitic coverage, he was told not the "give us this 'blood libel' business." The Conference dispatched Schindler to urge Begin to modify his policies and appoint a commission of inquiry. A State Department study of American Jewish leadership concluded that the pressure from a number of normally loyal leaders was partially instrumental in Begin's decision to authorize the inquiry.[46]

In trying to respond to the anti-Israeli critique, the Conference ran afoul of the powerful neoconservative Jewish elite that gained visibility after the election of Reagan. Offended by the fact that such leaders had constant access to the president, the Conference published a statement criticizing what was described as self-appointed "court Jews." However, the political direction of the Conference changed when, in 1986, Abram became the chairman. Unlike his predecessors who came from the relatively liberal NCRAC, the AJCongress and the Reform movement, Abram and his executive director Malcolm Hoenlein were recruited from the ranks of the assertive circle of Soviet Jewry activists. Abram had a good personal relation with the hard-line Yitzhak Shamir who replaced Begin in 1983. Hoenlein, an Orthodox Jew, was described as a pragmatic conservative who was popular with Likud politicians. Privately, Hoenlein became an advocate for the West Bank settlers' movement, helping in their fund-raising events and facilitating their lobbying efforts in the United States.[47]

The shift to the right of the Conference outraged its liberal members. Menachem Rosensaft, president of the Labor Zionist Alliance, described the Conference as "an organization which does not have by-laws, does not have a constitution" and no visible budget. He accused Abram of supporting the policies of the Israeli government, "sight unseen." Albert Vorspan, then senior vice president of the UAHC, created a stir when he publicized the inner struggle over Israel. In spite of moves to censure dissent, constituent members of the Conference continued to take independent positions. For instance, during the World Zionist Congress meeting in Jerusalem in 1983, the Hadassah group, another constituent of the Conference, joined the World Labor Zionist Movement in condemning the Likud's policy toward the Palestinians. In September 1985 the AJCongress, anxious to restart the peace process, sent a twenty-person delegation for an unprecedented meeting with the Egyptian President Hosni Mubarak and King Hussein of Jordan. The tour provoked the wrath of Shamir, by then Israel's foreign minister, and unease among the leadership of the Conference.[48]

Compared to the Conference, AIPAC was less susceptible to the divisive atmosphere in the community. Under the leadership of Lawrence Weinberg, its president since 1976, AIPAC increased its independence from other Jewish organizations. In a series of reforms, AIPAC raised the number of its members, made a major effort to increase its grass-root appeal, and doubled its executive committee. The latter step was designed to neutralize the Jewish organizational leaders on the executive committee, making AIPAC quite immune from communal pressure. In fact, most of the real power in the organization was concentrated in the hands of a small number of wealthy conservative donors known as "the officers' group."

Dine, the executive director of AIPAC who was hired by Weinberg in 1980, was credited with many of the new ideas for restructuring AIPAC. Before joining AIPAC Dine worked on the staff of two liberal senators and was a research fellow at the Brookings Institution. In the thirteen years of Dine's stewardship, AIPAC's staff grew from 24 to 158, paid membership rose from 8,000 to 55,000, and the budget increased from $1.7 to $15 million. Even more impressive was AIPAC's skillful use of a number of influence multipliers. Most of AIPAC's 55,000 contributors were enlisted as lobbyists and grass-roots organizers for pro-Israeli issues. Many of them could be also counted in helping in political campaigns of friendly legislators.[49]

AIPAC had also good links with many of the Jewish PACs, which worked to defeat "unfriendly congressmen." In what became a virtual crusade for Jewish activists, Charles Percy, the Republican senator from Illinois, was targeted and lost the 1984 election to the Democrat Paul Simon. In other cases AIPAC helped to undermine Paul "Pete" McClosky's senatorial race and defeated Findley (D-Ill.), the outspoken critic of Israel, in 1982. George McGovern, who angered AIPAC by voting for the sale of F-15s to Saudi Arabia, lost much of his Jewish financial support and his seat. In some of these cases AIPAC collaborated with John Terry Dolan, the head of the well-funded National Conservative Political Action Committee, which was created to end the political career of a number of liberal senators, including McGovern and Church. In other instances, AIPAC could rely on the considerable electoral heft of the Christian Right. AIPAC's skillful use of influence multipliers turned the organization into a formidable, albeit not-well-understood presence in the Jewish community. Indeed, in spite of its reputation in Washington, the 1984 American Jewish Population Survey (AJPS) found that over three-quarters of the respondents had no impression of AIPAC, compared to only 6 percent who had no impression of the UJA.[50]

However, AIPAC's relative independence could not protect it totally from tensions over Israeli foreign policy. During the war in Lebanon Dine praised the Reagan peace plans, which called for a freeze on settlements in the West Bank, and was immediately attacked by right-wingers in his own organization. Steven Rosen, who was hired on Weinberger's recommendation as the research director, along with some of the officers, was part of the hard-line group that supported Likud. Weinberger's own position was described as "difficult to classify." Although he struck up a good relationship with Begin, upon leaving AI-PAC in 1982 Weinberger established the Washington Institute for Near East Policy, which became the "stronghold of Labor thinking at the height of the Likud era." Weinberger's successors in AIPAC—Robert Asher, Edward C. Levy and Mayer "Bubba" Mitchell—were all conservative Republicans supportive of the hard-line policies of Likud. Working against this group, Dine managed to score some victories. When Senator Carl Levin and thirty of his colleagues wrote a letter to George Shultz criticizing Israel's unwillingness to trade land for peace, the conservative officers wanted to denounce the legislators in public. However, Dine urged quite diplomatically to diffuse the simmering resentment on Capitol Hill.[51]

AIPAC's efforts to strike a balance between a liberal and hard-line position did not satisfy its detractors. Left-wing Jewish critics denounced the organization in the harshest possible terms. Hertzberg went so far as to accuse AIPAC of sabotaging the peace process in order to safeguard its existence: "AIPAC is going to wake up one morning and discover peace in the Middle East . . . and then what will it do? Its job will be over. The fact is that what 'PLO Inc.' is to Palestinian nationalism, AIPAC has become to American-Israeli relations." Calling AIPAC the "Sorcerer's Apprentice," Hertzberg urged to disband the organization. Other critics accused AIPAC of stifling public debate and keeping files on Jewish dissenters. On the other hand of the ideological divide, groups like AFSI denounced AIPAC for showing a lack of vigilance in defending Israel's interests in the United States. Still, some critics acknowledged that AIPAC, caught between the government of Israel and the right and left wings of the community, faced an "agonizing dilemma."[52]

Israel's 1984 elections, which resulted in a Likud-Labor national unity government, aggravated the task of both the Presidents Conference and AIPAC. Labor's Shimon Peres was named prime minister and Shamir became foreign minister under an arrangement that was to rotate the positions after two years. Israelis described the foreign policy of the national unity government as a "two headed monster" and a "government of national paralysis." Peres, who declared that the continuing occupation of the West Bank was a grave threat to the security of Israel, used his time as Prime Minister to push for a deal with Jordan that paralleled the Reagan peace plan. When Shamir, who took a very hard-line position on the territories, became prime minister, he scuttled the Jordanian deal and expanded the Jewish settlements.

Caught between the clashing visions of Likud and Labor, the Conference and AIPAC could only make a pretense of supporting a unified Israeli foreign policy. The effort of Peres to conclude a deal with Jordan is a case in point. In April 1987 Peres, now the foreign minister, reached an agreement with King Hussein to return most of the West Bank to Jordan. Hussein wanted the deal to be sanctioned by an international peace conference and Peres asked American Jews to persuade the United States to back the arrangement. The AJC and the AJCongress both endorsed the deal, encouraging Peres to appeal to the entire Conference of Presidents in September. However, Prime Minister Shamir, who strongly objected to the Jordanian deal, warned Abram not to involve the Conference in an internal Israeli dispute.[53]

Legitimizing the divisions in the American Jewish community, the Israeli government of national unity accelerated a process of fragmenting and privatizing the Jewish lobby. Ever since, Breira and left-wing groups dissatisfied with the Conference and AIPAC had worked to create their own lobbying channels in Washington. These and other activists hoped to persuade the American government to apply economic and political pressure in order to change Israel's policy in the West Bank. Israeli peace activists had also favored such a strategy. For instance, David Shaham, the former editor of the Labor journal *Ot*, had publicly urged the Reagan administration to "apply discreet pressure" on Israeli leaders in order to force territorial concessions. Extending these efforts to Congress, a group of eighteen rabbis, including some Breira veterans, met in 1983 with twenty pro-Israeli congressmen to lobby against the Israeli government. In 1984, activists from the Berkeley branch of the NJA urged Congress to cut funds to Israel by the amount it spent on settlements outside the Green Line.[54]

Reacting to what was perceived as anemic support for Israel by the Conference and AIPAC, right-wing groups commenced their own lobbying activities in Washington. Using the well-connected network of Christian fundamentalists, these groups could count on the large number of conservative legislatures that were brought to Capitol Hill by the Reagan revolution. In a mirror image of the left, the right-wingers were urged by the settlers' organizations in Israel to plead their case before the American authorities. In one such instance, in the fall of 1985, AFSI organized a tour of the secretary general of Gush Emunim, who met with Senator Helms and other pro-Israeli conservative legislators. On tour for his Jerusalem Temple Foundation, Goldfoot urged evangelical audiences to lobby Congress for pro-Israel issues.[55]

The split in the Israeli government institutionalized these privatized lobbying practices. Relying on the advice of his chief of staff, the career diplomat Yossi Ben-Aharon, Shamir authorized the creation of an extensive network of contacts in America. Israeli diplomats, civil servants, and Likud party officials who became part of this independent lobby were personally accountable to Ben-Aharon rather than to the Israeli government. There is little doubt that the neoconservative influence in the Conference and AIPAC helped Likud's budding lobby efforts. But Labor's historical reluctance to get involved in the nitty-gritty of Jewish organizational life was also a boon to Likud. Rabin, who was once described as a "Canaanite," displayed a distaste for the "court Jew" function of the Conference and AIPAC. His successor Peres did not seek to establish a vigorous Labor presence to match the Shamir–Ben-Aharon network. A senior adviser to Peres subsequently acknowledged that this was a mistake: "We simply didn't think it was important, and the Shamir's people do [sic] whatever they wanted."[56]

The privatized lobbying contributed to the confusion and polarization in the community. For instance, when the AJC publicly sided with Peres in the Jordanian deal, it triggered a major uproar in America and Israel. But the contradictory voices emanating from Jerusalem created a sense that there was no objective Israeli national interest worth defending. Worse, as Spiegel, a leading expert on the subject, argued, by seeking support for their contrasting approaches, Israeli leaders destroyed the monopoly they used to enjoy on defining their own national interest. They turned American Jews from supporters to mediators in Israeli politics, a role that the community was totally unprepared to perform. Indeed, Spiegel found "no model in contemporary political theory for a community in one state to play an integral political function in another." In Spiegel's view American Jewish institutions were poorly equipped to play such a role because they lacked the ability to develop "detailed and sophisticated tactics for specific problems, or to deal with issues that require specialized expert knowledge." Spiegel and other thoughtful observers called for "institutional and intellectual reform" that would replace activism without substance, and give essence to "panaceas and slogans."[57]

As a piece of political science writing, Spiegel's analysis, which was part of a large February 1988 *Commentary* symposium on Israel and American Jewry, was a sound one. He hoped that reforms could stem the growing decline in the Jewish community and provide innovative channels of turning criticism and frustration with Israel into "productive channels of help." Unfortunately, American Jewry did not have the time to engage in the much needed communal healing and restructuring of its institutions. Two months before the symposium took place, the Palestinians embarked on a process of civil resistance to Israeli occupation that would soon become known as the Intifada. Although few could anticipate it at the time, the Palestinian uprising was destined to further the already deep polarization in American Jewry and radically change its relations with the state of Israel.

5

The Long Shadow of the Intifada: American Jews and the Palestinian Problem

Throughout much of the Arab-Israeli conflict American Jews had ignored Palestinian nationalism. As noted in chapter 1, Palestine was seen as a refuge for the survivors of the Holocaust. The occupation of a large Palestinian population in the wake of the Six Day War prompted some observers to worry that the absorption of more than a million Arabs would decisively affect the character of the Jewish state. However, as long as the Palestinians were viewed through the prism of PLO's terrorism, questions about long-term solutions to their problem could be avoided. Likud's settlement policies left many American Jews uneasy, but the communal consensus against an independent Palestinian state held firm. The outbreak of the Intifada, a massive civil rights insurrection in the West Bank and Gaza Strip, shattered this consensus. It forced American Jews to engage in a painful process of soul-searching that would ultimately change their attitudes toward the Palestinians, altered their relations with Israel and lead them to re-examine the bases of their own identity.

THE INTIFADA: U.S.–ISRAELI RELATIONS AND THE COMING OF AGE OF PALESTINIAN NATIONALISM

The Intifada, which started in December 1987 in the Gaza Strip and quickly spread to the West Bank, caught Israel by surprise. The Palestinians had never recognized the Israeli rule as legitimate, but the various intelligence reports in the 1980s did not predict the outbreak of a large civil disobedience movement in the territories. The Israeli handling of the Intifada, which involved the use of military force against unarmed civilians, many of the them stone-throwing children, was sharply criticized in the United States. When, in January 1988, the then-Defense Minster Yitzhak Rabin publicly announced a policy of "force, might, beatings" to put down the daily violence, widespread condemnation followed. The Israelis were also harshly criticized for their policy of deporting the leaders of the Intifada. Still, none of these tactics was effective in limiting the uprising, which, according to an IDF count, claimed some three hundred Palestinian lives by the end of 1988. An additional five thousand Palestinians were jailed and fifteen hundred were held under administrative detention. One year later the *New York Times* reported that more than six hundred Palestinians had been killed and some fifteen thousand to twenty thousand wounded. There were fifty thousand arrests and thirteen thousand Palestinians remained in jails.[1]

The Intifada posed a serious challenge to the Reagan administration and its relations with Israel. After the war in Vietnam, American foreign policy had developed a great sensitivity to issues of public legitimacy in friendly countries. Israeli handling of the Intifada, which involved violations of American-style human rights, provoked a sharp rebuke from the White House. The administration expressed strong opposition to the deportation policy and voted with the Security Council to condemn Israel's conduct in the territories. When, in May 1988, Israel expelled Mubarak Awad, a Mennonite-educated Palestinian-American who espoused civil disobedience, the State Department issued a sharply worded rebuke. Israel was left in the unhappy position of trying to dispel the "misperception" that Awad was a "dedicated disciple of Mahatma Gandhi and Martin Luther King Jr." State officials also deplored Israel's restrictions on media coverage of the Intifada.[2]

What bothered the administration most was the fact that the uprising seemed to be broadly based and not related to the PLO. Rabin himself admitted: "whatever started it, it started without any instructions from outside," and it took the PLO "two days to catch up." Secretary of State Shultz allowed that the origin of the problem was "essentially indigenous," created by "a large number of people in occupation who haven't had the basic rights of governance."[3] Although the administration, which had been rebuffed in its earlier peace efforts, was reluctant to get involved anew in its last year in office, the State Department proposed a modest plan. The so-called Shultz initiative envisaged a limited Palestinian self-rule in the territories as part of a five-year interim autonomy plan. Egypt and Jordan welcomed the land-for-peace proposal, which also involved an international peace conference, but Israeli Prime Minister Shamir took a hardline position for many reasons, not the least of which was the proposed participation of the PLO. In a sign of continuous division in the Israeli government, Foreign Minister Shimon Peres welcomed the idea of an international peace conference.

After the failure of the Shultz mission, on March 5, 1988, thirty senators, including some of Israel's staunchest friends, wrote a letter criticizing Shamir for his refusal to trade territory for peace. The letter—signed by Carl Levin (D–Mich.), Rudy Boschwitz (R–Minn.), Daniel Patrick Moynihan (D–N.Y.), Edward Kennedy (D–Mass.) and Alan Cranston (D–Calif.), among others—praised Peres and stated that "peace negotiations have little chance of success if the Israeli Government's position rules out territorial compromise." Shultz pressed his peace initiative in Congress where, on March 10, he urged Israel to change its notions of defense and face the "ticking demographic time bomb." The next day Shamir struck back, declaring that the "only word in the Shultz plan I accept is his signature." Upon arriving, on March 14, for a series of talks in Washington, he repeated his charge that the peace conference would not serve the cause of peace.[4]

In contrast to the frosty reception accorded to Shamir, Washington lavished praise on Peres, who visited in May. Shultz returned to Israel in June as part of a Middle East tour, where he warned that the occupation is a "dead end street." While in the Middle East, the secretary of state received an indirect endorsement from an emergency summit meeting of Arab states in Algiers. Although the summit resolution pledged to help the Intifada and affirmed that the PLO is the sole representative of the Palestinian people, the Arab leaders did not heed Arafat's demand to reject the peace plan, which did not envision an independent Palestinian state. As if to underscore the need for a solution, on July 31 King Hussein announced that Jordan would end its claim to the West Bank, thus recognizing the right of the PLO to form an independent Palestinian state.

The elections in Israel and the United States scheduled for the fall had put the peace process on hold, but the returns from the November 1 Israeli ballot dispelled any hope for a fresh start. The Likud bloc took forty seats as opposed to Labor's thirty-nine seats, with the religious parties that supported hard-line positions increasing their hold on the Knesset. The inconclusive results led to a new national unity government with Shamir as prime minister, Rabin in the defense ministry, and Peres in the finance ministry. Seven days later American voters picked George Bush and an activist foreign policy team, which was expected to inject new energy into the Middle East negotiations.

The new momentum accelerated when, in a dramatic change of attitude, Yasser Arafat recognized Israel's right to exist and promised to renounce terrorism in the beginning of December. On December 14, the United States reversed its Kissinger-era policy of shunning what was described as a "terrorist organization," and began a dialogue with the PLO. The Palestinian decision to recognize Israel came as no surprise to the administration, which, through intermediaries, had for months encouraged Arafat to take such a step. One day later, Robert H. Pelletreau, a senior State Department official, initiated contacts with the PLO. The international community received warmly the American decision, and the UN changed the PLO observer's status from "PLO" to "Palestine."

Reflecting on these developments, most observers noted that the Intifada provided the Palestinians, the PLO, and Arafat with the international legitimacy that had eluded them during decades of terrorism. This message was not lost on the Israeli government, prompting Shamir to engage in some damage control. He declared that the "philosophy of PLO had not changed—that is, [it is still dedicated to] the destruction of Israel." However, when Israeli efforts to dissuade the administration from talking to the PLO failed, Shamir, who also faced pressures from the European community, proposed a plan for negotiations on February 1, 1989. The two-stage proposal envisaged an interim autonomy for the Palestinians and a promise for direct negotiations between Israel, the Palestinians, and the Arabs states. During his early April meeting with President Bush, Shamir proposed elections in the territories to choose a delegation that would negotiate an interim period of self-government. Bush and his secretary of state, James Baker, welcomed the Israeli proposal but charged that "such elections are not the end of the road but the beginning of a process that would lead ultimately to resolution of the territorial dispute and the Arab-Israeli conflict."[5] The Palestinians countered with a plan that demanded the withdrawal of Israeli troops from population centers in the West Bank and Gaza Strip prior to an election to pick representatives to the Palestinian National Council.

In yet another testimony to the deep division in Israel, Shamir, upon returning home, faced a backlash from the hard-liners in his own party. Ariel Sharon, Deputy Prime Minister David Levy, and Planning and Economy Minister Yitzhak Modai warned that those responsible for the Intifada would be elected, but Rabin and Peres backed the plan. The Likud hard-liners wanted to ban the residents of East Jerusalem from the vote and demanded that there would be no commitment on the ultimate status of the territories. On May 14, after concessions to the hard-liners, the Israeli cabinet approved the plan. Still, among those voting against the plan were Sharon and Modai, who maintained that it would lead to a Palestinian state. As expected, the PLO dismissed the proposal as a "farce" designed to deceive world public opinion.

Israel's tepid efforts to move forward the peace process did not please Secretary Baker either. In a major address delivered on May 22 to the annual gathering of AIPAC, Baker called on Israel to "lay aside once and for all the unrealistic vision of a Greater Israel." Baker's remarks drew an angry response from Shamir, who rejected as "useless" the idea that Israel give up the quest of Greater Israel and Jewish settlements. Conversely, the Palestinians were pleased with the secretary's position and noted his courage in facing AIPAC down.[6]

Whatever limited hopes for a breakthrough were raised by the Shamir initiative were dashed when the plan's leading opponents in Israel took their fight to a special meeting of the Likud's Central Committee. Sharon, Levy, and Modai forced Shamir to accept a number of limitations on the peace proposal. Among them was the stipulation that East Jerusalem residents would not vote in the elections, that Jewish settlements would continue, that Israel would not give up any territory, and that a Palestinian state would never be established. Americans reacted with anger to the July 6 decision, and Baker charged that the conditions "give rise, at least in our minds, to a question about the seriousness of purpose."[7] Labor's threats to leave the coalition further muddied the waters. To avert such an outcome, the cabinet voted on July 23 to endorse Shamir's original plan, but did not force the prime minister to renounce the Likud-imposed conditions.

While the vote saved the national unity government, the strains between Likud and Labor over the peace process were becoming more pronounced. Labor wanted to use the proposed election to legitimize the PLO's participation in future negotiations, whereas Likud tried to structure the vote in a way that would exclude the PLO from the talks. As a result, Labor quietly encouraged American contacts with the PLO, a process that Likud vehemently opposed. After President Hosni Mubarak of Egypt proposed a ten-point plan to speed up the negotiations, Peres broke publicly with Shamir by insisting that the "Cairo points" can serve as a basis for talk. Among the points was the withdrawal of the Israeli army from the territories prior to elections, a moratorium on Jewish settlements, and a prior commitment of Israel to exchange territories for peace. When Egypt officially introduced the Cairo plan on September 15, the Israeli cabinet split, prompting Baker to meet separately with Peres and Likud's Moshe Arens. However, Shamir indicated that the Cairo plan was unacceptable and, on October 6, after a stormy debate, the Israel cabinet tied at six to six to defeat it.

The administration, gravely disappointed by Israel's rejection of the Mubarak plan, tried to salvage the peace process by proposing its own five points, designed to assuage some of the Israeli concerns. The PLO registered its misgivings with the American proposal, but did not formally reject the Baker-drafted plan. This role fell to Shamir, who, on October 17, told a Likud party gathering that Israel would "stand firm and not give in, even if we face a clash."[8] The prime minister accused the Bush administration of trying to get Israel out of the territories and force it to negotiate with the PLO. The State Department reacted critically to Shamir's comment, but pressed on with the peace plan, energizing Labor's own efforts to solve the Arab-Israeli conflict. Ever the optimist, Peres declared during his January 24, 1990, visit to Cairo that the two sides were near an agreement in their talks. Shamir, faced with a rebellion in his own ranks, was forced to deny this statement and had to defend his hard-line credentials during a stormy meeting of the Likud Central Committee on February 12. This prompted Labor's ultimatum to leave the government if peace negotiations did not commence by March 7. On March 11, Likud rejected Labor's demand that the cabinet vote on the Baker plan; two days later the Knesset defeated the Shamir cabinet in a no confidence vote.

American hopes for a breakthrough in the peace process was raised when Peres was asked on March 20 to form a new government. The State Department called on Israel to choose a government "capable of saying yes" to U.S. proposals, and Peres promised that, if successful, he would approve Baker's approach. But Shamir ridiculed Peres's argument that Likud's failure to say yes to Baker sabotaged the peace process and vowed to defend the territories by appealing to religious parties. At the end of March, Rabbi Eliezer Shah, the spiritual leader of the ultra-Orthodox Degel Hatorah party, refused to join a Labor-led government. Even so, Peres was able to cobble a coalition with the help of Agudat Israel, another ultra-Orthodox party. However, hours before the Knesset was to endorse the new Labor government, Rabbi Menachem Schneerson, the leader of the New York–based Lubavitch Hassidim who opposed territorial concessions, ordered Agudat Israel to stay away from the coalition. Aguda's defection cleared the way for Shamir to build a narrow sixty-two-seat coalition and, on June 1, the Knesset approved what was to become the most conservative government in Israel's history.[9]

The new government did not waste time in showing its priorities. Defense Minister Arens spent his first day in office visiting Jewish settlements in the West Bank and Roni Milo, the police minister, declared the Baker plan "not relevant." Baker responded by delivering what *Newsweek* magazine called the "sharpest public rebuke to an Israeli government since the 1956 Suez crisis." He charged that Shamir undermined the peace plans and offered the White House phone number, adding: "When you're serious about peace, call us."[10] Faced with the danger of being painted as an extremist, the Israeli government spent the months of June and July trying to improve its image. By ordering soldiers to stay away from Palestinian centers, the IDF managed to decrease the violence of the Intifada. David Levy softened his opposition to Israeli-Palestinian negotiations and Sharon, who became the housing minister in the new cabinet, refrained from a dramatic increase in settlement activity.

Still, it took the Iraqi invasion of Kuwait on August 2 to bring Israel back into Washington's good graces. Although Saddam Hussein tried to link the Kuwait crisis to the Arab-Israeli conflict, President Bush rejected the so-called linkage theory and refused to blame Israel for Iraq's aggression. The administration, which planned to ask Congress to authorize the use of force to dislodge the Iraqis, could not afford to alienate pro-Israeli legislators, on whose votes it counted. After the war began on January 16, 1991, President Bush personally called Shamir to dissuade him from retaliating against the Scud missile attacks that Iraq launched against Israel. An Israeli military response, which the Israeli Chief of Staff Dan Shomron did not rule out, would have destroyed the multinational coalition that the United States assembled against Iraq. Israel's restraint during the war improved its international image at a time that the Palestinians, who fervently supported Saddam Hussein, lost some of the goodwill earned during the Intifada. When the Gulf War ended on February 23 with the utter rout of the Iraqi army, the Palestinians suffered a serious setback in their efforts to present a more moderate façade.

However, Baker was resolved to use the post–Gulf War momentum to salvage his peace initiative. During a series of trips to the Middle East, Baker pushed for an international conference to settle the Arab-Israeli conflict. When Baker arrived in Israel on July 21, he had commitments from Egypt, Syria, Lebanon, Jordan, and Saudi Arabia to participate in a peace conference. On July 24 Shamir described the issue of Palestinian representation as the major stumbling block. Informally, Shamir was also reacting to the hard-line position adopted by the administration to the 1991 Israeli request for loan guarantees designed to help absorb Jewish immigrants from the Soviet Union. Still, the Shamir government came under additional pressure when the Palestinian National Council announced on September 23 its readiness to participate in the conference. After assuring Shamir that the PLO would not be represented at the gathering, the Israeli government agreed to Baker's plan on October 17. On October 18 the United States and the Soviet Union—the official hosts of the conference—announced that the meeting would convene in Madrid on October 30.

From an American perspective, the Madrid Conference was a major breakthrough in the ceaseless efforts to solve the Arab-Israeli conflict. The Bush administration could point to the fact that the Arab decision to attend represented a victory for moderate forces in the Middle East. The conference was also a crucial turning point for the Palestinians. Faisal El-Husseini, a moderate Palestinian leader, claimed that, after many past mistakes, the Palestinians were ready to move toward a more realistic posture: "We are heading toward political discussions, a new reality."[11] In spite of the momentum created by the Madrid Conference, the subsequent bilateral negotiations between the parties became bogged down in procedural and substantive problems. In particular, Israeli talks with the Palestinians had been marred by the continuing violence of the Intifada. At the beginning of January 1992 Israel expelled twelve Palestinians, triggering a sharp rebuke from the UN Security Council. The Bush administration joined the Security Council resolution of January 6 in spite of the strong language used to condemn Israel's action.

The administration was also unhappy with Israel's rejection of a detailed proposal for self-government that the Palestinians presented on March 3. Although Baker urged all sides to continue the negotiations, there was little hope in Washington that things would progress on Shamir's watch. This pessimism was also shared by many in the American Jewish community who were overwhelmed by the task of defending Israel's handling of the Intifada.

PROVING THE LEFT RIGHT: THE AMERICAN JEWISH DISCOURSE ON THE PALESTINIAN ISSUE

American Jews, like the Israeli government, were surprised by the intense Palestinian nationalism of the Intifada. For a minority, which had consistently advocated civil rights and self-determination, the widespread civil resistance presented special problems. The terrorist label of the PLO that for decades enabled American Jews to write off the Palestinians was quickly becoming obsolete. Only ten years before, a Presidents Conference report noted that peace talks should not be conducted with a "murderous band of terrorists who call themselves the Palestine Liberation Organization." But the new image featured an occupied people fighting an oppressor—the Israeli army—which was seen on "nightly news attacking stone-throwing children, demolishing houses, shooting rubber bullets at young people, and generally behaving like a stereotypical occupying army."[12]

Not surprisingly, the first to protest the Israeli conduct were the traditional left-wing critics of Israel. Michael Lerner, the editor of *Tikkun*, a magazine billed as a liberal response to *Commentary*, emerged as a forceful voice in the communal discourse. He called the occupation "immoral and stupid" and demanded the establishment of an independent Palestinian state. Hilda Silverman from the NJA established Act on Conscience for Israel/Palestine and Jerome M. Segal, a professor at the University of Maryland, created the Jewish Peace Lobby (JPL) to advocate for a Palestinian state. In 1988, nineteen peace groups formed the Passover Peace Coalition to create a more effective platform for a pro-Palestinian advocacy.[13]

As the Intifada dragged on, the idea that Israel should negotiate with the Palestinians gained currency in mainstream circles. Leading the way was the AJCongress, which in its October 1987 report described the status quo as "untenable." The Congress was one of the most ardent advocates of the land-for-peace formula and among the first major Jewish organizations to speak out publicly against Israel's policy in the territories. Theodore Mann, a past president of the Congress, was instrumental in creating the Nishma ("Let Us Listen") project in 1988, in conjunction with the Israeli Council for Peace and Security, a group of retired IDF generals who advocated a Palestinian state. Nishma (later the Israel Policy Forum) argued that a Palestinian state would not undermine the security of Israel. Menachem Rosensaft, a child of concentration camp survivors and the chairman of the International Network of Children of Holocaust Survivors, proved to be another effective voice for peace. Even some hitherto apolitical figures had been drawn into the fray. In a letter to the *New York Times*, Woody Allen expressed his shock at the Israeli behavior and urged to bear "every method of pressure—moral, financial and political—to bring this wrong-headed approach to a halt."[14]

Adding religious legitimacy to the pro-Palestinian advocacy were the leaders of the Reform and Conservative movements. Rabbi Ismar Schorsch, the head of the Jewish Theological Seminary, sided squarely with the land-for-peace formula. John Ruskay, from the UJA, noted his sense of sadness "that 40 years after the Holocaust we end up occupying thousands of Palestinians against their will." The 1988 annual convention of the Central Conference of American Rabbis (CCAR) sent a letter to Shamir denouncing the beatings of Arab protesters as "beyond the bond of Jewish moral values."[15]

Collectively, this advocacy introduced a number of novel themes into the American Jewish discourse on the Palestinians. First, there was a growing realization that despite Golda Meir's famous rhetorical query, "who are the Palestinians?" ignoring the Palestinians was no longer a viable option. Second, the Intifada introduced a civil rights dimension into the conflict. Mass arrests, deportation, and disclosure of torture of Palestinian prisoners, which *Tikkun* prominently publicized, was especially painful for American Jews, who not only prided themselves on high moral standards, but also fought for civil rights in the United States. As Eizenstat put it, "the prism through which many American Jews view the Israeli-Palestinian struggle is that of an underdog minority in the United States that depends on public tolerance and constitutional protection."

Vital explained that American Jews, unlike their Israeli counterparts, were part of the Western culture, "where respect for the rights of men and citizens" as well as a peaceful resolution of conflicts had become "infinitely more preferable" than the "darker principles" of military power. *The Yellow Wind*, a book by the Israeli journalist, David Grossman, which painted a harrowing portrayal of Israeli occupation, was widely discussed in the community.[16]

Third, the treatment of the Palestinians and the related issue of Israeli Arabs had become increasingly linked to the quality of Israeli democracy. Emet Ve-Emunah, the 1988 Conservative movement manifesto, proclaimed that the "litmus test of the character of a democratic Jewish state is the treatment of and attitude of religious and ethnic minorities." The notion that controlling a large and hostile Arab population would threaten the democratic nature of Israel was not new, but the measures needed to put down the Intifada-added urgency to the issue. The AJCongress was one of the scores of critics who pointed out that Israel was sitting on a demographic bombshell that would require a permanent system of undemocratic controls over a subjugated population. *Moment* magazine commissioned two articles to find out whether the occupation had "affected the soul" of Israeli democracy.[17]

In fact, such fears were not far-fetched. A study of democratic attitudes of Israelis concluded that the "Intifada and its dynamics has the potential for weakening the [Israeli] commitment to democracy." Particularly affected were such values as support for civil rights of Arabs and a related willingness to a use of force in dealing with the minority. There was even an increase in the number of Israelis who supported the "encouragement of Arabs to immigrate," a euphemism for a Kahane-style expulsion. American Jewish anxieties were also fueled by the West Bank Data project, whose director, Meron Benvenisti, gained international attention for his argument that the Jewish settlements made the annexation of the West Bank and Gaza "irreversible." The "irreversibility argument" and its implications for Israeli democracy were widely discussed in the Anglo-American press.[18]

Fourth, the Intifada, by turning the Palestinians into victims, enabled some critics to link Jewish and Palestinian oppression and victimhood. Lerner asserted that "we did not survive the gas chambers and crematoria so that we could become the oppressors of Gaza." *Tikkun* also suggested that a prayer for Palestinians should be included in the Passover service, because "we partially empty our cup of joy in sadness at the suffering of the Palestinians today." Activists from the NJA demonstrated in front of Holocaust memorials, and Silverman published a "Palestinian Holocaust Memorial" declaration. The Reconstructionist Rabbinical Association expressed the belief that "the Jewish people's own experience with historical persecution and homelessness should make us especially sensitive to the frustrated sense of national fulfillment felt by the Palestinians." Others argued that by pursuing a policy of brutality and colonialism, the Israeli Jews had forfeited their moral claims stemming from the Holocaust.[19]

Not surpassingly, the Holocaust-driven moral anguish became a focal point

in the American Jewish discourse. Some critics went so far as to blame the
"Holocaust theology," as espoused by Elie Wiesel, Emil Fackenheim, and Irving
Greenberg, for turning Jewish needs into a "moral absolute, without any reference to the legitimate needs of the Palestinian people." Because of his moral
stature, Wiesel was frequently pressured to speak out on the treatment of the
Palestinians, a task that he found painful. Wiesel's ethical stand was put to the
test during a *Midstream* symposium on the Intifada, where he refused to assume
the role "of a judge over Israel," preferring to "bear witness." This did not satisfy
a fellow participant who implied that Wiesel and, by extension, all Jews would
be guilty of double standards if they failed to speak out against Israel's treatment
of the Palestinians.[20]

Two developments helped Israel's critics to influence the communal discourse. One stemmed from the more moderate image projected by the Palestinians and the PLO. The Intifada, which brought forth such moderate, Western
style Palestinian figures as Hanan Ashrawi and El-Husseini, was partially credited with this image "makeover." More important was Arafat's December 1988
decision to renounce terrorism and enter negotiation with Israel. In fact, American Jewish activists were among those who helped to convince Arafat to change
course. In May 1987 Silverman and Segal spent ten days in Tunis talking to
Arafat and other top PLO officials. In early December, just days before Arafat's
historical about-face, Rita Hauser, a prominent international lawyer and a board
member of the International Center for Peace in the Middle East, Rosensaft, and
three others traveled to Stockholm for talks with the PLO chief. Henry Siegman,
from the AJCongress, refused to join the so-called Stockholm Five, but met with
Palestine National Council member Khalid al-Hassan. In mid-February 1989,
Robert Freedman, who met Arafat during a trip to Tunisia, found the PLO
genuinely interested in negotiations following the establishment of a Palestinian
state. American Jewish peace groups organized a number of joint events with
Palestinian moderates, including a 1988 conference called "Road to Peace" at
Columbia University.[21]

The second development pertained to the growing weight of the Israeli peace
movement in America. As noted in the preceding chapter, even after the war in
Lebanon, PN was still viewed by many American Jews as a "fringe" phenomenon. Peace activists such as Alouf Hareven, from the Council for Peace and
Security, and Mordechai Virshubski, a Knesset member from the left-of-center
Shinui party who traveled to the United States, were ignored by the mainstream
community. However, the Intifada legitimized the message of the Israeli peace
activists. Three months after the outbreak of the uprising, prominent Israeli intellectuals—Amos Oz, A.B. Yehoshua, and Elon—appealed to American Jews
to speak up for peace. B'Tselem (the Israeli Information Center for Human
Rights in the Occupied Territories), created by ACRI and some leftist Knesset
members, used *Tikkun* and the general media to publicize the human rights plight
of the Palestinians, including allegations of widespread use of torture.[22]

The Palestinians received an intellectual boost when the Israeli historian

Benny Morris published his revisionist account of the Arab-Israeli conflict. In a major article in *Tikkun* and in a book (*The Birth of the Palestinian Refugee Problem, 1947–1949*), Morris accused the leadership of the Yishuv of trying to create a "Jewish State without an Arab minority, or with as small an Arab minority as possible." Unlike traditional Israeli historiographers who have maintained that the Arabs fled on their own accord, Morris charged Ben-Gurion and the Israeli high command with authorizing a massive expulsion of the population. Morris and other revisionist historians portrayed Zionism as part of a larger white colonial movement set to subjugate indigenous populations in the Middle East and elsewhere. First articulated by Edward Said, a Palestinian-American scholar in his book *Orientalism*, the revisionist theme spread from academia to the broader community in both Israel and the United States.[23]

Perhaps most important from the perspective of the security-conscious American Jews, was the growing public involvement of senior IDF officers in the debate over the territories. On April 11, 1988, eleven retired generals, including Aharon Yariv, a former intelligence chief, and Motti Hod a past commander of the Air Force, declared on the front page of *Ha'aretz* that Israel should withdraw from the territories. Efraim Sneh, a former head of the civil administration of the West Bank and Gaza, asserted that the West Bank is not crucial to Israel's security. Nishma, which provided the Council for Peace and Security with access to American Jewish audiences, had skillfully used the testimonies of Yariv, Sneh, and Shlomo Gazit, another intelligence chief, to argue that a Palestinian state would not undermine Israeli security. Norman Podhoretz, the bitter critic of an independent Palestinian state, acknowledged the effectiveness of these tactics. He wrote that the "security argument—long a mainstay of American Jewish support—was undermined when many vocal Israeli intellectuals, now reinforced by many politicians and retired military men said Israel is strong enough to handle a Palestinian state."[24]

American Jewish nationalists for whom a Palestinian state was an anathema shared Podhoretz's frustration. Many subscribed to the view of Podhoretz—spelled out in his essay "Israel: A Lamentation for the Future"—that the creation of a Palestinian state would result in the destruction of Israel. Moreover, they accused the critics of the Likud government of complicity in such deed, or as Podhoretz put it, of having the "blood of complicity on our own Jewish hands." Alexander alleged that leftist critics admired and supported Arafat and the PLO and "hope to see them realize their goal" of destroying Israel. According to a source, a speaker at a ZOA dinner called Jewish critics of Israel "assimilated court Jews, Vichy Jews, galut Jews, Kapos, quislings—in short, traitors."[25]

Much of the right-wing anger was directed against Lerner, the Stockholm Five, and other high-profile peace activists. Alexander called Lerner a "favorite display Jew of the media: a kipah-wearing, rotund beard-plucker of vaguely 'rabbinic' appearance who could always be relied on to blame Israel and not the Arabs for the absence of peace." The ZOA dinner speaker contended that Hauser and other Jews who called for talks with the PLO "should be shot at dawn." Woody Allen was described as a marginal Jew whose op-ed on the Intifada was a "classic statement of self-pity among American Jews who identify as Jews only in order to criticize Israel" when they feel "embarrassed by the Jewish state." Indeed, the nationalists considered many in the peace camp to be assimilated Jews who had no right to be counted as part of the community, let alone criticize Israel. The Israeli peace activists had also been harshly attacked. Wisse, who admitted that Exodus was the "best international advertisement that Jews ever had," blamed Yehoshua, Oz, and Grossman's *Yellow Wind* for tarnishing Israel's image. Alexander accused Israeli liberals of "going well beyond John Stuart Mill in their readiness to accommodate libel and sedition." AFSI's monthly *Outpost* tried to discredit the peace groups and sent protesters to hand out literature at propeace meetings.[26]

In addition to blaming Israel's Jewish critics, the nationalists were also outraged at the media and the American government. Philip Hochstein declared that Israel "has been massively smeared by the media," by, among others, overrepresenting the popularity of the Intifada and misrepresenting the identity of the stone-throwers. Marvin Maurer stated that the media, including Ted Koppel from ABC, provided a biased anti-Israeli account. Andrea Levin from CAMERA was particularly upset with coverage of the Intifada produced by PBS. Joel Carmichael, who categorically rejected the land-for-peace formula, accused President Bush of pursuing "his obsession" in the Middle East and of pressuring Israel.[27]

Of course, the lion share of the right-wing critique was aimed at the Palestinians. In contrast to the inclusive universalists, the nationalists distrusted the Palestinians as the ultimate "other." They argued that Arafat had simply switched tactics in his crusade to destroy Israel. In this view, instead of pursuing the failed terrorist strategy, the new weapon of choice was what Podhoretz called the "barbarically brilliant" tactic of pitting children against soldiers with guns, which "took the heart out of American Jews." Others complained that the Palestinians appropriated Jewish and Zionist national symbols, topped by the February 1988 effort to organize a ship that "intended to echo the voyage of Exodus."[28]

Under normal circumstances, focusing on the threat that the Palestinian state presented to Israel would have been enough to stir up the community. However, the Intifada had clearly changed the equation. An increasingly large, albeit tentative, segment of American Jewry was ready to discard the long-standing litmus test of "no Palestinian state." As one observer put it, "former dissenters, those who advocated a Palestinian state and were called self hating Jews are welcome speakers in the synagogues." As the discourse on the Intifada came to resemble what Carl Bernstein called the "uprising of American Jewry," it had become clear that the organized community was itself badly divided over the Palestinian issue and struggling to contain the dissent.[29]

DISUNITY IN THE ORGANIZED COMMUNITY: HOW TO SUPPORT ISRAEL AND FACE THE INTIFADA

Faced with a blizzard of conflicting statements on the Intifada by its member organizations, the Conference of Presidents convened an emergency meeting on January 27, 1988, to hammer out a statement of support for Israel. After three days of marathon negotiations, four key members refused to sign unless Israel was not reprimanded, alongside the Palestinians. Some of the critics denounced the Conference's chairman Abram for putting a "kosher stamp on everything— shootings, deportations, excessive force." The compromise communiqué stood by "embattled Israel," but also expressed "concern" that there would be no departure from Israel's "long standing policy of restraint." Behind all this anxiety for correct phraseology was the fear that the Conference would publicly split. In another incident that took on peculiar significance, the Conference, ignoring Shamir's objections, sided with Peres and called for the peace process to move forward.[30]

In February, the NJCRAC endorsed the Reagan administration peace plan based on a limited autonomy and an international peace conference. However, the deep divisions between the Likud and Labor in the national unity government discouraged a sixty-person delegation that went to Israel to discuss the initiative. Vorspan, acting as one of the delegates, commented on the "schizophrenia on the highest level in Israel." To preserve a modicum of consensus, Abram expressed the official optimism in the "overall moral authority of the government in respect to its defense policy" and urged Jewish leaders not to publicize their criticism of Israel. The efforts of peace activists to persuade Arafat to moderate his stance further divided the Conference members. Alexander Schindler, who in January sent an open protest letter to the Israeli president, saw the missions as a "step in the right direction" and Siegman from the AJCongress noted PLO's "new willingness" to move toward peace. But ZOA president, Milton Shapiro called the Stockholm Five "renegades," and Abram accused them of giving "aid and comfort" to the enemy. There were even those who wanted to oust Rosensaft's Labor Zionist Alliance from the Conference. The ZOA was also quick to condemn Shultz, who lifted the ban on U.S. contacts with the PLO. Other members of the Conference were either reluctant to attack Shultz or actually supported the administration's gesture.[31]

Faced with a public relations problem, the Israeli government launched an offensive to discourage American-PLO talks. According to one source, the Likud government suppressed an Israeli military intelligence report in December 1988, which concluded that the PLO was ready to accept a two-state solution. Shamir then authorized Benjamin Netanyahu, a fast-rising Likud star, to enlist the help of American Jews to undermine the budding PLO-American relationship. Netanyahu's message that the PLO is using moderation as a ruse to regain Palestine was readily repeated by the Jewish nationalists, but did not alter the position of the mainstream, which was reluctant to challenge Shultz or the incoming Bush administration. What is more, the Jewish leaders, in the name of reasonableness, had long argued that, under very strict conditions a dialogue with the PLO should proceed. While some sincerely waited for Arafat to come around, others hoped that the conditions would create a "straight jacket" that would prevent any opening. When Arafat made the reluctant turnabout, they "had been hoist with [their] own petard."[32]

The rift between Israel and influential members of the organized community grew during the February 1989 meeting of NJCRAC, which narrowly defeated a proposition to express "deep concern over the profound consequences of a status quo in the territories." In the same month Rosensaft asserted in a *New York Times* op-ed that, as long as Shamir and Likud are in power, Israel would not move toward peace. He was rebuked by Seymour Reich, who replaced Abram as chairman of the Conference, for "undermining the Prime Minister." In early March the AJCongress and the ADL commissioned a study by the Jaffee Center for Strategic Studies at Tel Aviv University to analyze various solutions to the Palestinian problem. The report's recommendation that suggested the inevitability of negotiations with the Palestinians was welcomed by Peres and condemned by Shamir. The influential *American Jewish Year Book* was also stepping up the pressure. Its negative coverage of Israel's handling of the Palestinians had increased and it dropped the name of "Judea and Samaria" in favor of "occupied territories."[33]

Alarmed by the divisions in the community and the tepid response to his entreaties, Shamir took to denouncing his American Jewish critics. During the 1988 meeting of the Presidents Conference in Jerusalem, the prime minister declared that "every critical statement of Jewish leaders does much more harm that many violent demonstrations in Gaza and elsewhere." Deputy Prime Minister Levy and Foreign Minister Arens were sent to deliver the same message. Arens reminded the Conference that American Jews did not do enough during the Holocaust, and chastised those who met with the PLO. He asserted that the erosion of American Jewish sympathy for Israel was more dangerous than the rocks of the Intifada.[34]

To shore up support, the Israeli government conceived of a Solidarity conference of Jewish leaders before Shamir's first meeting with Bush in April 1989. The meeting, which took place from March 20 to March 22, was billed as a celebration of "Israel-Diaspora unity," but many of the invited leaders boycotted the meetings and there were serious disagreements among the more than twelve hundred delegates who attended. Proponents of negotiations felt vindicated when a published intelligence report concluded that the Intifada could not be put down by force and advised adopting political measures. The final document of the Conference that pledged support for the "democratically elected national unity government" was vague enough to satisfy the divergent views of the participants, but grumbling persisted. Robert L. Lifton, president of the AJCongress, declared that "waiting for peace on your own terms is not necessarily conducive to reaching peace" and Lerner called the conference "a grave disservice to the Jewish people and to Israel."[35]

When Shamir, during the April meeting with President Bush, unveiled his peace plan, most of the Jewish organizations expressed relief. Reich explained that the lack of unity in Israel had caused the "misunderstanding," noting that "Shamir speaks for the government of Israel." Given the hard-line opposition in Likud to Shamir's plan, this optimism was short-lived. Sharon, who arrived in the United States in June to organize opposition to Shamir's plan, received a chilly reception at the Presidents Conference. After Shamir was forced to accept the Likud party amendments to the peace plan, the Conference split in its assessment of the situation. Reich and Abraham Foxman from the ADL asserted that there was no change in the Israeli position, but AJC and AJCongress expressed concern. Rosensaft went so far as to urge Labor to leave the coalition, a step that Reich opposed. On the other end of the political spectrum, the Likud-Herut U.S.A. accused the Jewish leadership of "Holocaust-like" neglect of Israel's interests and blasted the left-wingers for legitimizing gentile hostility toward the Jewish state.[36]

Dissension in the ranks of the Conference prevented Reich from drafting a welcome ad for Shamir's November visit to Washington. Several organizations protested that the announcement was too supportive of Likud, forcing Reich to run a simple message wishing Shamir well in his negotiations. But the *New York Times*, which published the ad, also carried a message supportive of Shamir from B'nai B'rith International, of which Reich was the president. Reich's leadership of the Conference came under sharp attack during a November conference titled "Israeli Meshuggas and American Response: What Should American Jews Do in Response to the Current Policies of the Israeli Government?" Lerner, who sponsored the conference, declared his goal of "reclaiming Judaism from the organized community" and warned that the immoral Israeli actions would erode long-term support for Israel.[37]

Shamir's January 14, 1990, declaration that a "bigger Israel, a strong Israel, Eretz Yisrael" is needed to absorb the Soviet immigrants further complicated the relations in the Conference. Reich explained that Israel had no deliberate policy of settling Soviet Jews in the territories, but the annual meeting of NJCRAC held February 20 and 21 split down the middle over a resolution criticizing Israel's settlement plans. Theodore Mann, the former AJCongress president, introduced a resolution that condemned "the construction of new housing in the territories" on the grounds that it would hurt the Soviet immigration, but Reich called the resolution, which passed in a tie vote, "inappropriate and mischievous." The NJCRAC also divided over a resolution that favored a two-state solution to the Arab-Israeli conflict.

Still, when the Conference met late in February, Reich, in response to internal pressures, went on record to suggest that Israel should move faster to implement the peace process. Privately, delegates pressured Shamir to dispel any notion that the Russian Jews would be settled in the territories. Publicly, there was a hostile reaction to an appearance by Sharon, who threatened to resign from the cabinet over Shamir's willingness to negotiate with the Palestinian. Conversely, the Presidents Conference expressed satisfaction when it looked like Labor would be able to form a coalition. When Labor was frustrated by the intervention of Rabbi Schneerson, Reich argued that it was "reprehensible for anyone in the Diaspora to interfere with the Israeli political system." While this time around most of the left and moderate Conference members shared Reich's position, the nationalist and religious groups welcomed Shamir's efforts to form an ultraconservative government.

As if to underscore the perils of right-wing policies, on April 11, just before Easter, 150 Jewish settlers moved into the St. Johns Hospice in the Christian Quarter of Old Jerusalem. Partially financed by Moskowitz through Ateret Cohanim, the project was designed to "repopulate the Old City" with Jews. After the Israeli government changed its statement and admitted its involvement in financing the scheme, the Conference, followed by AIPAC, issued an unprecedented condemnation of the action. In spite of the official communal censure, Ateret Cohanim continued to receive support from right-wing circles in the United States. It even attracted Senator Alfonse D'Amato (R–N.Y.) and Jack Kemp as keynote speakers at fund-raisers for Ateret Cohanim in New York.[38]

The Gulf War temporarily united the members of the Presidents Conference, but the issue of the Soviet immigrant in the territories continued to fester. In February 1991 a plenary session of NJCRAC passed by a very close vote a resolution urging the Israeli government to refrain from settling immigrants in the West Bank. In March, responding to President Bush's appeal to consider the land-for-peace formula, both the Conference and NJCRAC issued statements praising the president's commitment to peace, but blaming the Arabs for the continuos conflict. But Nishma, three past presidents of the NJCRAC, and Hyman Bookbinder, formerly from the AJC, immediately challenged the approach of the umbrella groups; they all blamed Israel's settlement policy for the stalemate.

Adding to the perception of dissent and disarray was the unprecedented "ad wars," conducted by American Jewish organizations and individuals on the pages of major American newspapers. Ever since the war in Lebanon, paid advertisements, op-eds, and open letters had featured prominently in the communal discourse. However, Shamir's enthusiastic reception during his April 1988 visit to the United States added an important impetus to the public relation campaign. Supporters rallied outside his hotel, thousands turned out to hear him speak and the three thousand strong National Young Leadership Conference in Washington gave him a standing ovation. Although it was explained that the warm reception was a show of solidarity with Israel, the cheering, which was shown on Israeli television, enabled Shamir to claim that American Jews are behind him. To counter this impression some twenty Jewish organizations organized "A Rally for Peace" in New York and the Labor Zionist Alliance and AJC advertised the view that most American Jews support Labor policies. In his *New York Times* ad, Lerner called on Shamir to "end the occupation," prompting Kahane from the JDL to attack the liberals.[39]

The public relations intensified during Shamir's April 1989 visit to the United States. Although the ZOA mustered some two hundred well-wishes when Shamir arrived at the airport and B'nai B'rith published a full-page ad welcoming the prime minister, anti-Shamir groups considered picketing him outside New York Town Hall. *Tikkun* sponsored an ad in the *New York Times* that read "No, Mr. Shamir, don't think that American Jews support your policies toward the Palestinians." During his November visit to address the CJF in Cincinnati, Ohio, forty-one prominent Jews, including a number of past presidents of major organizations, published a letter warning Shamir not to "mistake courtesy for consensus, or applause for endorsement" of his policies. Although Reich contended that the letter did not reflect the mood of the mainstream Jewish community, the public relations campaign forced Shamir to stick to friendly venues of pro-Likud audiences and Orthodox Jews.[40]

With so much turmoil in the community, even the more autonomous AIPAC did not escape division and dissent. Much of it surrounded the Israeli request for $10 billion in loan guarantees to absorb the Soviet immigrants. American Jews, who had fought for more than two decades for Soviet immigration, enthusiastically supported the loan project. However, the matter became controversial after Shamir stated that a Greater Israel is needed to welcome the new arrivals, implying that some may be settled in the territories. Bush and Baker, eager to expedite the peace process, seized upon the loan guarantees to force Shamir to moderate his settlement policy. Ignoring a plea from some American Jews, on September 6, 1991, Israel formally submitted the request, prompting Bush to threaten a veto.

In spite of some internal unease, AIPAC decided to support the request, bolstered by dozens of organizations that appealed directly to Congress. On September 12, over a thousand Jewish activists arrived on Capitol Hill to lobby for the loan guarantees. On the same day President Bush asked for a 120-day delay in order to enable the administration to pursue the delicate negotiations over the Madrid Conference. In what many saw as anti-Semitic stereotyping, the president described himself as "one lonely little guy" and the activists as "some powerful political force." Shoshana Cardin, the new chairwoman of the Conference of Presidents, vowed to fight on, but AIPAC soon discovered that there were not enough votes to override the presidential veto. On September 20, a group of American Jewish leaders met with Israeli government officials to apprise them of the need to moderate their policy in the West Bank.[41]

AIPAC's humiliating defeat encouraged Israel's critics to mount a major offensive against the settlement policy. Activists from APN urged Congress to link the loan guarantees with a settlement freeze. Nishma issued a statement urging the Israeli government to impose a temporary freeze on the settlements in the interest of peace and security. Rabbi Eric Yoffie of the ARZA pointed out that Israel was prepared to jeopardize the Soviet Jewish immigration for the sake of settling the West Bank and Siegman from AJCongress stated that Israel has to choose between the loan and the settlements. Less publicly, many American Jewish activists complained that Israel put them in a tight spot by "sending them to play hardball with Bush." Shamir's scheduled appearance at the General Assembly of the CJF on November 21 gave the settlements' opponents a new forum for debate. Creating a stir, Nishma published a poll of federation leaders that showed overwhelming support for a freeze. APN released a letter signed by more that two hundred rabbis who declared that "continued settlement activities are not only detrimental to the peace process but also to the successful absorption of the new *olim* in Israel."[42]

Faced with internal dissension and a hostile administration, AIPAC and the Conference decided not to pursue President Bush's promise to reopen the loan case in January 1992. Reacting to what it perceived as a leftward slide in the organized community, AFSI, which had been long-warning against any pressure on Israel, released a poll, which indicated that a majority of American Jews were behind unconditional loan guarantees. Although some questioned the veracity of the poll, Cardin asserted that American Jewish leadership "remains unanimous in supporting Israel's request." In actuality, the issue of settlements bitterly divided the February 1992 meeting of NJCRAC. The AJCongress, the UAHC, and a number of local councils demanded a resolution that would urge a freeze on settlements. The Union of Orthodox Jewish Congregations of America vehemently objected to such a step; in a deeply emotional debate each side accused the other of endangering Israel's interests.[43]

Even before the NJCRAC impasse, Jewish groups were actively engaged in countervailing lobbying efforts in Washington. The APN created the Center for Israeli Peace and Security, an advocacy office in Washington, and urged to link loan guarantees to a settlement freeze during a congressional hearing. The ZOA and the National Council of Jewish Women sent delegations to Capital Hill to persuade lawmakers to vote for the loan guarantees. The Jewish Peace Lobby, which created its own PAC, circulated a letter signed by 250 rabbis urging the United States to oppose the settlements. To make matters worse, Likud and Labor politicians, in preparation for the Israeli election in June, appealed to groups sympathetic to their vision. The *New York Times* ran a front-page ad on the division in the Jewish community, pointing out that the loan debacles undermined the effectiveness of AIPAC.[44]

Indeed, even before the loan episode, AIPAC was criticized harshly by numerous elements in the community. On October 12, 1988, the *New York Times* revealed that in a letter to AIPAC, AJC, AJCongress, and ADL complained that AIPAC adopted positions outside the "consensus of the organized Jewish community" and threatened to establish a rival lobbying organization. Less than a year later AJCongress, the UAHC, and other groups blasted AIPAC for supporting an effort by Jesse Helms (R–N.C.) to block the State Department's contacts with the PLO officials who had terrorist backgrounds. Lerner claimed that AIPAC and other Israel defense organizations were filled with conservative "bigwigs" totally at odds with the sentiments of most American Jews. Most seriously, AIPAC was accused of limiting dissent in the community by creating a secret intelligence unit to gather information and intimidate those who were deemed critical of Israel. Although AIPAC's spokesmen vehemently denied the charges, first publicized in *Village Voice*, the notion that AIPAC had come to equate criticism of Likud with an attack of Israel were shared by others. In a public debate with Tom Dine, Fein accused AIPAC of stifling any opposition to Likud's foreign policy.[45]

There is some evidence that the communal divisiveness over the Palestinian issue had undermined AIPAC's legendary standing on Capitol Hill. To begin with, before publishing their letter, the thirty senators refused the request of Dine to delete a reference to the land-for-peace formula. In January 1988 a dozen Jewish legislators summoned the Israeli ambassador Moshe Arad to express their "deep concern" about Israel's treatment of Arabs. Later that year Senator John H. Chafee (R–R.I.) sponsored a successful amendment to the appropriation bill urging Israel to open Palestinian schools closed during the Intifada. Other senators were also increasingly willing to speak out against Likud. Patrick Leahy, the highly popular Democratic senator from Vermont, became a vocal critic of Israel's handling of the Intifada and Senator Robert Dole (R–Kans.) threatened to cut aid to Israel.[46]

Legislative critics of Israel took comfort from the fact that AIPAC could not repeat its "Percy act" in a number of high-profile senatorial races. Senator Frank Lautenberg, a Jewish Democrat from New Jersey, was targeted when, in 1987, he cosigned a letter to Secretary of State Shultz, urging him to seek a resolution to the Middle East conflict. He survived a Jewish-supported challenge from a conservative opponent. In 1990 Paul Wellstone, an ardent advocate of Palestinian self-determination defeated Senator Boschwitz (R—Minn.) a Likud supporter who was heavily supported by Jewish PACs. Senator Robert W. Kasten (R–Wis.), one of the Christian conservatives and a top recipient of Jewish PACs' money, lost the 1992 race to liberal Russell Feingold. Observing these and other races, some policymakers in Congress affirmed that the "great fear of AIPAC is gone."[47]

With so much divisiveness and dissension, the old question of who speaks for American Jews reemerged vigorously. As already noted, the voluntary membership and the permeable boundaries of the community complicated the issue of legitimacy and representation. In the discourse about the Intifada, participants often claimed that they alone represent the "American Jews," while denying legitimacy to their opponents. Leading the way were the nationalists who had claimed that they represented, as Podhoretz put it, the "silent majority" against the "noisy minority" that "chose liberalism over Israel." Leftists like Lerner responded that the established leadership stifles the "silent majority" that opposes the Shamir policy. Hauser of the Stockholm Five contended that organizational leadership no longer represented most Jews who supported accommodation with the Palestinians.[48]

The Israeli leaders were equally eager to claim popular legitimacy in America. Upon returning from the rousing reception during the 1988 UJA Young Leadership Conference, Shamir told the Israeli radio that the American Jews "all unanimously expressed support for me" and that they "expressed total support for everything I say and do." After receiving a letter from forty-one very prominent Jews warning him not to mistake the applause of the General Assembly for support of his policies, the prime minister sought to paint his critics as a "voluble minority." Shamir then went on to argue that the "vast majority of US Jews—I would say the entire Jewish community, other than a few exceptions— support . . . the views I expressed." When angered by AJCongress peace forays, Shamir called it a "peanut-sized organization," asking rhetorically "who elected them."[49]

Some observers evoked a variance of the voice-or-exist phenomenon to argue that most Jewish organizations had ceased to be representative of the community. Hertzberg explained that moderates, unwilling to fight the hard-liners in their organizations, had opted to leave. Goldberg added that a "small minority of Jews had been allowed to take over Jewish organizational infrastructure and turn it into an instrument of defensive nationalism." Robert Spero, in his exposé "Speaking for the Jews," implied that many of the groups represented in the Presidents Conference were essentially "paper organizations," that resorted to number bolstering. Those who compared the normally liberal position of NJCRAC, which included a large number of local level leaders, to the more hard-line Conference and AIPAC accused the national organizations of misrepresenting the lower-rung leaders.[50]

The bitter debate about representation had spurred a furious round of polls aimed at revealing the attitudes of American Jewish rank and file toward the Palestinians. In fact, with so much riding on the issue of popular legitimacy, the opinion polls became another important part of the discourse.

THE SLOW CHANGE: AMERICAN JEWS AND THE RELUCTANT EMBRACE OF PALESTINIAN LEGITIMACY

In trying to analyze the changes brought by the Intifada, Cohen's 1986 *Survey of American Jewish Attitudes toward Israel and Israelis* serves as a useful baseline. The survey found that 29 percent of the respondents supported a compromise in the West Bank in return for credible peace guarantees, whereas 36 percent disagreed and 27 percent were not sure. At the same time 48 percent of the sample agreed that the Palestinians have a right to a homeland in the West Bank and Gaza as long as it does not threaten Israeli security, 25 percent disagreed and 29 percent were not sure. A three to one majority—57 percent to 18 percent—of the respondents agreed that Israel should negotiate with the PLO if it renounces terrorism. Still, mistrust of Arabs ran quite high; 44 percent agreed that "you can never trust an Arab to make a real peace with Israel," 24 percent disagreed, and 33 percent had no opinion. Peres and the Labor party were more favorably evaluated than Shamir and Likud, but in both cases about half of the sample had no opinion, reflecting the apparent ignorance regarding Israeli politics. The affinity for Labor, which historically had run at least three to one, was explained by the fact that American Jews reflected the host culture's opprobrium for those "which seem to be inflexibly ideological and permanently nonconciliatory." In a sign of growing polarization, the Orthodox, who scored the highest on attachment to Israel, were also more likely to support hard-line positions toward territorial compromise.[51]

A month after the start of the Intifada, a January 1988 poll for the ADL found that 51 percent of American Jews thought Israel was responding too harshly to the Palestinian rioters. Around the same time a Yankelovich-*Time* poll revealed that 57 percent of Jews disapproved of the Israeli use of force and 77 percent felt that it hurt Israel's image. Two months after Shamir's speech at the UJA Young Leadership Conference on April 13, the *Los Angeles Times* published a more comprehensive poll of Jewish and non-Jewish opinion of the Middle East conflict. Over 60 percent of the Jewish sample of 1,018 respondents supported an international peace conference as part of the Shultz initiative; only 17 percent objected. Even the Orthodox who registered the highest rates of opposition to the conference supported the initiative by 41 to 23 percent. But the sample split 43 to 31 percent against giving up territories and a plurality; 45 percent to 29 percent opposed a Palestinian homeland. Thirty-five percent of the respondents felt that the continuing occupation of the territories would "erode Israel's democratic and humanitarian character," but 45 percent did not worry. In the 1986 poll only 6 percent of the respondents thought that the occupation would erode the democratic nature of the state.[52]

In the 1989 survey 38 percent agreed with the U.S. decision to talk to the PLO and only 28 percent disagreed. Fifty-eight percent wanted Israel to negotiate with the PLO provided it renounced terrorism; 18 percent objected and 24 percent were not sure. Moreover, 47 percent of the sample agreed that the Palestinians have a right to a homeland as long as it did not threaten Israel's security. Only 23 percent disagreed with this statement and 30 percent were not sure. In a related matter, 35 percent rejected Israel's settlement drive in the territories; 25 percent supported it, and 41 percent were not sure. Still, the growing embrace of Palestinian nationalism was a reluctant one. Sixty-two percent of the respondents agreed that the PLO was determined to destroy Israel and 86 percent said that the PLO was a terrorist organization. Almost half of the sample (49 percent) expressed the view that Arabs could not be trusted to make a real peace with Israel, as opposed to 20 percent who were ready to bet on the Arabs. In other words, security fears and mistrust of the Arab adversaries strongly qualified support for negotiations and a Palestinian state. Absent a more specialized study, it can only be speculated that, presented with the high human and political cost of the Intifada, an increasing number of American Jews, like their counterparts in Israel, had reluctantly conceded that Palestinian sovereignty was inevitable.[53]

A 1990 survey of affiliated Jews in nine communities carried out by Brandeis University confirmed the trends revealed in the national sample. Seven out of ten respondents agreed to trade some of the territories for credible peace, six out of ten rejected new settlements, and the same number were willing to see a Palestinian state if it posed no threat to Israel. Tested on a composite scale of seven items, four out of ten respondents scored as doves, two as hawks, and five were in the middle range. Raab and Sternberg concluded that affiliated Jews were very concerned with the status quo and wanted some solution to the Palestinian problem, albeit without hurting Israel's security interests.[54]

The Gulf War and Palestinian support for Iraq hardened American Jewish attitudes without erasing the basic split in the community. Cohen's 1991 survey indicated that only a very slim plurality (35 percent to 34 percent) supported territorial compromise, but 30 percent agreed that Israel should expand settlements, leaving 29 percent to oppose it. Skepticism about Arabs and Palestinians had increased. Fifty-one percent agreed with the statement that Arabs could not be trusted to make a real peace with Israel, and 23 percent were willing to trust. A full 83 percent of the respondents felt that the PLO wanted to destroy Israel; only 4 percent disagreed, and 13 percent were not sure. There was also a corresponding decline in concern that continuing occupation would destroy the democratic character of Israel; 55 percent rejected the statement, 14 percent agreed, and 29 percent had no opinion. Using his "hawk-dove" scale, Cohen was able to correlate attitudes toward the Arab-Israeli conflict with socioeconomic characteristics of his respondents. The dovish group, closely corresponding to the more universalistic Jews, was composed of younger (under forty years old) respondents with higher levels of education who described themselves as liberal. The hawkish-nationalist group was weighted toward older, less educated Jews and those who defined themselves as conservatives. Also predominant among the nationalists were the Orthodox and the more active members of the community, leading Cohen to conclude that hawkishness is strongly associated with greater involvement in Jewish life. Such a profile is in line with the definition of the tribal-nationalist view that puts Israel's survival above all other imperatives. Filtered through this prism, Likud's policies in the territories were considered appropriate for Israel's survival needs and morally justified, since such Jews saw Israel's survival as a high moral imperative in its own right.[55]

Going beyond rank and file, a number of studies probed the attitude of communal leaders at the local and national level. A 1990 study of American leaders and Israel, commissioned by the AJC, found that 62 percent thought that Israel should talk to the PLO, given credible security guarantees; 53 percent felt that Israel should offer territorial compromises; and 47 percent agreed that continued Israeli occupation would erode Israel's democratic character. Only 11 percent wanted Israel to annex the West Bank, a move opposed by 52 percent. A surprising 58 percent of the leaders disclosed that they had spoken critically of Israel's handling of the Intifada in the past two years. A leadership study by Cohen and sponsored by the Israel-Diaspora Institute at Tel Aviv University, found similar patterns among its 780 respondents who were polled in November 1989. An overwhelming number rejected forcible deportation of Palestinians (78 percent), opposed the expansion of settlements in the West Bank (78 percent), and the annexation of the West Bank (78 percent). Fifty-nine percent wanted Israel to offer a demilitarized state and three-quarters agreed that Israel should be ready for territorial compromises. Still, most of the leaders whom Cohen named "dovish" were deeply suspicious of the PLO and were reluctant to criticize Israel publicly. A 1991 study of rabbis and rabbinical students revealed that the attitudes toward the territories were correlated with denominational affiliations. Fifty-nine percent of Conservative rabbis and 51 percent of rabbinical students rejected the statement that Israel should hold on to the occupied territories. The percentage among Reform rabbis and rabbinical students was 61 and 69 respectively, and among the Reconstructionists the numbers were 80 and 76 percent. Surprisingly, 34 percent of Orthodox rabbis disagreed with holding the territories, although 84 percent strongly agreed that God promised Judea and Samaria to Israel.[56]

In the same year, Cohen and Seymour Martin Lipset conducted a study of 339 top leaders of the Jewish community under the auspices of the Wilstein Institute of Jewish Policy Studies at the University of Judaism. Nishma, which commissioned the project, wanted to disprove Shamir's repeated assertion that the vast majority of American Jews supported his position. The survey, released just before the Israeli prime minister was due to address the meeting of the General Assembly in November 1991, reaffirmed trends found in the previous studies. Seventy-six percent of those polled agreed that continued Israeli rule over 1.8 million Palestinians would make Israel less democratic and 64 percent said that the costs and risks of continued Israeli rule over the West Bank outweighed the benefits. Fifty-nine percent felt that the presence of so many Jewish settlements in the West Bank would make reaching a peace agreement more difficult. Some 85 percent of the sample disagreed with Shamir's claim that Israel should not give up "one each" of the territory, and 66 percent wanted to impose a freeze on settlements in return for the end of the Intifada. Moreover, 88 percent thought that Israel should compromise in the West Bank and Gaza in return for credible peace guarantees. By a large margin, the leaders had an unfavorable opinion of Gush Emunim and a much more favorable opinion of PN. Asked about a hypothetical vote in Israeli elections, 53 percent preferred Labor or one of its allies, and 22 percent declared that it would have supported Likud or one of its allies.[57]

These results received wide media coverage in Israel and the United States and were entered into the *Congressional Record*. While most of the commentary was positive, the Wilstein study did not please everyone. Cardin described the sample as "self-selecting" and some Jewish newspapers complained that surveys provided the Arabs with a "trump card" to pressure Israel. As expected, the loudest criticism came from the nationalist segments of the community. Lawrence Black, the president of AFSI, asserted that the poll "did not represent the Jewish stance." Jonathan Tobin the then-national director of Techiya, U.S.A., a radical right-wing Israeli party, called the poll a "self-serving stunt." Willie Rapfogel, director of the Orthodox Union's Institute for Public Affairs, quoted in the *Forward*, described the survey as unrepresentative and "carefully crafted."[58]

The reaction of Shamir and his supporters was equally dismissive. Asked about the poll, the prime minister repeated that the U.S. Jewish community always received him with great enthusiasm and that his critics were a "certain minority that disassociate themselves from the Jewish community's overall support for [his] stance." Shamir also asserted that "U.S. experts assured me that the [survey] is of little importance against the welcome that I received from the majority." An editorial in the *Jerusalem Post*, under the ownership of the right-wing Canadian Jewish tycoon Conrad Black, went even further. The *Post* called the poll "ludicrous" and an effort to undermine Shamir's standing in the community by the "unelected opposition."[59]

That a survey designed by Cohen, the premier pollster of American Jews, and Lipset, one of the most prominent political scientists in the United States, could evoke such bitterness was one more indication of how extremely divisive the peace process had become. But the debate about Israel's foreign policy was also symptomatic of the larger revaluation of Israel's role in American Jewish identity.

JEWISH IDENTITY REVISITED: THE END OF THE "SACRED UNITY"

The Intifada could not have come at a worse time for the Jewish community. The 1990 National Jewish Population Survey (NJPS) confirmed many of the long-standing fears about the dwindling number of Jews. The core Jewish population was estimated at some 5.5 million, compared to the 5.4 million in 1970, a number that, according to the researchers, reflected low fertility levels, conversion to other religions, and high intermarriage rates. The intermarriage rates, estimated at 52 percent for those married since 1985, created particular alarm, especially as only 28 percent of children of intermarriage were raised as Jews.

Sidney Goldstein, one of the authors of the report, referred to the findings as a "silent Holocaust," a theme that was repeated in the extensive coverage of the issue. Even before the official results were published, the expected demographic shrinkage had unleashed a public controversy over the problems of Jewish identity reminiscent of the discourse in the sixties. One commentator compared American Jews to a "wee cube of sugar or a grain of salt floating in a soothing bath" and predicted that "the little bit of stuff would eventually melt altogether, or be reduced to a religiously committed kernel."[60]

While it was easy to link the demographic decline to the attenuation of Jewish identity, there was no consensus on what had accelerated the assimilationist trend. Orthodox critics were quick to compare American Judaism to an empty vessel, a charge repeated by the Israeli American commentator, Ze'ev Chafets. In his controversial book, Chafets wrote: "Judaism doesn't seem to be about anything. It is a holding operation—an effort to wring one more generation of allegiance from people who are no longer sure what being a Jew is all about." Even those who took a more lenient view could not hide their disappointment at the failure of the Israeli-centered solutions to the Jewish identity problem touted so highly after the Six Day War. They argued that Jewish identity was ill-served by the "quick fix" of Israel and the Holocaust. Earl Raab described as "extravagant hopes" the notion that Israeli and American Jews would become "bonded as one in religious, cultural, and tribal affinity." Another leader wrote: "the Diaspora had imagined that the State of Israel had promised it that the children of the activists in its cause would remain Jewish in Topeka, Los Angeles or Seattle. By the 1980s, this was clearly not true."[61]

Empirical evidence from the NJPS and commercial polls had confirmed that indeed, as compared to the past, a certain amount of distancing had taken place. In the 1986 survey Cohen found that 20 percent of the respondents felt very close and 42 percent fairly close to Israel; 33 percent reported being "not very close," and 5 percent were not sure. In 1991 17 percent felt extremely attached, 23 percent very attached, 44 percent somewhat attached, and 15 percent were not sure. Though the overall level of affinity was still quite high, Cohen discovered that the younger cohorts are less close to Israel than their elders. The 1988 Los Angeles poll found the same age-related pattern: almost half of those over sixty-five years old declared themselves to be very close to Israel, but only about a quarter of the eighteen to forty age group felt the same way. The forty-one to sixty-one age group placed itself somewhere in between. Whatever degree of closeness American Jews professed to have toward Israel, the behavioral indicators belied these sentiments, leading Cohen and others to wonder whether the responses were part of a "socially acceptable" answer. The surveys found that, with the exception of the Orthodox, the level of ignorance about Israeli society and politics was very high and the knowledge of even rudimentary Hebrew very low. For instance, after probing the attitudes of his sample toward the Arab-Israeli conflict, Cohen noted that "few possess the rudimentary information necessary to make reasonably well-thought-out judgments about a particular policy or leadership alternative."[62]

Concluding that support for Israel was "deep but superficial and fragile," Cohen identified three profiles of affinity. About one-third of his sample was indifferent, or even hostile; about one-third passionately attached; and the rest were pro-Israel in a reflexive, but not particularly committed or thoughtful way. Since commitment to Israel was correlated with the degree of orthodoxy and age, it is safe to assume that among the passionately attached were a large number of nationalist hard-liners and older Jews. Among the younger, secularized and less attached, Israel was a harder sale. Cohen's conclusion that the findings "ought to alarm any supporter of Israel who cares either for Israeli security or who believes that American Jewish involvement with Israel is important" was echoed by others. Indeed, one observer urged Israeli officials and American leaders to accept that "most young American Jews do not see Israel as their spiritual center.[63]

Participants in the anguished debate that followed the findings identified a number of factors that, in their opinion, had contributed to the disappointment with the Israeli-centered Jewish identity. One explanation was derived from the cohort-based view of Israel. Whereas the older generation, which had personal experience of the defining events of the Holocaust and the creation of the Jewish state, the younger and more assimilated American Jews had no historic memory to nourish their emotional attachment to Israel. For them, Israel was not a David fighting a Goliath, but a country identified by the lexicon of the 1980s of "Sabra and Shatila, Lebanon, Pollard and ultimately Intifada." Worse, unlike the old "Jewish Camelot of the Six Day War and the Entebbe raids," this new Israel was a "place worn down by an endless Palestinian uprising and horrible images of Israeli soldiers breaking the bones of Arab children."[64]

Another explanation alluded to a process of maturation and realism in the relations between American Jews and Israel. A Hadassah study guide (*Israeli and American Jews. Understanding & Misunderstanding: A Study Guide*) noted that American Jews, who for three decades had perceived Israel as an "ideal and idyllic society led by politicians and military commanders of unsurpassed bravery, wisdom, fairness and competence," were willing to take a more realistic view. Fostering this growing sense of realism were some Jewish American leaders and intellectual elites. Among them were communal leaders discouraged by years of dealing with the Israeli political system, with "its arcane bureaucratic structure and its convoluted nexus of personal fiefdoms and rewards." American Jewish literature on Israel, augmented by such books as Philip Roth's *Counterlife*, had grown in sophistication. One expert credited such works with "rescuing" Jewish-American fiction about Israel from the realm of the "conventional Zionist propaganda novel, a la Leon Uris's *Exodus*." Even some neoconservatives gave up on the idealized version of the Jewish state. Midge Decter described "her personal odyssey from believing that Israel was a miraculous place unlike any other" to accepting the fact that it was an "extremely messy" Western democracy under pressure.[65]

Lurking behind this newly found realism were the demographic changes in Israel. Although grumbling that the increasingly Sephardi character of the state had declined since the days of Begin, some Jewish observers were willing to admit that the sense of a common heritage was lost. The leading demographer Calvin Goldscheider explained that the feeling of ethnic commonality diminished because non-European Jews came to dominate Israel. A contributor to the Hadassah study guide wrote that in 1948 the Israeli and American Jews were removed by one generation from common roots and, in many cases, literally related. But as Israel had transformed into a largely Sephardi country and American Jews became more Americanized, a process of distancing took place. Milton Himmelfarb added that in the past, both groups had grandparents who spoke

Yiddish, but the grandparents of most contemporary Israelis spoke Arabic. Vital noted that the Israelis had become the "ever more remote cousins" of American Jews. Such distancing was also evident in Israel. A 1983 survey of Israeli Jewish attitudes toward their American counterparts showed the emergence of two very different publics with very different memories.[66]

The struggle over religious pluralism had further tarnished the image of Israel as an enlightened Western enclave in the Middle East. The long-simmering debate on the status of Conservative and Reform Jews in Israel came to a head after the inconclusive 1988 election. In an effort to sweeten its coalition offer, Likud agreed to the demand of the religious parties to amend the Law of Return specifying that only those converted through an orthodox practice could be considered Jews for the purpose of aliya. Although the practical effects of such a change were negligible, the symbolic delegitimation of their faith infuriated the American Conservative and Reform Jews. The CJF and the UJA took out ads in Israeli papers warning about rupture in relations with the Diaspora, a theme that was reiterated in a statement of Conservative leaders. A coalition of twenty-seven American Jewish organizations charged that the acquiescence to the Orthodox "would inflict enormous danger, actual and symbolic on the Jewish of the Diaspora." An unprecedented number of delegations went to Israel to lobby against the amendment and there were threats to withdraw contributions. The 1991 NSAJ found widespread opposition to Orthodox forces in Israel and an adamant desire to have an American-style separation of state and church.[67]

This around-the-clock pressure deterred the Knesset from changing the Law of Return, but the strains in the relations persisted. Many in the community were outraged by the revocation of a kosher certification of a conservative youth hostel in Jerusalem and the harassment of American Jewish women who tried to pray at the Western Wall. The right of the Women at the Wall became a cause celebre in the Jewish feminist circles in the United States. A communal leader asserted that "we cannot be one people when the forms of Judaism practiced by the majority of American Jews are disenfranchised in the Jewish homeland itself." Adding insult to injury in this view was the fact that the Lubavich Hassidim and other orthodox groups in America were allegedly involved in the efforts to change the "Who is a Jew" law. According to some observers, the Orthodox could not win the battle against assimilation in America, so they took their fight to Israel.[68]

As expected, liberal critics of Israel's foreign policy seized upon the demographic findings to denounce the Israeli-focused Jewish identity. Asserting that the Israeli-centered chauvinism with its cries of "never again" was a wrong focus for Jewish identity, Fein called for a return to liberal-universalistic values as a more effective way to assure communal survival. In the same vein, Vorspan declared: "We have ceased to be Jewish champions of social justice and became cheerleaders for failed Israeli policies." In an amazing candid *New York Times* confession, Vorspan, a Reform spokesman, revealed that American Jews suffered "shame and stress" because of the developments in Israel, and wanted to disassociate themselves from the "political and moral bankruptcy" of Israel policies. Allan C. Brownfeld noted that American Jewish life became so dominated by Israel and Middle East politics that a spiritual gap developed, leading many younger Jews to turn away from Judaism. Gershon Cohen, a former chancellor of the Jewish Theological Seminary, described the pretense of the "centrality of the state of Israel on the life of the Jewish people" as an "absurd shibboleth." Neusner, who once called the Israelis "dull-witted and brutish" and deplored their "arrogance and self-righteousness," reiterated his thesis that America is a much better place for Jews than Israel. He noted the Israelis lack "the most routine, commonplace courtesy" taken for granted in the United States. Neusner pointed out to the "irony of religious passion's being lavished by mainly secular people upon a state, which, like all other states, is a contingent and this-worldly fact." Another commentator argued that Israel had not resolved the Jewish Question: "Israel has not become the spiritual beacon for world Jewry . . . Israel has not remade the Jewish people into a 'working nation;' if anything it is transforming Israeli Jews into a parasitic class pied noirs battening off cheap Arab labour and massive foreign subvention."[69]

Those and other observers made it quite clear that the Intifada and Israel's refusal to pursue peace had contributed to the failure of the Israeli-centered Jewish identity to attract younger Jews. Fein charged that, as they "became virtuosos at euphemisms, at excuses and alibis," many Jews had become alienated not just from Israel, but from Judaism itself. The journalist Thomas Friedman, once a poster boy of Israeli-centered identity, contended that "Israel in the eyes of American Jews has gone in twenty years from substitute religion to a source of religious delegitimation, and from a source of political identity to a source of political confusion." As one communal activist summed it up, "the Intifada complicated Israel for a lot of Israeli supporters. No longer was it possible to rehearse the same old lines that Israel was always right, Arabs always wrong . . . many people simply disengaged from Israel." Worse, as another observer claimed, because of the Intifada, "Israel is becoming much less 'like us' and more 'like them,' " another Middle Eastern country. Even Cardin acknowledged that the "nachas" from Israel diminished because of the problems in the territories. The authors of an empirical study concluded: "the confusion among some about how to relate to Israel had an effect on how to relate to Judaism. Liberal Jews have been frustrated with the Israel political scene. Part of the frustration has been converted into a frustration with Judaism."[70]

Adding to the sense of malaise was the growing chorus of criticism coming out of Israel. Some of the bad feelings were apparently related to the ambivalence Israeli Jews felt over the involvement of their American counterparts in Israeli foreign policy. Shimoni, of the Institute of Contemporary Jewry at the Hebrew University, noted that though Israeli officials bragged about the influence of the Jewish lobby in Washington, they often brushed off criticism by describing the same activists as "self-appointed nonentities." The partisan splits in the Israeli and American Jewish foreign policy circles did not help. For instance, during the loan guarantee campaign, a visiting Likud cabinet member publicly accused American Jews for being less than sufficiently active, a fact that he attributed to opposition to settlements. At about that same time, a left-wing Israeli politician criticized the American Jewish lobby for its "vulgar mistake" in pressing for the loan guarantees. He charged that the episode was responsible for the increase in anti-Israeli and anti-Jewish sentiments in the United States.[71]

Israeli disenchantment with American Jews reached a peak during the Gulf War. Faced with the threat of Scud missiles, most American Jews (with the exception of the Orthodox) cancelled their trips to Israel. Although a solidarity mission was belatedly organized, the Israelis felt abandoned and pointed out that Christian tourists had not been deterred by the danger. The Israeli novelist Yehoshua used the theme of abandonment to argue that the Israeli Jews and the Diaspora have the same history, but a different destiny. The sense of betrayal led some Israeli spokesmen to accuse the American Jewish community of hypocrisy and hollow sloganeering from the safety of American homes. Uri Gordon, a Jewish Agency official, questioned the slogan "we are one," a theme previously raised by the journalist Hirsch Goodman who emphatically argued that "we are not one." Another Israeli journalist insisted that the slogan "we are one" had "become completely hollow."[72]

The Israeli journalist Matti Golan elaborated on these themes in his book *With Friends Like You*, a scathing criticism of American Jewry. Golan described with considerable bitterness how American Jews—even Eli Wiesel—came to "identify" with Israel and then returned, leaving the Israelis to shoulder the burden of the conflict. In an allusion to the cultural chasm, Golan asserted that, public pronouncement of unity notwithstanding, in the privacy of their homes American Jews consider Israelis to be "arrogant," "aggressive," and "loudmouthed." In short, "you [American Jews] don't exactly consider me the type you'd would like to spend a vacation with or have as a long-term house guest." Responding to such accusations, one critic pointed out that, at the subconscious level, the rage of being abandoned during the Gulf War was recombined with the "historic, carefully nurtured Zionist contempt for the Diaspora to form a virulent anger such as we see in Golan's book." An American born rabbi who lived in Israel complained about the "feeling of hostility verging on contempt toward American Jews."[73]

Finally, all throughout the Intifada American Jews had to face the fact that the American public was quite annoyed with Likud's hard-line policy. Those in the community who were sensitive to cognitive dissonance or allegations of double loyalty took little comfort from opinion polls which showed that, for the first time in the history of the Middle East conflict, Americans were becoming more sympathetic toward the Palestinians. In an April 1988 and 1989 Roper poll the percentage of those who felt that Israel was wrong in refusing to negotiate with the PLO went up from 27 to 32. The same polls showed a drop in sympathy for Israel—48 percent to 36 percent—and an increase in sympathy for the Arabs. Most alarming, the general public favored, 44 percent to 37 percent, withdrawing of military or economic support in order to pressure Israel to make concessions. The comparable figures for Jews were 80 percent to 12 percent respectively. By 1991 the polls showed that Americans came to regard Israel as more of an obstacle to peace than the Arabs countries. A Chicago Council on Foreign Relations survey of foreign policy elites found a similar development. In 1991 sympathy for the Palestinians went up to 35 percent as opposed to 33 percent for Israel; in 1981 the numbers were 26 percent for Palestinians and 42 percent for Israel.[74]

Coming at the heel of the Bush administration's well-publicized clashes with Shamir, such numbers were bound to create a sense of unease in the community. An AJC analyst described these results as "sobering" and an indication of "a significant erosion from the traditional American view that Israel held the moral high ground." Summing up this and other developments, Wertheimer posited that American Jews are "disillusioned with Israel because it does not contribute to the enrichment of their lives. When Israeli policies do not conform to their standards and when "they evoke criticism from non-Jewish sectors within American society," some distancing takes place. That a right-wing Israeli foreign policy was bound to offend many American Jews was also evident from opinion polls which showed that the Jews were consistently more liberal than other whites. Despite fears of Jackson's influence on the Democratic party, Jews voted two to one for Michael Dukakis in the 1987 election; the only group that exceeded this record were African Americans.[75]

As befitting a vigorous communal discourse, some commentators disputed this diagnosis of the problems in Israeli-American Jewish relations and others flatly denied that there was erosion of support for the Jewish state. Understandably, apprehension about "sacred unity," the cornerstone of communal life of American Jews, was more prevalent among organized Jewry. In particular, Fein's analysis of American Jewish alienation from Israel was attacked by a number of critics, with some calling it simplistic and misleading. But even if alienation from Israel did not play an essential role, the surveys indicated that American Jews were once again changing their views about their identity. In the *Los Angeles Times* poll 50 percent of the respondents said that "social equality" was most important to their Jewish identity. The other half divided among different options, with 17 percent listing Israel as the most important aspect of their identity. Stephen Cohen's 1989 sample chose "leading an ethical and moral life" as a top value, with "support for Israel" ranked eight out of twenty choices. In 1983, eight out of ten said that "caring about Israel" was the most important part of their Judaism. This shift away from the Israeli-centered identity was most pronounced among the younger and more secularized Jews.[76]

Overall, the reshuffling of the values scale was indicative of a more privatized identity, which researchers had first identified in the early 1980s. Indeed, Cohen found that the younger respondents exhibited a "telling inconsistency" between their relatively high level of belief in God, ritual practice, and other Jewish values and a low attachment to Israel. In other words, younger Jews came to prefer the more privatized elements of their identity to the more public and communal Israeli-centered "civil religion." Cohen and others felt that such an identity structure left little hope that attachment to Israel will grow with age as part of the life cycle change of an individual. Steven Bayme, an expert on Israel-Jewish American identity in the AJC, agreed with these findings. He wrote: "Israel represents the public agenda of American Jews. However, that public agenda is perhaps the least important aspect of insuring Jewish continuity."[77]

Given these findings many observers called for an urgent reexamination of the foundations of Jewish identity and Israel's role in Jewish communal life. But, as always, the discourse on the role of Israel was closely intertwined with the peace process. And it was here that the debate became highly complicated as American Jews were forced to grapple with the historic Israeli-Palestinian Oslo peace accord.

6

The Oslo Agreement: Cementing the Split in the American Jewish Community

During the long tenure of Likud, American Jews, faced with a chorus of criticism of the Begin and Shamir policies, struggled to preserve a modicum of unity around Israel. However, the Oslo agreement made the split official, pitting nationalist and Orthodox segments of the community against the Labor government and its supporters in the United States. In the resulting titanic struggle between competing visions of the peace process and indeed, of Israel, a new paradigm of relations between Israel and the Diaspora emerged.

THE ROAD TO OSLO: PROMOTING PEACE BY LEGITIMIZING THE PALESTINIANS

After years of inconclusive results, the June 23, 1993, election gave Labor a clear victory over Likud and a mandate to solve the persistent Palestinian problem. Yitzhak Rabin, the head of the new Labor-led coalition, announced that he would change the national priorities by furthering peace and shifting investment from the settlements to social and economic needs within the Green Line. On July 13, during his inauguration speech, Rabin called to end Israel's international isolation and promised peace and reconciliation. The new prime minister also urged the Palestinians and the Arab states to join in his quest for a peaceful resolution to the Arab-Israeli conflict.

After years of dealing with Begin and Shamir, Washington greeted the Labor victory with relief. Wasting little time, the Bush administration dispatched Secretary of State James Baker to the Middle East to revive the peace process. On July 25 Syria, Jordan, Lebanon, Egypt, and the Palestinians welcomed

Baker's tour and signaled interest in pursuing talks with Israel. On August 10 Rabin met President Bush in his summer residence in Maine, a move that was designed to symbolize a better personal relationship between the Israeli and American leaders as well as their countries. Speaking later at the National Press Club, Rabin promised to expedite the negotiations over Palestinian autonomy. His deputy foreign minister Yossi Beilin, also a major proponent of a peace deal with the Palestinians, declared that the "Arabs won't find a more moderate Government that the current one," and urged them to seize the opportunity.[1]

When the sixth round of talks with the Palestinians opened in Washington on August 24, Israel offered a set of proposals for self-rule, including elections for an administrative council that was a response to a Palestinian demand for a 180-member parliament. However, the Palestinian delegation to the talks rejected the proposals because Israel refused to address the issue of Jerusalem and Palestinians' right to land. Eli Rubinstein, the Israeli negotiator, expressed frustration with the Palestinians for failing to realize a "sea change" in the Israeli position. Rabin blamed the PLO leadership in Tunis for making it difficult for the more pragmatic Palestinians in the territories to reach a deal.

The government's resolve to move the peace process along was not limited to the issue of the Palestinians. On August 3, the Middle East expert Itamar Rabinovich was nominated to head the talks with the Syrians. At the beginning of September, Rabin indicated in a number of public statements Israel's willingness to return parts of the Golan Heights. Speaking during a Knesset debate in which he rejected charges of a "sellout," Rabin asserted that the Likud approach of peace-for-peace would never persuade the Arabs to make peace, and defended the Labor's formula of land-for-peace. In an interview on September 10 Rabin, proclaimed that Israel was ready for certain territorial comprise with Syria in exchange for a peace treaty with open borders and normal diplomatic relations. On September 14, Israel presented an eight-page outline of its vision of peace with Syria and soon after Rabin announced that UN Resolution 242, which called for return of territory, would apply to the Golan Heights. In spite of the fact that there was no breakthrough, the sixth round of talks ended with a sense of progress.

The seventh round of talks began on October 21, but there was an understanding on all sides that, with the elections in the United States scheduled for November 3, there would be little momentum. Although Bill Clinton, who won the race against Bush, urged Israel and the Arabs to proceed in their efforts to solve the long-standing conflict, the interregnum in Washington offered little incentives. As expected, the seventh round of talks ended on November 19 with no progress, and the prospects for the eighth round, scheduled for December, looked even worse. On December 7 a terrorist group ambushed and killed three Israeli soldiers and Israel quickly closed off the Gaza Strip to search for the killers. Responding to the new tensions, the fundamentalist Hamas organization kidnapped and subsequently killed an Israeli border policeman, prompting the government to deport 415 Palestinians with links to the militant Islamic group to Lebanon. While the Israeli public opinion convulsed with anger over the killings and supported the deportation, the Arabs boycotted the final session of the eighth round to protest the policy.

The new wave of deportations had put the Israeli government at odds with the international community and the outgoing Bush administration. On January 4, 1994, UN Secretary General Boutros Boutros-Ghali warned that his organization was considering punitive measures against Israel, and Yasser Arafat called on Arab states to boycott the peace talks. However, Clinton, sworn in as the new president on January 20, tried to solve the problem through quiet diplomacy. Partially as a gesture to the incoming administration and partially as a response to international pressure, Rabin announced on February 1 that a hundred of the deportees would be able to return to Israel, and promised that the rest would be able to return in a year. Clinton's secretary of state, Warren Christopher, described the Israeli formula as a "breakthrough" and announced a new American diplomatic initiative in the Middle East.

Meanwhile, on March 15 Rabin arrived in Washington for his first visit with President Clinton. Following the three-hour meeting, Rabin declared that "we have a friend in the White House," and Clinton expressed optimism that the peace process would go forward. A new wave of Palestinian violence, which claimed the life of fifteen Israelis in March alone, undermined this rosy assessment. Rabin cut his visit to Washington short and returned to Israel, where he promised the outraged Israeli public to wage an "all-out-war" against terrorism. Still, in what was a testimony to Israel's resolve to proceed with the peace talk, the Rabin government decided to join the ninth round of negotiations in Washington, scheduled for April 27. Foreign Minister Peres, spoke optimistically about reaching an autonomy agreement with the Palestinians and hinted at progress with Syria. On their part, Arafat and the Palestinian leaders in the West Bank were eager to show some results in order to block the growing political appeal of their fundamentalist opponents. But on May 10, under pressure from the Islamic radicals, Arafat demanded a return of the deportees and cut his negotiation team from fourteen to three, de facto ending the ninth round of talks.

The tenth round of talks started on June 15, but there was little optimism for a breakthrough. To expedite things, the Clinton administration announced a new initiative, which sought to flesh out the functional, rather than the territorial, aspects of Palestinian authority. Both sides rejected the draft paper and ended the round of talks on July 1 amid mutual recrimination and criticism of the United States. At the end of July Christopher went back to the Middle East to revive the flagging process and, upon return to Washington, announced that the sides were ready to resume talks on August 31.

While all sides were preparing for the official track, rumors of a major breakthrough in the Israeli-Palestinian negotiations spread in Washington. On August 28 Peres flew to the United States to inform Christopher of the top secret Declaration of Principles (DOP) reached in Oslo, Norway. The low-level Oslo track was initiated by two Israeli academics and Palestinian intellectuals and was supervised by Peres, Beilin, and the director general of the Foreign Ministry, Uri Savir. According to the agreement, Israel recognized the PLO as a legitimate representative of the Palestinian people and promised to relinquish control of Gaza and Jericho as a first step toward Palestinian self-rule. In exchange, the PLO recognized Israel's right to exist in peace and security, renounced the use of acts of violence, and promised to discipline any of its loyalists who broke the pledge.

Although the administration was not privy to the historical breakthrough, President Clinton eagerly welcomed the proposed accord and offered to hold the historic signing ceremony in the White House. On September 13, in front of some three thousand guests, Rabin and Arafat exchanged the famous handshake while Peres and a PLO official, Mahmoud Abbas, signed the Declaration of Principles. In what was widely described as a "stirring oration," Rabin spoke about the fact that the two people were destined to live together and called to exchange the suffering and bloodshed for a peaceful coexistence. Arafat pledged that the PLO would use peaceful means to pursue its dream of a fully independent state with East Jerusalem as its capital. For his part, Clinton praised both leaders for their "brave gamble" for the future and described the ceremony as the most important milestone in the Middle East peace since the Israeli-Egyptian peace treaty.

To bolster the chances of the agreement, the Rabin government urged the United States and other countries to underwrite the costs of building an infrastructure for the incipient Palestinian entity. A World Bank report indicated that the Palestinians would need some $3 billion over eight years to upgrade basic services like water and healthcare. Palestinian economists estimated that an additional $6 billion would be needed to build housing and develop local industry. A forty-two–nation conference, which convened on October 1 in the State Department, promised $2 billion in aid over the next five years. Summing up the thinking behind the economic initiative Secretary Christopher spoke of the need to "demonstrate the tangible benefits of peace" so that the "advocates of peace" would be strengthened and, the "enemies of peace" isolated and discredited.[2] For its part, the United States pledged $500 million over five years, and Israel pledged a grant of $25 million and a loan of $50 million.

The Israeli-Palestinian accord generated additional dynamics in the Middle East conflict. On September 14 Jordan signed its own Declaration of Principle with Israel. At the beginning of December, Christopher met with the Syrian ruler Hafez Assad and secured some humanitarian concessions. Assad promised to investigate the fate of seven Israeli soldiers missing in action since the war in Lebanon and to grant exit visas to some eight hundred members of the Syrian Jewish community. On December 9, Christopher revealed that Syria had agreed to resume talks with Israel. Five days later the Israeli government allowed the remaining two hundred Palestinian deportees to return back, ending the long festering episode. To crown the progress toward peace and normalization, on December 27, Israel and the Vatican announced an agreement to establish diplomatic relations. Commenting on the historic breakthroughs of 1993, Beilin, one of the Oslo architects, noted that Israel was on the way to a long-awaited normalization.

THE "HANDSHAKE EARTHQUAKE": AMERICAN JEWISH REACTIONS TO THE OSLO AGREEMENT

A number of opinion polls on the attitudes of the Jewish community taken immediately after the White House ceremony indicated a widespread support for the peace process. A Marttila & Kiley, Inc. poll for the Israel Policy Forum (IPF) conducted from September 19 through September 23, 1993, showed that 82 percent of the respondents approved of the DOP, and only 11 percent disapproved. Moreover, 56 percent favored the creation of a Palestinian state and 26 percent opposed it. Rabin was rated very favorably by 61 percent and favorably by 33 percent of the respondents, and 82 percent said that the Israeli prime minister was moving at about the right speed in his negotiations. Harking back to the debate about Israeli security, 45 percent of the sample felt that Israel would be more secure if IDF troops would withdraw from populated areas in the territories and the Palestinians were allowed to have self-rule.[3]

A survey of the AJC found a similar pattern. Eighty-four percent of respondents supported the Israeli peace initiative and only 9 percent opposed it. Eighty-seven percent felt that Israel was right in negotiating the agreement with the PLO; an even higher number (90 percent) considered the mutual recognition between Israel and the PLO to be a positive development. There was also an increase of support for Labor's land-for-peace formula. Sixty-eight percent welcomed the land-for-peace exchange and only 27 percent of the respondents rejected it. In addition, 73 percent of American Jews stated that the DOP increase the chances for peace. These results represented a significant change from 1991, when only 45 percent supported the land-for-peace exchange, 27 percent opposed it, and 27 percent were not sure.

Despite high levels of support for Oslo, there was some residual mistrust of the Palestinians. Forty-two percent believed that the PLO could not be relied upon to refrain from terrorist activity, 35 percent trusted the Palestinians, and 25 percent were not sure; 34 percent felt that the PLO is determined to destroy Israel. Still, these numbers represented a significant decline from the 1989 and 1991 surveys, which found that 83 and 62 percent respectively believed that the PLO is out to destroy Israel. Equally interesting was the fact that most of the respondents were prepared to face the possibility of an independent Palestinian state. Sixty-six percent of the sample believed that the Oslo agreement would lead to the creation of a Palestinian state. Some 57 percent favored such an option. There was much less enthusiasm for Israel's efforts to negotiate a peace treaty with Syria, primarily because of the reluctance to give up the Golan Heights. Twenty-seven percent of the sample opposed giving up any part of the Golan, 30 percent wanted to concede only a small part of it, and 29 percent some of it. Only 5 percent would have given up most of the Golan Heights and 2 percent all of it. The question of Jerusalem was also difficult for American Jews. Asked whether, within a permanent peace agreement with the Palestinians, Israel should compromise over Jerusalem, 62 percent said no and 30 percent said yes; 8 percent were not sure.[4]

Followup studies revealed that, in spite of the difficulties in implementing the Oslo accord, support for the Israeli-Palestinian rapprochement had remained high. An AJC poll taken in August 1994 showed that 77 percent of the sample supported Rabin's handling of the peace process. Seventy-nine percent supported the handling of the negotiations with Jordan, 70 percent with the Palestinians, and 62 percent with Syria. Sixty-six percent felt favorably disposed toward the Palestinian autonomy plan and 61 percent thought that the accord would increase the prospect of peace. As for the prospect for Palestinian sovereignty, 60 percent of the respondents believed that the peace process would lead to an establishment of a Palestinian state; 53 percent supported such an outcome. Fifty-nine percent accepted the principle of trading territories for peace and 35 percent rejected it. The round of terrorist attacks carried out by Hamas against Israeli civilians had increased the level of mistrust against the Arabs in general, and Palestinians in particular. Fifty-one percent of American Jews agreed that Arabs were determined to destroy Israel and 65 percent said that the PLO could not be relied upon to carry out the agreements. Fifty-three percent believed that the PLO was determined to destroy Israel. The Syrians ranked the lowest on the trust scale; 47 percent said that the Syrians were not interested in "true peace," as opposed to 33 percent who said that they were. Questions about Syria also reflected attitudes toward the Golan Heights. As in 1993, 32 percent opposed the return of any part of the Heights and 27 percent wanted to give up only a small part; 4 percent were willing to concede most of it and 3 percent all of it.[5]

A May 1995 poll conducted by Luntz Research Companies, and presented at the 1995 annual AIPAC conference, showed that despite further problems with Palestinians there was still widespread support for the peace process in the community. Seventy-six percent of American Jews represented in the sample were in favor of the negotiations and only 18 percent opposed it. Nevertheless, there was growing skepticism about PLO's ability to deliver on the Oslo accord. Fifty-five percent felt that the negotiations had been largely unsuccessful as opposed to 42 percent who defined the accord as successful. The distrust of Arafat was high: 61 percent of the respondents said that they had "no trust" or "little trust" in the PLO chairman. The suspicion of Syria and Assad ran even higher, with 62 percent of respondents reporting that Assad cannot be trusted to keep a peace agreement. Opposition to a land-for-peace deal with Syria was also stiff. A majority of the sample (51 percent) refused to consider withdrawing from all or most of the Golan Heights, while only 39 percent would have sanctioned some territorial concessions.[6]

The AJC survey of August 1995 found that only 68 percent of the American

Jews interviewed supported Israel's government handling of the peace process as compared to 84 percent in 1993. Support for the negotiations with Syria stood at 62 percent. With the exception of the Jordanians, the distrust of Arabs and Palestinians was high. Fifty-six percent agreed that the Arabs were bent on destroying Israel and 71 percent felt that the PLO could not be relied upon to honor its agreements with Israel. Influenced by the brutal terrorist attacks of Hamas, this increasingly negative perception of the Palestinians reduced the percentage of those supporting a Palestinian state to forty-six. In addition, 91 percent of the sample claimed that the Palestinian authority was not doing enough to fight terrorism. The relatively hard-line position on Syria continued with 33 percent who were unwilling to give up any part of the Golan Heights and 28 percent who were willing to concede a little. In contrast, 26 percent favored giving up some and 3 percent most of it. The question of compromising over Jerusalem within a framework of a permanent peace treaty with the Palestinians elicited the same two to one rate of rejection as in 1993 and 1995. Sixty-two percent said "no" to a divided Jerusalem as opposed to 33 percent who said "yes." But there was little immediate interest in moving the American embassy to Jerusalem. Only 20 percent of the sample favored an immediate relocation of the embassy and 45 percent supported such a step in the future, in conjunction with progress in the Israeli-Palestinian peace talk. Twenty-five percent did not want to move the embassy and 10 percent were not sure.[7]

Virtually all commentators noted that for the large and liberal segment of American Jewry, the election of Rabin and his deal with the Palestinians was a welcome relief from the dissonance forced on it by Likud policies. As one observer argued, after years of tensions between Israel and the United States, "there was an audible sigh of relief from American Jewish liberals. Once again they could support Israel as good Jews, committed liberals, and loyal Americans." The community "could embrace the Jewish state without compromising either its liberalism or its patriotism."[8] It was thus not a coincidence that those who supported the peace process most eagerly tended to be less religious, younger, more affluent, and more educated. Such respondents were also less emotionally attached to Israel.

Conversely, older and less educated Jews and the Orthodox were least supportive of the Oslo agreement and more likely to oppose territorial concessions. For instance, in the 1993 AJC poll, 84 percent of Conservatives, 90 percent of Reforms, and 83 percent nondenominational Jews backed the Oslo agreement, while only 53 percent of Orthodox did so. Likewise, support for further Jewish settlements in the West Bank was strongest among respondents with lower household incomes, lower levels of education, and the Orthodox. These respondents were also least likely to trust the Arabs and the Palestinians, and more likely to insist on the unity of Jerusalem. The 1995 survey revealed an almost identical pattern. Respondents who reported that they felt very close to Israel were also likely to be more wary of the peace process. The 1995 AJC poll showed a clear correlation between emotional distance from Israel and opposition to Palestinian autonomy. Among those who felt very close to Israel, 36 percent opposed autonomy, but only 15 percent who felt fairly/very distant objected. Those close to Israel were also more likely to be suspicious of Arabs and disliked the idea of negotiations with what they viewed as Israel's enemies. Thus, 20 percent of the sample that felt very close rejected negotiations as opposed to 4 percent that felt fairly/very distant.[9]

Superficially, the division mirrored the split in the Israeli society. However, there is little doubt that the "rejectionists" in the surveys fit the profile of the nationalists and the Orthodox camp who had been the most ardent supporters of Israel. The peace advocates were largely disaffiliated and passive Jews. They were described as "disengaged from Israel in all but sentimental ways," whose voices are "expressed only in answers to opinion polls." In contrast, the peace skeptics were, largely, highly engaged members of the community and the most audible voices in the peace discourse. In fact, the handshake earthquake promoted an extremely forceful reaction from the American Jewish right.[10]

Leading the way, Podhoretz argued that the Oslo accord would increase the probability of war rather than peace, an argument that was shared by Isaac, who declared that Israel already paid "an extremely high price" for the agreement with Egypt. These and other critics attacked the land-for-peace model and warned of the dangers of appeasing the Arabs and creating a foothold for the Palestinians to destroy the Jewish state. Podhoretz contrasted Rabin's willingness to give up territory with Shamir's steadfastness in the face of pressure, adding that "Jewish people need a 'mean little prick who could say no' and that God had answered this need by creating Yitzhak Shamir." Shortly before Oslo, *Commentary* announced a new feature, "Israel Watch," created to comment on the negotiations. Others described the peace process as a "hallucination" and an assured path to another war.[11]

Borrowing a page from the successful struggle of the left-wing groups against the Likud government, secular nationalists and their religious counterparts had launched a major campaign to register their objections to the peace process. On October 10, 1993, opponents of the PLO-Israel accord met in Arlington, Virginia for the American Leadership Conference for a Safe Israel. Herbert Zweibon from AFSI, who was one of the organizers, proclaimed that the "thirteenth of September is a date that will live in infamy. A great people prostrated itself before a bankrupt thug." Another organizer stated that the aim of the conference was "to try and puncture the air of euphoria, to try to make people think of the difficult unresolved issues that will be coming up."[12]

The anti-Oslo protest reinvigorated many of the nationalist groups and lead to the creation of a number of new ones dedicated to "preserving Israel's security and territorial integrity." Rusty Mostow, the executive director of Pro-Israel, disclosed that the response to post-Oslo solicitation mailing was "off the charts." Pro-Israel used the proceeds to advertise in Jewish and general press, including an ad entitled "Architect of Peace or a Catalyst for War" in the February 4–10, 1994, issue of the *Boston Advocate*. Word Committee for Israel (WCI), which was funded by the Miami millionaire Manfred Lehmann, was also involved in media advertising. It took out a full-page ad in the November 12, 1993 issue of the *New York Times* to criticize the Oslo accord. The Jewish Action Alliance, an ad hoc umbrella organization of Oslo opponents, listed among its members AFSI, Jerusalem Reclamation Project, American Academics for Israel Future, Pro-Israel, American Friends and Families of Efrat, Academic Alliance for Israel, Women in Green USA, Students for Israel, International Committee for Safeguarding our Holy Sites, Lema'an Tzion/American Jewish Coalition for a Safe Peace, and others.

The Freeman Center for Strategic Studies and its monthly publication the *Maccabean*, which featured American and Israeli right-wing commentators and politicians, offered a harsh critique of Labor's foreign policy. The *Maccabean* also published news and analysis from alternative right-wing news services like Information Regarding Israel's Security (IRIS) and Independent Media Review & Analysis (IMRA). Bernard J. Shapiro, the executive director of the Freeman Center, was linked to AFSI and, in turn, AFSI's Zwiebon and Isaac served on the Board of Directors of the Center. Likewise, Dov Hikind, a New York assemblyman, used his organization, Save Our Israeli Homeland (SOIL), to protest the agreement.[13]

Important segments of the Orthodox community shared many of the same misgivings. Taking an early stand, the powerful National Council of Young Israel organized a conference of rabbis in New York where, on September 19, 1993, a decision to launch a major struggle against the Oslo agreement was made. The Union of Orthodox Jewish Congregations in America, the Rabbinical Council of America, and Agudat Israel all denounced the peace process and the Lubavitch Hassidic movement announced a multimillion dollar campaign against it. Joining them were Operation Chizuk and the Committee for the Preservation of Eretz Hakodesh. Many Orthodox Jews cut their donations to the UJA in order to send money to settlement-oriented charities such as the Jerusalem Reclamation Project, Yesha-One Israel Fund, and Operation Kiryat Arba. In 1995 a group called Friends of Yesha took out an ad urging shifting UJA donations to the One Israel Fund/Yesha Heartland Campaign. Others called for a referendum in Israel to repeal the accord and, in early November, 150 Orthodox rabbis went to Israel to lobby against the deal.[14]

From the perspective of the Orthodox community, the DOP was not just an affront to the sanctity of Eretz Israel, but also a personal threat. Some 15 percent of the settlers were Orthodox immigrants from the United States, and since 1967, intensive links had developed between the two communities. The journalist Ya'kov Kornreich wrote of the horror of watching "as the homes of 130,000 Jews [in the territories] were, potentially, signed away with a stroke of pen." Rabbi Moshe Gorelick, president of the Rabbinical Council of America and a leader of the delegation, explained that Labor policies were putting Jewish settlers at risk. To stress the personal connection, the Orthodox community developed an "adopt a settlement" program, which was announced in a February

1994 New York rally. Israeli officials and loyalist American Jews interpreted this move as an open rebellion against the Rabin government.[15]

Both secular and Orthodox rejectionist groups benefited from the willingness of affluent American Jews to underwrite the antipeace activities. Irving Moskowitz—who had supported American Friends of Ateret Cohanim/Jerusalem Reclamation Project, American Friends of Everest Foundation, and other settlement-oriented projects—intensified his efforts through his Irving I. Moskowitz Foundation. The foundation had also contributed to AFSI, the ZOA, Pro-Israel, the Center for Security Policy (a conservative think tank founded by Frank Gaffney), the Freeman Center, and other groups involved in the anti-Oslo discourse. Hikind called Moskowitz a "wonderful and very special person" concerned about Jerusalem, and Gaffney credited Moskowitz with emphasizing an "alternative view . . . not well represented among the established Jewish institutions." Rose Mattus of the Haagen-Dazs ice-cream fortune became another important benefactor. Mattus explained that "everything changed when Yitzhak Rabin signed the Oslo accord," which she described as an act of appeasement that "American Jews had learned from the Holocaust, is the sure road to war." The Häagen-Dazs heiress, who proclaimed herself to be "a staunch supporter of Benjamin Netanyahu," was involved with AFSI, the ZOA, and other nationalist and settler groups. In 1997, the ZOA nominated her as a candidate for elections to the WZC. Albert Wood, a Philadelphia philanthropist, helped to fund the Middle East Forum, a right-of-center think tank on the Middle East.[16]

Shimon Peres and Beilin, who were widely perceived as the true authors of the Oslo accord, became the favorite targets of right-wing critics. An AFSI editorial called Peres a "ridiculous buffoon," and Beilin was described as one of Israel's most "flamboyant and reckless sloganeers and posturers." Peres was derided for allegedly thinking of himself as the foreign minister of the region and the "hired defense attorney for Yasser Arafat." He was also accused of committing "sedition and treason." Rabin's illustrious military background had not shielded him from attacks. Moskowitz once described the peace process as "a slide toward concession, surrender and Israeli suicide" and compared Rabin to Chamberlain. AFSI's publication, the *Outpost*, carried articles that accused Rabin of cowardice, alcoholism, and a lifetime of "psychological and military retreats." Sam Domb, a New York businessman and major Likud supporter, described Rabin as "a man seemingly devoid of honor, self-respect, compassion, common sense and a sense of history" who was "spiritually destroying the Jewish people." On December 13, 1993, during a demonstration sponsored by the WCI and addressed by Domb, Hikind and Rabbi Abraham Hecht, a noted rabbinical leader in New York, some participants described Rabin as "worse than Hitler" and demanded that he be killed.[17]

There were other extreme forms of protest. Itamar Rabinovitch, the Israeli ambassador to Washington, complained about the hostility that he encountered among some Jewish audiences. Speaking at an Orthodox synagogue on the eve of the White House ceremony, he was shouted down by cries of "Rabin is a traitor" and "Go to Hell," while some threw tomatoes and eggs at him. Colette Avital, the Israeli consul general in New York, was called a "traitor" and a "Nazi." Tali Lador, the consul for public affairs in the consulate was also publicly vilified. Shulamit Aloni—the head of the Meretz party and the minister of commination, culture, and science in Rabin's cabinet—was allegedly physically assaulted when she tried to speak at the 1995 annual Israel Day Parade in New York. The parade was sponsored by Domb and chaired by Jack Avital, the vice president of the WCI.[18]

The protest was taken to a higher level when, on January 5, 1994, bombs were found in front of the offices of APN and NIF in New York. Notes condemning the peace process signed by two hitherto unknown groups, Ma Squad and Shield of David, were attached to the devises, one of which exploded without hurting anyone. Before the bombing, the APN and other leftist groups had received a large amount of hate mail and death threats. Colette Avital asserted that the incidents were triggered by the verbal and physical abuse heaped against the Rabin government by certain sections of the community. Letty Cottin Pogrebin, chairwoman of APN, blamed Likud for using terms like "traitor" to delegitimize the Rabin government. Shamir responded that even had the bombs gone off, the damage would have been less significant than that caused by PN.[19]

When soon after, on February 25, Baruch Goldstein, an American-born settler, killed and wounded dozens of Muslims in the Tomb of Patriarchs in Hebron, some in the Orthodox circles called for a repudiation of extremism in the service of Eretz Israel. However, the tensions between the critics of the peace process and the majority of American Jews who supported the Oslo accord did not abate. As the Labor government was to discover, the popular mandate that the public opinion polls conferred on its efforts, proved to be elusive at the level of the organized community. In the words of Gedal, "most of the organizations representing the Jewish community fail to reflect the overwhelming support for the peace process that polls indicate among American Jews."[20]

THE DISINTEGRATING CENTER: THE JEWISH
ORGANIZATIONS AND THE PEACE PROCESS

In trying to explain why there was little enthusiasm for the peace process at the level of organized community, observers borrowed from organizational theory to point out to four interrelated factors. First, starting in the eighties, the relatively liberal leadership and the professional staff of many Israel-oriented organizations had been progressively replaced with individuals who fitted the nationalist-religious profile. More generally, because of their philanthropic engagement and activism, the Orthodox and the "residual Orthodox" had become prevalent in the ranks of professionals in Jewish institutions. Moreover, after more than a decade of Republican administrations in Washington and an even longer tenure of Likud in Israel, the top echelons of AIPAC and the Conference were staffed by conservative hard-liners who were skeptical of Labor's peace overtures. A number of top officials in AIPAC and some top donors were associated with the National Jewish Coalition, an organization aimed at attracting Jews to the Republican party.[21]

Second, the Oslo agreement promised to normalize Israeli relations with Washington and improve its world standing. For some American Jewish leaders, accustomed to playing a key role in representing Israel, the peace process looked like a threat to their organizational raison d'être. One journalist captured this sense well when he wrote: "pro-Israel lobby sees roles shrink as enemies turn into friends." Rabin might have added to a perception of redundancy when he declared that Israel does not need intermediaries in Washington. Peres created even more of a commotion when he stated that Oslo made *hasbara* ("public relations") obsolete, and Uri Savir, his director general, embarked on dismantling the apparatus of public relations in the Foreign Ministry. To those in the Israel defense organizations, who were in the forefront of numerous public relations campaigns, such sentiments spelled an end to a well-entrenched tradition. Commenting on this development, one observer noted that "in a span of only nine months these policies took the sail out of American Jewry." Another one added that many of the leaders became invested in the status quo of "Israel under siege" and accustomed to playing the role of an intermediary. While they found many aspects of Likud's policy troublesome, the "wholesale change" promised by Oslo was too much to comprehend.[22]

Losses of personal standing aside, some leaders were also worried that a peaceful Israel would detract from communal fund-raising. One senior official noted that "not having a major Jewish crisis, which is often the point when Americans rally around Israel with their dollars, presents a problem." In this sense, peace threatened Jewish organizations which, according to some, were set up "as a vast machinery of defense, a blunt weapon that sought out and punished the enemies of the Jewish state." Such worries had some basis in reality. Barry Shrage, the president of Boston's Combined Jewish Philanthropies, noted that for "some American Jews it has been a lot easier to support war than peace." Leonard Fein described the fear of the peace process as the "crisis of the ordinary," explaining that most American Jews could not relate to an Israel which was not in crisis. Steven Rosen, AIPAC's director of foreign policy issues, revealed that, following Oslo, it was much harder to ignite grass-root level activism for Israel. Malcolm Hoenlein, the executive vice-chair of the Conference, agreed that "you can always rally people against" but it is "very hard to rally people for."[23]

Some experts, including the sociologist Egon Mayer, urged that the community find alternatives to the "mobilization model" based on a beleaguered Israel. This theme was taken up by a conference entitled "Israel Advocacy in the 90s: Challenges and Opportunities," held at Brandeis University on November 13, 1993. Mayer, as well as a number of participants, advised some organizations to go out of business "gracefully," but few were willing to preside over their own organizational demise. As one observer put it, for much of the organized leadership "doom and gloom is better than peace." Striking a sarcastic note, Arthur Hertzberg noted that he had a nightmare in which "Israel made peace with the Arabs, the Soviets allowed all Jews to leave, and Israel struck oil." Such "joyous news would leave the organized American Jewish community unemployed and totally disoriented." Hertzberg added that his nightmare had mostly come true.[24]

Third, organizational leaders and activists whose perceptions of the Middle East conflict fitted the nationalistic-religious profile were more reluctant to accept the fact Israel was dealing with the PLO, which for years was described as the worst enemy of Israel. The same leaders had also warned for years against the existential threat posed by giving up the Golan Heights and the establishment of a Palestinian state. Labor's optimism notwithstanding, it was hard for them to let go of the old fears. In what was a typical line, Bayme, the Israel expert at the AJC, cautioned against the "euphoria surrounding the September 13 handshake." He warned "the prospect of a Lebanese-type experience on the Gaza Strip or the West Bank ought to be most sobering to those who foresee a new era of Arab-Jewish coexistence." More important, the peace process undermined the three "nos" that formed the boundary of organized Jewry: no independent Palestinian state, no Syria on the Golan, and no divided Jerusalem. One Jewish journalist explained that being let down on the three "nos" left many supporters of Israel "disappointed, confused and saddened," and wary of any message coming out of Israel. The rabbi whose congregants attacked ambassador Rabinovitch noted that, after being told for twenty years that the PLO was out of bound, people cannot be expected to "turn on a dime." Indeed, sudden turns in Israeli policy were hard even for peace enthusiasts. The dovish Theodore Mann recalled how he and other leaders had felt used by Jerusalem during the Camp David process. After a major effort by the American Jewish community to persuade Washington that air bases were essential for Israeli security in the Sinai, Begin gave it up as part of the peace treaty with Egypt.[25]

Observers noted that this type of psychological mechanism could explain why it was hard on some of the "organizational Jews" to give up the image of the Palestinians as the reincarnation of the traditional anti-Semites. It would have been even more difficult if they were convinced that Jewish group solidarity depends on "keeping the dread of Gentiles in the minds of the Jews." Sklare once defined such Jews as those whose fear of a Holocaust-like calamity is ever present, and who are determined not to give Hitler a final victory. Added to this was the suspicion that the Arabs in general and the Palestinian in particular were using the peace process to pursue their historical quest of annihilating Israel. As Zoe Danon Gedal pointed out, it is not uncommon for Diaspora groups who are deeply committed to the welfare of their "ancestral home to advocate extreme solutions. Even worse from this perspective was the fact the Oslo accord called for what one historian described as the "muting of the differences between the national narrative of the Palestinians and the Jews." Such a change was almost impossible to achieve within the context of the Holocaust and anti-Semitism paradigm of Jewish history.[26]

Four, Labor's foreign policy had triggered a major rearrangement in the hierarchy of the Israel defense organizations. After years of being marginalized or cast as pariahs, APN, NIF, JPL, and other left-wing groups were suddenly elevated and legitimized at the expense of some more mainline groups. APN—which testified in Congress against the loan guarantees and whose president, Gail Pressberg, served with the Foundation for Middle East Peace, an organization reviled by some in the community for its alleged Palestinian sympathies—is a case in point. Following Oslo, the APN and the foundation—which had sponsored Israeli leftist politicians like Haim Ramon, a member of the Labor inner circle—could claim to be on the "right-side" of history. What is more, the Clinton White House hired some Jewish American peace activists, prompting complaints of imbalance from more mainstream groups. Commenting on this reversal, Ian Williams noted that "only a year ago American Jews espousing views like Rabin's were accused of thought-crimes by AIPAC leaders."[27]

The Rabin government was slow to realize the traumatic impact of Oslo on the organized community. Many Labor politicians were buoyed by the public opinion polls that supported their handling of the peace process and annoyed by the small but vocal minority. Ephraim Sneh, a Labor Knesset member, accused some American Jews of "nostalgia for Shamir" in a *New York Times* op-ed. Although some Israeli diplomats were concerned by the amount of opposition, Rabin was hampered by his disdain for the Diaspora, a stand that was compounded by Ambassador Rabinovitch's failure to achieve much traction with the community. One sympathetic Jewish activist commented that, unlike Likud, Labor neglected to cultivate ties, creating a "vacuum," which left some people "ignored."[28]

Belatedly recognizing the public relations failure, the Labor party set up an "American desk," which, among others, sent Labor Knesset members on speaking tours of U.S. Jewish communities. In September 1993 Peres, in an address to the Presidents Conference, sought to quiet qualms about Israel's security, a move that was repeated by Rabin during the November General Assembly of the CJF. Helping with Labor's public relations effort were some of the American Jewish Oslo supporters. Most effective was Nishma, which in August 1993 placed an ad signed by over one hundred prominent Jews stating that "when it comes to Israel's security, nobody knows more than Yitzhak Rabin. Nobody." One month later Nishma organized a large Jewish-Arab conference, featuring the PLO's Nabil Sha'ath, the Israeli ambassador to the UN, Gad Yaacobi, and over six hundred leading Arab and Jewish American figures. Early in 1994 IPF brought together the visiting King Hussein of Jordan and a diverse group of American Jewish leaders.[29]

Still, the Labor campaign did not mollify the hard-line opponents of the Oslo agreement who were wowed by a vigorous Likud counteroffensive. In November 1993, two top Likud leaders—the former Prime Minister Shamir and

Sharon—traveled to the United States to denounce the peace agreement. Speaking before the Conference of Presidents, Shamir called on American Jews to reject the peace process. Sharon, referring to the UJA as "United Jericho Appeal," asserted that the Jewish settlers were denied basic services while the Jewish community was asked to help the Palestinian. Later, a leading Washington public relations firm, Preston, Gates, Ellis, Rouvelas and Meads, was hired to bolster the Likud case in America. The Anglo-Jewish press also helped to fan anti-Labor sentiments. According to Berthram Korn, a former executive editor of the *Jewish Exponent*, many of the Jewish papers, including the leading *Forward*, "expressed skepticism of the land-for-peace policies enshrined in the 1993 Oslo accord" in spite of the pressure of the Israeli Foreign Ministry. It is entirely possible that some of these editors were reacting to the sentiments of their readers who flooded the papers with letters attacking the Israeli policy. As one editor noted, "getting a pro-government piece is like pulling teeth."[30]

Nowhere was the problem of adjustment manifested more clearly than in AIPAC and the Conference of Presidents. AIPAC, which, until the early nineties, was the undisputed arbiter of Israel's defense in the United States, found itself under particular pressure. Rabin, whose dislike for the "court Jew" style mediation was well known from his tenure as Israeli ambassador in Washington, was also incensed by what he saw as a heavy Likud bias among AIPAC officials. Beilin, the deputy foreign minister who doubled as the liaison for Israel-Diaspora relations, had his own grievance to nurse. Prior to the 1992 election, Beilin—who was a leading member of Labor's peace faction, *Mashov*, along with Ramon, Yael Dayan, and others—was allegedly ostracized by mainline Jewish leadership which, as already described, had scoffed at "Peace Now types." Rabin used a secret meeting with AIPAC leaders in 1992 to chastise them for their hard-line position on the peace process and for creating unnecessary antagonism in Israeli-American relations by pushing Shamir's loan guarantees scheme. He also promised to pursue direct relations with Washington. When the Israeli paper *Davar* leaked the encounter, an unapologetic AIPAC spokesman described Rabin as "naïve" for not appreciating AIPAC's importance. Although Rabin later apologized for his critical comments, the notion that Israel should give up territory in exchange for peace did not sit well with the organization.[31]

The peace process also triggered a major power struggle within AIPAC. In spite of the fact that AIPAC picked Steve Grossman, a liberal Democrat, as its new president in 1992, the pro-Likud leaders, Larry Weinberg, Robert Asher, Edward Levy, and Mayer Mitchell retained considerable power in the organizations. To bolster their reach, they created in 1992 the position of a managing director to which Howard Kohr, a conservative Republican, was appointed. The "gang of four" overruled Grossman, who wanted AIPAC to fight the right-wing "peace obstructionists" and, according to sources, both Kohr and the "gang" lobbied Congress against policies of the Labor government. The Reform leader Rabbi Schindler charged on the pages of the *New York Times* that "unreconstructed hawks" in AIPAC did not support the peace process. An AIPAC vice president, Harvey Friedman, was forced to resign after accusing Rabin of having "chutzpa" to give up territories and calling Beilin a "little slime ball." The ZOA subsequently nominated Friedman as a candidate for the World Zionist Organization. For his part, Beilin argued that in spite of some "dovish views" AIPAC "is essentially identified with the Republican Party."[32]

In yet another sign of internal strife, Dine, the longtime AIPAC executive director, was eased out in June 1993, ostensibly because of a slur against Orthodox Jews which was reported by the journalist David Landau. However, some observers argued that the "gang of four" instigated the dismissal because of Dine's effort to bring AIPAC into line with Labor's foreign policy. The four officers tried to appoint Kohr to fill Dine's position, but Grossman and a group of Democrats within the organization blocked them by arguing that the AIPAC should be more responsive to the leftward shift in Washington and Jerusalem. Grossman's pick, Neal Sher, the liberal former chief of the Nazi-hunting Office of Special Investigations at the Justice Department, had little experience in Middle East affairs and was easily outmaneuvered by the conservatives. Sher, who was also attacked by the ZOA and other right-wing groups for his support of the peace process, resigned in 1996. Some insiders alleged that Sher was forced out by the hard-liners on the board of directors and replaced with Kohr. The internal tension became so great that some observers proclaimed the once mighty lobby all but "paralyzed by a lay leadership that reflects Middle East hawks and doves."[33]

Even if the leadership could collaborate on developing a more "Labor friendly" course of action, there was considerable resistance from the AIPAC rank and file. Although there were opinion polls taken of AIPAC's more than fifty thousand members, anecdotal evidence indicates that many of them were highly suspicious of the land-for-peace formula that was at the heart of Labor's foreign policy. After meeting with Rabin in Jerusalem, Grossman and Kohr stated that "they were assured by Israel's leaders that the security of the state and all its citizens constituted '110 percent' of their concern in crafting the agreement." Gedal, who reported on this and other similarly cautious statements, found it "remarkable" that an American Jewish organization would have to reassure its members that an Israeli government is concerned about the security of its citizens. In yet another effort to persuade its reluctant members, the AIPAC leadership reminded its members that the Oslo agreement was reached by a "democratically elected Israeli government." When Ambassador Rabinovitch said in the 1993 AIPAC annual meeting that Israel would have to make concessions to advance peace, he was greeted with stony silence. The same assembly gave a standing ovation to Jan Willen Van der Hoven, the head of the Christian Embassy in Jerusalem, who supported the vision of Greater Israel. Dine was accused of working for the Arabs and of trying to organize a PLO takeover of AIPAC. Grossman was booed when he refused to commit AIPAC to a fight with the administration over an UN resolution which called East Jerusalem an "occupied territory." During the 1996 meeting, Peres was warmly welcomed, but observers found that the sessions "revealed a clear split in loyalty among American Jews." According to an Israeli journalist, the AIPAC bureaucracy could not impose control over its rank and file.[34]

The struggle to contain the internal split in AIPAC paled in comparison with the competitive frenzy experienced by the Conference of Presidents. The loosely structured body became the main arena where the clashing visions of the left and the right played themselves out. Much of the vigorous debate could be attributed to ZOA's president Morton Klein, a brilliant strategist and gifted speaker. In an early incident Klein strenuously objected to the Conference's plan to admit the left-leaning APN on the grounds that the group espoused Palestinian independence, testified against the loan guarantees, and favored concessions on Jerusalem. Calling the APN an "extremist in moderate clothing," Klein argued that the organization was at odds with the majority of American Jews and the Israeli government. However, supporters of the APN pointed out that its platform was virtually identical to Meretz, a Labor coalition partner, and that some APN activists were part of the Clinton administration. The APN was finally admitted in March 1993, but the raucous discourse did little to dispel the notion that the Conference was deeply divided.[35]

Adding to the picture of disarray was the difficulty that the Conference faced in imposing the civility on the peace debate. Under organizational guidelines, members were cautioned to use restraint in public discourse, putting Hoenlein in the middle of some bitter exchanges. For example, when Colette Avital demanded that the Conference censure the harsh attacks of some Orthodox spokesmen on Rabin, Young Israel and the ZOA urged Hoenlein to remain neutral. In the end, a reluctant Hoenlein published a statement of censure, which had virtually no effect on the Orthodox community.[36]

With so much riding on the perceived consensus of the Jewish community, the Conference leadership made numerous efforts to negotiate differences between its disparate members. Although surveys indicated an overwhelming support for the Oslo agreements, the deep divisions between the proponents and opponents of the peace process could not be breached or resolved in a democratic manner. As already noted, the voluntary nature of the community and its complex organizational structure tended to distort the public mandate. Worse, the Conference was powerless to stop individuals and groups from private lobbying of Congress, a dynamic that transformed Capitol Hill into a major arena of Jewish infighting.

JEWISH LOBBY VERSUS JEWISH LOBBY: THE CONGRESS AS A BATTLEGROUND

Since the success of the DOP hinged on financial help to the fledgling Palestinian authority, much was riding on congressional willingness to allocate resources promised by the administration. The Jewish organizations that tried to influence the peace process understood this imperative very well. On the left,

the APN launched it action Alert Network and Adopt-a-Congressperson programs. The religious and the nationalists groups showed even more vigor, turning their often-disparate lobbying efforts into a virtual rival of AIPAC. A
consortium of seven Orthodox organizations—Orthodox Union, National Council of Young Israel, Rabbinical Council of America, Poalei Agudat Israel, Religious Zionists of America, and Amit Emuna—established a strong presence in
Washington, along with the ZOA and AFSI. Perhaps most interesting was the
institutionalization of the Likud lobby, which was started by Shamir. In addition
to Yossi Ben-Aharon, it featured Yigal Carmon, a former Shamir adviser on
terrorism and Yoram Ettinger, a former congressional liaison at the Israeli embassy in Washington.[37]

Even before Oslo the right-wing groups clashed with AIPAC and the Conference over some of the Clinton foreign policy appointees, including Dennis
Ross, Samuel Lewis, Aaron Miller, and, in particular, Strobe Talbott, whom the
ZOA's Klein accused of anti-Israeli bias. In spite of the fact that the Israeli
government and AIPAC decided not to challenge the administration over Talbott's appointment as deputy secretary of state, the ZOA forced the issue by
involving the Senate. Talbott was compelled to apologize, embarrassing AIPAC
and the Israeli government.[38]

The nationalist and Orthodox lobby also locked horns with AIPAC over the
reaction to a UN resolution condemning the Hebron killings by Baruch Goldstein. In the preamble to the resolution, the UN referred to Jerusalem as "occupied territory," a term that the Clinton administration was willing to overlook
at the behest of Rabin, who was reluctant to impede the ongoing negotiations.
The Israeli government asked AIPAC and the Conference of Presidents to refrain
from lobbying the administration to veto the resolution, but ZOA persuaded
eighty-three senators to urge the president to impose a U.S. veto. Faced with a
fait accompli, AIPAC was forced to reverse course and the Clinton administration had to insist on a rare paragraph-by-paragraph vote for the UN resolution
that passed unanimously on March 18, 1994.[39]

The nationalist alliance was even more eager to challenge the various pro-
visions contained in the DOP. The most important item pertained to the financial
aid to the Palestinian Authority (PA). Under the Oslo provision, a $2 billion
fund to restore the Palestinian economy was established, of which a quarter was
to come from the United States. Rabin, who, along with many experts, believed
that poverty fomented Islamic fundamentalism in the territories, personally lobbied for American help. The Congress responded by passing the Middle East
Peace Facilitation Act (MEPFA). But Klein from the ZOA, Mandell I. Ganchrow of the Orthodox Union, and other activists urged Congress to condition
the aid on the PA's compliance with the DOP. Such a move was in line with
the nationalist-Orthodox claim that the PA is undemocratic and corrupt and
could not be trusted to implement the peace accord. The Israeli government, the
Clinton administration, and AIPAC objected to the compliance provision. However, largely due to Klein's efforts, the Congress passed on July 29, 1994 the

Specter-Shelby amendment, which required the State Department to certify the PA's compliance. Senator Arlen Specter (R–Pa.) became the co-chair of the ZOA–conceived congressional Peace Accord Monitoring (PAM) group to which some fifty-six members belonged. The amendment virtually insured future intracommunal quarrels in Congress. On June 13, 1995, a delegation of one hundred Orthodox rabbis went to Capitol Hill to lobby for a delay in the funding. When, on September 20, 1995, the Committee on International Relations convened to debate a MEFPA extension, the public squabbling among the Jewish organizations came to a head. AIPAC, which, at Israel's request, failed to get the hearing cancelled, supported the extension; the ZOA opposed it, and the Orthodox Union wanted to withhold the money until the Palestinians complied with their DOP obligations.[40]

Claiming that ZOA's actions threatened its role as the community's official lobby for Israel, AIPAC expressed outrage. It charged that Klein acted in "an amateurish and hostile fashion" and that he "put the entire pro-Israel agenda at risk." AIPAC asked the Conference of Presidents to take disciplinary action against the ZOA, but Klein refused to attend the Conference's special meeting. He contended that, in the absence of a consensus in the community, individual groups should be free to pursue their own strategies. The ZOA also rejected the Conference's new lobbying guidelines, which stipulated that all Israel-related issues had to be first cleared with AIPAC, a stand that was also questioned by the Orthodox groups.[41]

Klein's actions angered both the Israeli government and its American Jewish supporters, who accused the ZOA of being a Likud ally out to scuttle the peace process. However, asserting their independence from AIPAC, Klein and likeminded activists had turned the compliance issue into a major public relations exercise. The ZOA, which had denounced the Congress-mandated State Department reports on the PA as a "whitewash," took the lead in publicizing its own evaluation of Palestinian violations of the Oslo accord. Many of these violations were reported by alternative news networks in Israel and the United States, including Carmon's Middle East Media Research Institute (MEMRI), IMRA, and IRIS. These actions frustrated Labor officials, including Chaim Ramon, who used a CJF General Assembly forum to accuse the aid opponents of "cooperating with the extreme parts of Israel." In turn, Klein argued that "Chaim Ramon is an extremist in demanding we ignore Arafat's pro-terrorist behavior."[42]

Closely related to the issue of aid was the demand that the United States pressure the PA to extradite Palestinian terrorists accused of killing American citizens in Israel. At the initiative of the ZOA, numerous legislators urged the Clinton administration to force Arafat to hand over such perpetrators. The nationalists, who made the extradition issue one of their priorities, also demanded that the State Department post the names of Palestinians terrorists on its want list. The emotionally charged issue of terrorism proved successful with lawmakers who periodically sent letters to the White House, but was less than welcome by the Labor government, anxious to proceed with the peace negotiations.[43]

In yet another sign of dissension, the right wing mounted a vigorous campaign to preempt any plans to facilitate a possible Israeli deal with Syria over the Golan Heights. In the 1980s, a number of retired Israeli generals suggested that a Sinai-style deployment of a Multinational Force and Observers (MFO) might be used as a model to safeguard Israel's security on the Golan. The Rabin government which, parallel to the Palestinian track, tried to negotiate a peace treaty with Syria, apparently favored such an arrangement. To thwart this possibility, Gaffney's Center for Security Policy released on October 25, 1994, a special report that strongly objected to the scheme. In addition to a number of retired U.S. military officers, Douglas J. Feith, the former assistant secretary of defense in the Reagan administration, Gaffney, and Perle signed the document. Published in the December 1994 issue of *Commentary*, the report was followed up by a detailed piece by Dore Gold, a foreign policy adviser to Netanyahu. These and other critics argued that the stationing of American soliders on the Golan would expose them to terrorist attacks reminiscent of the bombing of the marine barracks in Beirut. They also contended that a possible deal with Syria would cost American taxpayers $5 billion in a financial package to Israel.[44]

The ZOA, AFSI, and Ettinger used the same arguments to demand that Congress debate the issue prior to any possible deal. Writing in AFSI's *Outpost*, Gaffney urged a congressional debate of the Rabin peace initiative with Syria because of its implications for U.S. national interests, taxpayers, and military personnel. Ettinger faxed a letter to Capitol Hill that contended that "Israeli withdrawal from the Golan Heights would not moderate the Mideast nor would it advance U.S. national security interests." Ironically, a group of anti-Israeli legislators led by Findley had used the same argument to fight the deployment of American soldiers during the Kissinger-brokered Israeli withdrawal from the Sinai dessert. The strenuous right-wing lobbying forced AIPAC to send a letter to all 535 members of Congress asking them not to hold hearings on the issue. Although AIPAC prevailed, Gaffney, Zweibon, and others complained bitterly that the "intense pressure" of AIPAC and the Israeli ambassador Rabinovitch helped to dissuade "key committees on Capitol Hill" from allowing careful scrutiny of the issues. Zweibon warned that delaying the hearings would be "tragic" because American lives would be lost.[45]

Nowhere were the differences between the nationalist-Orthodox camp and the official Jewish lobby more pronounced than on the issue of the American embassy in Jerusalem. Ostensibly, all Israeli governments and the American Jewish community had expressed their desire that the American embassy should be moved from TelAviv to Jerusalem. However, when, in 1984, Senator Daniel Patrick Moynihan (D–N.Y.) introduced a bill to force relocation, AIPAC was caught by surprise. To make matters worse, AIPAC leaders were divided between those who wanted to fight for the issue, and critics who felt that such a high-profile case would damage the relations with President Reagan, who opposed the embassy move. In the end, faced with a reluctant Israeli government and a veto threat from the administration, the Congress passed a nonbinding resolution. By 1995, when Robert Dole, the Senate majority leader, was running for president, the National Jewish Coalition, the ZOA, and other right-wing activists renewed the embassy campaign despite the dismay of the Labor government and AIPAC. According to one source, Kohr, contravening the official position of his organization, joined in lobbying Dole. In the end, a bipartisan group in Congress passed the Jerusalem Embassy Relocation Act, which mandated the embassy move by May 1999.[46]

Peace activists criticized the step as "destructive" and accused Kohr of using the embassy issue to bolster Dole's presidential chances against Clinton. The Conference, which officially kept a low profile, was also implicated in the fight. According to reports, Hoenlein and others in the Conference leadership actually welcomed the legislation, a move that the Israeli government was reluctant to fight in public, especially as the issue resonated with many in the community. It was left to Pogrebin from APN to repeat her charge that such emotionality stifled all rational discourse on the issue, in favor of what she called the "Three Forevers": Jerusalem shall be forever untied, forever the capital of the Jewish state, and forever under Israeli sovereignty.[47]

The Embassy Relocation Act was illustrative of the new dynamics of lobbying for pro-Israeli causes in the Republican-dominated Congress. The influx of conservative lawmakers, which came to dominate both Houses in 1994, had given the nationalist-Orthodox coalition a certain advantage over the mainstream AIPAC and the Conference. As already noted, many of the legislators were foreign policy hard-liners who mistrusted the Palestinians and other former Arab allies of the Soviet Union. Those who had Jewish constituencies or depended on Jewish PAC money had to be sensitive to the right-wing Jewish voices, which often overwhelmed the more liberal channels. Reflecting the larger problem of American Jewish representation, it was difficult for congressmen to make a clear determination as to who spoke for whom in the community. For instance, Nita Lowey, a Democrat from New York and one of the most liberal members of Congress, was persuaded to cosponsor the Specter-Shelby amendment out of concern for hard-liners in her Queens district.

The fact that many of the conservative legislators were supported by Christian fundamentalists was an added boon for the Jewish opponent of peace. The National Unity Coalition for Israel and the Christian Israel Public Action Campaign (CIPAC) lobbied vigorously against aid for the PA and American deployment on the Golan, not to mention the embassy move. In August 1995 CIPAC organized a conference to develop a grass-root lobbying system, to which AFSI was invited to contribute. In the same year a newly formed Coalition for a Secure U.S–Israel Friendship, composed of Jewish and Christian groups, lobbied for legislation that would bar the use of American soldiers in the Golan. Beth Gilinsky from the Jewish Alliance Action listed CIPAC as a member of her group that worked against aid to the PA.[48]

While ideology played a major role, there were additional factors that drove Congress to side with the nationalist-Orthodox camp. Observers noted that many of the congressmen were ignorant of the issues involved in the Arab-Israeli conflict and were easily swayed by pressure from vocal groups. Some lawmakers were not aware that "these nationalist-maximalist leaders were urging positions contrary to what the Israeli government wanted." Others asserted that the use of "flamboyant pro-Israeli rhetoric" was a cynical ploy to raise funds and defeat rivals. As one commentator put it, "Palestinian bashing is low risk for these guys. Everyone likes to hook up with Israel because it's good for their careers, good for their fundraising and good foreign policy." Jay Footlick, a former special assistant for Jewish affairs in the Clinton administration, added that there were those in Congress who "tr[ied] to out-Israeli the Israelis." He described them as not having a "particularly sophisticated view of politics in Israel. What they think they have is an understanding of Jewish power in Washington and fund raising."[49]

Finally, the hard-liners in the Jewish community could count on the large number of isolationist legislators who were reluctant to support any new international initiatives, especially if they involved large financial outlays or troop deployment. An analyst wrote that the "lobby's message fit well with the popular disinclination to place American boys at risk in foreign countries." Indeed, speaking before the 1994 General Assembly of the CJF, Prime Minister Rabin accused right-wing Jewish lobbyists of straightening isolationist tendencies in American politics and thus damaging Israel's national interest.

Congressional bias against the Oslo process upset many peace proponents. One complained that "these congressmen" are generally out of step with the "mainstream of the Jewish community," adding that the peace process is supported by a majority of U.S. Jews. Others stated that "certain members of Congress became representatives of the pro-Likud segment of the community." Lerner declared the Republican Congress to be "the most anti-Israel and the most anti-Jewish Congress we've had in a very long time precisely because of its willingness to knee-jerk to the demands of the right wing in Israel." The input of fundamentalist Christians infuriated many liberals, especially in light of a 1994 ADL report that accused the Christian Coalition of trying to erode the separation between church and state. Summing up the novel situation, one journalist noted that the most vocal debate seems not to be between the State of Israel and the Arabs but between the State of Israel and its [Jewish] friends" in Washington. They call for the "Israeli government to be more aggressive" on the issue of PLO compliance, oppose American troops on the Golan, and lobby for the American embassy in Jerusalem, making them "more Catholic than the pope on these issues."[50]

The lobbying battles in the Congress angered some lawmakers. Alcee Hastings (D–Fla.) protested that "Israeli political pressures are spilling over into the U.S. political agenda." He proclaimed himself to "be disgusted by the attempt by opposition parties in Israel to manipulate the sincere concerns of American Jews in order to further their political agenda." Senator Joseph Lieberman (D–

Conn.), an Orthodox Jew and a target of much of this cross-lobbying, complained that settlers "are investing vast sums in propaganda." AIPAC, whose
standing in Congress had eroded because of competing voices, shared these
sentiments. Sher, AIPAC's executive director, charged that it was problematic
"when there are efforts to lobby Congress against the duly elected government
of Israel." On a 1995 visit to Israel, AIPAC officials met with Netanyahu to
express their anger at Ben-Aharon, Ettinger, and Carmon's lobbying on behalf
of Likud. Even Hoenlein became alarmed that too much independent lobbying
would damage Israel's interests by placing Congress in the middle of "inter-
Jewish battles," noting that lawmakers "may just throw their hands up and say
'forget all of you clowns.' "[51]

While the frustration of these and other critics was palpable, the mainline
organizations could do little. The new lobbying dynamics reflected the fact that
the American Jewish community had become more pluralistic and polarized.
Despite the Jewish opinion polls that continued to reflect a strong support for
the peace process, the organized community could not prevail against the right-
wing opponents of Oslo. To begin with, the peculiarities of congressional politics put a premium on dedicated activism and it was here that the ZOA and
other nationalist and Orthodox groups had an advantage. As Goldberg put it, "it
was true that only one Jew in ten was opposed to the peace accord, but only
one Jew in four or five participated regularly in the affairs of the organized
community. And that one-fourth included most of the peace opponents." Rabbi
David Saperstein, director of Religious Action Center of Reform Judaism, subsequently acknowledged that peace supporters were too slow to respond, allowing "opponents to control the political discourse, even though they were a
minority."[52]

The organized community could also do little to dissuade right-wing Jews
from taking positions that were inimical to other Jews or the government of
Israel. When AIPAC or the Conference called to tow the official line, they
overlooked the fact that, in lobbying Congress, the ZOA, AFSI, and Orthodox
activists acted not as American Jews but rather as American taxpayers. For
instance, Rabbi Steven Pruzansky who led a delegation of 100 Orthodox rabbis
to lobby against aid to the Palestinians, stated that "as an American taxpayer I
demand a right and a voice in where money is distributed."[53]

What is more important, the outcry over the lobbying battles in Congress
overshadowed a more profound change in the relations between Israel and
American Jews. It was at this more basic level that the Oslo accord accelerated
the emergence of a new paradigm of Israeli-American Diaspora linkage.

FROM CRITICISM TO LIMITED SOVEREIGNTY: A NEW
PARADIGM OF ISRAEL-DIASPORA RELATIONS

The open discord over congressional lobbying had added a new twist to the
continuous debate about the limits of pressure that U.S. Jews could apply in
order to shape the peace process. Podhoretz, who during the Likud tenure in-

sisted on respect for the democratically elected government of Israel, reversed his position. He argued that, since the criticism from the right does not help the Arabs in the way that left-wing critique had done, it was incumbent upon him to warn about the dire consequences of Oslo. However, peace proponents accused Podhoretz and others conservatives of rank hypocrisy for turning against Labor after years of lambasting left-wing critics of Likud. More neutral observers noted that the latest spat was an inversion of an old cycle whereby the right and the left take turns protesting "the inherent indecency and impropriety" of criticizing the sitting government of Israel. Other analysts blamed the Israeli politicians who, with striking consistency, had demanded the support of American Jews when in power but, when in opposition, had turned to their U.S. friends to agitate against the duly elected government. A high-ranking Jewish official argued that the fiction of communal unity should be put to rest. He added that most Diaspora Jews now recognize "that it is counterproductive to parrot mindless support for every single policy promoted by Israeli governments."[54]

Interestingly enough, some senior Labor politicians welcomed this vigorous communal debate as a way to promote a new covenant between Israel and Diaspora Jewry. In their various appearances between Jewish audiences in the United States, they argued that the Oslo agreement should be used to phase out the old model based on charitable donations and political activism built around the Arab-Israeli conflict. Beilin, the intellectual architect of the new approach, asserted that the institutional structure of the Jewish community is antiquated and not representative of the rank and file. Describing a "significant number of the groups" in the Conference of Presidents as "little more than post-office boxes," he argued that professionals who collect substantial salaries run groups which reward large donors by simply rotating their presidency. Beilin complained that, in order to raise donations, Israel had been often presented as a backward and poor country, pointing out that the president of the Atlanta Jewish Federation once rode a camel during Israel's Independence Day celebration. Speaking before a gathering of Women's International Zionist Organization in December 1993, Beilin declared that the monies collected for Israel would be better spent to insure American Jewish continuity. Both Rabin and Peres pleaded with their U.S. Jewish audiences to stem the rate of assimilation and offered Israel's leadership to lead the fight.[55]

Avraham Burg, another Laborite and the incoming chairman of the Jewish Agency, unveiled a proposal to restructure the Agency along these lines. His seventy-four–page proposal "Brit Am—A Covenant of the People" lamented the high rate of intermarriage and the fact that three-fourths of American Jews had never visited Israel. Burg proposed to create a Jewish Peace Corps and other vehicles for enhancing Jewish identity. A Diaspora-Israel conference organized by the Israeli president Ezer Weitzman in June 1994 echoed similar themes. The two-day dialogue of some two hundred organizational and intellectual leaders focused on the ways in which the Jewish state could help the survival of world Jewry. Weitzman and other Israeli representatives used the occasion to call for Western immigration to Israel as the best way to assure Jewish continuity. The conference established a twelve-member committee to work out practical means to help Diaspora Jews to retain their identity; one such example was Beilin's proposal to provide young American Jews with free visits to Israel.[56]

While the Labor leaders were genuinely concerned about the state of the Diaspora, they also used their new model to fight the Oslo critics. The antipeace agitation reached a peak before the signing of the Oslo II agreement on September 28, 1995, which promised to transfer more of the territories to the Palestinians. During that summer the *Jewish Press*, a Brooklyn-based weekly with a mainly Orthodox readership, attacked Rabin in its editorials. On June 21, the newly created International Coalition for Israel, a group of Orthodox rabbis, announced that the peace process had violated Jewish law. Rabbi Hecht, president of the Rabbinical Alliance of America, publicly stated that Jewish leaders who gave away land deserved to die. Soon after, Rabbi Moshe Tendler from Yeshiva University issued a public opinion claiming supporters of the peace process violate Jewish law because they aid and abet Arabs who murdered Jews. In spite of a meeting between some rabbis and Israeli leaders in July, the tension remained high. On October 9, in an interview with *New York* magazine, Rabbi Hecht reiterated that, according to Jewish law, any person who "consciously hands property or wealth of the Jewish people to an alien people" is guilty of sin. Thus, "if a man kills him, he has done a good deed."[57]

Coming on top of the fight against aid to the Palestinians, such resistance to the peace process upset Rabin. He called some of the extremist rabbis "ayatollahs" and intensified his efforts to urge American Jews to stay out of Israeli politics. Following the White House Oslo II ceremony, Rabin lambasted the Jewish groups that "pressure Congress against the policies of the democratically elected government of Israel." Proclaiming such efforts "loathsome," Rabin implied that, with the exception of paying for immigration to Israel, Diaspora Jews should have no involvement in domestic Israeli matters. Peres was equally blunt when he said "I don't understand American Jews. They want to sit in Brooklyn and defend Hebron and Shechem [Nablus] from there." An Israeli consular official echoed the complaints in an article published in the Washington *Jewish Week*. Responding to the charge that the Labor government and its supporters had forsaken the land of Israel, he wrote that the people of Israel "have lived their lives in sacrifice for the sake of maintaining a Jewish state." He further pointed out that Jews who opted to live in the United States had actually abandoned the land. Commenting on these exchanges, one critic noted that the Jews of the Diaspora, or what he called the Jewish "foreign legion," are fighting the Middle East conflict "from the comfortable barracks in the posh residential areas" in the West.[58]

The efforts to limit the Diaspora input into Israeli domestic politics did not please many in the community. The group of Zionist women before whom Beilin argued against American charity reacted with anger. In a quick rebuttal,

the World Zionist Executive warned that the "greatest mistake Israel can make
is to separate Diaspora Jewry from the State of Israel and to callously stop the
contributions of Diaspora Jewry to the ingathering of exiles and building of the
State of Israel." The reaction to Weitzman's conference was even sharper. American Jewish leaders ridiculed Beilin's proposals and described the Israeli president as woefully ignorant of Jewish life outside Israel. Cardin, now the former
chair of the Presidents Conference, complained that American Jews are viewed
as "fodder for aliyah."[59]

However, the nationalist-Orthodox circles presented the greatest challenge to
Labor's maneuvers to limit Diaspora's foreign policy activism. Drawing on what
they saw as a clear divine mandate, these advocates argued that Israel is not
entitled to full sovereignty over the Land of Israel because the Land is under
Hashem's sovereignty (God's sovereignty). As a result, the "Land is held in
perpetuity as a covenant between G-d and Abraham and cannot be traded from
some temporary false peace. Eretz Yisrael belongs to the whole of Am Yisrael
(People of Israel for all eternity)." Rabbi Shneerson was among those who asserted that the "[Israeli] Prime Minister has no right to give away the land of
Israel because it does not belong to him." These and other critics also complained that Rabin, like many Israeli leaders, were insensitive to the "spiritual
dimension of our heritage." Ambassador Rabinovitch noted that "from this novel
perspective, the government of Israel was no longer seen as a sovereign, un-
challenged decision maker. The Land of Israel and Jerusalem were seen as the
sacred property of the Jewish people, temporarily managed by the government
of Israel."[60]

Although not well-understood at the time, the limited sovereignty doctrine
was a radical departure from the Ben-Gurion–Blaustein agreement, which, as
noted, sought to stop Israel and the American Diaspora from mutual interference.
Equally important, the peace opponents used limited sovereignty to justify their
efforts to shape the broader political culture in Israel. Right-wing critics pointed
out that Labor and its ally, the Meretz party, were in the forefront of post-
Zionism, an ideological movement that, in their view, wanted to "normalize"
Israel by undermining its Jewish character. Alexander contended that the Israeli
left built up a "terrific energy of resentment" against religious Jews and "Zionism itself." He added that the "people who rule the new Israel, culturally as
well as politically, are Hebrew speaking Gentiles." Isaac called Peres a "post-
Zionist par excellence," who discarded "any notion of Israel as a state whose
mission is to fulfill a Jewish nationalist and religious identity." Irving Kett denounced Amos Oz and other Israeli intellectuals who called nationalism a
"curse," and explained that the cosmopolitan Jews who control Israel "prefer
the strengthening of the Arab position in Israel" as a "counterweight to the
religious Zionist position." Others bemoaned the fact that Rabin and Peres turned
Israel into a secular dictatorship that harassed the *haredim* and the settlers. As
Rabbi Mordechai Friedman, head of the Orthodox American Board of Rabbis,

declared, "the Israeli Army has been transformed into the ultra-radical left-wing Rabin/Peres militia."[61]

Given the belief system of the nationalist-religious segments of the community, the vision of Israel as the guardian of sacred Jewish values was highly logical. However, such a vision was an anathema to the secularized majority which, as already noted, preferred to see Israel as an embodiment of Western, liberal, and democratic virtues. It was thus inevitable that these contrasting images of Israel would become intertwined in the ongoing debate on Jewish identity in America.

FAR AND AWAY: ISRAEL, JEWISH IDENTITY, AND THE CONTINUITY IMPERATIVE

The bitter polarization brought on by the peace process, coupled with the decline in threats to Israel's security, had accelerated the debate about the attenuation of Jewish identity. Sociologists, social psychologists, and other experts who analyzed the 1990 Jewish population survey in depth argued that the community should develop new and more transferable forms of Jewish identity. Fleshing out this newly minted continuity imperative had preoccupied a number of Jewish organizations, leading one observer to suggest that "Jewish continuity has become the biggest growth industry in the Jewish community." The much-awaited 1994 report of the North American Commission on Jewish Identity and Continuity, an eighty-eight–strong body of experts created by the CJF, listed a number of "formative" and "transformative" Jewish experiences. The Wilstein Institute of Jewish Policy Studies released a book of essays on the subject and the Center for Modern Jewish Studies at Brandeis University issued a report on the organizational underpinnings of Jewish identity. Although these and numerous other writings failed to produce a clear consensus on the ways to reverse the attenuation of Jewish identity in America, some trends had emerged.[62]

By far, the most popular remedy suggested was Jewish education. In the 1994 Wilstein Institute study "The Power of Jewish Education," Seymour Martin Lipset demonstrated a correlation between Jewish schooling and Jewishness. Subsequent community efforts had mounted a major effort to enhance Jewish literacy for both children and adults. Another often-proffered solution was a revival of religious commitment, spurred by a National Council of Synagogue Youth survey that showed that only 2 percent of Orthodox Jews intermarry. Conservative critics of what Jack Wertheimer termed "Judaism without limits" argued that American Jews had diluted their core identity by experimenting with New Age religions or by embracing "ferocious secular liberalism." As Elliott Abrams put it, "many American Jews confuse the Democratic Party Platform with the Law of Moses." Another conservative commentator charged that American Jews had grown comfortable with a religion that "entails no restrictive personal requirements, does not interfere with their social lives. . . ." Writing in a *Commentary* symposium on the beliefs of American Jews, Michael Medved went even further. He argued that the "sum total of their [American Jews] commitment, the beginning and end of their ideological identity as adherents of what is still misleading described as the Jewish faith" is the rejection of Jesus as the Messiah. The leading sociologist Calvin Goldscheider concurred, adding that "they're Jewish because they're not Christians." Even such moderates as Eric H. Yoffie who succeeded Schindler as the head of the Reform movement, warned that without return to religion the community will not survive. He complained that "continuity" and "identity" are empty slogans without a straightforward call "for religious commitment and for an embrace of Torah and mitzvot."[63]

Not surprisingly, the role envisaged for Israel in the Jewish continuity imperative was quite modest. In his eighty-six–page study entitled *What Will Bind Us Now? A Report on the Institutional Ties between Israel and American Jewry*, Samuel Norich, the director of YIVO, detailed the declining relations between the American Diaspora and Israel. Bayme, a leading expert on the subject, allowed that there had been "too much confidence placed in the Israeli experience at the centerpiece of the Jewish continuity agenda." Others were more blunt. Harry Wall, the Israeli representative of the ADL, proclaimed that "the country is no longer going to be the Disneyland of Jewish delights that serves a rallying point for American Jews." He and other observers explained that Israel, more Westernized and prosperous, ceased to be less exotic and, thus, less attractive to American Jews.[64]

However, many of the analysts blamed the raucous political and religious divisions in Israel and the United States for the alienation. Isi J. Leibler, the chairman of the governing board of the World Jewish Congress, wrote that the polarization and divisiveness, including wholesale name calling, eroded the spirit of *ahavat yisrael* ("brotherhood of Israel") and frightened American Jews. Leibler, who was also a critic of what he called the "extreme secularism" of the "Hebrew speaking Canaanites," described as "naïve" the urge to rely on Israel as a "panacea for all the Diaspora's ill." Elazar blamed the Israeli "militant secularists" and their drive to "become normal like everybody else" for an attempted "radical de-Judaization of the Jewish people." Hillel Halkin declared that the Oslo accord would most likely put an end to "Ahad Ha'Amism," his term for the "Zionist triumphalism" that underpinned the Israeli-centered Jewish identity after the Six Day War. The noted commentator pointed out that, out of the forty-eight contributors to the *Commentary* symposium on Jewish identity, about half either did not mention Israel or mentioned it in a very casual way. Another analyst painted a bleak picture of the Israeli-Diaspora relations under the provocative title "American Zionism in Extremis."[65]

Empirical evidence seemed to support some of the observations. In the 1993 survey of the AJC, 79 percent of the respondents said that caring for Israel was a very important part of their Jewishness. Sixty-eight percent agreed with the statement that the destruction of Israel would amount to one of their greatest tragedies. In a 1993 survey of attitudes toward the peace process, 27 percent reported feeling very close to Israel, followed by 48 percent of those who felt fairly close. Still, 69 percent declined to describe themselves as Zionists, and 67 percent reported that they had never visited Israel. In a similar 1994 survey the percentage of those who felt very close and fairly close was 25 and 41 respectively; 74 refused to define themselves as Zionists and only 35 percent visited Israel.[66]

Attachment to Israel was probed in the August 1995 AJC survey where a large majority of respondents reported feeling either very close (26 percent) or fairly close (43 percent) to the Jewish state. In addition, 78 percent agreed that caring about Israel is a very important part of being Jewish; 67 percent of the sample reported that the destruction of Israel would have translated into a major personal tragedy. These numbers did not match the behavioral profile of the sample since 63 percent had never visited Israel and a large percentage lacked basic knowledge about Israel. When asked whether Peres and Netanyahu belong to the same party, 7 percent answered in the affirmative, and 53 percent were not sure; only forty answered correctly. Almost 50 percent did not know that Israel declared independence in 1948, and 64 percent did not know that the West Bank came under Israeli control in 1967. These figures confirmed the long-standing discrepancy between attitudinal and behavioral factors, which, as already noted, led Steven Cohen to speculate about socially desirable responses to the items that probed relations to Israel.[67]

The 1995 survey had also demonstrated that, as in the past, both attitudinal and behavioral manifestations of closeness to Israel were not equally distributed across the sample. In the younger cohorts (age thirty-nine and below) only 22 percent felt very close to Israel, compared to 22 percent in the middle age cohort (between the ages of forty and fifty-nine) and 37 percent in the older group (sixty years and older). In the younger group, 38 percent felt either fairly or very distant from Israel, compared to 31 in the middle range group and only 14 in the older cohort. Religious affiliation was even more of an important predictor of attitudes toward Israel. Seventy-two percent of Orthodox respondents felt very close to Israel, as compared to 32 percent of Conservatives, 17 percent of Reform, and 15 of "just Jewish." The Orthodox had also scored the highest on the behavioral indices, with 76 percent visiting Israel (59 percent more than once), and 72 knowing that Peres and Netanyahu do not belong to the same party. Only 24 percent of "just Jewish," unaffiliated respondents visited Israel and only 32 percent knew the political difference between Peres and Netanyahu.[68]

Related research indicated that knowledge about Israeli culture was modest at best. In spite of decades of efforts to popularize Hebrew, most American Jews did not master the language. U.S. Jews were equally unimpressed by Israeli literature, even when translated into English. One analyst noted that Israeli literature failed "to become part of the intellectual discourse and cultural repertoire of the American Jewish community," adding that in Europe and even in Germany, where there were few Jews, Israeli writers were more widely read. A report on Israel education in Jewish schools, commissioned by the AJC found

that, although the majority of school principals were verbally supportive of Is-
rael, there was a great deal of confusion, ambivalence, and lack of interest.
Michele Alperin, the author of the study, noted that schools moved from the
Israel-centered curriculum because of the Intifada, increased distance from the
Holocaust, and the establishment of the state of Israel and Israel's disdain of
liberal Judaism.[69]

Responding to such findings, some community leaders urged to develop novel
efforts to rekindle a passion for Israel among the younger and unaffiliated cohorts. Borrowing some themes from the Beilin and Burg reform agenda, Charles
Bronfman and other Jewish philanthropists called for programs that would send
young American Jews to Israel for a short visit. Bronfman declared that the
"Israel experience holds great promise for heightening awareness, strengthening
identity and making a significant contribution to contemporary Jewish life, education and Jewish community." Bronfman's proposals, which eventually led to
the Birthright Israel program, were taken up by the 1994 General Assembly of
the CJF, where Rabin famously challenged the participants to "Let My People
Be Jewish." The Jewish philanthropists and other advocates were able to point
out that the more limited Israel Experience program had served Jewish youth
from the United States by immersing them in kibbutz life and other "authentic"
Israeli venues.[70]

Critics doubted that a short visit to Israel could strengthen Jewish identity or
heal the frayed relations between the two communities. One observer stated that
for the "vast majority of American Jews Israel is a Jewish theme park. They
visit Israel like they visit Disney World." Another one used the Disneyland
analogy to caution that Israeli experience is a "great time in a theme park, but
nothing that touches one's core." Many in the Jewish continuity movement argued that that the casual model of Israel Experience should be reversed to account for findings that indicated that it was a strong Jewish identity that had
lead the younger people to sign up for the program in the first place. After
analyzing the AJC polls, Raab concluded that the majority of Jewish youth had
difficulty incorporating Israel into their generally weakening identity, except in
"defensive terms." Moreover, this defensive motive needed "stronger reinforce-
ment, such as independent [of Israel] search for identity and community." Raab
speculated that, whatever "tribal sense develops" around the Israeli endeavor,
has mostly to do with the bonds that American Jews form among themselves
while working for Israel. Indeed, according to research he quoted, one-half of
all federation members said that they felt very close to other American Jews,
but only one-third felt very close to Israelis.[71]

A study designed to find why there was little enthusiasm for Israel Experience
trips in the New York area indicated that attitudes ranged from apathy to antipathy. Moreover, many of the young respondents did not see Israel as a critical
factor in forging their Jewish identity. The only rigorous study of American
Jewish participants in Israel immersion programs found some correlation between a visit to Israel and an enhanced Jewish identity. However, Mittelberg,

the author of the study, cautioned that the linkage is by no means simple, as it reflected additional factors like self-selection and other life experiences. In his words, the critical factor is "who goes to Israel or what happens there." Mittelberg's finding that Jewish identity depended on what "happens there" went to the heart of problem.[72]

As already noted, the community was deeply divided as to what Israel should become and the direction in which it should proceed. The assassination of Rabin on November 4, 1995, had only deepened these differences. While immediately after the killing there was a show of unity, the spirit of common bereavement barely concealed the bitterness of the peace camp against Rabin nationalist-Orthodox opponents in the United States and Israel. To liberals like Lerner, the assassination was the beginning of a "civil war" over the soul of Israel. For his part, Lerner proclaimed himself equally repulsed by the crass Westernization and materialism of the secular Israel and hypernationalism of what he termed "settler Judaism." He also castigated American Jews who supported this nationalist Israel, calling them "super-militant Zionists-in-absentia."[73]

Going on the defensive, most of the Oslo opponents denounced the murder in the strongest possible terms, but there was a reluctance to give up the idea of Greater Israel or bless the peace process. When consul Collette Avital proposed to organize a memorial service for the slain prime minister, the project was almost derailed because some nationalist and religious groups expressed reservation about what they viewed as too much emphasis on peace. When the organizers refused to give opposition spokesmen an official part at the rally, the ZOA and the National Council of Young Israel took out an ad in the *New York Times* emphasizing the partisan nature of the event. At the insistence of propeace activists at the Conference of Presidents, twelve former chairpersons of the organization sent a letter to the two dissenting organizations calling their ad "unacceptable" and "censurable." The letter added that, while "it is your right to have sought to change the program or opt not to participate . . . you sought to undermine this communal endeavor."[74]

In claiming to represent the community, the Presidents Conference had the opinion polls behind it. The January 1996 AJC survey indicated that 79 percent supported the Labor government handling of the peace process, an 11 percent rise from October 1995. There was also a majority for continuing U.S. aid to the Palestinians and, for the first time since 1993, the opposition to Oslo within the Orthodox community had declined from 64 percent to 56 percent. Still, as in all previous polls, the older cohorts, the nationalists, and the Orthodox were the most skeptical of the peace process.[75] This segment, highly vocal and dedicated to the vision of Israel as a guardian of the land of Israel was ready to play a major role in reversing the Oslo process by helping the Likud party to regain power in Israel.

7

Lurching to the Right: Responding to Netanyahu's Vision of the Peace Process

Slightly more than three years after the Oslo agreement, a victory of Likud changed once again the Middle East politics. In what became a noticeable lurch to the right, the community was asked to support the peace plans of the Likud government, putting it at odds with the foreign policy vision of the Clinton administration. To escape the problems of cognitive dissonance and preserve the Oslo achievements, the peace camp had encouraged the administration's pressure on the Israeli government, a move that was bitterly contested by the nationalist-religious segments. As each side sought to prevail, the peace process, and, by extension, the vision for Israel's future as a Jewish state, had emerged as the most divisive issue among American Jews.

TRIMMING THE SAILS OF THE PEACE PROCESS: NETANAYAHU AND AMERICAN JEWS

The Israel elections of May 29, 1996, gave a slim edge to Likud's Benjamin Netanyahu over his Labor opponent, Shimon Peres. The election of Netanyahu, a vigorous critic of the Oslo accord, was met with mixed feelings among the U.S. Diaspora. The nationalists and Orthodox Jews felt elated and vindicated. Morton Klein declared that Likud's 9 percent point margin among Jewish voters proved that the ZOA was "representative of the Jewish mainstream all along." An editorial in AFSI's *Outpost* described the result as a fulfillment of on "ardent hope." Bernard Shapiro from the Freeman Center for Strategic Studies titled his editorial "Victory at Last—Israel Saved."[1]

The right-wing camp was doubly pleased because it was instrumental in Netanyahu's victory. According to reports, Netanyahu had a large network of American friends, some dating to his childhood, in a suburb of Philadelphia. One of them, Stephen Friedman, went on to become Likud's official attorney and fund-raiser in the United States. Friedman was credited with helping Netanyahu during his tenure as Israel's ambassador to the UN to establish a network of donors who contributed to his primary and election victories. Among them were a number of wealthy Jews, including Ronald Lauder; Irving Moskowitz; Rose Mattus; Marc Belzberg; a Canadian-born corporate investor, Mervyn Adelson; chairman of Lorimar-Telepictures; Joseph Mermelstein, a New York businessmen; Joseph Gutnick, an Australian mining magnate and an emissary of the Lubavitcher movement; Steve Wynn, the chairman of the Mirage Resorts in Las Vegas; Murad Zamir, a New York diamond dealer; Jay Zises; Henry Kravits; and Marvin Josepheson. Although a 1994 law banned Israeli political parties from receiving direct donations; the American contributors were allegedly able to evade the prohibition by using charitable and nonprofit organizations. For instance, the Shalem Center, a right-wing think tank sponsored by the Ronald S. Lauder Foundation and led by the philosopher Yoram Hazony, was apparently linked to Netanayahu's campaign. Three Likud charities supported by Lauder and others contributors—Israel Development Fund, Education Fund for Israel, and Youth Towns of Israel—were also implicated in the 1996 election. The same reports linked Lauder to the political consultant Arthur Finkelstein, who created many of the commercials that questioned the credibility of Peres and the peace camp. Itzhak Fisher, Netanyahu's treasurer, had subsequently became Lauder's business partner and an investigation into Netanyahu's finances alleged that Lauder helped him buy an apartment in Jerusalem.[2]

Nationalist activists explained that they had felt compelled to intervene in the Israeli elections in order to undo the Oslo damage. Dov Hinkin, the New York assemblyman, described how he used the methods developed in Brooklyn's elections to consolidate the Orthodox support in Israel behind Netanyahu. Gutnick insisted that Oslo's main achievement was to "legitimize a terrorist organization responsible for killing more Jews than anyone since Stalin and Hitler." Shapiro asserted that he and others were privileged to participate in the battle for Eretz Yisrael against the "forces of darkness who wished to dismember their country in the name of pseudo-peace." For its part, the new Likud government reciprocated by lifting the ban on Rabbi Abraham Hecht and others who were involved in the anti-Rabin incitement.[3]

The right's hope of undermining the Oslo agreement dismayed the leftist peace advocates who were reeling from the unexpected defeat of Peres. The most dovish elements in this group agreed with the call of the journalist Walter Ruby that American Jews should immediately state "openly and forcefully" that they cannot support the new prime minister's stand on the peace process. The APN took a wait-and-see attitude, but warned the Netanyahu government that it would consider any expansion of settlements to be a breach of the spirit of Oslo. Most of the mainstream organizations tried to minimize the concerns that a right-wing government would derail the peace process. The AJC noted that Netanyahu's "desire for peace is surely as passionate as that of Mr. Peres," and Abraham Foxman from the ADL explained that Netanyahu's pursuit of peace is "local lane," as opposed to Labor's "express lane." Speaking on behalf of the consensus seeking Conference of Presidents, Malcolm Hoenlein declared that "the American Jewish majority doesn't identify with Labor and or Likud but with the State of Israel."[4]

In his first visit to the United States in July Netanyahu reassured American Jewry that Israel was committed to the peace process, but promised to be a tough negotiator who would hold the Palestinians accountable to the Oslo accord. This pleased the ZOA's Klein who expressed satisfaction that "Arafat's violation of the peace accords" would become "a central theme for achieving a real and durable peace." However, David Harris, the executive director of the AJC, worried that the new prime minister, whom he described as a "work in progress" might not command the necessary support of American Jews in time of crisis.

An opinion poll released by the IPF during Netanyahu's visit revealed that 81 percent of American Jews supported the Rabin-Peres approach and 95 percent felt that its continuation was important for the United States. Although 59 percent of the respondents said they would have voted for Labor, 62 percent had a favorable view of Netanyahu. Sixty-four percent felt that he was sincerely committed to the peace process, and 85 percent thought that the process would continue, albeit at a slower pace. In view of the executive vice-president of the IPF, the poll showed that Netanyahu was perceived as a moderate.[5]

Such expectations suffered a blow when, in September, Netanyahu's government authorized the opening of an entrance to the Hasmonean tunnel in East Jerusalem. The work on the archeological tunnel was part of a larger project of Irving Moskowitz, Belzberg, and other contributors to American Friends of Ateret Cohanim which, through its subsidiary, the Jerusalem Reclamation Project, sought to acquire properties in the Moslem Quarter. Moskowitz had also used his American Friends of Everest Foundation to settle Jews in the Quarter. According to reports, the decision to open the tunnel was a political payoff to Moskowitz, Belzberg, and other right-wing American supporters of Netanyahu. During the secret opening ceremony, donors from Jerusalem Reclamation Project, Ateret Cohanim, and two additional foundations created with the help of Moskowitz—Society for the Development of East Jerusalem and the Fund of the Heritage of the Wall—were present.[6]

The tunnel touched off a wave of Palestinian protest in which scores of Palestinians and fourteen Jews were killed. In reacting to the violence, the American Jewish community split along predictable lines. The most dovish groups blamed Netanayahu for the provocation and urged his governments to take the lead in reducing tensions. Following the disclosures of the *Miami Herald* and the Israeli press about the alleged political payoff, peace activists also pointed the finger at Moskowitz and others in Netanyahu's "millionaire club." Most of the mainstream organizations questioned the wisdom of the Israeli decision, but accused the Palestinians of a disproportionate reaction. For the nationalist groups, the firing on Israelis by armed Palestinians proved that the Oslo accord was not working. The ZOA took the lead in criticizing the Likud government for insufficient zeal. During an October ZOA fund-raiser, the Israeli ambassador to Washington, Eliahu Ben-Elissar was heckled for asserting that under the territorial concession of the Oslo accord "not everything can be saved."[7]

With the stage set for a new round of negotiations over the Israeli withdrawal from Hebron, a step strongly urged by the United States, a new test of the Netanyahu government's peace intention was offered. When, in mid-December, the Israeli cabinet decided to build more homes in the West Bank, Bill Clinton, fresh from his resounding victory in the November election, publicly criticized the move during a December 16 press conference. Though uneasy about Clinton's public stance, most of the mainstream organizations such as the AJC, the ADL, AIPAC, and the Conference, refrained from criticizing the president. The peace advocates, who had become convinced that Netanyahu was sabotaging Oslo, praised Clinton for his comments. Still, when the Hebron accord was signed in mid-January 1997, the mainstream community was eager to point out that Netanyahu's strategy of slowing down the process did not kill Oslo. Martin Raffel, associate vice-chairman of the NJCRAC, expressed hope that the Hebron accord would "alleviate concern by some that this Israeli government's approach to the peace process would lead to deadlock." An IPF poll found that 64 percent of American Jews supported the Hebron deal and 80 percent approved of the administration's role in securing the agreement.[8]

What pleased the moderates had upset the hard-line nationalists, who castigated Netanyahu for abandoning Hebron. A group of activists protested outside the Israeli consulate in New York demanding that the Likud government reveal "its true self." The Freeman Center published an article that asked, "how does a government, elected on a platform guaranteeing continued Jewish development in Hebron, literally strangle the existing Jewish community?" In the end though, the nationalists went along with Netanayhu's decision and Gutnick even facilitated the deal by donating a large amount of money to refurbish houses in the 20 percent of Hebron allocated to Jewish settlers.[9]

The Hebron agreement offered but a short respite from the tensions surrounding the peace process. In early March 1997, the Israeli government unveiled a plan to build a Jewish neighborhood in Har Homa in southeastern Jerusalem, which provoked Palestinian protest and a UN rebuke. Clinton, though not explicitly condemning the plan, made it clear that the United States did not welcome the new Jewish construction. Touching on the sensitive issue of Jerusalem, Har Homa undermined whatever little consensus over Netanyahu's policies that the community had managed to preserve. The Conference of Presidents declared that all of its fifty-three members backed Israel's right to build in Jerusalem, but did not mention the Har Homa project by name. Hoenlein also praised the U.S. decision to veto the UN resolution that would have condemned Israel, but the dovish members of the Conference publicly criticized Hoenlein's proclamation.

The issue of Jerusalem provoked another bitter communal debate. On December 21, 1996, the *New York Times* ran a full-page advertisement by Churches for Middle East Peace that called for Jews and Palestinians to share Jerusalem. The ad was part of a broader campaign by the liberal National Council of Churches to influence Congress, the U.S. government, and public opinion. Most of the mainstream American Jewish organizations denounced the advertisement and sent letters of protest, but the APN and the JPL, which in the past had urged to consider the idea of a shared capital, was supportive. A *Tikkun*-sponsored roundtable declared that the Palestinians were not given the "same power and voice in shaping a solution to Jerusalem," adding that Jerusalem is a symbolic center of all cultures and should be a city with shared sovereignty. Right-wing spokesmen like Daniel Pipes asserted that Jerusalem had little spiritual meaning to the Moslems and the Palestinians. Others were even more scathing in their assessment of the situation. Manfred Lehmann stated that the ad was an anti-Semitic ploy to take Jerusalem away from the Jews. The co-founder of the World Committee for Israel expressed confidence that "the current controversy helps finally to ferret out the people who for years pretended to be Zionists and shared the Israeli government's faith in a united Jerusalem under undivided Jewish rule."[10]

Equally controversial was the ongoing debate about U.S. aid to the Palestinians. With the MEPFA due to expire in August 1997, right-wing and religious groups were pushing hard to cut off funding to the PA. They reiterated that, unlike Israel, the PA had not upheld its commitment to Oslo, and they pointed to the fact that the overall level of terror had actually increased since 1993. A number of suicide bombings carried out by the Islamic terrorist organization Hamas that killed and injured a large number of Israeli civilians dramatized this argument. Helping the ZOA and others to keep count of the infringements was the newly established Media Analysis Center. A unit in the prime minister's office under Netanyahu's chief media adviser David Bar-Ilan, the center published periodical reports of PA violations of the Oslo agreements. Itamar Marcus, the director of the privately funded Palestinian Media Watch, had also provided meticulously researched papers on anti-Israeli incitement in PA's media and school textbooks.[11]

Closer to home, the nationalists could point to the fact that the *Near East Report*, an AIPAC newsletter, published a two-page critique of Palestinian violations. A ZOA press release of June 24, 1997 noted that "the world must know the truth about Arafat's pro-terrorist behavior and praised AIPAC and the Israeli government for adding their voice to "this crucial issue." Nevertheless, peace advocates like Michael Lerner pointed out that the United States and Israel hampered Yasser Arafat in his fight against Hamas terror by holding him accountable to "normal standards of civil liberties." Due to such deep divisions, the Presidents Conference decided not to vote on the aid issue.[12]

With the rancor between the left and right running high, the Conference had faced difficulties in imposing its civility code on the communal discourse. In one widely publicized case, Klein criticized the ADL's plan to invite the journalist Thomas Friedman to address its December 1996 annual dinner. Klein, who cited a number of statements of Friedman that he viewed as anti-Israeli, called for public protest should the ADL refuse to cancel the speech. Gaffney's Center for Security Policy backed Klein, expressing outrage at the "prospect of a persistent defamer of Israel being honored by the Anti-Defamation League." Netanyahu's communication director Bar-Ilan joined the fray by asserting that Zionist organizations should not give a platform to Friedman. Besieged by protesters, ADL's Foxman accused Klein of being the "attack dog of the thought police" and of lowering the discourse "to a new level of personal intolerance." Foxman wanted the community to ostracize Klein, but after the ZOA appealed to the Conference of Presidents on the ground that Foxman violated its 1995 civility rules, the ADL chief was forced to apologize. A special committee of the Conference issued a statement expressing regrets that the incident hurt the community, but the continuous turmoil over the peace process made it clear that the Conference's ruling was largely ignored.[13]

Using the round of celebrations of the 40th anniversary of the Conference in September 1996, critics from the left and the right of the political spectrum harshly attacked the organization for being unrepresentative of the community. Mimicking the left-wing critique, the right-wing activist Rabbi Avi Weiss complained that the Conference did not represent the "will of the people" and was timid to the point of refraining from controversial debates and decisions. Weiss also decried the secretive and nondemocratic election process of the Conference. Referring to the glittering anniversary gala in New York, Weiss urged the community to stand up and declare that "the Emperor Has No Clothes."[14] Similar sentiments were expressed by APN, which sent a letter to the Conference urging it to reflect Jewish popular opinion on the peace process.

In an effort to address such demands, the Conference in July 1997 picked Melvin Salberg, a prominent attorney and a former chairman of the ADL, over the right-leaning Lauder to head the organization. Some observers, including Foxman, welcomed Salberg's election, calling it a "victory for moderation at the time for polarization." Salberg was praised for his efforts to reform the decision-making process, introduce accountability to members, and improve the general atmosphere. However, even these goodwill measures could not restore civility to the intensely bitter communal discourse. When the Smithsonian Museum announced plans for a series of lectures on Israel's fiftieth anniversary, which were cosponsored by the NIF, the nationalists attacked the plan. AFSI, which was particularly incensed by a proposed lecture, "Jerusalem: To Unify a Divided City," declared that the Smithsonian had been duped by the "far-left." AFSI leaders compared the NIF-inspired lecturers to Louis Farrakhan and David Duke. The ZOA and other right-wing groups prevailed upon Representative Michael Forbes (R–N.Y.), a member of the House Appropriations Committee, to pressure the museum to cancel the show. When the Smithsonian director backed down, Anthony Lewis from the *New York Times* accused the right of "Jewish McCarthyism." Charges of censures were also made when the editor of the Wisconsin *Jewish Chronicle*, a Jewish federation-sponsored paper, was allegedly pressed to resign after criticizing Netanyahu.[15]

THE ROAD TO WYE: ENCOURAGING CLINTON TO PRESSURE ISRAEL

The diplomatic language of the exchanges between Israel and the United States could not conceal the growing tension in the relations between the two countries. When Netanyahu arrived in the United States in April 1997, the president challenged the Israeli prime minister to speed up the peace process. Clinton also refused to recant his opposition to the Har Homa project. Alarmed in July by another suicide bombing that killed fifteen people in Jerusalem, the administration became convinced that, without a significant American push, the peace process would dissipate amid mistrust and violence. On August 6, Secretary of State Madeleine Albright announced a new initiative that challenged both sides to speed up the peace process by merging interim agreement arrangements with final solution status talks. Most Jewish leaders welcomed Albright's condemnation of Palestinian terror. Yet the peace camp was especially encouraged by the fact that the speech opposed "unilateral acts" by either side, a clear reference to Har Homa and other settlements and to the demand that Israel make further withdrawals from the West Bank. In an ad in the *New York Times* on August 10, the IPF (recently merged with Nishma) thanked Albright for her initiative.

On her visit to Israel on September 10 and 11, following another suicide bomb in Jerusalem, the secretary of state extracted a pledge from Arafat to curtail terrorism. She also warned Netanyahu's government to abstain from "provocative steps." When in mid-September Israel announced plans to construct three hundred new units in Efrat and reinstated subsidies to settlers, which were halted by the Labor government, Albright openly condemned the step and called for a "time out" in the territories. Even to the most disinterested observers these high-handed tactics signaled that Clinton, a president with a proven pro-Israel record, was ready to repeat Bush's act of pressuring Shamir.

In embarking on this new strategy, the administration benefited from the division in the community. Likud's settlement policy mobilized the proponents of Oslo, with APN, the IPF, and other peace activists accusing Netanyahu of sabotaging the peace process. During a heated debate at the annual conference of NJCRAC in February 1997, the delegates adopted a resolution in support of the peace process and urged the Netanyahu government to show "maximum restraint" on settlements. Among others, NJCRAC called to end subsidies to settlers, freeze the growth of the extant settlements, and impose a ban on new constructions. However, the construction in Har Homa and Efrat pleased the nationalists and religious circles that helped to elect Netanyahu. Chaim S. Kaminetzky, the President of National Council of Young Israel, praised the prime minister for his resolve in Efrat and urged him to settle the territories. Hoenlein acknowledged the obvious when he stated that "there's no consensus on settlements" and that the differences "were long-held" and broken down along "traditional lines."[16]

The community was equally spilt over the proper response to Clinton's resolve to push Israel along the Oslo path. As expected, right-wing groups appealed to the Conference to speak out against the pressure tactics used by Clinton and Albright. Right-wing activists also vented anger at Martin Indyk, the assistant secretary of state for Near East and the former American ambassador to Israel, whom they viewed as all too eager to enforce the American policy of twisting Netanyahu's arm. The ZOA criticized Indyk's "insulting, demeaning, and patronizing statements about Israel," and the Center for Security Policy accused him of a "contemptuous attitude toward Israel." But APN, which described Indyk as a devoted "public servant," and IPF/Nishma praised him and the president for what one APN official described as his concern for Israel's best interest.[17]

In fact the peace camp asked its members to urge Clinton to pressure the Netanyahu government. Some Clinton Democratic donors, including S. Daniel Abraham from the Center for the Middle East and Economic Cooperation, had worked behind the scenes to impress on the White House that an urgent action was needed to salvage the peace process. Prior to Albright's September visit to the Middle East, forty American Jewish leaders urged her in a letter to press the Likud government for concession. In addition to Theodore Mann, the signatories included Alexander Schindler and Eric Yoffie from the Reform movement and the Conservative leader Ismar Schorsch. These and other advocates pointed out that the majority of American Jews would support a more activist policy by the administration. Based on political soundings taken during the summer and fall, the administration concluded that the community would tolerate increased pressures on the Israeli government, "as long as it would be perceived as reasonable and equal and greater pressure would be applied on the Palestinians."[18]

The AJC's American Jewish Population Survey of February 1997 showed a high level of support for the Hebron agreement (59 percent versus 24 percent). There was also a fair amount of optimism with regard to the peace process: compared to the previous year, some 58 percent reported the same level of optimism, 17 percent felt more optimistic, and 23 percent were less optimistic. In the wake of the Hebron accord, Netanyahu's handling of the peace process was evaluated positively by 61 percent and negatively by 24 percent. Some 14 percent said that Arafat's support for the peace process was strong and 48 percent felt that it was somewhat strong. Still, the Labor party received a positive rating from 60 percent of the sample, compared to 41 percent for the Likud. In spite of the White House criticism of the Israeli government, 23 and 67 percent of the respondents respectively felt that the relations between Israel and the

United States were very positive or somewhat positive. An IPF poll taken at the end of September 1997 found that 57 percent of American Jews had a favorable view of Netanyahu and 84 percent had a negative view of Arafat. Still, a vast majority wanted the United States to continue with the peace process; 84 percent agreed that the United States should "apply pressure" on both leaders, and 89 percent thought that the United States "must be even-handed when facilitating negotiations." In addition, 85 percent of the sample supported Albright's demands that Arafat crack down on terrorism and Netanyahu impose a moratorium on settlements.[19]

The IPF findings served as a background to a meeting, convened on October 6 in the White House, which featured the visiting Israeli president Ezer Weitzman and a group of American Jewish leaders. The guests included representatives from mainstream organizations, but there were also some prominent peace activists like Daniel Abraham, IPF's Jack Bendheim, and Sara Ehrman from the APN. According to reports, the Jewish leaders encouraged Clinton to be more forceful with Netanayahu and assured him that the community would not be adverse to such a move. Noting that the Conference's Salberg came out in favor of pressing both Arafat and Netanyahu to "restore the peace process," some observers called the White House gathering a "watershed" in the history of relations between American Jews and Israel. As Jonathan Broder put it, never before had the "community's top leadership given a president the green light to pressure Israel." Indeed, Clinton felt so sure of the American Jewish support that he took the unprecedented step of refusing to meet with Netanyahu during his November visit to the United States. The decision raised only minor objections at the time. Thomas Friedman wrote that "the White House knows there's a new mood out there among American Jews," many of whom felt that the Israeli leaders have "more in common with Larry, Moe and Curly than with David Ben-Gurion, Menachem Begin and Yitzhak Rabin." [20]

Observers noted that Netanyahu's perceived personal shortcomings played a part in the disenchantment of American Jews. The Israeli leader was accused of arrogance, of failing to consult with the organized community, and of presiding over a number of blunders like the tunnel incident, the Har Homa project, and the failed attempt to assassinate a Hamas leader in Jordan. The close association between Netanyahu and some of his right-wing donors had also alarmed the Jewish mainstream. In December 1996, CBS's "60 Minutes" ran an exposé on Moskowitz and his efforts to further Jewish settlements in the Moslem Quarter and in the West Bank. Jewish peace activists called for a probe of Moskowitz's dealings, emphasizing that most of his donations came from the Bingo Club in Hawaiian Gardens, an impoverished Latino community in California. Rabbi Gerald Serotta, one of the organizers of the anti-Moskowitz group Coalition for Justice in Hawaiian Gardens and Jerusalem, pointed out that most of the money from the bingo operation went overseas "to do damage to the Jewish people and the future of Israel." The Central Conference of American Rabbi (CCAR), the organizational arm of the Reform movement, issued a scathing condemnation of the use of gambling money to fund "activities that cause agitation and threaten peace in the holy city of Jerusalem."[21]

There was concern in the community that such political use of donations would bring a close scrutiny to the larger philanthropic effort on behalf of Israel. An Associated Press inquiry noted that, in 1995 tax exempted contributions to settlements in the West Bank, the Gaza Strip, and the Golan Heights reached $11 million. Among them were the Moskowitz-supported American Friends of Ateret Cohanim and American Friends of Everest Foundation, as well as One Israel Fund, Israel Community Development Foundation, American Friends of Yeshivat Harav Meri, and the Hebron Fund. More alarm was raised when, in September 1997, Moskowitz moved three Jewish families into a building in the Ras al-Amud neighborhood of East Jerusalem just days after the United States called upon the Israeli government to take a "time out." Faced with a storm of protest, Netanyahu had to engage in a humiliating weeklong negotiation with the American philanthropist over the removal of the families.[22]

Netanyahu's very public association with evangelical Christians added insult to injury. As already noted, many American Jewish liberals were unhappy with the close ties of Likud leaders like Menachem Begin and Yitzhak Shamir with the Christian Zionists. Netanyahu furthered these anxieties when, in April 1997, he addressed some three thousand evangelicals at the annual conference of Voices United for Israel. The organizing committee of the gathering included Pat Robertson, Jerry Falwell, Ralph Reed from the Christian Coalition, and other evangelical stalwarts. During his speech and in a letter to Esther Levens, the head of the National Unity Coalition/Voices United, Netanyahu praised the organization for its embrace of Israel's security needs. When, upon arriving in the United States in January 1998, Netanyahu first visited Falwell—an outspoken critic of the peace process and President Clinton—many in the community took it as a personal slight. ADL's Foxman implied that some of Falwell's pronouncements were either anti-Semitic or "crude" and "curious," a sentiment that was apparently shared by other Jews. The 1997 AJC survey corroborated that 22 percent of the respondents perceived "most" of the "religious right" to be anti-Semitic and 25 percent perceived that "many" were anti-Semitic.[23]

The liberals were equally upset by the high-profile stand of the evangelicals over Jerusalem and the settlements. Articles in the Anglo-Jewish press alerted the community to the fact that the Canaan Land Restoration of Israel, an institute established by Clyde Lott, an ordained minister with the National Pentecostal Assemblies, was working with the Temple Mount Faithful to breed red heifers destined for Temple sacrifices. The press also reported on the Christian Friends of Settlements in Judea, Samaria and Gaza headed by Ted Becket, which, through its Adopt-A-Settlement program, funneled funds to some forty-two settlements. An April 10, 1997 ad in the *New York Times* announced a "Christian Call for a United Jerusalem." Falwell promised to mobilize 200,000 evangelical Christians to lobby Congress to stop pressure on Israel to cede any more land to the Palestinians. The Christian fundamentalists had also supported the Women in Green, the radical settler group that stepped up its activities after the Hebron accord. Liberal anger boiled over after it was disclosed that some evangelical bodies stepped up contributions to compensate for the falloff in donations to Israel caused by the Conservative and Reform unhappiness over the issue of conversion.[24]

Most significantly, the old specter of cognitive dissonance drove many American Jews to seek progress in the peace process. The administration's distaste of Netanayahu was well known. Albright allegedly called the Israeli prime minister a "liar," and Clinton was said to use terms like "ridiculous," "despicable," and "untrustworthy" to describe him. The president also apparently complained that Netanyahu did not understand which of the two countries—Israel or the United States—was the superpower. Anxious to avoid a repeat of the vintage "Reagan or Begin" AWACS dilemma, a substantial segment of the community was ready to support tacitly the administration's maneuvers to bring Israel to the negotiating table. As one observer put it, Netanyahu had "become not only an embarrassment and a danger to Middle East peace, but more important, a threat to their own peace of mind as non-Christian minority in the United States."[25]

But it was the renewed struggle over religious pluralism in Israel that had greatly aggravated the unprecedented alienation of American Jews, more than 80 percent of whom were either unaffiliated or belonged to the Conservative or Reform movements. Dormant since the Shamir era, the issue became front-page after a 1995 Israeli Supreme Court decision opened the door to non-Orthodox conversion. To forestall such a possibility, Shas, a Sephardi Orthodox party in the Likud-led government, proposed an amendment to the Law of Return that would have given full conversion power to the Israeli Orthodox Rabbinate. While not banning non-Orthodox conversions abroad, the proposed legislation would have prevented Israeli citizens from seeking such recourse. More than in the previous rounds of the "who is a Jew" controversy, the new discourse was fraught with extreme anger and bitterness. The attempts at mixed prayer at the Wall of the Conservative and Reform community in Israel led to well-publicized attacks by ultra-Orthodox yeshiva students. Reports of abuse suffered during the attacks, including offensive physical and verbal assaults, filled the pages of the general and Anglo-Jewish presses. Members of the Conservative and Reform movements were also aware of the fact that, stirred by the liberal trends in the community, some American Orthodox circles welcomed this newest effort to delineate the boundaries of Judaism. The high rates of intermarriage, which were described as a form of auto-genocide, and the Reform's controversial decision to legitimize patrilineal descent had especially distressed American orthodoxy. In an effort to buttress the conversion bill in Israel, the small Union of Orthodox Rabbis of the United States and Canada held a press conference in March 1997 to declare that the forms of Judaism practiced by the non-Orthodox were inauthentic. Some went so far as to assert that the Reform and Conservative movements were deviant shoots of Judaism.[26]

Responding to what they perceived to be an effort to delegitimize their faith, Conservative and Reform leaders harshly attacked the Israeli orthodoxy and the Netanyahu government. Some called the chief Israeli rabbis "medieval" and Rabbi Ismar Schorsch, the chancellor of the Jewish Theological Seminary, demanded the abolition of the chief rabbinate on the grounds that it "had no scintilla of moral worth." Rabbi Yoffie, who replaced Schindler as the head of the Reform movement, argued that he did not mind that Orthodox rabbis did not accept him personally. But he added that when Israel, which "is the state of the entire Jewish people" suggests "that only one group stood at Sinai, only one group is legitimate, and chooses to exclude me from its official recognition, that is very serious matter indeed."[27]

Leonard Fein declared that the "who is a Jew" controversy left many American Jews feeling betrayed by Israel. Rabbi Ammiel Hirsh, executive director of ARZA, predicted that the legislation would prompt American Jews to "disengage" from Israel. Yoffie elaborated upon his sense of estrangement by noting that "American Jews look at Israel and ask what exactly does Israel have to do with them." Schindler warned that "liberal Judaism and liberal rabbinate will not long be negated in Eretz Yisrael." He added that even though the non-Orthodox Jews in Israel have no electoral strength, they should be protected in the same way that the Bill of Rights protects American Jews in the United States. In an unprecedented move, Conservative and Reform leaders threatened to ban from their synagogues any Israeli lawmaker who would vote for the conversion bill. Calls to divert support from the UJA to Conservative and Reform-oriented charities in Israel had contributed to a $20 million UJA shortfall.[28]

Taken aback by the uproar, which culminated in a session of the February 1997 NJCRAC plenum entitled "Challenges to the American Jewish-Israeli Relationship," the Netanyahu government was forced to devise a compromise. Accordingly, there would be a simultaneous moratorium on the conversion bill and the Reform and Conservative challenges in the courts, while a commission chaired by Finance Minister Ya'akov Ne'eman was tasked with providing a long-term solution. Although the Ne'eman commission eventually came up with a "conversion institute" that represented all the three denominations, the Israeli Orthodox circles dismissed it. To make matters worse, on the eve of the 1997 Jewish New Year, four U.S. Orthodox organizations—Agudat Israel, the National Council of Young Israel, the Rabbinical Council of America, and the Union of Orthodox Jewish Congregations—issued a statement supporting the Israeli orthodoxy. The group asserted that prayer at the Western Wall should be conducted in an Orthodox manner and charged that the "political, economic and social pressure" of American Jewry on Israel had "created a climate of ill-will."[29]

The high-profile fight over the legitimacy of their denominations forced many American Jews to take a closer look at the array of political parties in the Likud government. Even though the urbane, English-speaking Netanyahu cut a dashing figure compared to Begin, the pivotal place of the Shas party, which represented the growing Sephardi-Orthodox population, stirred up some of the old discomfort about the political culture of Israel. The attitudes of the Sephardi Orthodox leaders added to the anxiety. Delivering a biblical commentary in July 1996 Eliahu Bakshi Doron, the chief Sephardi rabbi of Israel, was reported to have praised the biblical figure Pinchas, who killed Zimri for having a relation with a gentile woman. Alarmed leaders of the Reform movement claimed that the sermon could be viewed as a license to kill Reform Jews. Yoffie, the President of the UAHC, asked the Israeli attorney general to prosecute Bakshi Doron on charges of sedition. Complaining of a "blood libel," Bakshi Doron denied that he considered Zimri to be the "first Reform Jew." Still, the Sephardi chief rabbi reiterated his claim that the "greatest danger facing the Jewish people is the shocking increase of intermarriage," which "could lead to the demographic collapse of the Jewish people."[30] Baskhi Doron also asserted that converts processed by the multidenominational conversion institute proposed by Ne'eman would not be "real converts." The Shas party had threatened to quit the government if the conversion bill as well as another bill that barred non-Orthodox representatives from the powerful municipal religious councils should not pass Knesset.

Even for those not well versed in the complexities of Israeli politics, such demands served as a reminder that the peace process and the collations that it spanned was part of a larger struggle over the future of the Israeli polity. As Broder put it, the political elites in Netanyahu's government "represented to American Jews someone different—not the familiar European Ashkenazi Jews that Jewish Americans have grown accustomed to. Rather, they have risen from the ranks of Israel's dark-skinned Sephardi Jews, its recent Russian immigrants, and its black-coated ultra-Orthodox." Visiting Labor officials emphasized the connection between the peace process and the political culture of the Jewish state. Haim Ramon pointed out that Labor's refusal in 1981 to commit itself to a change in the Law of Return had enabled Likud to attract enough Orthodox voters to win the election and wage the war in Lebanon. He subsequently reminded American Jewish audiences that Peres jeopardized his political chances by refusing a request of Shas to rejoin the Labor coalition in 1995 in return for the conversion bill. By the spring of 1998, it became commonplace to comment on the linkage between religious pluralism, the peace process, and the alienation of American Jews.[31]

While the conversion issue helped to mobilize the Reform and the Conservative Jews on the side of Clinton's efforts to pressure Israel, the nationalists and the religious camp launched a major counterattack. Leading the way, the ZOA placed an ad in the *New York Times* arguing that "the United States should pressure America's enemy—the PLO—and not America's friend and ally—Israel." AFSI and other right-wing groups published similar ads in the general and Anglo-Jewish presses. Betty Ehrenberg, director of the International and Communal Affairs at the Orthodox Union, issued a statement in support of Israeli policy. Klein and other activists portrayed Clinton as "another Bush," and wondered why Clinton should be widely perceived as an "Israel friendly" president. Others chastised the Jewish leaders for "defecting" to the administration's side. These and other critics emphasized the fact that peace activists like Daniel Abraham played a prominent role in the October White House meeting.[32]

To demonstrate that pressuring Israel had little backing in the community, Arthur J. Finkelstein & Associates published a poll of Jewish voters in September 1997. Designed to contradict the IPF poll, the survey did not ask questions about U.S. pressure on Israel, but the large number of statements contrasting Netanyahu and Arafat brought out the community's underlying mistrust of the Palestinians. Some 77 percent agreed with Netanyahu's position that terror needs to stop before peace negotiations can resume. Fifty-eight percent felt that Arafat could not stop terrorism if he wanted, and 72.2 percent argued that terrorism would not stop even if the "Palestinians have their own country." The *Middle East Quarterly*, published by the Middle East Forum, sponsored another poll. Carried out by an associate of Finkelstein, John McLaughlin & Associates, the January 1998 survey revealed that 65 percent of American Jews opposed Clinton's pressure on Israel and 65.7 percent disapproved of Clinton's refusal to meet with Netanayahu. Seventy-four percent of the sample opposed signing a peace treaty with the Palestinians if it required giving up part of Jerusalem, 64 percent opposed such a treaty if it required giving up the West Bank, and 68 percent opposed it as long as terrorism continued. Commenting on the poll, Pipes, the editor of the *Middle East Quarterly* and a leading scholar of Islam, stated that "President Clinton is on a collision course with a majority of American Jews."[33]

Likud's own network in the United States helped to wage the counteroffensive. According to reports, Netanayahu, who described the White House refusal to meet with him as "unbecoming" conduct insulting the state of Israel, mobilized the pro-Likud activists in the Conference and AIPAC. These tactics seemed to have paid off by putting the leadership of the Conference on the defensive. Various spokesmen denied that their organizations' failure to respond to Clinton's pressure amounted to a tacit endorsement. In March 1998, the Conference, in a twenty-seven to three vote, decided to send a letter to Clinton accusing the administration of complicating the negotiations and creating a perception of "shift in U.S. policy toward Israel." Netanyahu scored an even more resounding victory during the annual AIPAC meeting in May. Many of the right-leaning delegates gave him a warm welcome and Howard Kohr, the executive director, declared that public pressure on Israel is counterproductive. The hard-liners also prevailed on the issue of Palestinian sovereignty. In an effort to change AIPAC's long standing opposition to a Palestinian state, the leadership managed to pass a modified resolution which would have urged the United States to oppose the establishment of a Palestinian state with "full, unlimited sovereignty." However, on a second vote, the resolution was defeated amid concerns that it would give a green light to the Palestinians. Mandell I. Ganchrow of the Orthodox Union and Klein—leaders in the effort to defeat the move—expressed satisfaction with the outcome, prompting headlines reading "AIPAC Veers Right."[34]

The stiffening position of the Israel defense organizations gave pause to the administration, which by early 1998 devised a "breaching proposal" to nudge the peace process forward. The United States wanted Israel to relinquish a further 13 percent of the territory and agree on a deadline for an Israeli-Palestinian conference. To dispel the perception that the administration was "pushing Israel," Secretary Albright met with Jewish leaders and, in an unprecedented move, asked the Conference to intercede with Netanyahu. While the White House had no hope of swaying the hard-liners, the maneuvers appeared to be aimed at preventing an antiadministration consensus from developing in the community.

As it turned out, the administration had little to fear on this score. The right-wing victory came at the price of further polarizing the community. APN and other pro-Oslo advocates mounted a major effort to prove that the Conference and AIPAC were not representative of popular sentiments. In a May 13, 1998, letter, APN accused both organizations of backing the policies of the Netanyahu government and urged them to reflect more closely the propeace opinion of the majority of American Jews. Labor politicians added to the ruckus by repeating the charge that AIPAC had become a pro-Likud stronghold. A visiting delegation led by Yossi Beilin and Ehud Barak, the new party leader, accused AIPAC of being too right-wing; Shlomo Ben-Ami, a Labor member of Knesset (MK), asserted that AIPAC leaders did not understand the "true need of the country." As usual, the pages of the general press were the preferred venue for waging the "Jewish wars." For instance, when Netanyahu arrived in the United States in January 1998, millions of dollars were spent on advertising to either denounce or encourage Clinton's efforts to pressure Israel.[35]

Another favorite venue was Congress, in which the Oslo opponents had a competitive edge. Netanyahu was a personal friend of the House speaker Newt Gingrich, and had a good relationship with Benjamin Gilman (R–N.Y.), the powerful chairman of the House International Relations Committee. When Netanyahu addressed a joint session of Congress in July 1996, the Republicans enthusiastically cheered him. Many of the lawmakers were especially receptive to Netanyahu's contention that the real question was not whether Israel should make peace with the Palestinians, but rather whether peace with the Palestinians was possible in the absence of democracy in the Palestinian Authority. The ZOA, the National Jewish Coalition, JINSA, and other groups that lobbied Capitol Hill on Palestinian noncompliance with the Oslo accord had also vigorously pushed the theme of peace-and-democracy. Jim Nicholson, the chairman of the Republican National Committee and the target of much of this lobbying, was quite receptive. After returning from a trip to Israel, organized by the Republican-aligned National Jewish Coalition, Nicholson declared his belief in "peace through strength, peace through compliance." In February 1998 Sam Brownback (R–Kans.), chairman of the Senate Foreign Relations Middle East Subcommittee, scheduled a hearing to review the Oslo accord and possible sanctions against PA for noncompliance. Congressional support for Netanyahu was also evident in the high-level delegation that went to Jerusalem to celebrate Israel's fiftieth anniversary. Gingrich, who once called Albright a "Palestinian agent," wanted to use the occasion for a symbolic cornerstone-laying ceremony for the American embassy. After intense pressure and threats of violence, the House speaker scrapped his plans, but still proclaimed himself in favor of legislation that would have established the "indivisibility of Israel."[36]

Such sentiments were not shared across the board. According to some sources, many lawmakers were upset with Netanyahu, who had a reputation for arrogance, and were convinced that Israel was dragging its feet on the peace process. However, they were unwilling to risk alienating the Jewish constituency whose vocal elements opposed Oslo or the Jewish PACs. Worse, open criticism of Israel would have brought a swift retaliation from the fundamentalist Christians. Choosing the path of least resistance, they were all too happy to let Clinton "play the bad cop" and take "all the heat." Capitalizing on the complex political calculus on Capitol Hill, the National Jewish Coalition (NJC) launched a Senate initiative, sponsored by Connie Mack (R–Fla.) and Joseph Lieberman (D–Conn.), to send a letter opposing Clinton's efforts to pressure Israel. After a lobbying blitz by AIPAC, 81 senators signed the letter in April 1998, and more than 150 House members penned a similar message. The letter infuriated the administration, which viewed it as a cynical Republican ploy to goad Clinton and a slap on the face of the secretary of state, who had asked American Jewry to refrain from "portraying us as if we are shoving something down Israel's throat."[37]

Jewish peace proponents were equally outraged, moving vigorously to counter the impact of the senators' letter. They were helped by the Labor party, which, in a belated effort to emulate Likud, established its own lobbying network on the Hill. Alon Pinkus, the foreign policy adviser of Ehud Barak, and Stanley Ringler, head of the Labor party's North American desk, were among some of the Labor personalities that were making rounds on the Hill. Heading the pro-peace effort was Representative Sam Gejdenson (D–Conn.), a son of Holocaust survivors who was close to the Labor party and the IPF. A letter signed by thirty-three members of the House, including fifteen Jews, noted that "it would be one of the great failures of American Jewry in our times" if the peace process "collapsed" in part due to the administration backing away out of "fear of political retribution from our community." Caught in the middle was the Conference of Presidents, which thanked the senators for the letter, but did not endorse it.[38]

The competition between the Oslo proponents and opponents had become so fierce that public opinion polls published in the course of 1998 did little to settle the issue. The AJC's annual survey released in March 1998 revealed that 56 percent of the respondents supported Netanyahu's "current handling" of the negotiations with Arafat, 34 opposed it, and 10 percent were not sure. Sixty-nine percent wanted the United States to apply pressure on Arafat to advance the peace process but 28 percent objected. As for American pressure on Israel, 45 percent supported it and 52 percent objected, with 3 percent being "not sure."

Some 94 percent felt that Arafat was not doing enough to control terrorist activity, and there was also an increase in pessimism over the peace process. Thirty-nine percent felt less optimistic than the year before and 55 percent reported feeling the same; only 5 percent felt more optimistic. The drop in optimism was attributed to continuing terrorism and to the perception that Arafat was not strongly interested in peace. More that half of the sample (55 percent) felt that Arafat either somewhat opposed peace or strongly opposed the peace process. Thirty-seven percent were of the opinion that the PA chairman somewhat supported the peace process, but only 3 percent felt that Arafat had a strong commitment to peace.[39]

A poll commissioned by the *Los Angeles Times* and the Israeli paper *Yediot Aharanot* in conjunction with Israel's fiftieth anniversary showed that 41 percent of the American Jewish sample felt less optimistic about the peace process than the year before. This was mainly due to the perception that the peace process made Israel less, rather than more, secure (35 percent versus 18 percent). Netanyahu was found to be more sincere in his quest for peace than Arafat (60 percent versus 37 percent). Still, 36 percent stated that Netanyahu had made relations between Israel and the United States worse. As for the peace process, 66 percent approved of Oslo and 68 percent were willing to approve an independent Palestinian state. Although American Jews did not want to give up all the territories for peace, 68 percent thought that Israel should not continue to expand settlements in the West Bank.[40]

A May 1998 poll sponsored by the IPF found that an overwhelming majority of American Jews—80 percent—supported the Clinton administration's "current efforts to revive Israeli-Palestinian negotiations." Fifty-four percent believed that the "current level of American diplomatic pressure" on Netanyahu was about right and 33 percent said it was too much. Large numbers of respondents felt that, in helping to move the peace process forward, Clinton would not compromise Israeli security (39 percent strongly agreed and 41 percent somewhat agreed). As for Netanyahu, 19 percent had a very favorable opinion of the Israeli prime minister and 54 percent had a somewhat favorable opinion. Opinions about Arafat were on the whole negative: 31 percent had a somewhat unfavorable opinion, 39 percent had a very unfavorable opinion. Only 4 percent had a very favorable opinion and 21 percent had a somewhat favorable opinion. At the same time, 81 percent of the sample said that it was very important to achieve a stable peace between Israel and the Palestinians, and an additional 15 percent said it was somewhat important. To this end, 41 percent felt that it is very important for the United States to propose bridging proposals for the peace process and 42 percent felt that it was somewhat important.[41]

A secondary analysis of the AJC surveys published by the *Middle East Quarterly* chose to focus on the increased pessimism of the Oslo process since 1993. Yale Zussman, the author of the analysis, argued that the decline in support correlated with the "growing belief among American Jews that the Palestinians remain more intent on destroying Israel than in establishing peaceful relations with it." Zussman also claimed that American Jewish dissatisfaction with the Israeli government's handling of the negotiation stems from the perception that Netanyahu was too conciliatory, rather than too hard-line. To bolster his conclusions, Zussman quoted data from a September 1998 poll of leaders represented in the Conference of Presidents. A sizable group believed that Arabs had no intention of living in peace and found Netanyahu too soft. Those who advocated more concessions though they did not believe that the Arabs did not want a real peace formed another category, followed by those who believed that, in insisting on reciprocity from the Palestinians, Netanyahu jeopardized the peace process. Using his reinterpretation of the surveys, Zussman charged American Jewish liberals with overrepresenting the support for the peace process and for creating the impression that the community had embraced Clinton's pressure on Israel. He also argued that the "dissenting voices were nearly drowned out" or presented as "right-wing ideologues, or apologists for the Orthodox." Noting that dissatisfaction with the peace process was spreading to the mainstream, Zussman warned that the "foreign policy establishment" would have a more difficult time claiming that it had the support of the community.[42]

Whatever merit Zussman's analysis might have had, the proliferation of opinion polls whose questions were not comparable made it easier for the administration and its American Jewish backers to claim a mandate for further pressure on the Israeli government. With a community sharply divided and "ad wars" continuing unabated, the White House felt safe in taking the initiative that ultimately led to a new peace conference between Israel and the Palestinians.

THE WYE AGREEMENT AND THE "JEWISH WARS": PLEASING SOME AND EMBITTERING OTHERS

From the standpoint of American foreign policy there were a number of urgent imperatives to proceed with the peace process. The most compelling one was the threat by Arafat to declare unilateral independence on May 4, 1999, the Oslo target day for completing the final-status negotiations. Security officials in the administration had fanned the May 4 anxiety by warning about violence and chaos, an estimate that was shared by their Israeli counterparts. Such an outcome would have threatened the stability of the region and further undermined the fraying American-led coalition against Iraq. Much of the same conclusion was reached by a 1997 report sponsored by the Council on Foreign Relations entitled *U.S. Middle East Policy and the Peace Process.* The report argued that the situation had deteriorated to a perilous point and, without strong and determined American leadership, the region could plunge into renewed chaos.[43]

Brokering an agreement between Israel and the Palestinians was also important on a personal level to the president, who was deeply mired in the Monica Lewinsky affair. Indeed, political observers in the United States and Israel had wondered whether the administration, paralyzed by the scandal, could mount a serious effort to resuscitate the comatose peace process. The centerpiece of the administration's proposal that Israel give up an additional 13 percent of the territory was effectively defunct after Netanyahu managed to mobilize Congress to defeat Albright's May 1998 ultimatum. The political impasse in Washington also worried the American Jewish peace camp, which used the Oslo anniversary on September 13, 1998, to mount a show of support. More than four hundred representatives from various Jewish groups, including Theodore Mann from IPF and Seymour Reich, a former chairman of the Conference, joined Leah Rabin, the widow of the slain Israeli prime minister, to express their steadfast support for peace. APN published a letter urging Clinton to "pursue a robust American strategy," a theme that was also pressed by Beth Shalom, an ad hoc organization of sixteen peace groups. According to its leaders, Beth Shalom was formed in protest over the alleged failure of the official Jewish lobby to pursue peace. More to the left was Break the Silence, an ad-hoc group organized by Rabbi Mordechai Liebling, former executive director of the Reconstructionist Federation; Arthur Wascow, the director of the Shalom Center; and Cherie R. Brown, director of the National Coalition Building Institute. The group placed ads in the *New York Times* and the *Forward* criticizing Netanyahu and urging American Jews "to speak out against the current Israeli government's return to a policy of fear and noncooperation with her Arab and Palestinian neighbors." Peace activists were so worried that, on September 12, they met with Leon Feurth, Vice-President Al Gore's foreign policy adviser, to question him whether the president, who faced impeachment, would be able to engage in Middle East diplomacy. When the president surprised them by joining the meeting, the activists urged him to intensify the peacemaking effort and reassured him that an overwhelming majority of American Jews supported Oslo.[44]

Encouraged by such efforts and anxious to avoid a Middle East meltdown on its watch, the administration intensified its pressure on Netanyahu to meet with Arafat at the Wye River Plantation in Maryland. The Wye Memorandum, signed in Washington on October 23, showed compromise on both sides. Israel promised to withdraw from an additional 13 percent of the territories in exchange for a Palestinian promise to curtail terrorism, amend the 1968 Palestinian National Charter that called for the destruction of Israel, and curb incitement. A trilateral committee of Palestinians, Israeli, and American representatives was charged with implementing the anti-incitement clauses of the Memorandum. According to a poll, three-quarters of Israelis approved of the Wye outcome.

The Wye agreement was well-received by the American Jewish peace camp and the mainstream community which, as already indicated, was anxious to avoid being caught in the middle of a struggle between Israel and the United States. Actually, the 1998 AJPS indicated that the community was in the process of developing a case of cognitive dissonance. When asked to evaluate the relation between the two countries, 14 percent said it was very positive, 70 percent described it as somewhat positive, 14 percent said it was somewhat negative, and 1 percent very negative. In 1997 the comparable figures were 23 percent very positive, 67 percent somewhat positive, and 9 percent somewhat negative.

The Jewish Council for Public Affairs (the former NJCRAC) praised the agreement as "an important achievement, adding that the pact "renews our hope that the ultimate vision of Oslo . . . can yet be realized." The ADL and the AJC also welcomed the agreement.[45]

What looked like a positive development to the peace camp amounted to a grave disappointment to Netanyahu's staunch supporters on the right. Even before the terms of Wye became known, a group called Israeli Support Network warned Netanyahu in a *New York Post* ad that any withdrawal would amount to a "fundamental breach of trusts" that the "Republicans in Congress, the fundamentalists Christians and 2 million right-wing American Jews have placed in him." Gutnick, the Lubavitcher emissary, asserted that Netanyahu, who was elected because of opposition to Oslo, was "still a prisoner of this historic blunder, shackled to an accord which threatened to drain the lifeblood of Israel." Pipes expressed disappointment that Israel was willing to give new benefits to Palestinians in spite of the fact that they failed to fulfil earlier promises. The *Forward* was dismayed because Netanyahu abandoned his demand that democratization of the Palestinian Authority should precede any negotiations. Feith described the Wye accord as "mushy drafting," replete with "undefined terms, unaddressed contingencies, unauthorized interoperations and loopholes."[46]

AFSI and the Freeman Center, already rattled by the Hebron agreement and the Ras al-Amud incident, were openly looking to replace Netanyahu as the standard-bearer of the nationalist right. In a gesture reminiscent of the reaction to Rabin, three prominent rabbis—Aaron Soloveitchik, Moshe Tendler, and Herschel Reichman—wrote in an ad in the *New York Post* that Jewish law prohibited the ratification of an agreement to give up Jewish land. The advertisement, which was coordinated by Joseph Frager from the Jerusalem Reclamation Project, called for a new leadership "which will be loyal to the Jewish people, to the land of Israel and the Torah of Israel." Dore Gold, Netanyahu's representative to the UN, was heckled during a ZOA dinner and Harvey Friedman, an honoree at the same dinner, called the Wye agreement "disastrous." Carl Freyer, a national board member of the ZOA, claimed that in Wye the Netanyahu administration was humiliated by Arafat and "left with an Arafat-imposed land-for-more-nothing agreement."[47]

Some of the nationalist Jews put their faith in the Land of Israel Front, a group of seventeen right-wing Knesset members who broke with Netanyahu over Wye. Michael Kleiner, one of the group's leaders, had met with Gutnik and received a promise of financial support for a new party. An editorial in AFSI's *Outpost* expressed hope that a "serious nationalist party" led by Kleiner and Benny Begin, the son of the former prime minister, would bring "meaningful change in Israel." There were also reports that Moskowitz was ready to finance an alternative right-wing religious party that would oppose withdrawal from the territories. Others, like ZOA's Klein, accepted the Wye agreement but promised vigilant monitoring of the PA's compliance with the accords. Writing shortly after the Maryland conference, Klein noted that Arafat had not moved fast enough to comply with a long list of infractions, including halting anti-Jewish incitement and curbing terrorism. The ZOA president asserted that "Arafat intends to violate the Wye agreement just as frequently as he has violated the Oslo accord." Klein and others also complained that, in spite of a history of noncompliance, the Wye agreement was expected to bring the Palestinians an additional $900 million in aid. They warned that, because of the corruption in the PA, the money would do little to benefit ordinary Palestinians. The ZOA also took a lead in lobbying Congress against the establishment of an independent Palestinian state, which, in its opinion, would pose a grave security risk to Israel.[48]

The issue of noncompliance was also at the center of the Israeli government's Palestinian policy. On December 20 Netanyahu decided to suspend the second pullback until the PA met a number of conditions. While the right wing of the American Jewish community welcomed the step, the peace camp denounced it as a thinly disguised maneuver to torpedo the Oslo. Even before the official suspension, the APN, emulating a favorite ZOA tactic, issued a "score card" on the Wye Memorandum. It praised the Palestinians for being ahead of time in fulfilling the accord, but gave the Netanyahu government a failing grade for backsliding and for creating new demands. The APN and other propeace groups emphasized that the Palestinian National Council took the historical step of changing the Palestinian charter, long a focus of attacks by the Jewish right wing. But Shoshana Bryen, the executive director of JINSA, accused the APN of acting as a "mouthpiece for a terrorist organization."[49]

In spite of the Wye suspension, Netanyahu could not save his coalition. The right wing of the Likud and other Israeli nationalists were angry with the prime minister for abandoning the dream of Greater Israel. The center and the left accused Netanyahu for not going far enough to save the peace process. On December 23 the Knesset voted eighty to thirty to dissolve itself, paving the way for a new election scheduled for May 1999. While the Israelis embarked on a bitterly divisive campaign, the American Jewish community, reflecting the same cleavages, continued its own battle over the peace process. As before, the focal point of the struggle was the relocation of the American embassy and U.S. relations with the PA. The Jerusalem embassy relocation law stipulated that the State Department should start the construction of a new embassy by March 31, 1999, or forfeit half of its construction and maintenance budget. With the European Union challenging Israel's right over all of Jerusalem and the 2000 election kickoff, Clinton signaled his readiness to sign a waver on the law, a move that was welcomed by the American Jewish peace camp. APN's Mark Rosenblum asserted that implementing the law would be equivalent to throwing a "grenade in the middle of very sensitive negotiations" and would "help scuttle Oslo and give Hamas a new issue around which to rally." However, right-wing activists bitterly opposed Clinton's plans and lobbied Congress to pass a new Embassy Relocation Law that would have dispensed with the waiver provision. Among those who were receptive were two hard-line supporters of Israel, Jon

Kyl, a Republican senator from Arizona, and James Saxton, a Republican House representative from New Jersey.[50]

Underlying the embassy issue was the larger problem of Jerusalem's unity, long a sacred principle in American Jewish politics. With the Israeli election in high gear and the Labor party gaining in the polls, the American peace camp was emboldened enough to push the vision of a shared Jerusalem. The APN was particularly active in pointing out that the rights of the Palestinians in East Jerusalem were encroached on by the intensive campaign of constructions undertaken by the Likud government in Har Homa, Silwan, and other neighborhoods. However, Oslo opponents chastised the left for what they saw as efforts to Judenrein Jerusalem. Leading the way, Klein published an open letter to APN in which the ZOA leader complained that the organization used the term "Judaizing Jerusalem" in its fundraising letter.[51] The American Friends of the Women for Israel's Tomorrow/Women in Green called for a large rally under the banner of Jerusalem's Eternal Position as the Undivided Capital of the Sovereign State of Israel. The rally, held in Washington, D.C., in April 1999, attracted the support of numerous religious and right-wing groups.

U.S. relations with the PA had added fuel to the communal discourse. During a visit to Gaza in December 1998, Clinton gave a speech in which he compared the suffering of both Palestinian and Jewish children left fatherless because of the protracted struggle set off a fiery controversy. Lewis Roth, the assistant executive director of APN, praised the parallel drawn by Clinton and expressed hope that mutual recognition of suffering would expedite the peace process. Even those not well-versed in the arcane language of the peace discourse had to notice that, in evoking the sufferings of both sides to the conflict, Clinton borrowed a favorite line of the peace camp. Such a development was not lost on Lionel Kaplan, AIPAC's president, Foxman from ADL, or anyone in the nationalist camp that attacked the so-called "moral equivalency" speech. The Jewish Council for Public Affairs, B'nai B'rith, and the AJCongress issued a statement applauding the revocation of the PLO charter that coincided with Clinton's visit, but did not mention the speech.[52]

More heated debate followed congressional maneuvers to deflect Arafat's presumed plans to declare a Palestinian state in May 1999. Right-wing activists joined AIPAC in urging the House of Representatives to pass a resolution asking President Clinton to call on the PA to avoid unilaterally declaring independence. The resolution, passed by a 379–24 vote in early March, was bolstered by a similar measure in the Senate. The ADL expressed the sentiments of many in the community, when it noted that the declaration "sends a clear signal to Chairman Arafat that the Congress of the United States views abandonment of this principle as a treat to peace." However, others, like Gejdenson, sought to broaden the resolution to include language warning against "unilateral action by either party." Gejdenson, like many in the peace camp, felt that the Palestinians had made considerable progress in complying with the Oslo and Wye agreements and feared that the negative congressional language was not helpful.

When AIPAC sought to censure the congressman from Connecticut, APN, IPF, and other peace groups came to his defense. Thomas Smerling, the Washington director of the IPF, argued that "it seems very destructive for any pro-Israel organization to be attacking a Jewish pro-Israel member of Congress over a nuance like this." The deputy executive director of the National Jewish Democratic Council, Stephen Silberfarb, worried that the fight over the resolution marked another low in Jewish activism in Washington. He noted that "what we're heading to is AIPAC versus IPF on Capitol Hill. I think that's bad for our community."[53]

Other observers decried the continuous rancor and acrimony that was becoming a staple of the American Jewish discourse. A Jewish newspaper editorialized that the swings from Labor to Likud government and back have "revealed hypocrisy in all circles, as Jewish American doves and hawks took turns chastising each other for speaking against the Israel government." The editorial exhorted the community to search with the same fervor for "common ground and shared identity" as it did "exhibit while arguing over their political and religious difference." Others urged to end the divisiveness in the name of Jewish unity. However, it was quite clear that the simmering passions swirling around Israel had seriously dented the communal façade and strained the relation of the American Jewry to Jewish state.[54]

ISRAEL AT FIFTY: TAKING STOCK OF A TROUBLED RELATIONSHIP

Ironically, the forthcoming fiftieth anniversary of Israel provided a convenient platform for analyzing the changing attitudes of the U.S. Diaspora toward the Jewish state. Even a cursory look at the numerous articles and symposia devoted to the topic revealed that the official celebratory mood was underlain by what one observer described as an "impatient, if not downright surly tone." Most of the participants in a large *Moment* symposium entitled "Is Israel still Important to American Jews?" agreed that Israel had became more marginal to the concerns of individual members of the community. A special issue of the *Jewish Spectator* found that the "gap widens between American Jews and Israel," and noted that the "discontent" was caused because the "old heroic Israel" was gone and the new realities were "not palatable." A *Tikkun* roundtable reached the same conclusion, with many of the contributors emphasizing the distance between Israel and the real concerns of the community. The *American Jewish Year Book* openly focused on the "disenchantment of U.S. Jews with Israel." Even the conservative *Commentary* magazine questioned the depth of the relation. Hillel Halkin summed up the tenor of the debate by noting that about 25 years ago Israel was proclaimed central to the "civic religion of American Jews, today this faith is losing its congregation."[55]

The AJC surveys of 1997 and 1998 showed a decline in attachment to Israel. Asked in 1997 how close American Jews felt toward Israel, 23 percent stated that they felt very close, 46 percent felt fairly close, 23 percent fairly distant, and 8 percent very distant. The 1998 figures were 25 percent very close, 44 percent fairly close, 23 percent fairly distant, and 8 percent very distant. However, when queried about the future in 1997, 31 percent felt that American Jews and Israel would become closer, 13 percent felt that they would drift apart, and 54 percent thought that the relation would stay the same. In 1998 only 26 percent said that Israel and American Jews would become closer, 19 percent felt that the relation would drift apart, and 51 said it would stay the same. As in the past, the behavioral indices of closeness as measured by visits to Israel were much lower than the verbal one. The survey showed that 21 percent of the respondents went to Israel once and 18 percent more than once. A 1998 National Survey of American Jews carried out by Steven Cohen on behalf of the Jewish Community Center Association found that just 9 percent of the sample felt extremely emotionally attached and 18 felt much attached. When asked about closeness to Israelis, only 8 percent felt very close and 41 percent felt close to some extent. Just 20 percent thought that is was essential for good Jews to support Israel and 18 percent thought it was important to visit. Noting that Israel is important to only about a fifth to a quarter of the sample, Cohen emphasized the "limited extent to which Israel figures in the private lives of American Jews."[56]

Age and income levels had also influenced the degree of attachment to Israel. Older and poorer respondents reported the highest degree of closeness whereas the younger cohorts and the better off were more remote. Among those aged sixty or more, 28 percent were very close and only 5 percent very distant. In the age group under forty, 23 percent felt very close and 11 percent felt very distant. Twenty-nine percent of those in the category making less than $30,000 felt very close, as opposed to 17 percent of those earning more than $30,000 a year. Perhaps the most interesting finding came from the question about intermarriage. Those who were married to other Jews were more likely to feel close to Israel (23 percent) than those who were married to non-Jews (13 percent). Only 21 percent of intermarried Jews felt very distant from Israel as opposed to 54 percent of those who married outside of Jewry.[57]

The *Los Angeles Times* survey confirmed many of these trends. Nearly half of the "high observers" felt very close to Israel and 83 percent felt very/somewhat close, but only 9 percent of the "low observers" felt very close. While the older cohorts (sixty-five and older) were overwhelmingly close to Israel, the younger cohorts (ages eighteen to twenty-nine) were almost evenly divided, with 51 percent feeling close and 48 percent feeling distant. Some 68 percent of the high observers reported visiting Israel at least once, compared to 22 percent of low observers. The mostly Orthodox high observers also reported having relatives and friends in Israel, compared to 48 percent of Conservatives and 39 percent of Reform Jews. The more observant respondents were also more likely to rate the relations between American Jews and Israel as good or excellent (59 percent); 23 percent predicted that in the next three to five years the relationship will get even closer.[58]

In trying to explain the growing distancing from Israel, especially among the younger cohorts, scholars pointed to the larger changes in Jewish identity. According to Charles S. Liebman, the postmodern "privatized" form of identity was gaining dominance over the ethnic-communal model centered on Israel. Cohen explained that the "self had the right to decide whether, when and how to be Jewish" and that this selection is based not on the *halacha* or what is good for the Jewish community, but rather on what is "personally meaningful to the self." As a result, ethnicity had to compete with other identities of American Jews. This privatized Judaism became increasingly less significant in a person's life, a "matter of choice, a leisure activity." Because "privatized" religious identity put a premium on spirituality, it had less use for Israel, which came to "occupy a smaller and narrower place in the conciseness of American Jews." Cohen and Liebman used the survey results to prove their theory that the ethnically driven "mobilization model" of American Jewish identity which flourished in the 1967–77 period lost its appeal, especially among the baby-boomers and their children. Liebman also pointed out that since 1983 the AJC surveys showed a steady decline in the number of those who reported being close to Israel. He speculated that, as anti-Semitism and its psychological twin—the sense of a beleaguered Israel—would decline, there would be even more estrangement between the two communities, ending "the romance."[59]

Those who advocated a more dramatic shift toward a domestic "continuity" imperative seized upon the diminished role of Israel in the "public square" of American Jewry. Lerner wrote: "for much of the past 50 years the real object of worship . . . has been Israel and Zionism. Unfortunately, like all false gods, this one has failed to satisfy the spiritual hunger of the Jewish people. If many Jews turn away from Judaism today, Israel has played no small part in that process. Judaism may be one of Israel's most important casualties." Lerner and other left-wing American Jews urged the community to return to *tikkun olam*, that is, "social justice as the core Jewish identity."[60]

While the left-wing interpretation of the growing alienation between the American Diaspora and Israel was predictable, the position of the Reform movement was less expected. As already indicated, the movement, a champion of a universally oriented Judaism, was historically reluctant to adopt the ethnopeoplehood definition of Jewish identity and its implied Zionism. However, shocked by the demographic hemorrhage of the assimilationist era and swept by the euphoria of the Six Day War, Reform Jews became hesitant converts to an ethnically based Judaism centered on Israel. But the failure of Israel to bolster Jewish identity and communal growth spurred Reform leaders to resurrect some of their original reservations against identifying Judaism with ethnic nationalism. Speaking in 1997 Rabbi Yoffie, the Reform leader, declared that that "the age of ethnicity is over." Judaism must reach out for the "spiritual, the transcendental, the holy." Though stopping short of calling Israel a "false God," as some of the left-wing critics had done, Yoffie urged to fill the vacuum left by "Israel worship" with a "serious reflection on God and on mitzvah and on the meaning of life."[61]

Not surprisingly, Orthodox and conservative commentators reached a very different conclusion from the trend revealed in the surveys. They agreed with their more secularized counterparts that ethnicity was a poor substitute for a true Jewish religion, but pointed out that the highly observant were more likely to have strong ties to Israel. Indeed, the AJC surveys indicated that closeness to Israel was correlated with the degree of orthodoxy. In the 1997 poll 62 percent of Orthodox Jews said that they were very close to Israel as compared with 32 percent of Conservative and 13 percent of Reform Jews. Among those who labeled themselves "just Jewish," only 12 percent felt very close to Israel. Conversely, only 4 percent of Orthodox felt very distant from Israel as opposed to 15 percent of Conservatives, 38 percent of Reform Jews, and 50 percent of "just Jews." Supporting this claim was a survey of alumni of the National Conference of Synagogue Youth, the youth movement of the Orthodox Union, which showed that 78 percent of them visited Israel. According to the Orthodox and conservative observers, such surveys were proof that a strong religious Judaism was the only answer to the waning connection to Israel. They used this reversed casual model to argue that, with or without Israel, the universalistic, socially oriented formula of Judaism as advocated by Yoffie and others was a misguided effort to restore the faith and stop the demographic attenuation. Elliott Abrams asserted that continuity programs cannot work "unless they are centered on faith in God," and chastised Reform Jews for investing "liberal politics with sacred values," adding that this type of "politicized left-wing Judaism will fail."[62]

The divergent interpretations of the survey trends were further testimony that the cleavage that opened in American Jewry between the newly resurgent orthodoxy and the seculars had colored the commentary on the relation between Israel and its American Diaspora. These divisions were projected onto the Israeli political scene and, in turn, reinforced by the bitterly split Israeli citizenry. Daniel J. Elazar was among the first to comment on the new alliance that had formed between Israel and the Diaspora. The distinguished scholar argued that the new division would run between those—both in Israel and the United States—who were "Judaizers" and those who were "normalizers." As both sides fought to legitimize their belief systems, the Judaizers wanted Israel to assume a more Jewish character and the normalizers wanted to "deJudaize" it. Schorsch put it succinctly: "Israel is the battlefield, but the war is in America."[63]

It is through this "battleground" perspective, that American Jews came to evaluate their relations to the Jewish state. For those who wanted Israel to evolve into a full-fledged liberal democracy, the peaceful resolution of the Arab-Israeli conflict was the key. Although liberal American Jews did not accept the more radical parts of the post-Zionist critique, they assumed that once the peace process took root, Israel would embrace civic equality and religious pluralism. The unfinished battle over conversion standards proved to many in this group that the road to religious equality could not be traversed without lowering the nationalist and Jewish profile of the state. Ezrachi made the connection clear, arguing that during the decades of nation-building and struggle for survival, the liberal, individual, and pluralistic ethos in the Israeli democracy took a back seat.[64]

To recall, the NIF and other left-wing groups had advocated civic equality and other Western-style liberties in Israel for more than a decade. In the early nineties a group of American Jewish donors was persuaded to contribute to a reform campaign that led to the direct election of the prime minister. Ostensibly, the move was designed to make the Israeli system more Americanized, but unofficially there was hope that the reform would reduce the influence of religious parties in the coalition. However, in 1996 the new law gave Netanyahu a small edge over Peres, enabling him to put together a nationalist-religious coalition. Shas, with the blessing of Orthodox circles in the United States, used its executive power to press for a change in the Law of Return. It did not help matters when Shlomo Benizri, an influential Shas Knesset member, declared that the Reform and the Conservative movements were "a new religion" with which there could be no compromise. Chief Sephardi Rabbi Bakshi Doron followed this statement with the even more incendiary assertion that Reform Judaism had done more damage than the Holocaust.[65]

Dismay in the community over what was seen as a drift toward an Israeli nationalist theocracy was fueled by reports of serious strife between the secular and the *haredi* sectors of the Israeli population. The Anglo-Jewish press was filled with accounts of verbal and physical threats against leading Israeli peace politicians, refusal of the religious camp to commemorate the death of Rabin, and attacks against Supreme Court justices who ruled in favor of the Reform conversion. Commenting on such divisiveness, Stanley K. Sheinbaum claimed that the "implosion of Israel" caused the distancing of American Jews who felt that "Israel itself is no longer the Israel it was and which they could be proud of." The popular American-born Israeli commentator Ze'ev Chafets pointed out that many of the ultra-Orthodox rabbis and an increasing number of modern Orthodox leaders "have made it clear that they consider Western-style democracy, with its civil rights and constitutionalism, to be inherently opposed to God's law and His Torah." Chafets went on to add that these rabbis "despise the secular, modern materialistic culture of Tel Aviv, distrust the outside world, and dream of making Israel a theocracy."[66]

But it was precisely the Western style culture that many observers viewed as a necessary condition for maintaining the allegiance of American Jews to the Jewish state. Jerold S. Auerbach wrote that "the more Western liberalism and American consumerism Zionism absorbs, the easier it will be for American Jews to renew their identification with Israel. It must be an Israel that "reaffirms liberalism as the salient attribute of Judaism in order to make American Jews comfortable." Another observer added that "exporting" American models of democracy and pluralism to Israel would "enable people to love Israel, and to honor it, not just because it exists, but because of what it is." In his controversial book on Jewish character, Arthur Hertzberg warned that the "new messianism and the ultra-Orthodox are not only misleading Israel," but also are a threat to the Jewish world. The veteran peace activist and Harvard professor Herbert C. Kelman noted that a post-Zionist Israel, "while maintaining its Jewish character . . . would be a state primarily committed to protecting and advancing the interests of its citizens, regardless of ethnicity." In his view, a post-Zionist Israel would upgrade the status of non-Jewish citizens and downgrade the status of the Jewish ones. Raffel predicted that the status of the one million Arab-Israeli citizens would receive increased attention, adding that American Jews could identify with the plight of a minority group. Yet another commentator expressed hope that in the post-Zionist period, Israel would grant all the nonhalachic Jews equal status. One observer went so far as to assert that Israel's slide into theocracy can be "partially halted by the vigorous intervention of enlightened American Jews." The *Los Angeles Times* poll had affirmed an overwhelming American Jewish support for a liberal pluralistic system in Israel. By very large majorities, the respondents also demanded equal statutes for Conservative and Reform rabbis in Israel.[67]

But not all those who wanted Israel to "normalize" were sure that a peaceful, Western capitalist style country envisioned by Beilin and other peace prophets would be attractive to American Jews. The sociologist Samuel Heilman wondered whether a "MacDonalized" Israel, where the kibbutzim turned into Price Clubs, a reference to kibbutz-run shopping malls, could serve a spiritual homeland for its Diaspora. Others, who wanted Israel to retain a vague, generic Jewishness, were equally uneasy. With the Birthright Israel program getting ready to issue its first free vouchers, such musings were not merely academic. As Hillel Halkin put it, when, with "voucher in hand, young Bruce or Jennifer steps off the plane and finds a nation of Yossi Beilins, what profits him or her to have left Philadelphia?" To be sure, even some advocates of a more Westernized—Jewish Israel were hard pressed to define what Jewishenss should look like. At least one of them, Alan Dershowitz in his popular book *The Vanishing American Jew*, admitted that most of the Jews who wanted to preserve the "Jewish character" of Israel did not quite know "what that Jewish character is supposed to be."[68]

Of course, as already noted, it was the nationalists and Orthodox Jews who had a firm vision of what a Jewish Israel should look like and used it to harshly criticize the post-Zionist "normalizers." Repeating the charge that the "Oslo regime" was a conspiracy between the leftist elite in Israel and the Arab minority to dilute the Jewish character of the state, nationalist commentators accused Israel's intellectual elite of contempt for Judaism. They agreed strongly with the thesis of the Shalem Center's director Hazony, who postulated that, with the collapse of Labor Zionism, religious Zionism became the only viable and coherent ideology in Israel. Both the AJC survey and the *Los Angeles Times* poll showed that, like in the past, the self-described conservatives and Orthodox respondents had a much more favorable opinion of the Likud government and its handling of the peace process. The highly observant Jews had the most favorable opinion of Netanyahu (65 percent) as opposed to the low observant Jews (33 percent). The nationalist critics were particularly incensed by what they saw as a wholesale rewrite of history inspired by the revisionist New Historians. They pointed out that revisionist accounts found their way into textbooks where history was deconstructed to show the Palestinians as victims of European colonialism. The ZOA went so far as to release a study refuting the long-standing charges that during the 1948 war the Israelis committed atrocities in the Arab village of Deir Yassin. Right-wing groups had also protested the NIF-sponsored screening of *Tekuma*, a twenty-two part documentary produced by the Israeli television for the independence celebrations, on the grounds that it showed a pro-Palestinian bias.[69]

With the unconditional closeness epitomized in the slogan "we are one" replaced by contradictory visions of what Israel should be, it was only a question of time before the Israelis joined the discourses. Beilin reiterated his well-known view that American Jews should wean themselves from the old habit of relating to Israel through war and adversity. He offered a new model whereby the "post-conflict" Israel of high technology and prosperity would become a source of pride for the Diaspora. However, Daniel Doron, the head of a conservative think tank, rebuked the Conservative and Reform movements for a "self-serving" drive to promote religious pluralism in Israel and accused the NIF of "importing" U.S. style feminism and gay rights. More generally, he charged that the politicized American charity had divided and corrupted Israel and that the Jewish Agency, "a costly failing body" had encouraged "failing socialists experiments." Bar-Ilan questioned whether Israel should follow American dictates of religious pluralism. He stated that while the Reform and Conservative movements may constitute the majority of American Jewry, they do not necessarily form the majority "among the subset concerned with Israel-Diaspora relations."[70]

Concerned with the increased strife, the General Assembly of the CJF that met in Jerusalem in November 1998 tried to restore the frayed relations. In spite of a show of unity, symbolized by the signing of a "covenant" of the Jewish people, tensions over conversion and the territories were close to the surface.[71] In any event, formulaic expressions of unity did not prevent the different camps in the United States from trying to implement their vision for the Jewish state. The Israeli elections scheduled for May 1999 provided a fertile ground for such attempts. Aiming at repeating their success in 1996, the nationalist-religious groups launched a major effort to re-elect Netanyahu and to increase the presence of nationalist parties in the Knesset. In January 1999 Moskowitz led a large delegation to encourage the splintered right wing to unite behind Netanyahu. The American Jewish liberals and the peace camp mounted a vigorous campaign to elect Barak and diminish the influence of Shas and other religious parties. As the bitterly fought elections in Israel unfolded, all pretenses of objectivity vanished across the Atlantic. Articles in the Anglo-Jewish press reminded the readers that, for the first time, what was at stake was not just the size of Israeli borders, but its political culture as well. With so much passion and money poured into the campaign by American Jews, it became clear that either a Labor or a Likud government would face an uphill battle to unite the community behind it.

8

Lurching to the Left: Responding to Barak's Vision of the Peace Process

Barely three years after the Israeli elections produced a shift to the right, the American Jewish community was faced with adjusting to what was arguably the most radical peace vision in the history of the Arab-Israeli conflict. Driven by the efforts of the Labor government to reach a final peace agreement with Syria and the Palestinians, the far reaching concessions, including an offer to relinquish sovereignty on Temple Mount, had demoralized the already badly split community.

OSLO REINCARNATED: BARAK'S REVOLUTION AND THE AMERICAN JEWISH COUNTERREVOLUTION

The Knesset election of May 17, 1999 generated a great deal of anticipation in the segment of the American Jewish community that had strong convictions about the peace process. Borrowing a page from right-wing activists who helped Benjamin Netanyahu in 1996, the peace camp launched an all-out effort to elect Ehud Barak and his Labor party, renamed One Israel. Though the Israeli law made foreign contributions illegal, reports listed Charles and Edgar Bronfman, Michael Sonnenfeld, Jack Bendheim, Stanley Gold, S. Daniel Abraham, Haim Saban, and Lord Michael Levy from Great Britain as major donors to the Barak campaign. Like in the case of Likud, much of the money was channeled through nonprofit organizations such the Roved Association. Since Israel had no absentee ballot, Kesher Inc., a group organized by Udi Behar and funded by the Shefa Fund, offered subsidized airfares to left-leaning American Israelis, a countermove to Chai L'Yisrael, which filed voters favorable to Likud. James Carville,

Stanley Greenberg, and Bob Shrum—political consultants with strong ties to the Clinton administration—helped to form One Israel's winning strategy and were said to be paid by American Jews. Many of Barak's contributors also donated large sums to Bill Clinton, extending the impact of the administration on the election. With the right wing contributing to Netanyahu's campaign, AJCongress chairman Phil Baum, its president Jack Rosen, and other communal leaders criticized the role of "American Jewish millionaires" in Israeli elections. Still, according to estimates, Americans contributed between $10 to $15 million in 1999 as opposed to some $6 to $8 million in the 1996 election.[1]

The unexpected large-margin victory for Barak delighted the peace camp which worked hard to elect One Israel. APN declared that the Israeli ballot proved that "Bibi's 'empire' of messianic settlers, religious zealots and political extremists" didn't "strike back," adding that many in the Barak cabinet came from the ranks of PN. The AJCongress professed to have "great expectations for Barak and noted that his government is "widely representative, stable and effective," and IPF cashed on its connection to the new prime minister by attracting large crowds of donors to its fund-raising events. In fact, Barak; Yossi Beilin, the minister of justice in the new government; and Haim Ramon, another key Labor figure, seemed to favor the IPF, NIF, and other peace groups over some of the more mainline organizations. What is more, the leftist groups were elated by Barak's message that he would not wait for the Palestinians to become "Jeffersonian democrats" before "Israel can make peace with them."[2]

Barak's close association with the peace camp sent a signal to Israel's defense organizations that they were again faced with the psychologically arduous task of retooling their policy. Barak's charge that AIPAC is a "Likud oriented organization that has never supported the peace process" was not forgotten. The comments of his foreign policy adviser, Alon Pinkus, that AIPAC played a partisan role on behalf of Netanyahu, added fuel to the fire. When AIPAC, which scheduled Netanyahu to address its May 1999 convention, changed its mind and invited Barak, he declined. Although Barak assured AIPAC that he was ready to bury the hatchet, he made it known that he expected the organization to "thwart efforts in Congress by forces in the American Jewish community" who opposed his peace plans. Faced with the prospect of being bypassed in favor of IPF, AIPAC moved swiftly to readjust its policies. It dropped the opposition to a Palestinian state and declined to support a congressional showdown over Clinton's waiver, avoiding the May 31 deadline for moving the American embassy to Jerusalem.

The relations with the Presidents Conference, which picked Ronald Lauder— a strong Netanyahu supporter—as its new chairman in 1999, promised to be equally troubled. The Conference leaders were particularly upset by Barak's plans to meet only with some of its constituent members and by his insistence on a conjoint meeting with the IPF, which was not a Conference member. In a compromise move, Barak held two separate meetings, but his message to both audiences was tough. He wanted American Jews to accept the results of the

Israeli elections and unify behind the peace process. In a secret meeting, the new prime minister allegedly urged to end all pressure to move the embassy. Barak carried the same message to the General Assembly of the CJF, where in a televised address he proclaimed that "today, to be pro-Israel is to be pro-peace." To avoid a public split, Lauder promised to work closely with Barak and Malcolm Hoenlein, the executive vice chairman, adding that the Conference works "with the democratically elected government of Israel, whatever that government is."[3]

In adopting a conciliatory tone toward the new government the Israel defense organizations took into consideration the opinion polls. The AJC annual survey released just before the elections showed that 44 percent supported Palestinian statehood and 39 percent felt that Israel should accept a unilateral Palestinian declaration of independence. Forty-two percent of the sample felt that Israel should compromise on the status of Jerusalem within the framework of a permanent peace agreement and 53 percent supported dismantling some Jewish settlements in the West Bank. However, 88 percent of the respondents stated that the PA was not doing enough to carry out the peace agreement and 66 percent agreed with the statement that the "goal of the Arabs is not the return of the territories but the destruction of Israel.[4] A more detailed IPF poll conducted in late June indicated that 67 percent strongly supported the peace process and 21 percent somewhat supported it. Twenty-two percent said they would have voted for Netanyahu and 58 percent favored Barak. Barak was also expected to do a better job of moving the peace process forward than Netanyahu: 37 percent felt that he would do it much better and 36 percent felt he would do somewhat better. Twenty percent also felt that U.S.–Israeli relations would get much better under Barak and 27 percent thought that he would do somewhat better.[5]

While left-wing activists used these numbers to argue that Barak had the support of American Jews, nationalists remained skeptical of the Israeli leader. AFSI, which described itself as a watchdog of Israeli security, pledged to monitor the "red lines" in negotiations with the Palestinians. Joseph Frager, the head of the American Friends of Ateret Cohanim, warned against giving up settlements and vowed to accelerate construction in East Jerusalem. On the day that Barak was elected, construction began on a lot owned by Irving Moskowitz in Ras al-Amud, followed by preparations to build a two hundred–unit Jewish settlement in Abu Dis, an area rumored to be a possible site of a Palestinian capital. Morton Klein reserved the right to continue to monitor PA compliance with the Oslo accords and pressed Congress to link U.S. aid to the Palestinians to a number of new conditions. Among them was compensation to the families of thirteen Americans killed in terrorist attacks in Israel and the extradition of twenty-three Palestinians whom the ZOA accused of being responsible for the killings.[6]

Undaunted by the right-wing critique, Barak was determined to proceed with his comprehensive peace plan. In his inaugural speech on July 6, the prime minister called on "all regional leaders to take our outstretched hands and build a peace of the brave."[7] During a July 15 meeting with President Clinton the two leaders agreed on an ambitious agenda that included a possible agreement with the PA, Syria, and Lebanon. An important part of this plan was realized when, on September 5, Israel and the PA signed an agreement, known as Wye II, in Sharm el-Sheikh. The new protocol provided for Israel's withdrawal from an additional 11 percent of the West Bank, the release of Palestinian prisoners from Israeli jails, and the opening of a "safe passage" from Gaza to the West Bank. Wye II also called for an immediate assumption of final status talks, with a statement of principles drafted by February 15, 2000, and a final agreement to be completed by mid-September 2000. To sweeten the pot, Congress was expected to approve a $1.9 billion aid package, which the United States pledged during the original 1998 Wye agreement. The aid included $1.2 billion for Israel, $400 million for PA, and $300 million for Jordan.

Although the Wye II accord was praised by the usual array of peace groups and many of the mainstream Jewish organizations, the right wing lashed out against it and vowed to fight the aid package in Congress. AFSI declared that Wye II was tantamount to the process of "cleansing" Jews from the territories and a prelude to transferring Jews from the Golan. The ZOA reiterated its charge that the United States should not subsidize a brutal regime in the PA, which "tramples on the principles of freedom and democracy that Americans cherish." The powerful Christian Zionist lobby, including the National Unity Coalition for Israel and CIPAC joined the protest, which was also helped by Likud's Washington lobbyist, Yossi Ben-Aharon and Yoram Ettinger. Both the Jewish and Christian groups emphasized their concern that the aid package would weaken Israel and hurt American taxpayers. American Friend of the Women for Israel's Tomorrow/Women in Green asserted that the Wye fund would "cleanse Jews" with U.S. taxpayers' money. AFSI argued that "if Israel chooses to take perilous risks for peace," American taxpayers should not "foot the bill." The National Unity Coalition described the aid as "an unfortunate commitment of . . . dollars that belong to the people of the United States—the final endorsement to handing over Israeli territory in return for more empty promises."[8]

To prevent such an occurrence, the anti-Wye coalition launched a major lobbying campaign in Congress. Esther Levens from the National Unity Coalition urged members to write letters to their members of Congress to protest that U.S. funding for Wye as a "flagrant misuse of American tax dollars." She explained that "Congress is in a position to impose some common sense and financial accountability on the Oslo process." Richard Hellman from CIPAC appealed to his followers to lobby wavering House members, most of whom already came under strong pressure from right-wing Jewish groups, to vote against the aid bill. Such calls resonated well with top legislators who, like majority Senate leader Trent Lott (R–Miss.), expressed concerns about PA's ability to live up to its commitments. Tom DeLay (R–Tex.), the majority House whip, and Sonny Callahan (R–Ala.), the chair of the House Appropriation Foreign Operations

Subcommittee, had already voiced concerns that foreign layouts would hurt Social Security and other domestic programs. When the bill was defeated, the anti-Wye lobby expressed satisfaction. But critics—noting that DeLay and Ron Paul (R–Tex.), another ardent foe of aid, had poor voting records in Israel—charged that peace opponents were playing into the hands of isolationists in Congress.[9]

The failure of the aid package enraged the Barak government and its American Jewish supporters. Deputy Defense Minister Efraim Sneh accused the National Unity Coalition for Israel, the right-wing Jewish groups, and the Likud lobbyists of sabotaging the bill. Barak, in an address to the IPF, argued that to wait for the Palestinians to tone down their anti-Israeli rhetoric would lead to an indefinite postponement of peace. Labor ministers met with lawmakers and Barak in a joint press conference with Secretary of Defense William Cohen, and urged Congress to pass the bill. ADL's Abraham Foxman accused right-wing Jewish activists of using Congress to win a fight that they lost in Israel. He and others worried that the spectacle of Jewish groups lobbying against an Israeli government would cripple Israel's standing on Capitol Hill and erode the political clout of American Jewry. A senior Jewish source close to the White House complained that the community abandoned the Congress to right-wingers. Indeed, the wrangle over Wye proved so bitter that even the Likud party had second thoughts. Addressing the November General Assembly of the United Jewish Communities (the former CJF), Ariel Sharon, Netanyahu's successor as Likud leader, promised to end all lobbying by the opposition. Prodded by the Israeli government, AIPAC launched a major offensive to reverse the decision. The ADL followed up with a large-scale campaign, including advertisements in two Capitol Hill newspapers. Martin Raffell, a senior official with the Jewish Council for Public Affairs (JCPA), asked its constituent members to lobby their local legislators. These combined efforts produced a bipartisan embrace of Wye II. The House of Representatives passed the aid package on November 5 and, on November 18 and 19, Congress approved an omnibus appropriation bill that included the regular aid to Israel, and Egypt.[10]

With the community still recovering from the battle over Wye II, the Israeli government's plans to negotiate a peace treaty with Syria opened new fissures. Following an intelligence assessment that Israel's military power created a window of opportunity for an agreement with Syria, whose land and naval forces were judged to be fundamentally weak Barak offered to resume talks disrupted by the death of Rabin. With the help of Clinton, Barak and Syrian Foreign Minister Faruk al-Shara met in Washington in December 1999 and agreed to resume negotiations in January 2000 in Shepherdstown, a historic site in West Virginia. Despite the fact that the conference failed, there was widespread expectation that the aging Syrian leader Hafez Assad would be likely to conclude a peace treaty based on an Israeli offer to return most of the Golan Heights. Press reports estimated that an American aid package necessary to underwrite the deal would range between $20 to $100 billion over several years, with some of the money going to Syria. As before, there were also speculations that American forces might be stationed on the Heights to police the peace pact.

Propeace groups welcomed the prospect of an Israeli-Syrian peace accord and were eager to support an appropriate aid package. Mainline groups like AIPAC and the Conference of Presidents were more guarded, but mindful of their role as representatives of the Israeli government, tried to show balance. Lauder and Hoenlein, the Conference leaders, issued a statement welcoming the talks, which was seconded by AIPAC. However, such restraint was not binding on the right-wing camp, which simply dusted off its anti-Syrian campaign of the Rabin years, even when it became known that Lauder had secret negotiations with Assad on behalf of Netanyahu. In fact, right-wing groups had lobbied against American involvement in the Syrian deal well before the Shepherdstown conference convened. An *Outpost* article called peace with Syria a "kind of suicide," and the Center for Security Studies issued a new warning on stationing U.S. peace-keeping troops on the Golan Heights. Likud's lobbyist Ettinger met with congressional staffers to discuss the Syrian threat, and the National Unity Coalition for Israel repeated its opposition to the stationing of American troops on the Heights. The coalition also circulated a letter suggested by Ettinger to the effect that a peace treaty with Syria would jeopardize 30 percent of Israel's water resources, evict Jewish communities from the Golan, and put American trust in a dictator. JINSA sponsored a trip by thirty high-ranking American military experts who declared that "whether directly or through the provision of economic assistance . . . the expansion or upgrading of Syrian forces would be a source of instability in the region."[11]

To block American aid to Syria, the ZOA had endorsed a bill introduced by Michael Forbes (R–N.Y.) to halt all U.S. aid to Syria until it withdrew its forces from Lebanon. An organization called the International Coalition for Missing Israeli Soldiers demanded that the issue of Israeli soldiers missing since the war in Lebanon should be raised with Syria. Representative Tom Lantos (D–Cal.), often sympathetic to hard-line positions, wrote a letter to the State Department noting that under U.S. law, aid to Syria should take into account its willingness to assist in locating and returning the missing soldiers. The ZOA also raised the problem of the Syrian record of Holocaust denial, a highly emotional issue in the community, made even more poignant by the Holocaust denial trial in London. Elie Wiesel, a prominent Holocaust researcher; Hoenlein; Lionel Kaplan; AIPAC's president; and others signed ZOA's letter condemning Syria's denial of the Holocaust, which was published in the *New York Times* on February 9, 2000. Opponents of the Syrian deal had also lobbied Congress to hold hearings in order to discuss these and other issues. Foremost among them was the footing of the bill of the Syrian deal which Yigal Carmon's MEMRI estimated at between $20 and $100 billion. On February 8, 2000, more than a hundred volunteers from AFSI, National Unity Coalition, and CIPAC made the rounds on Capitol Hill and emphasized that the pact could cost $100 billion. To up the ante, ZOA asked lawmakers to sign a letter that emphasized that Syria was linked to terrorists organizations in the Middle East. As in the Wye case, Conservatives and isolationists in Congress welcomed the entreaties against a deal with Syria. Jesse Helms, the chairman of the Senate Foreign Relations Committee, wrote that "the peace between Israel and Syria must come on its own terms—not because the countries believe that they can temporarily push aside their fundamentalist bilateral problems in return for U.S. dollars."[12]

Such vigorous lobbying upset peace proponents and embarrassed AIPAC. Debra DeLee, the APN president, accused "hard-line Jews" of adopting isolationist positions in order to sabotage the Syrian peace treaty, a theme reiterated by Sonnenfeld, the chairman of IPF. AIPAC urged Congress members not to sign the ZOA letter, noting that its timing would jeopardize the negotiations between Israel and Syria. Responding to critics, Klein described AIPAC's opposition as "perplexing" since AIPAC's own policy called on the United States to condition its relation with Syria on Syria's efforts to end terrorism. AFSI's president Herbert Zweibon was much more blunt. He stated that "it's irrelevant what American Jews think. Its relevant what Congress thinks," adding, "If I wanted to convince anybody, it would be the Christian community."[13] These and other statements showed that Israel's renewed peace-initiative balkanized the Jewish community into autonomous fiefdoms which brokered no central authority. Worse, Israel's umbrella organizations were internally divided and harshly criticized by both ends of the communal spectrum, further undermining their legitimacy.

WHOSE VOICE IS IT ANYWAY? THE ORGANIZED COMMUNITY, CONGRESS, AND THE PEACE PROCESS

With mutual suspicion and hostility on the increase, the Conference and AIPAC came under intense scrutiny, turning their functioning into an exercise in continuos controversy. The tone was set after Lauder's ties to Netanyahu were publicized by the *New York Jewish Week*. Although Lauder denied the allegations and was subsequently confirmed, left-leaning leaders like Howard Squadron from the AJCongress and Mark Rosenblum from APN demanded that Lauder be investigated. The Conference came under withering criticism from leftists when it refused to admit the dovish group Meretz USA, the affiliate of the Israeli Meretz party. Its plan to downgrade the status of three leftist groups—Labor Zionist Alliance, the National Committee for Labor Israel, and the Women's League for Israel—for allegedly not meeting membership standards, provoked more accusation of right-wing bias. However, right-wing groups like AFSI accused the Conference of failing to bolster Israel and being preoccupied with the fact that the new chairman "is too supportive of Benjamin Netanyahu." The Anglo-Jewish press was filled with complaints about the oligarchic nature of the Conference under the stewardship of Lauder and Hoenlein, accompanied by the old charges that the organization had no clear bylaws or itemized budgets and that its decision-making process was murky. One editor, Jonathan Tobin, wrote that the Conference was a "bloated joke. There are dozen of so-called 'major' organizations and the group is paralyzed by division and ultimately speaks for no one."[14]

AIPAC fared only marginally better when it tried to adjust its policy to Barak's peace offensive. The message that the Jewish community should unite behind the Israeli government was delivered during AIPAC's annual conference in May 2000 from a number of quarters. Speaking via satellite, Barak argued that "when we are united we are much stronger" and AIPAC's Kaplan pledged support to Barak, noting that "we stand ready to do anything." However, Klein reiterated his objection to Israel's giving up land for an uncertain peace, and other participants complained about the proposed displacement of Jewish settlers in the Golan and the territories. AIPAC's effort to secure aid for the PA and Syrian peace deal was bitterly questioned. Murray Kohl, publisher of the rightist newsletter *Israeli & Global News*, wrote that AIPAC was asking Congress to spend tax-payers' money on "an ephemeral peace," which would "ultimately transfer Israel into a military basket case." Right-wing participants also challenged AIPAC's decision to invite Al Gore but not Republican George W. Bush to address the conference, calling it "partisan." Those and other critics made it clear that AIPAC's resolve to support the Israeli government was less than welcome, leading some to wonder "what it means to be an Israeli supporter these days."[15]

Indeed, even if the defense organizations could unite around a clear plan, the fragmentation of the community would have made imposing discipline difficult, if not impossible. Continuing unilateral lobbing of Congress was a case in point. In June 1999 ZOA persuaded forty-two legislators to demand that the United States block aid to Jordan until it extradites Abu Daoud, who was the mastermind in the 1972 killing of Israeli athletes in Munich. Jordan denied sheltering Daoud and propeace organizations protested holding Jordan to higher standards than Israel or America, which were less than vigilant in prosecuting terrorists. In its letter to ZOA, AIPAC leaders protested: "the gratuitous attack on Jordan's eligibility for U.S. assistance intimated in your campaign is damaging not only to Jordan itself, but also to important American Israeli interests."[16] Right-wing groups had also persisted with their efforts to force the PA to comply with the Oslo and Wye agreement, despite the fact that the Barak government dismantled the department established to oversee PA records on incitement. Jews for Truth Now demanded in an ad that the PA replace their message of incitement with the "message of peace." Vigorous lobbying was also used to keep the issue of American victims of Palestinian terror alive and to publicize the plight of Israeli victims. In a series of ads a new group called American Friends of Victims of Oslo accused Clinton of creating a terrorist state in the PA.[17]

Perhaps the most intensive lobbying involved Jerusalem. In spite of Barak's well-known reservations about moving the American embassy to Jerusalem, AFSI, the ZOA, the Orthodox Union, One Israel Fund, and B'nai B'rith International, among others, urged Congress to dissuade the administration from using the waver. Anthony Weiner (D–N.Y.) was persuaded to sponsor a motion to recognize Jerusalem as Israel's capital and there was an initiative to have Congress mandate the State Department to record the birth of American citizens in Jerusalem as Israelis. Countering these efforts were peace groups such as IPF that commended Clinton on repeatedly delaying the embassy move. The Reform movement noted that there are "understandable reasons" for the president's decision not to move the embassy. The APN and the Jewish Peace Lobby went so far as to try and mobilize congressional opinion behind the idea of dividing Jerusalem. On February 11, 2000, APN hosted on Capitol Hill a "Conference on Jerusalem," which was cosponsored by Senator Daniel Inoyoue (D–Hawaii) and Representative Robert Wexler (D–Fla.).[18]

The cross-lobbying of Congress triggered the usual round of complaints that the community's standing on the Hill was being undermined. Editorial writers were particularly worried that lawmakers would have a difficult time determining which Jewish group to listen to. In the words of Jonathan Tobin: "most members of Congress worry about being caught between the Jewish peace-process skeptics and the Jewish peace-process cheerleaders—who often disagree on what is or is not pro-Israel." Even relatively minor matters resulted in major confrontations between the warring Jewish camps. When Samuel Berger, Clinton's national security adviser, mentioned in a speech that clashes between Israeli and Palestinians are "both the blessing and the curse of the Israeli-Palestinian conflict," the ZOA urged Congress to press for Berger's dismissal. However, the ADL, APN, and the Religious Action Center of Reform Judaism circulated their own letter defending Berger. Misgivings about sawing confusion on Capitol Hill notwithstanding, Labor and Likud actively encouraged unilateral lobbying efforts. Although the Israeli government publicly disavowed Beilin's plans to cut AIPAC's "super embassy" to size, it was common knowledge that Labor preferred to rely on IPF and other sympathetic groups to make its case in Washington. As for Likud, Sharon's call to end Israel's partisan lobby in the United States was short lived. In March 2000, anticipating the resumption of talks with Syria, Sharon urged American Jews to defeat any financial outlays for a peace deal. In June, a delegation of Likud and Shas legislators lobbied Congress to oppose Barak's proposed concession to the Palestinians.[19]

There was also apprehension that the passions unleashed by the peace process would further erode the standards of civility in the communal discourse. In one highly publicized case, the APN accused some of the constituent members of the National Unity Coalition for Israel, such as Friends of Israel, of proselytizing Jews. The implication that Jewish groups who collaborated with the Coalition colluded in such tactics was not lost on the right-wing organizations that noisily protested the use of McCarthy tactics of "guilt by association." Another high-profile incident was prompted by Hadassah's decision to bestow an award on Hillary Rodham Clinton, who was criticized by some right-wing circles for being pro-Palestinian. ADL's Foxman singled out ZOA for sharp criticism, prompting Klein to lodge an official complaint with the Presidents Conference and demand an apology from the ADL chief. The development surrounding the annual Isaiah Award of the United Jewish Communities (UJC) illustrated best the atmosphere of communal tension. A leaked story that the UJC planned to give the award to Arafat created a storm of protest and promoted its president, Stephen Solender, to hire Kroll Associates to investigate the leak. Still, many Jewish leaders ridiculed the idea of hiring a private eye and bemoaned the level of mistrust and hostility in the community.[20]

Indeed, the level of mistrust was so great that questions about bias and representation had become a major part of the peace discourse. The Orthodox leaning *Jewish Press* accused the Jewish Telegraphic Agency of "following too quickly the Israeli Barak–friendly media." The Forward Association and the philanthropist Michael Steinhardt, who funded the *Forward*, fired its conservative editor Seth Lipsky. Lipsky, an admirer of the Revisionist leader Vladimir Jabotinsky, was accused of bending facts to suit his ideological agenda and promoting flamboyant positions such as a demand to arrest Hafez Assad during his meeting with President Clinton in Geneva.[21] Coming on top of the wide use of alternative, right-leaning information networks by Oslo opponents, the community shared precious little common perceptual ground, making its voice even more fractious. Even the opinion polls, traditionally relied upon to gauge the attitudes of the American Jews, were less than helpful because of the genuine ambiguity of the respondents and partisan sponsorship of the surveys. Focusing on different issues and employing different wording, peace proponents and opponents could claim that they represented the communal sentiments most faithfully. ZOA's Klein used a poll published in the September 1999 issue of the *Middle East Quarterly* to prove that his organization, far from being radical, had reflected positions shared by the majority of American Jews.[22]

Sorting out competing claims to represent a balkanized community made up of ontologically diverging groups was challenging enough for academic analysts, not to mention for Congress. Never an easy task, things promised to get even more difficult when the Barak government entered what was billed as the final stage negotiations with the Palestinians in Camp David in July 2000.

CAMP DAVID II: SLAYING THE LAST SACRED COWS

In spite of the news blackout at Camp David, it soon became clear that the Israeli government was prepared to offer far-reaching concessions to the Palestinians in return for a final settlement of the century-long conflict. The scope of the proposed settlement had elicited predictable responses from the ends of the communal spectrum. The left hailed Barak's resolve to reach a peace agreement with the Palestinians and described the occasion as historic. Aware of the Jewish community's hesitation to support massive concessions, Leonard Fein argued that such sacrifices are justified because they would bring an end to a bitter and bloody conflict. The right attacked Barak in articles, editorials, and paid advertisements. A *Jewish Press* editorial called Barak "pathetic" and Friends of Families of Victims of Oslo placed ads in the *Jewish Voice* that referred to Barak, along with Yasser Arafart and Clinton, as Israel's most "dastardly trio." FLAME (Facts and Logic about the Middle East) claimed that it was the Arabs, not Israel, who needed to sacrifice for peace. The Center for Security Policy called the outcome of Camp David II "Assisted Suicide for Israel." A new organization called Victims of Arab Terror International (VAT) announced that it would physically oppose the removal of Jewish settlements. A VAT spokesperson disclosed that the group was raising money to buy military equipment for settlers and providing military training for American Jewish youth willing to make aliya and defend the settlements.[23] While most right-wing spokesmen blamed either Barak or Clinton's desire for a legacy for the rush to achieve a peace agreement, Daniel Pines argued that the Israeli readiness to make far-reaching concessions had a more popular base. Pipes was one of the first to contend that the Israeli public was tired of the prolonged conflict and susceptible to defeatism vis-à-vis the Palestinians. Noting that the Israeli reputation for heroism was "sadly out of date," he argued that, weary of constant loss of life, young people are less than enthusiastic to serve in the military, creating serious morale problems in the IDF. Pipes compared this atmosphere of defeatism to the climate of appeasement in Europe in the 1930s and the Vietnam War in America.[24]

Whatever the diagnosis of the "Israeli malaise," as Pipes put it, right-wing activists made it clear that they would continue to challenge Camp David II in Congress. Rumors that Clinton was ready to promise up to $40 billion to underwrite the agreement gave them new ammunition. Americans for Responsible Foreign Spending took the lead in arguing that the American people would rather spend $40 billion to rescue the social security system. The Center for Security Policy and MEMRI were among a long list of groups that joined the antiaid movement. Others tried to emphasize the security risks of the proposed deal by appealing to Senator Sam Brownback (R–Kan.), the chair of the Foreign Relations Near Eastern and South Asian Affairs Subcommittee, to hold a special hearing on the subject. They were helped by Likud politicians like MK Michael Kleiner and his colleagues who visited Capitol Hill to lobby against Camp David II. Kleiner reported that many Congress members had "difficulty understanding how Israel can allow itself to give up strategic assets without which the country will be in danger."[25]

In staging a major campaign against Camp David II nationalist activists had benefited from considerable doubts in the mainstream community. ZOA scored a coup when, on June 23, it published an open letter to Barak signed by thirty American Jewish leaders, including two past chairmen of the Conference, top officials of AIPAC, ADL, the State of Israel Bonds, and other moderate officials. One of them, Julius Berman, stated that the letter was a "wake-up call, a plea to Barak" to heed the concerns of leaders who considered themselves a centrist constituency. The text listed concerns voiced by the Israeli Interior Minister Nathan Sharansky, who resigned from the government over Barak's alleged willingness to surrender more than 90 percent of the territories, uproot thousands of settlers, and give Arafat control of Abu Dis and parts of Jerusalem. The letter embarrassed AIPAC, whose chairman of the executive committee, Gerald Charnoff, was one of the signatories. After Charnoff was forced to resign, AIPAC spokesmen emphatically stated that the letter did not represent the views of the organization. Still, observers noted that the 463 members of AIPAC's executive committee, who spanned the entire political spectrum, were deeply divided on the peace process.[26]

More importantly, the controversy over the letter revisited the older question of whether American Jews have the right to criticize the democratically elected government of Israel. Theodore Mann and Seymour Reich attacked the ZOA letter, claiming that "recent assertions that American Jews oppose the Prime Minister's efforts to reach an agreement with the Palestinians are inaccurate." Neal Sher, a former executive director of AIPAC who asked to have his name removed from the letter, noted that, as a Diaspora Jew, he believed that decisions about Israel's security should "rest on the shoulders of the duly elected officials." A *Forward* editorial pleaded that the Israelis and the Palestinians be given the "space they needed to go the last mile" and avoid the urge "to circle our wagons, rattle our swards or . . . rush to Washington with new initiatives to punish the Palestinians." Melvin Salberg, a past chairman of the Conference, advised American Jewish critics of Barak to "pipe down," adding that in life-and-death situations, the only decision makers should be the Israeli people and their leaders. To make sure that such voices were heard, the IPF organized a letter of support for Camp David II. It was signed by 384 leaders, including six former chairs of the Conference, twenty-four AIPAC officials, and senior leaders of scores of Jewish organizations. The letter emphasized that an overwhelming majority of American Jews supported the peace process and expressed confidence in Barak's "visionary leadership."[27]

However, critics such as Jacob Schreiber, the editor of the *Atlanta Jewish Times*, pointed out that by asking American rightists to "shut up," Barak's defenders follow the well-worn routine of the "shoe is on the other foot." He referred to the notion that American Jews have no right to voice opinions because they do not live in Israel as "recycled garbage of the week," and stressed that Diaspora Jews and Zionist pioneers "teamed up to establish Israel and that "Israel belongs to the entire Jewish people." Invoking the doctrine of limited sovereignty, Schreiber asserted that it is the obligation of the Diaspora to "actively engage in this historic Jewish enterprise."[28]

Mindful of such sentiments, the Barak government tried to promote more vigorously his vision of peace. While the Israeli prime minister was secluded in Camp David, his envoy to the Diaspora, Michael Melchior, toured a large number of communities and held meetings with Jewish members of Congress. However, such efforts could not overcome Labor's notoriously poor record of reaching out to U.S. Jews. By all accounts, the Israeli ambassador to Washington, David Ivry, the former head of the Israel Air Force, was not well qualified for the task. Described as "shy and taciturn," he was said to have an adversarial relation with the Anglo-Jewish press, and was reluctant to appear in public.

Shmuel Sisso, the Israeli consul general in New York responsible for media and the city's large Jewish community, was also less than an inspired choice. An alleged protégé of the Foreign Minster David Levy, Sisso, a former mayor of a small Israeli town, had poor English skills and no diplomatic background. A report of Israel's state comptroller found a lack of coordination in the North American section of the diplomatic service, and Barak's own National Security Council was critical of the outreach to the Jewish community.[29]

Improving the public relations campaign would have undoubtedly been helpful, but the Barak government faced an uphill battle in persuading the community to accept its far-reaching compromises for peace. Analysts noted that for some thirty years Jews had been "weaned on" AIPAC's "Myths and Facts about the Middle East." Among its mantras was the strategic importance of the Golan Heights, a fact that was also "drilled" into the heads of every American Jew who has "visited the plateau." Consequently, many in the community had a hard time conceiving how it can been "traded for Syrian promises of good will." Even more shocking to Jewish sensibilities was Labor's willingness to divide Jerusalem, long the most sacred of the "sacred cows." Some commentators advised the community to face the fact that Barak "is not singing along with chorus and the traditional text" and accept the new reality in which Jerusalem "is the eternal divided capital of Israel." However, the issue had sent shock waves through the community.[30]

In addition to the usual right-wing critics like ZOA and Orthodox groups, Hoenlein declared that "the position of the Jewish community remains the same as it always has been—a unified Jerusalem, the capital of Israel." Shoshana Cardin, a former chair of the Conference, added that she had not changed her beliefs that Jerusalem should stay united. ADL's Foxman allowed that "an Israeli compromise on Jerusalem" would be troubling to a "lot of people," but for the sake of a final settlement, "most members of the American Jewish community would swallow and say, okay." The rank and file was equally divided. The AJC's annual Survey of American Jewish Opinion conducted in September 2000 found that 57 percent of the sample refused to compromise with the Palestinians over the status of Jerusalem and 36 percent were willing to do so. Yet only 17 percent of the compromisers were willing to relinquish sovereignty over the Old City within the framework of a permanent peace with the Palestinians. Commenting on these fissures, one communal leader urged American Jews to come to grips with the fact that "community consensus around Israel has completely broken down."[31] However, the failure of Camp David II and the outbreak of Palestinian violence following the visit of Sharon to Temple Mount on September 27, gave communal unity a temporary reprieve.

THE EL AQSA INTIFADA: RESTORING UNITY TO THE AMERICAN JEWISH COMMUNITY?

The refusal of Arafat to accept what was regarded as an exceptionally generous Israeli offer united most of the community in criticizing the Palestinians.

Although some peace activists criticized Sharon and blasted the harsh IDF response to the Palestinian protest, the violence and brutality of the second Intifada was widely condemned by almost the entire spectrum of American Jewry. The lynching of the two Israeli soldiers and the destruction of religious shrines located in PA areas had a special resonance in the community. One Jewish leader declared that "right now American Jewish opinion is unanimous that what has happened so far is unacceptable." Echoing the Six Day and the Yom Kippur wars, there were solidarity rallies in many communities, and the November General Assembly of the UJC cancelled some of the planned activities to accommodate a number of pro-Israeli events. Privately, some leaders were reported to have been relieved that the show of loyalty for Israel had replaced the highly divisive issues originally scheduled. Fund-raising officials were also hopeful that Israel could be restored to the center of the Jewish philanthropic agenda, which had suffered a decline in the previous few years.[32]

Underlying this more consensual approach was a powerful shift in the dynamics of the peace process discourse. In yet another of the sudden reversals in the Middle East conflict, the Intifada II had vindicated many of the reservations that the Oslo opponents had voiced for years. This change was even more remarkable given the fact that just three months before the outbreak of violence even some right-leaning observers conceded that in the historical debate between the American left and right, the left-wing had won. As one of them put it, the center and the right had to face the fact that the American left—"those who advocated sharing Jerusalem and a Palestinian state"—were about to win.[33]

Standing to profit most from this gain in credibility was ZOA's Klein, who for years had criticized PA's lack of compliance with Oslo and Wye. A White Paper published by the Barak government detailed a long list of Palestinian violations such as sheltering terrorists, failure to collect illegal firearms, incitement to violence, and condoning large scale criminal activities, most notably car theft and tax fraud. A secret report submitted to the Mitchell committee, which was appointed to investigate the outbreak of the violence, added participation of Palestinian police in attacks on Israelis, destruction of Jewish religious sites, incitement to violence, and hatred to the list. An Israeli Foreign Policy Ministry video shown at the General Assembly made the same points, prompting Klein to note that during the 1999 UJC meeting he was threatened with arrest for trying to show similar videotaped evidence. Norman Podhoretz, another persistent Oslo detractor, could also claim that his predictions had come true. Much like Pipes, Podhoretz blamed Israeli war weariness for the evasion of the "unbearable reality" that the Arabs in general and the Palestinians in particular did not share in the yearnings for peace. In an ironic reversal, it was the turn of the right-wingers to accuse the peace camp of being a "messianic movement." According to one critic, the peace movement shared with other messianic movements an urge to suppress any information that "calls into question the arrival of blissful era."[34]

While peace proponents were not ready to accept that "peace within reach" was a fundamentalist messianic belief, they freely admitted that the Intifada II served as a serious reality check. The dovish John Ruskay, a high-ranking UJA official, admitted that, like Oslo, which shattered the fantasies of Greater Israel, the new Palestinian uprising "challenged if not shattered the fantasies of an early, quick, peaceful coexistence between Israelis and Palestinians." Other veteran peace proponents were even more outspoken. Gary Rosenblatt, the editor of the *New York Jewish Week*, confessed that the tendency to ignore what the Palestinians were saying was a mistake. Quoting Itamar Marcus from the Palestinian Media Watch, Rosenblatt agreed with the statement that the Palestinians were quite open in their intentions, which amounted to the "delegitimation of Israel's right to exist and the need to continue the revolution." He also repeated Marcus's assertion that Palestinian leaders denied the Holocaust and that they had planned for an uprising well before Sharon's visit to Temple Mount. Menachem Rosensaft, one of the Stockholm Five, wrote about his change of heart in the *Washington Post*, and the AJCongress took out an ad in the *New York Times* to retract their unequivocal support for Oslo. Rabbi Alexander Schindler charged that "Arafat was waiting for an excuse" and compared the Palestinian riots to Kristallnacht in 1938 when "Hitler really wanted to firebomb all the synagogues and was just waiting for the right moment to do it." APN published a statement blaming the PA for failing to take "significant steps to build support for the peace process among its own people" and for lacking in commitment to defeat anti-Israeli terrorism."[35]

Although not all on the left and the center agreed with the nationalists and the Orthodox that the conflict is existential, the focus on Palestinian behavior had legitimized the right-wing notions that democratic norms do matter after all. The commentator Hillel Halkin captured the new perception well in his description of the Palestinian society that "in the form of its street mobs, its politicians, or its supposed intellectuals, seems so easily incitable . . . so incapable of distinguishing between truth and falsehood or subjecting itself to the slightest degree of self-criticism or self-analysis." Coupled with reports about the use of children in the riots and the culture of martyrdom that fueled the uprising, such observations changed the moral prism through which the conflict had been viewed since the first Intifada. Rather than powerless victims of the Israeli occupation, the Palestinians came to be perceived by many in the community as willful authors of their own misery, resurrecting the old adage that "the Palestinians have never missed an opportunity to miss an opportunity." Though some peace activists still urged to balance Jewish pain with the Palestinian narrative of a people "contained and disconnected by a series of Bantustatans," they fought an uphill battle.[36]

The new communal paradigm negated most of the assumptions on which the Oslo process was based. As one critic pointed out, the "naïve Oslo script" expected that Palestinians not risk their hard-won international respectability and prospects of independence by reverting to their old terrorist ways. Instead of the "fantasies about a new Middle East," the Oslo experiment gave birth to

a terrorist and corrupt political entity where billions of dollars were misappro-
priated by the Palestinian "kleptocracy." Pipes, who had all along questioned
the political maturity of the Palestinians, explained that in the Arab culture
where family honor was pivotal, political suicide and martyrdom were considered the highest form of honoring ones family. What is more, the new paradigm
reestablished the traditional view of Jews as victims of Arab violence, an image
underscored by brutal terrorist attacks on Israeli civilians.

More important, the new paradigm had fed into the old ambivalence about
the real motives of the Arabs. Even before the outbreak of the violence, AJC
surveys showed that 69 percent of the respondents agreed with the statement
that the "goal of the Arabs is not the return of occupied territories but rather
the destruction of Israel." The violence had hardened the American Jewish views
of the Palestinians, while at the same time giving a blessing to Israel's handling
of the Intifada. A March 2001 survey showed that 77 percent of the respondents
condemned the use of Palestinian children in the forefront of protest; only 37
percent felt that Israel was overreacting in trying to contain the violence. In a
potentially more significant development, the settler movement had managed to
mobilize segments of the mainstream American Jewish community. Reversing
decades-old policy, some local federations began to offer aid to settlements
across the Green Line.[37]

In spite of the emerging consensus that the Palestinians had shown themselves
woefully unprepared for embracing peace, the community remained divided over
possible solutions. The new fault lines did not follow the traditional left-right
cleavages. Despairing of the possibility of a peaceful coexistence, some veteran
peace activists took to advocating total separation between the Israelis and the
Palestinians, replete with concrete walls and barbed wire. But others, including
the Reform movement, continued to insist that "holding out for a sea change in
the mentality of the Palestinians" and a "democratic transition in the PA" would
prolong the conflict and contribute to more bloodshed. In fact, the UAHC established a three-year peace project designed to explore the "core issues where
Palestinian anger came from." High among the core issues were Jewish settlements "buried in the heart of the Arab population." The Reform leadership
emphasized that "by speaking out, the peace camp may wipe out the veneer of
'unity' and 'solidarity' that has enveloped the Jewish community since violence
broke out."[38]

As usual, Jerusalem generated the most pronounced disagreements. As early
as September 2000, the Conference's front man, Hoenlein, made a speech critical of Israel's compromise over the sovereignty of the Temple Mount in September 2000. He warned that "in future years, all of us will have to answer to
our children and grandchildren when they ask us why we did not do more to
stop the giving away . . . the birthright, the geographical heart and the spiritual
soul of the Jewish people for 3000 years." Hoenlein's statement was welcome
by the National Council of Young Israel, the Rabbinical Council of America,
and the Orthodox Union, but got little traction in the mainstream community.

However, three months later, the ZOA, in response to a statement from the Israel Foreign Minister Shlomo Ben-Ami that the Temple Mount would be shared, sponsored an ad stating that "Israel Must Not Surrender Judaism's Holiest Site." Among the thirty-five signatories were many moderates, including six past chairpersons of the Conference of Presidents, a high-ranking official of the Conservative movement, and a onetime consultant to the IPF. The ad stated that "no Israeli leader has the right to give away the essence of the Jewish people that is embodied in the Temple Mount."[39]

Evoking the doctrine of limited sovereignty, the ZOA's chief charged that Barak "has no moral right to surrender the Temple Mount or any other territory to Yasser Arafat. We have a sacred obligation to future generations of Jews to keep and protect Judaism's holiest site, the Temple Mount." Klein threatened that if Barak agreed to hand over the Temple Mount, he and others would try to undermine its implementation. While it was not clear whether the more moderate signatories shared this view, the issue of Jerusalem clearly cut across the traditional ideological divide. Observers noted that giving up control over the Temple Mount would threaten American Jewish identity and strain the already delicate relations between Israel and its Diaspora. Charles Liebman explained that it would be equivalent to saying to American Jews that "nothing Jewish is sacred to Israel, and therefore nothing Jewish is sacred to the Jewish people." Rabbi David Clayman, the director of the AJCongress office in Jerusalem, added that American Jews "attached themselves to the issue of Jerusalem" because it is easy to idealize.[40]

Important as such symbolism was, some in the community disagreed with the notion that Israel had no right to trade Temple Mount for peace. The Jewish Peace Lobby organized a statement of one hundred rabbis who asserted that Judaism does not demand exclusive Jewish sovereignty over the Mount. IPF's Thomas Smerling insisted that Israel had full sovereignty to negotiate over its territory, and Jeffry Mallow, the president of the Labor Zionist Alliance, urged Jews to "allow Israel to negotiate the holy sites." ADL's Foxman argued that it "was nice say that the Temple belongs to the Jewish people," but it was the Israelis who laid down their lives to defend it. He also insisted that "American Jews should respect the right of the democratically elected government of Israel . . . to make decisions concerning its future." Clayman charged that "Israel is a make-believe land for American Jews . . . a symbol," but not a place "where they send their sons to the army." These and other communal leaders warned that by claiming Jewish rather than Israeli sovereignty over the holy sites, American Jews could turn the conflict from one between Israel and the Palestinians to a broader struggle between Judaism and Islam.[41]

As expected, the Jerusalem issue had further complicated the relations between the Conference and the Labor government. According to reports, relations between Barak and Lauder virtually broke down and some Labor politicians denounced what they regarded as a right-wing takeover of the organization. When Sharansky, the leader of the opposition Yisrael b'Aliya party, urged Lauder to participate in a January 8, 2001, rally for a united Jerusalem, Labor MK Colette Avital attacked the Conference chairman for what she described as blatant partisanship. In turn, Likud's politicians described Avital's criticism as "chutzpa in the extreme," reminding her that many American Jews had contributed to Labor's election campaign and helped to organize its huge peace rallies. However, Labor officials challenged the rally organizers, including One Jerusalem, to disclose the list of donors, most of them American Jews. In his address, Lauder declared that he spoke for "tens of millions" of Jews throughout the world "who oppose dividing Jerusalem." Such phraseology created a storm at the Conference, which had previously voted against Lauder's plans to speak in the name of the organization. Some of the constituent members accused their chairman of false representation and nondemocratic practices, but others praised him for defending Jerusalem.[42]

Labor's irritation with what was perceived to be U.S. Diaspora meddling was not limited to Jerusalem. Beilin told the editorial board of the *Forward* that American Jews should stop acting "more Israeli than Israelis" when undermining Arafat. He was reacting to an ad taken out by ADL stating that Arafat was not a credible negotiating partner because of the PA's incitement to hatred and violence. This promoted Foxman to note that Beilin himself championed the right of the Diaspora Jews to voice their own views. Others complained that the Barak government created confusion by claiming that Arafat is both bad and a legitimate negotiating partner. These acrimonious exchanges lead Ami Eden to note that U.S. Jews are "stuck between Barak and hard place."[43]

Quite surprisingly, the victory of the hard-line Sharon in the February election 2001 had restored a measure of harmony to the relations between Israel and its American Diaspora. American Jewish leadership quickly expressed support for the new prime minister, with some dovish groups like the Congress pointing to the huge size of his victory. Rabbi Marc Schneider, a former Barak supporter, pointed out that the American Jewish community, like the people of Israel, is "disillusioned, disenchanted, and disgusted" with the Palestinian refusal to make peace. He added that it was "Yasser Arafat who elected Sharon." Such sentiments had strengthened the right-wing tendencies in the Israel defense organizations. According to observers, AIPAC, which had to make a painful effort to support Barak's peace vision, felt much more comfortable with the hard-line approach of Sharon and the renewed focus on Israel's security. The Conference of Presidents elected the right-leaning Mortimer Zuckerman as its new chairman despite considerable opposition from liberal members. The right-wing resurgence had translated into a renewed push to mobilize Capitol Hill against the Palestinian Authority. A number of bills pending before Congress demanded that aid to the Palestinians and U.S. diplomatic relations with the PA should be conditioned on Arafat's willingness to fight terror. AIPAC, which in the past had fought efforts to make aid conditional, affirmed that the U.S.–Palestinian relations should be linked to the "PA and PLO compliance with commitments made to Israel and the United States," leaning toward a cut of aid. The ZOA moved closer to realizing its demand that the State Department post rewards for the capture of Palestinian killers of American citizens in Israel. Separate legislation was introduced to create a unit within the Justice Department devoted to capturing and prosecuting Palestinian killers of American citizens.[44]

Such right-wing inroads angered peace activists and liberal segments of the community. Reform leader Eric Yoffie, who emerged as the major voice of dissent, while condemning Arafat, called for a freeze on settlements, and APN condemned efforts to cut off diplomatic relations with the PA. Yoffie was the driving force to derail the candidacy of Zuckerman, a move that reportedly angered Hoenlin, who complained that contention in the Jewish community was "counterproductive." The Reform and the Conservative movements also took the unusual step of urging President George W. Bush to disregard the advertizing campaign against his ambassador-designate to Israel, Daniel Kurtzer, spearheaded by the ZOA. Right-wing activists accused Kurtzer, an Orthodox Jew and a career diplomat, of being associated with the "failed Oslo process" and of pressuring Israel to make one-sided concessions.[45]

As in the past, the communal squabbles over the peace process and the concomitant efforts on the part of the leadership to maintain a united façade had promoted criticism. Rosensaft commentator denounced the "ill-conceived perennial attempts . . . to delegitimize those . . . who hold views that call into question some absolutist dogma or other." He decried the "various apparatchiks and modern-day commissars" who "lecture us about what we, individually or collectively."[46] Other observers warned that efforts to stifle the discourse would have a corrosive impact on the communal moral. Still, the El Aqsa Intifada exposed a more fundamental weakness in the relation with Israel at a time when American Jewry embarked on yet another of its periodical quests to reverse the decline in Jewish identity.

FROM CENTRALITY TO MARGINALITY: ISRAEL AND THE RENAISSANCE IMPERATIVE

Four years after the North American Commission on Jewish Identity and Continuity issued its report "To Renew and Sanctify: A Call to Action" in 1995, concerns about the dwindling Jewish population and the underlying identity crisis were raised again. Surveys bore out such worries. A majority in the 2000 AJC survey stated that they did not oppose interfaith marriages and 80 percent agreed with the statement that "intermarriage is inevitable in an open society." Although 67 percent thought that Jews had an "obligation to urge other Jews to marry Jews, a clear majority felt it was racist to oppose interfaith marriages; three-fourths of the sample said that a rabbi should officiate in such marriages. Even the long-planned 2000 Jewish population survey fell victim to the complexities of Jewish identity in America: it had to be rescheduled as researchers wrestled with the question of "who is a Jew" and how to count marginal Jews.[47]

A new round of communal discourse generated a number of identity-building initiatives that became known as the renaissance imperative. Most of them were focused on synagogue transformation and Jewish education. One of them, the Synagogue Transformation and Renewal (STAR), was underwritten by the philanthropic partnership of Edgar Bronfman, Steinhardt, and Charles Schusterman. The Reform movement devised the Experiment in Congregational Education (ECE), and Synagogue 2000 aimed at transforming worship and services. There was also an increased emphasis on Jewish education, the epicenter of the continuity imperative. Partnership for Excellence in Jewish Education (PEJE) redoubled its efforts to increase attendance in Jewish day schools and there was more effort invested in adult Jewish education. Although the renaissance imperative attracted its share of critics, there was a communal consensus that the old formula for identity building—anti-Semitism, commemoration, the Holocaust, and Israel—does not attract the young.[48]

In fact, the AJC survey had indicated that Israel's centrality in American Jewish life reached an all-time low. Only 28 percent reported being very close to Israel, followed by 46 percent of fairly close. Although 80 percent agreed with the statement that caring for Israel is an important part of Jewish identity, only 3 percent said that support for Israel was the most important part of their Jewish identity. Only 58 percent reported visiting Israel, a figure that indicated the continuing attitudinal and behavioral disconnection. A study of one thousand, five hundred Conservative youth in 1995 and 1999 showed the same slide in feelings toward Israel. Some commentators used these results to talk about "de-Israelization of American Jewry," and others asserted that the "ghost" of the anti-Zionist American Council for Judaism was winning the day. Even those who did not share such a pessimistic forecast had to agree that Israel's perceived value as an identity builder suffered a serious decline. Planned before the outbreak of El Aqsa Intifada, the General Assembly of the UJC had few panels devoted to Israel. The newly created Overseas Needs Assessment and Distribution Committee (ONAD), responding to domestic concerns, had cut the allocation to Israel to some 35 percent of the total UJC fund.[49]

In what became a ritualized round of commentary cum finger pointing, observers split in assessing the root causes of the growing alienation between the Israeli and American Jews. The Orthodox and the nationalists repeated the charge that, under the leadership of Barak, Israel had drifted further into the post-Zionist era of "normalization." Much attention in this context was devoted to Yoram Hazony's book *The Jewish State: The Struggle for Israel's Soul*, in which the Shalem Center president charged that the secular Ashkenazi elite had tried hard to de-Judaize the educational system and erase the achievements of Zionism. Like Hazony, these critics blamed the drive to universalism and "normality" for the decline in Israel's national morale and the push to conclude a peace agreement at all costs. But liberals reiterated their view that Israel was not universal and liberal enough to attract the younger generation of American Jews. Commenting on the Birthright Israel program, one critic wrote that sending "kids to Israel" would not be successful without a new understanding of

Zionism. He insisted that the "mass-marketed Zionism of the Hebrew school and Israel tour" fails to address the realities of young American Jews. He called to develop a series of Zionist visions such as Liberal Zionism, Ethical Zionism, Green Zionism, Spiritual Zionism, and Traditional Zionism. Another analyst urged Israel to reformulate Zionism and "Jewish principles of a just and egalitarian society" to prevent it from "evolving into a pale copy of an American consumerism ethos." Matters came to a head during a March 2001 symposium on "Israel Historical Revisionism from Left to Right," sponsored by the New York Center for Jewish History. Some Israeli scholars argued that American Jews took "an overly alarmist and pessimist view of Israel" and accused them of wanting to fight until the last Israeli."[50]

Failure to advance the case of religious pluralism had added to the disenchantment of the secularized elements of the community. Barak's decision to include the Shas party in his coalition, coupled with the refusal of Interior Minister Ramon to help the Conservative and Reform movements, convinced many that "not even the election of a secular dove" would advance the cause of pluralism in Israel. As if to underscore this opinion, in May 2000 the Chief Sephardi Rabbi Eliahu Bakshi Doron denounced a Supreme Court ruling that allowed women to pray at the Western Wall and both Shas, and the ultra-Orthodox United Torah Judaism introduced a bill in Knesset designed to override the Supreme Court decision. Rabbi Meir Porush, the United Torah leader, had also demanded that Israel should put a stop to fund-raising on its behalf by the U.S. Conservative and Reform movements, which he described as "cults" because the money raised was used for the "purpose of estranging unsuspecting Jews from their beliefs." A series of arson attacks on Conservative and Reform synagogues in Israel in the summer added to the sense of malaise in the relations, with some editorials in the Anglo-Jewish press drawing parallels with the infamous Kristallnacht.[51]

Perhaps more significantly, some analysts felt that, hard as it tried, the mainstream Jewish community could not come to terms with the Israel of the Sephardi Shas and the Russian immigrants. Clayman of the AJCongress noted that the "new Israel does not correspond to the picture of the typical Israeli as they understood it, and they can't relate to this." Yossi Alpher, the Israel director of AJC who resigned in protest, made the same point. He argued that his U.S. bosses did not really abandon their "mythical misconception of a 'heroic' Israel," and described their effort to bridge the gap between the two communities as "little more than a rearguard action." But other commentators pointed out that letting go of the "old Israel" was also difficult for the veteran Ashkenazim and secular Israeli Jews. After Shimon Peres lost the election to the largely ceremonial post of president to the Sephardi Moshe Katsav, the *Forward* editorialized that that "deep feeling of loss voiced by Mr. Peres's liberal backers" sounded as "though they had lost not just a political battle, but a homeland." Conversely, the nationalists among the American Jews welcomed the new "homeland." An advertisement of Friends and Families of Victims of Oslo congratulated the people of Israel because the president was a "Jew and a religious Jew," adding a PS for Peres that read "Good Riddance to Bad Rubbish."[52]

A series of incidents that involved Rabbi Ovadia Yosef demonstrated that the changed political landscape of Israel could be uncomfortable to the largely Ashkenazi American Jewish community. In August the spiritual leader of Shas, who previously stated that the name of the dovish Minister of Education Yossi Sarid should be wiped out off the face of the earth like Haman, described Holocaust victims as "reincarnated souls of Jews who sinned in the past." He also called the Palestinians "snakes" and Ishmaelite, adding that "they are all accursed" and that the "Holy One is sorry he created them." The comments created a storm in Israel and in the Diaspora, leading the ADL to ask Yosef to curtail his comments. Critics noted that Yosef might have reacted to the Ashkenazi elite dominating of the Barak government and its handling of the peace process. They also voiced disappointment that Katsav did not rebuke the Shas leader. Although Katsav vehemently denied that his circumspection was due to the crucial support of Shas for his presidential bid, the sense that Israel was engaged in a cultural war between the beleaguered secular Ashkenazim and a resurgent Sephardi-religious community lingered. A series of articles in the general and Anglo-Jewish presses about the use of cabalistic mysticism in Shas circles and the political power wielded by the 96-year-old Rabbi Yitzhak Kaddouri, a leading cabalist, added to the discomfort. That such a development was not pleasing to many American Jews was only natural, given the political profile of the community. According to a Zogby International survey conducted in the winter of 2000, some 49 percent identified themselves as "liberal" or "very liberal," and under one-quarter said they attended services at least once a week. When asked by the 2000 AJC survey who was responsible for the sharp increase in tension in Israel between secular and Orthodox Jews, 72 percent blamed the Orthodox, 7 percent blamed the secular, and 12 percent assigned equal blame to both.[53]

Even more offensive to the U.S. Jewish community were the remarks of Katsav during a September conference on Jewish assimilation and continuity organized by Bar-Ilan University. The Israeli president charged that Israel had given the Diaspora a "seal of approval" so it could "use Diaspora Jews for their money and politics." Noting that such a legitimation of the Diaspora was among the reasons for the high assimilation rate, the Israeli president called on Western Jews to make aliya as the only way to safeguard Jewish continuity. Katsav dismissed all other solutions to the demographic decline, including Jewish education, which he described as a stopgap measure that "could last two or three generations." The remarks generated widespread protest from American Jews, with a *Forward* editorial describing "Katsav's tirade" as a crude rendition of the classic Zionist doctrine of "negating the Diaspora." A spokesman for the Avi Chai Foundation, an organization dedicated to Jewish education, blasted the president for denigrating Diaspora education. Although Katsav retracted his comments following intense pressure from U.S. Jewish leaders, the controversy opened old wounds dating back to David Ben-Gurion. As one critic pointed out, most Israeli leaders have come to recognize the "emptiness of the dreams" of mass immigration from the West, but "made no effort to incorporate this reality into their thinking." Another critic added that a "society whose agenda is determined by mystical rabbis and by the distribution of amulets will find it very difficult to attract the Western engineers, scientists and intellectuals whom Israel so strongly needs."[54]

As pointed out, the Intifada crisis had restored a measure of unity between the American Jewish community and Israel, at least at the symbolic level. For their part, the Israeli elites, including Barak's National Security Council, had acknowledged that the Diaspora Jewry is a strategic asset for the state. Sharon's long-standing notion that American Jewry should be viewed as a central instrument of Israeli foreign policy and his self-definition as "a Jew first and then as an Israeli" had provided a personal dimension to the newly upgraded relations.[55]

At the same time, Palestinian terrorism had dramatically curtailed American Jewish travel to Israel, leading more and more Israelis to feel abandoned by their North American "family." Unofficial statistics indicated that, with the exception of the Orthodox and the Birthright Israel programs, the number of Jewish visitors to Israel in all categories, including tourism, youth, and college study programs had been drastically down. Following on the heels of the controversial decision of Yoffie to cancel the Reform youth programs in Israel, an ugly dispute erupted over the reluctance of American athletes to attend the 16th Maccabiah Games. In fact, critics accused Yoffie and the group that lobbied for postponing the games of delivering a victory to terrorists who were seeking to isolate Israel. Others simply noted that "if we're indeed family, now's the time to show it." They pointed out that both Orthodox Jews and Christian pilgrims had continued to arrive in Israel. The paltry tourist record made the call of prominent Israeli leaders for more immigration from North America sound particularly hollow.[56]

Going beyond visits to Israel, observers commented on the anemic attitude of American Jews, the sparsely attended solidarity rallies, and the virtual failure of other attempts to mobilize the divided community. As one editorial put it, with the exception of the passionate minorities "deeply committed to competing visions of Israeli security," the "larger population has simply given up and tuned out." The apathy among the younger cohorts created a particular alarm and spurred a renewed effort to instill Israel as a core part of the Jewish identity. One such effort, Collegiate Leadership Internship Program (CLIP) described its mission as "fighting ignorance about Israel" and passivity among Jewish college students. CLIP strove to equate Judaism with a prioritization of Israel in the core identity of its participants by promoting education about Israel, coupled with pro-Israeli activism on campuses. Nevertheless, even in this highly controlled environment, the dissension over the peace process had run afoul the official show of unity. Some students criticized the right-wing bias of the speakers and others complained about feeling marginalized because of their sympathy for the Palestinians.[57]

The attack on the United States on September 11, 2001, and the unprecedented wave of suicide bombing in Israel in the first months of 2002 had a profound impact on the relations between American Jews and Israel. From the low point of pro-Israeli feelings documented in this and other work, there has been a significant increase in identification with what has been perceived widely as the beleaguered Jewish state. The annual survey of the American Jewish Committee conducted in November-December 2001 found that 29 percent of the sample feels very close and 43 percent fairly close to Israel. Seventy-two percent of the respondents stated that caring about Israel is an important part of being Jewish. An emergency rally in support of Israel on April 15, 2002, echoed the genuine anguish of American Jews during the Six Day War. Mortimer Zuckerman, the chairman of the Presidents Conference, declared that the "very existence of Israel is at stake."[58]

More important, Arafat's rejection of the Barak proposal at Camp David II and the extreme and indiscriminate violence of the suicide bombings had again shifted the balance between the right and left wings of the community. The first Intifada had proved to many that giving up most of the territories was the only way to achieve a peaceful solution to the conflict. The second Intifada demonstrated to a large segment of the community that territorial compromise was not enough to placate the Palestinians. In fact, it revived the old suspicion that the Arabs and the Palestinians are out to destroy Israel was revived. Seventy-three percent of the AJC sample agreed that the goal of the Arabs is not to return the territories but to destroy Israel, and 71 percent either opposed or strongly opposed the statement that Yasser Arafat wants peace. Moreover, 44 percent of the respondents agreed that Arafat was Israel's Bin Laden. The support for the government of Ariel Sharon reached 65 percent, and there was an increase in those who argued that American Jews need to support the elected government of Israel, regardless of their own point of view.[59]

The right-wing shift at the grass-root level was underpinned by a corresponding move in the organized community, including the Conference of Presidents and AIPAC. More surprising was the right-wing turn of the historically dovish AJCongress. Eric Yaffie, the head of the Reform movement, offered a "mea culpa" for thinking that Arafat could be a peace partner. The new mood in communal discourse had vindicated ZOA's Morton Klein, Norman Podhoretz, Daniel Pipes, and others who have warned for almost a decade that the Palestinian Authority would become a terrorist entity. The moderate American Jewish Committee published a report titled *Intifada II: The Arab Campaign to Destroy Israel*, which repeated many of the charges made some years ago by the ZOA. A report by the Israeli Ministry of Defense based on documents seized by the IDF during its incursion into the West Bank in April 2002, expressed "astonishment at the scale of the involvement of the leaders of the Palestinian administration against Israel." These spokesmen were also bolstered in their stand against Arab and Palestinian anti-Semitism. Middle Eastern anti-Semitism, largely ignored by the peace camp, had come under belated scrutiny by scholars who found it a mixture of medieval blood libel and Nazi propaganda.[60]

Yet, the newfound unity had not erased the underlying divisions in the community, especially concerning settlements. Commenting on the suicide bombing of Passover guests in the Park Hotel in Netanya, an editorial linked it to the Passover celebration in the Park Hotel in Hebron in 1968 that started the settlement movement. Asked whether in return for a permanent peace Israel should return the territories, 9 percent of the AJC sample agreed to return all, 53 percent agreed to return some, and 34 percent none. These divisions prompted ADL's Foxman to note that "if God willing, we'll move into the era of peace and tranquility, those differences will surface again."[61] As the concluding chapter makes clear, such cleavages are inevitable because the American Jewish community had become split along competing visions of the Jewish state.

9

Conclusion: Competing Visions of Israel in American Jewish Identity

This work attempted to illustrate how the changing identity needs of American Jews, as mediated by the realities of Israel's handling of the Arab-Israeli conflict and the input of the American polity, have shaped their perception of Israel and the peace process. By following the complex triadic relations since 1948, it was possible to track how Israel and its handling of the peace process had been transformed from a symbol of communal unity, and indeed, the center of its civic religion, to a topic of deep division and much bitterness. So fundamental has this split become that one observer wondered as to what "pro-Israel" means. Another commentator noted that the image of "continued Jewish solidarity, clinging to its traditional posture of invariability supporting the Israeli Government . . . appears increasingly divorced from reality.[1]

As demonstrated, at the core of the problem is the split in U.S. Jewry between the more secularized element in the community, who define their Judaism through a liberal-universalistic religiosity, and the hard core, composed of nationalists and the Orthodox. The former want to use the peace process to secure a truly democratic, Western, and liberal Israel where enlightened citizenship and religious pluralism are the rule. The latter seek a solution that would guarantee the Jewish rather than civic character of the state and fulfill as much as possible the vision of Greater Israel. In what became part of the larger struggle for "the soul of Judaism" in America, both sides have worked hard to implement these competing images of Israel by shaping the peace process accordingly. This effort reached a peak in the years following the Oslo agreement, which all but eroded the communal consensus around Israel.

A number of factors have exacerbated the split in recent years. To begin with, the American Diaspora is a voluntary community based entirely on a network of "confederate" associations. As a result, there is no single hierarchy or pyramidal structure, but a "matrix consisting of many institutions and organizations tied together by a crisscrossing of memberships, shared purposes, and common interests, whose role and power vary according to situation and issues." In such a loosely knit voluntary structure, persuasion rather than coercion and power are the only tools for making and executing decisions.[2] Individuals and groups who break with communal consensus are free to pursue alternative advocacy in whatever form or manner. This built-in pluralism has been enhanced by recent changes in patterns of Jewish funding and philanthropy. Traditional umbrella groups have been increasingly passed over for smaller organizations where donors have greater control over the agenda. According to some observers, the community is in danger of being taken over by a number of wealthy donors and megadonors who either purchase offices by virtue of the "fattest checkbook" or operate their own private foundations.[3] Nowhere is this phenomenon more visible than in the field of peace advocacy which, as detailed in the book, has been driven by a host of groups and large donors that at times overshadow both AIPAC and the Presidents Conference. This shift in the balance of power between the "sanctioned" umbrella organizations and the "boutique" groups had eroded the traditional commitment to a loyal support of the democratically elected governments of Israel. With both the right and the left wings willing to put their principles above loyalism, it was only a matter of time before Oslo opponents developed the doctrine of limited sovereignty. As noted, this doctrine has been applied to the issues of Jerusalem and other territorial concessions.

Such fragmentation has affected the functioning of the umbrella organizations that represent Israel's interests in Washington. AIPAC, which in the mid-1990s was rated as the second most powerful lobby in America, had seen its membership stagnate and its influence curtailed by internal bickering and open challenge from ZOA and other groups. The Presidents Conference, whose membership has expanded to include many of the specialized advocacy groups, has been virtually paralyzed by the constant clashes between strong peace proponents and groups that oppose the land-for-peace formula. Mutual recriminations and accusations of bad faith and duplicity have marred the public image of the organization. Characteristic of this atmosphere was the sharp reaction to Ronald Lauder's appearance during the Jerusalem rally amid apprehension that that excessive partisanship would spell doom for the Conference.

The matrix of institutions and organizations that compose the community make it difficult to ascertain the lines of legitimacy and representation. The question of who speaks for the community and the extent of the popular mandate that such individuals or groups enjoy has been constantly open to challenges. The study shows how opinion polls taken to ascertain American Jewish attitudes toward the peace process had, over time, become contentious, with allegation of bias leveled by both the right and the left. As Gedal noted, data can be held suspect "because some samples contained only connected Jews" (that is, those who belonged to an organization), whereas others "had an indiscriminate mix of connected and unconnected Jews."[4] In a broader sense, such charges touch upon the issue of the permeable boundaries of the community and the related question of who should be counted as a member of the community for the purpose of expressing views about Israel. While most surveys sample American Jews at large, this and other studies show that the participants in the Israel discourse are the more activist members of the community whose political input vastly outweigh that of the marginally affiliated.

Such a lopsided input has skewed the balance of power between the peace camp and their opponents. As the book demonstrates, while the peace process has enjoyed considerable support in the Jewish community, those who passionately care for Israel hail, by and large, from the nationalist and the Orthodox circles. Other observers noted that the nationalistic groups tend to attract single-minded individuals, whereas the peace groups have to compete for universalists who have multiple agendas.[5] This imbalance is most evident in the fact that, fueled by nationalist megadonors, right-wing groups outnumber the left-wing ones by a ratio of some six to one. The collapse of the Oslo agreement had exacerbated this trend by promoting the withdrawal of discouraged liberal peace advocates from the discourse. A hard-line Israeli government may create so much cognitive dissonance in the secularized and marginal parts of the community that a massive "exit" cannot be ruled out, leaving the "voice" firmly in the nationalist court.

The cleavage in the American Jewish community has been reinforced by the deep polarization of the Israeli electorate. The analysis presented earlier indicates that both the Israeli right and left wings have used sympathetic segments in the American Jewish community to further their foreign policy goals. Likud, which, along with the settlers, enjoys a substantial advantage over Labor, institutionalized the procedure during the national unity governments period in the eighties. While it has been tempting for both sides to use American Jews as influence multipliers in domestic politics, the practice has muddled the perception of a national Israeli interest around which the community can rally. Worse, as the peace process lurched right and left, the call to support the duly elected Israeli government of the moment has often been undermined by the opposition, especially the Likud, which openly appealed to the U.S. Diaspora to defeat the policy of its opponent. This conflicting lobbying, often carried out with the help of the specialized advocacy groups, has also hurt the standing of AIPAC and the Conference of Presidents, which are nominally dedicated to a loyalist position.

The internal turmoil in the community, compounded by the divisions in Israel, has also affected the communal interaction with the foreign policy domain of the host country, the United States. Conventional wisdom has it that the Diaspora does best when it is united behind a well-defined national interest of the homeland, a factor that drove the establishment of AIPAC and the Presidents Conference in the 1950s. However, this formula is based on the assumption that the administration and Congress act as a unitary actor with regard to key foreign policy issues. When the legislative and executive branches diverge, even a united ethnic lobby can run afoul of a larger policy context. This was certainly the case when conservative Democrat and Republican lawmakers used the Jackson-Vanick amendment to torpedo Richard Nixon's détente policy. More recently, the divided American Jewish community became a boon for Republicans on Capitol Hill in their fight against Bill Clinton's foreign policy. With the expectation of aid to Israel that enjoys bipartisan support, isolationist Republican lawmakers had welcomed the right-wing Jewish campaign against funding for Oslo, Wye, and a possible peace deal with Syria as both a way to shrink foreign aid and sabotage Clinton's expansive brand of internationalism. Even without such ulterior motives, congressmen, with their more local views of politics, have been susceptible to the appeals of the nationalist camp. As noted, lawmakers tend to err on the side of caution by preferring to assume that the nationalist advocacy represents the Jewish interest of their districts, particularly when the more moderate voices are not normally heard.

The trends analyzed here have some major implications for the future. First, they cast doubt on the ability of American Jewry to function as an extension of Israel's national security, an assertion made by Israel's NSC in January 2001. Beyond some issues like financial aid and support during a major crisis in Israel, the community is not expected to behave like the cohesive unitary actor that was envisaged in the official NSC document. Second, and more important, the continuous tension over the competing visions of Israel would further diminish Israel's attractiveness as a symbol of Jewish identity and unity, particularly among the younger generation, which has shown signs of growing apathy if not outright alienation, the Birthright program notwithstanding. In what may be the ultimate irony, the struggle over the Jewish state may hurt the identity and demography of the Diaspora.

Notes

INTRODUCTION: AMERICAN JEWISH IDENTITY, THE PERCEPTIONS OF THE STATE OF ISRAEL AND THE PEACE PROCESS

1. Samuel Freedman, *Jew vs. Jew: The Struggle for the Soul of American Jewry* (New York: Simon & Schuster, 2000), 27.

2. Gabriel Sheffer, "A New Field of Study: Modern Diasporas in International Politics," in Gabriel Sheffer, ed., *Modern Diasporas in International Politics* (New York: St. Martin's Press, 1986), 8–11.

3. Daniel J. Elazar, "The Jewish People as the Classic Diaspora: A Political Analysis," in Sheffer, *Modern Diasporas*, 215.

4. Sheffer, "New Field," 10.

5. Zoe Danon Gedal, "The American Jewish Community and U.S.–Israeli Relations: Maintaining Influence in the Face of Increasing Pluralism" (Ph.D. diss., Brandeis University, 1997), 284.

6. Elazar, "Jewish People," 216.

7. Giandomenico Majone, *Evidence, Argument, and Persuasion in the Policy Process* (New Haven: Yale University Press, 1993), 161–164.

1: WARMING UP TO THE JEWISH STATE

1. David Goldberg and Harry Sharp, "Some Characteristics of Detroit Area Jewish and Non-Jewish Adults," in Marshall Sklare, ed., *The Jews: Social Patterns of an American Group* (Glencoe, Ill.: The Free Press, 1958), 107–119; Bezalel C. Sherman, *The Jews within American Society: A Study in Ethnic Individuality* (Detroit: Wayne State University, 1961).

2. Simon D. Herman, "Criteria for Jewish Identity," in Moshe Davis, ed., *World Jewry and the State of Israel* (New York: Arno Press, 1977), 171.

3. Bernard C. Rosen, "Minority Group in Transition: A Study of Adolescent Religious Conviction and Conduct," in Sklare, *The Jews,* 336–347; Marshall Sklare, *Jewish Identity and the Suburban Frontier* (New York: Basic Books, 1967), 53–94; David Kaufman, *Shul with a Pool: The Synagogue-Center in American Jewish History* (Hanover, N.H.: University of New England Press, 1999), 5.

4. Will Herberg, *Protestant, Catholic, Jew: An Essay in American Religious Sociology* (Garden City, N.Y.: Doubleday, 1955); Melvin I. Urofsky, *We Are One! American Jewry and Israel* (Garden City, N.Y.: Doubleday, 1978), 219–220; Eugene B. Borowitz, *The Mask Jews Wear: The Self-Deception of American Jewry* (New York: Simon and Schuster, 1973), 37; Edward S. Shapiro, "The Ordeal of Success: American Jewry Since World War II," *American Jewish History* 81, no. 1 (1993): 81–100.

5. Charles S. Liebman, *The Ambivalent American Jew: Politics, Religion, and Family in American Jewish Life* (Philadelphia: The Jewish Publication Society of America, 1983), 24–26, 44–45, 149–150.

6. Jerold S. Auerbach, "Are We One? Menachem Begin and the Long Shadow of 1977," in Allon Gal, ed., *Envisioning Israel: The Changing Ideals and Images of North American Jews* (Jerusalem: The Magnus Press, 1996), 335–351; Bernard Susser and Charles S. Liebman, *Choosing Survival: Strategies for a Jewish Future* (New York and Oxford: Oxford University Press, 1999), 75; Jerold S. Auerbach, *Rabbis and Lawyers* (Bloomington: Indiana University Press, 1990), 60.

7. Urofsky, *One!,* 238–240; Arnold M. Eisen, "Israel at 50: An American Jewish Perspective," in *American Jewish Year Book,* vol. 98 (New York: American Jewish Committee, 1988), 47–52; Seymour Martin Lipset and Earl Raab, *Jews and the New American Scene* (Cambridge: Harvard University Press, 1995), 131.

8. Joyce R. Starr, *Kissing through Glass: The Invisible Shield between Americans and Israelis* (Chicago: Contemporary Books, 1990), 147; Steven J. Gold and Bruce A. Phillips, "Israelis in the United States," in *American Jewish Year Book,* vol. 96 (New York: American Jewish Committee, 1996), 51–101.

9. Shoshana Cardin, "The New Agenda for Jewish Leadership," in Earl Raab, ed., *American Jews in the 21st Century: A Leadership Challenge* (Atlanta: Scholars Press, 1991), 111–118; Alan M. Dershowitz, *The Vanishing American Jew: In Search of Jewish Identity for the Next Century* (Boston: Little, Brown, 1997), 251; Moshe Ben-Eliezer, "Political Metaphors Used by American Jews for the State of Israel" (Ph.D. diss., New York University, 1981), 53–54; Emil L. Fackenheim, "Post-Holocaust Anti-Jewishness, Jewish Identity and the Centrality of Israel," in Davis, *World Jewry,* 28.

10. Jonathan D. Sarna, "A Projection of America as it Ought to Be: Zionism in the Mind's Eye of American Jews," in Gal, *Envisioning Israel,* 59; Jerold S. Auerbach, "Are We One? American Jews and Israel," *Midstream* 44, no.1 (January 1998): 20–24.

11. Auerbach, "Are We One? Menachem Begin," 339; Gal, "Overview: Envisioning Israel—The American Jewish Tradition," in Gal, *Envisioning Israel,* 21; Elan Ezrachi, "Israel and Identity Building: Educating American Jews About Israel," *The Reconstructionist* 62, no. 2 (1998): 5–11; David Ellenson, "Envisioning Israel in the Liturgies of North American Liberal Judaism," in Gal, *Envisioning Israel,* 125.

12. Ben-Eliezer, "Political Metaphors," 138; Steven M. Cohen, "Romantic Idealism to Loving Realism: The Changing Place of Israel in the Consciousness of American Jews," in William Frankel, ed., *Survey of Jewish Affairs* (Rutherford, N.J.: Fairleigh

Dickinson University Press, 1985), 172; Inis L. Claude Jr., *National Minorities: An International Problem* (Cambridge: Harvard University Press, 1955), 106–109.

13. Andrew Scott Furman, "Israel through the Jewish-American Imagination: A Survey of Jewish-American Literature on Israel, 1948–1993" (Ph.D. diss., Pennsylvania State University, 1995), 52; Urofsky, *One!*, 242; Liebman, *Ambivalent*, 27.

14. Eytan Gilboa, *American Public Opinion toward Israel and the Arab-Israeli Conflict* (Lexington, Mass.: Lexington Books, 1987), 241; Marshall Sklare and Benjamin B. Ringer, "A Study of Jewish Attitudes toward the State of Israel," in Sklare, *The Jews*, 437–451; Sklare, *Jewish Identity*, 215–249.

15. Lucy S. Dawidowicz, "United States, Israel and the Middle East," in *American Jewish Year Book*, vol. 61 (New York: American Jewish Committee, 1960), 101–110; Urofsky, *One!*, 244; Alexander Dushkin, "Implications of the Jewish State for American Jewish Education," *Jewish Education* 19, no. 2 (1948): 2–5.

16. Cohen, "Romantic Idealism," 172; Hugh Nissenson et al., "Jewishness & the Younger Intellectuals—A Symposium," *Commentary* (April 1961): 306–359.

17. Urofsky, *One!*, 65.

18. Ibid., 10; Jonathan J. Goldberg, *Jewish Power: Inside the American Jewish Establishment* (Reading, Mass.: Addison-Wesley, 1996), 128; Jack Wertheimer, "Jewish Organizational Life in the United States since 1945," in *American Jewish Year Book*, vol. 95 (New York: American Jewish Committee, 1995), 3–98.

19. Philip Bernstein, *To Dwell in Unity: The Jewish Federation Movement in America, 1960–1980* (Philadelphia: Jewish Publication Society, 1983), 15; M.Z. Frank, "American Jewish Community and Israel," in *American Jewish Year Book*, vol. 53 (New York: American Jewish Committee, 1952), 178–186.

20. Borowitz, *Mask*, 154; quoted in Urofsky, *One!*, 267; Dawidowicz, "United States," (1960), 101–110; Louis Shub, "The United States, Israel and the Middle East," in *American Jewish Year Book* vol. 65 (New York: American Jewish Committee, 1964), 145–159; Jacob Sloan, "American Jewish Community and Israel," in *American Jewish Year Book*, vol. 54 (New York: American Jewish Committee, 1953), 114–125.

21. The Conference of Presidents, the Presidents Conference, and the Conference all refer to the same organization and will be used interchangeably throughout the book. Louis Shub, "Zionist and Pro-Israel Activities," in *American Jewish Year Book*, vol. 54 (New York: American Jewish Committee, 1953), 153–161; Michael Reiner, "The Reaction of U.S. Jewish Organizations to the Sinai Campaign and Its Aftermath," *Forum* 40 (1980/81): 29–38.

22. Quoted in Goldberg, *Jewish Power*, 153; Gedal, "American Jewish Community," 57.

23. Roberta Strauss Feuerlicht, *The Fate of the Jews: A People Torn between Israeli Power and Jewish Ethics* (New York: Times Books, 1983), 91; Wertheimer, "Jewish Organizational Life," 55.

24. Wertheimer, "Jewish Organizational Life," 14, 17; Liebman, *Ambivalent*, 104; Goldberg, *Jewish Power*, 15; Lawrence Grossman, "Transformation through Crisis: The American Jewish Committee and the Six Day War," *American Jewish History* 86, no.1 (1988): 27–54.

25. Robert Jervis, *Perception and Misperception in International Politics* (Princeton: Princeton University Press, 1976), 117, 195, 281.

26. Urofsky, *One!*, 207; Sklare, *Jewish Identity*, 215; Sklare and Ringer, "Study," 437–451; Gilboa, *American Public Opinion*, 250.

27. Lucy S. Dawidowicz, "The United States, Israel and the Middle East," in *American Jewish Year Book* vol. 58 (New York: American Jewish Committee, 1957), 203–219; Steven M. Cohen, "Israel in the Jewish Identity of American Jews: A Study in Dualities and Contrasts," in David M. Gordis and Yoav Ben-Horin, eds., *Jewish Identity in America* (Los Angeles: University of Judaism, 1991), 128; Susser and Liebman, *Choosing Survival*, 60.

28. David J. Forman, *Israel on Broadway: America Off-Broadway: Jews in the New Millennium* (Jerusalem: Gefen, 1998), 23; Melvyn H. Bloom, "Image Israel: Then and Now," *Journal of Jewish Communal Service* 75 nos. 2/3 (1999): 145–149; quoted in Susser and Liebman, *Choosing Survival*, 60.

29. Jeremy Salt, "Fact and Fiction in the Middle East Novels of Leon Uris," *Journal of Palestine Studies* 14, no. 3 (1985): 54–63; Furman, "Jewish-American Imagination," 54; Arthur Hertzberg, "The Illusion of Jewish Unity," *New York Review of Books*, June 16, 1988.

30. Urofsky, *One!*, 206–207.

31. Bernstein, *To Dwell*, 24.

32. Forman, *Israel*, 68; Urofsky, *One!*, 226; David Mittelberg, *The Israel Connection and American Jews* (Westport, Conn.: Praeger, 1999), 7; Cohen, "Romantic Idealism," 172; Wertheimer, "Jewish Organizational Life," 16.

33. Shub, "Zionist and Pro-Israel Activities," in *American Jewish Year Book*, vol. 52 (New York: The American Jewish Committee, 1951), 110–124; Wertheimer, "Jewish Organizational Life," 3–98; Helen Ann B. Rivlin, "American Jews and the State of Israel," *Middle East Journal* 30, no. 3 (1976): 369–389; Paul Findley, *They Dare to Speak Out: People and Institutions Confronting Israel's Lobby* (Chicago: Lawrence Hill, 1989), 272–273; Robert Cotrell, "I.F. Stone and Israel," *South Atlantic Quarterly* 80, no. 2 (1987): 159–168; Ofira Seliktar, "Conceptualizing Binationalism: State of Mind, Political Reality, or Legal Entity?" in Ilan Peleg and Ofira Seliktar, eds., *The Emergence of Binational Israel: The Second Republic in the Making* (Boulder, Colo.: Westview, 1989), 3–38.

34. Findley, *They Dare*, 272–273.

35. Wertheimer, "Jewish Organizational Life," 29; Urofsky, *One!*, 249.

36. Richard P. Stevens, *American Zionism and U.S. Foreign Policy 1942–1947* (New York: Pageant Press, 1962), 206.

37. Robert O. Friedman, *Zealots for Zion: Inside Israel's West Bank Settlement Movement* (New York: Random House, 1992), 222.

38. Naomi W. Cohen, *American Jews and the Zionist Idea* (New York: Ktav Publishing House, 1975), 101; Lucy S. Dawidowicz, "The United States, Israel and the Middle East," in *American Jewish Year Book*, vol. 59 (New York: American Jewish Committee, 1958); Gilboa, *American Public Opinion*, 250.

39. N. Cohen, *American Jews*, 101; Lucy S. Dawidowicz, "The United States, Israel and the Middle East," in *American Jewish Year Book*, vol. 60 (New York: American Jewish Committee, 1959), 108–120; Noam Chomsky, *The Fateful Triangle: The United States, Israel & the Palestinians* (Boston: South End Press, 1983), 21.

40. Stephen Green, *Taking Sides: America's Secret Relations with a Militant Israel* (New York: William Morrow, 1984), 182.

41. Lucy S. Dawidowicz, "The United States, Israel, and the Middle East," in *American Jewish Year Book*, vol. 63 (New York: American Jewish Committee, 1962), 214–225; Nathan Glazer, *American Judaism* (Chicago: The University of Chicago Press,

1957), 15; Jonathan L. Teller, "Zionism, Israel and American Jewry," in Oscar I. Janowsky, ed., *The American Jew: A Reappraisal* (Philadelphia: The Jewish Publication Society, 1967), 320; Urofsky, *One!*, 289.

42. Quoted in Urofsky, *One!*, 341; Jacob J. Petuchowki, *Zion Reconsidered* (New York: Twayne Publishers, 1966), 31–72.

2: THE SIX DAY WAR AND THE EMERGENCE OF "SACRED UNITY"

1. Edward Tivnan, *The Lobby: Jewish Political Power and American Foreign Policy* (New York: Simon and Schuster, 1987), 61; Sidney Goldstein, "American Jewry, 1970," in *American Jewish Year Book*, vol. 72 (New York: American Jewish Committee, 1971), 3–88; Peter Y. Medding, "Equality and the Shrinkage of Jewish Identity," in Davis, *World Jewry*, 125.

2. Wertheimer, "Jewish Organizational Life," 65; Urofsky, *One!*, 338.

3. Goldberg, *Jewish Power*, 65; Charles Zibbel, "Suburbia and Jewish Communal Organization," *Journal of Jewish Communal Service* 38 (1961): 69–79; John Slawson, *Toward a Community Program for Jewish Identity* (New York: American Jewish Committee, 1967), 10–11; Urofsky *One!*, 338.

4. Simon Rawidowicz, *State of Israel, Diaspora, and Jewish Continuity* (Hanover, N.H.: University Press of New England, 1998), 53; Urofsky, *One!*, 338; Goldberg, *Jewish Power*, 65; Hillel Halkin, "Ahad Ha'Am, Herzl, and the End of Diaspora Zionism," in Michael Brown and Bernard Lightman, eds., *Creating the Jewish Future* (Walnut Creek, Calif.: AltaMira Press, 1999), 101–111; Jonathan S. Woocher, *Sacred Survival: The Civil Religion of American Jews* (Bloomington: Indiana University Press, 1986), 76–80, 100–101, 114–115.

5. Cohen, "Romantic Idealism," 170–171; Earl Raab, "Israel Connection," in Raab, *American Jews*, 70; Earl Raab, "Changing American Jewish Attitudes toward Israel," *Journal of Jewish Communal Service* 75, nos. 2/3 (1998/99).

6. Arthur Hertzberg and Aron Hirt-Manheimer, *Jews: The Essence and Character of a People* (San Francisco: HarperCollins, 1998), 243, 253; Stephen Sharot and Nurit Zaidman, "Israel as Symbol and as Reality: The Perception of Israel among Reconstructionist Jews in the United States," in Gal, *Envisioning Israel*, 149–172; Borowitz, *Mask*, 151.

7. A.F.K. Organski, *The $36 Billion Bargain: Strategies and Politics in U.S. Assistance to Israel* (New York: Columbia University Press, 1990), 59.

8. Tivnan, *Lobby*, 76; Norman Podhoretz, "Israel: A Lamentation for the Future," *Commentary* (March 1989): 15–21; Jerold S. Auerbach, "Thomas Friedman's Israel: The Myth of Unrequited Love," in Edward Alexander, ed., *With Friends Like These: The Jewish Critics of Israel* (New York: S.P.I. Books, 1993), 60; Dershowitz, *Vanishing American Jew*, 240; Marie Syrkin, "How Israel Affects American Jews," *Midstream* (May 1973): 27; Cardin, "New Agenda," 113.

9. Gilboa, *American Public Opinion*, 244; Susser and Liebman, *Choosing Survival*, 59; Milton Himmelfarb, "In the Light of Israel's Victory," *Commentary* (October 1967): 53–61; Stuart E. Eizenstat, "Loving Israel—Warts and All," *Foreign Policy* 81 (1990–91): 92; J. Goldberg, *Jewish Power*, 144; Lipset and Raab, *Jews* 119; Robert S. Wistrich, "Israel and the Holocaust Trauma," *Jewish History* 11, no. 2 (1997): 13–20.

10. Starr, *Kissing*, 46; Joyce R. Starr, "Why Israelis and Americans Misunderstand Each Other," *Moment* (June 1991): 46–7; quoted in D. Goldberg, *Jewish Power*, 134; Matti Golan, *With Friends Like You: What Israel is Really Think About American Jews*, trans. Hillel Halkin (New York: Free Press, 1992), 24; Eizenstadt, "Loving Israel," 90.

11. Chaim I. Waxman, "All the in the Family: American Jewish Attachment to Israel," in Peter Y. Medding, ed., *A New Jewry? America Since Second World War*, vol. 8 (New York: Oxford University Press, 1992), 134–149; Urofsky, *One!*, 363; Raab, "Changing Attitudes"; Jacob Neusner, "Zionism and the Jewish Problem," *Midstream* (November 1969): 34–45.

12. Irving Greenberg, "The Interaction of Israel and American Jewry," in Davis, *World Jewry*, 272; Tivnan, *Lobby*, 76; N. Cohen, *American Jews*, 143; Samuel Heilman, "Separated but Not Divorced: American Jews and Israel," *Society* 36, no. 4 (1999): 8–15.

13. Lipset and Raab, *Jews*, 129; Wertheimer, "Jewish Organizational Life," 32, 66.

14. Waxman, "Family," 140; Gilboa, *American Public Opinion*, 245; Peter L. Grose, *Israel in the Mind of America* (New York: Knopf, 1983), 309.

15. Sharot and Zaidman, "Israel"; Rachel T. Sabath, "Identity and the Post Modern American Jews," *Jewish Spectator* 62, no. 4 (1998): 36–37; Yosef I. Abramowitz, "Distant Relatives: Bridging the Gap between American Jews & Israel," *Moment* (December 1995): 54–57, 81, 84–85, 88; Liebman, *Ambivalent*, 101; Arthur Hertzberg, "Israel and American Jewry," *Commentary* (August 1967): 69–73, 72.

16. Halkin, "Ahad Ha'Am," 108; Michael Brown, "Israel and the Diaspora: An Introduction," in Brown and Lightman, *Creating the Jewish Future*, 79; Cohen, "Romantic Idealism," 172.

17. Goldstein, "American Jewry"; Elihu Bergman, "The Jewish Population Explosion," *Midstream*. (October 1977): 9–19; Mittelberg, *Israel Connection*, 5.

18. Raab, "Israel Connection," 31; Marshall Sklare, *Observing America's Jews* (Hanover, N.H.: Brandeis University Press, 1993), 126; Wertheimer, "Jewish Organizational Life," 32; S. Cohen, "Israel in Jewish Identity," 125; Gideon Shimoni, "How Central Is Israel," *Moment*, (October 1991): 24–27; Ezrachi, "Israel and Identity," 5–6.

19. Neusner, "Zionism"; Daniel J. Elazar, *Community and Polity: The Organizational Dynamics of American Jewry* (Philadelphia: The Jewish Publication Society of America, 1976), 83; Immanuel Jacobovits, "A Reassessment of Israel's Role in the Contemporary Jewish Condition," in Davis, *World Jewry*, 283; Borowitz, *Mask*, 162; David Vital, *The Future of the Jews* (Cambridge: Harvard University Press, 1990), 153; Charles S. Liebman, "Diaspora Influence on Israeli Policy," in Davis, *World Jewry*, 324; Waxman, "The Centrality of Israel in American Jewish Life: A Sociological Analysis," *Judaism* 25 (Spring 1976): 175–187; Charles S. Liebman, "The Role of Israel in the Ideology of American Jewry," *Dispersion and Unity* no. 10 (winter 1970): 19–26. Aharon Lichtenstein, "Patterns of Contemporary Jewish Hizdahut Self-Identification," in Davis, *World Jewry*, 183–192.

20. Woocher, *Sacred Survival*, 67; Waxman, "Centrality": Charles S. Liebman, "American Jews and the Modern Mind," *Midstream* (April 1981): 8–12; Urofsky, *One!*, 449; Heilman, "Separated," Jacob Neusner, *Israel in America. A Too-Comfortable Exile?* (Boston: Beacon Press, 1985), 18.

21. Urofsky, *One!*, 430; Gilboa, *American Public Opinion*, 249–250.

22. Gilboa, *American Public Opinion*, 250; Raab, "Changing Attitudes."

23. Quoted in J.J. Goldberg, *Jewish Power*, 204; quoted in Arnold Forster and Benjamin R. Epstein, *The New Anti-Semitism* (New York: McGraw-Hill, 1974), 3–5, 324;

Lee O'Brien, *American Jewish Organizations & Israel* (Washington, D.C.: Institute for Palestine Studies, 1986), 97; Nathan and Ruth Ann Perlmutter, *The Real Anti-Semitism in America* (New York: Arbor House, 1982), 155–57.

24. J.J. Goldberg, *Jewish Power*, 140; Raab, "Changing Attitudes"; Urofsky, *One!*, 379; Perlmutter and Perlmutter, *Real Anti-Semitism*, 125.

25. Perlmutter and Perlmutter, *Real Anti-Semitism*, 155–157; Hertzberg, "Israel and Jewry"; Borowitz, *Mask*, 57–61.

26. Lipset and Raab, *Jews*, 119.

27. Gilboa, *American Public Opinion*, 251.

28. Theodore Draper, "Israel and World Politics," *Commentary* (August 1967): 19–48.

29. J.J. Goldberg, *Jewish Power*, 155–62; Nadav Safran, *Israel: The Embattled Ally* (Cambridge: The Belknap Press, 1978), 437.

30. Urofsky, *One!*, 322.

31. Seliktar, *New Zionism and the Foreign Policy System of Israel* (London: Croom Helm, 1986), 95–101; Michael Prior, *Zionism and the State of Israel* (London: Routledge, 1999), 91–95.

32. O'Brien, *Organizations*, 59, 70; Wertheimer, "Jewish Organizational Life," 54–55; Gedal, "American Jewish Community," 274; Marla Brettschneider, *Cornerstone of Peace: Jewish Identity and Democratic Theory* (New Brunswick, N.J.: Rutgers University Press, 1996), 99.

33. Tivnan, *Lobby*, 72.

34. Walter Laqueur, "Israel, the Arabs, and World Opinion," *Commentary* (August 1967): 58.

35. Mohammed K. Shadid, *The United States and the Palestinians* (New York; St. Martin's Press, 1981), 112–118.

36. Yehoshafat Harkabi, *The Position of the Palestinians in the Israeli-Arab Conflict and Their National Covenant*, trans. J. Kraemer (Tel Aviv, 1970); Nimrod Novik, The *United States and Israel: Domestic Determinants of a Changing U.S. Commitment* (Boulder, Colo.: Westview, 1986), 25; Gilboa, *American Public Opinion*, 181–183; Grose, *Israel in the Mind*, 314–315.

37. Safran, *Israel*, 316.

38. Gilboa, *American Public Opinion*, 250.

39. Mitchell Geoffrey Bard, *The Water's Edge and Beyond: Defining the Limits to Domestic Influence on United States Middle East Policy* (New Brunswick, N.J.: Transaction Publishers, 1991), 198–204.

40. Wertheimer, "Jewish Organizational Life."

41. Seliktar, *Failing the Crystal Ball Test: The Carter Administration and the Fundamentalist Revolution in Iran* (Westport, Conn.: Praeger, 2000), 37–42.

42. Ronald Radosh, *Divided They Fell: The Demise of the Democratic Party 1964–1996* (New York: Free Press, 1996), 160; Steven S. Powell, *Covert Cadre: Inside the Institute for Policy Studies* (Ottawa, Ill.: Green Hill Publishers, 1983), 248, 252–253.

43. Safran, *Israel*, 438–439; J.J. Goldberg, *Jewish Power*, 245.

44. Radosh, *Divided*, 175–179; I.M. Destler, Leslie H. Gelb, and Anthony Lake, *Our Worst Enemy: The Unmaking of American Foreign Policy* (New York: Simon and Schuster, 1984), 59.

45. Norman Podhoretz, *Breaking Ranks: A Political Memoir* (New York: Harper & Row, 1979), 291, 351; Wertheimer, "Jewish Organizational Life," 45; Andrew and Leslie

Cockburn, *Dangerous Liaison: The Inside Story of the U.S. Israel Covert Relationship* (New York: HarperCollins, 1991), 187–188.

46. Michael Saba, *The Armageddon Network* (Brattleboro, Vt.: Amana Books, 1984); O'Brien, *Organizations*, 203.

47. Bard, *Water's Edge*, 66, 69; Russell Warren Howe and Sarah Hays Trott, *The Power Peddlers: How Lobbyists Mold American's Foreign Policy* (Garden City, N.Y.: Doubleday, 1977), 326.

48. J.J. Goldberg, *Jewish Power*, 174; Tivnan, *Lobby*, 88; David Howard Goldberg, *Foreign Policy and Ethnic Interest Groups: American and Canadian Jews Lobby for Israel* (New York: Greenwood Press, 1990), 51.

49. Feuerlicht, *Fate of the Jews*, 162ff; Joseph Puder, "The New Israel Fund: Financing Palestinian Nationalism," in Alexander, *With Friends*, 225–261; Urofsky, *One!*, 372–377.

50. Earl Raab, "Is the Jewish Community Split?," *Commentary* (November 1982): 22; J.J. Goldberg, *Jewish Power*, 203; Laqueur quoted in Feuerlicht, *Fate of the Jews*, 161.

51. Feuerlicht, *Fate of the Jews*, 168; Tivnan, *Lobby*, 94.

52. Marie Syrkin, "Sign Language from the PLO", *Midstream* (April 1977): 53–56; Tivnan, *Lobby*, 90–97; Feuerlicht, *Fate of the Jews*, 280; Arthur Hertzberg, *The Jews in America: Four Centuries of an Uneasy Encounter* (New York: Simon and Schuster, 1989), 384; Wertheimer, "Breaking the Taboo: Critics of Israel and the American Establishment," in Gal, *Envisioning Israel*, 397–419; Carolyn Toll, "American Jews and the Middle East Dilemma," *The Progressive* (August 1979): 28–35; Brettschneider, *Cornerstone*, 45; Findley, *They Dare*, 266.

53. Shmuel Katz, *Battleground: Facts and Fantasy in Palestine* (New York: Steimatsky/Shapolsky, 1985).

54. Rael Jean Isaac and Erich Isaac, "The Rabbis of Breira," *Midstream* (April 1977): 3–17; Rael Jean Isaac, "The Institute for Policy Studies: Empire on the Left," *Midstream* (June/July 1980): 7–18; Brettschneider, *Cornerstone*, 46; Friedman, *Zealots*, 76.

55. Quoted in Tivnan, *Lobby*, 80; Liebman, "Diaspora Influence"; Jacobovits, "Reassessment," 289; Feuerlicht, *Fate of the Jews*, 168–169.

56. Organski, *Bargain*, 61; Hertzberg cited in Tivnan, *Lobby*, 72; Borowitz cited in Urofsky, *One!*, 389, 435.

57. Cohen, "Romantic Idealism," 169–182; Tivnan, *Lobby*, 96; J.J. Goldberg, *Jewish Power*, 208; quoted in Urofsky, *One!*, 404–405; Chomsky, *Triangle*, 29.

58. Liebman, *Ambivalent*, 92; Brettschneider, *Cornerstone*, 88.

59. Joachim Prinz, "On Dissent," *Moment* (October 1976): 59–60; J.J. Goldberg, *Jewish Power*, 205.

3: STRAINING THE "SACRED UNITY": AMERICAN JEWS IN THE ERA OF LIKUD

1. Leonard Fein, "At the Beginning," *Moment* (September 1977): 10; Borowitz, *Mask*, 170; Interview with Alexander Schindler, *Moment* (January-March 1977): 16–17.

2. Hertzberg, *The Jews*, 384; Carl Bernstein, "The Agony over Israel," *Time*, no. 7 (May 1990).

3. David Gleicher, *Louis Brandeis Slept Here: A Slightly Cynical History of American Jews* (Hewlett, N.Y.: Gefen Publishing, 1997), 109; Auerbach, "Are We One? Men-

achem Begin," 342; Auerbach, "Are We One? American Jews," 20; J.J. Goldberg, *Jewish Power*, 210, 296.

4. Irving Greenberg, "Freedom, Power and Affluence: On the Jewish Way," in Raab, *American Jews*, 95–109; Milton Viorst, *Sands of Sorrow: Israel's Journey From Peace* (New York: Harper & Row, 1987), 42; Feuerlicht, *Fate of the Jews*, 234; Bernard Avishai, *A New Israel: Democracy in Crisis 1973–1988: Essays* (New York: Ticknor & Fields, 1990), 46; Fein, "Beginning," 10–12; Fein, "What, Then, Shall We Do," *Moment* (April 1983): 13–24; Urofsky, *One!*, 267.

5. Tivnan, *Lobby*, 109, 249; Gedal, "American Jewish Community," 99; Fein, "What Then," 15.

6. "The Rabbi and the Prime Minister: An Interview with Alexander Schindler," *Moment* (November 1982): 17–20; Greenberg, "Freedom, Power"; Podhoretz, "Israel: Lamentation," 21.

7. Heilman, "Separated"; Feuerlicht, *Fate of the Jews*, 228.

8. Avishai, *New Israel*, 75; Viorst, *Sands*, 42, 47; Tivnan, *Lobby*, 250.

9. Bergman, "Population Explosion"; Perlmutter and Perlmutter, *Real Anti-Semitism*, 280; Woocher, "The Civil Judaism of Communal Leaders," in *American Jewish Year Book*, vol. 81 (New York: American Jewish Committee, 1981), 149–169.

10. Brettschneider, *Cornerstone*, 2; Auerbach, "Are We One? Menachem Begin," 351; Auerbach, "Are We One? American Jews; Tivnan, *Lobby*, 107; Hertzberg, "Israel and the Diaspora: A Relationship Reexamined," *Israel Affairs* 2, no. 3 & 4 (1996): 169–183.

11. Woocher, "Civil Judaism"; Bloom, "Image Israel"; Menachem Kaufman, "Envisioning Israel: The Case of the United Jewish Appeal," in Gal, *Envisioning Israel*.

12. Paul Cowan, "American Jews and Israel: A Symposium," *Commentary* (February 1988): 21–75.

13. John Dumbrell, *The Carter Presidency: A Re-evaluation* (Manchester: Manchester University Press, 1993), 119; John G. Stoessinger, *Crusaders and Pragmatists: Movers of Modern American Policy* (New York: W.W. Norton, 1985), 263.

14. George Gruen, "The United States, Israel, and the Middle East," in *American Jewish Year Book*, vol. 79 (New York: American Jewish Committee, 1979), 120–151; Tivnan, *Lobby*, 112.

15. Alexander Schindler, "The Odd Couple: Begin and I," *Moment* (December 1978): 22–26; Tivnan, *Lobby*, 112.

16. Steven L. Spiegel, "Carter and Israel," *Commentary* (July 1977): 35–40; Tivnan, *Lobby*, 100; Feuerlicht, *Fate of the Jews*, 170.

17. Tivnan, *Lobby*, 119–120; Feuerlicht, *Fate of the Jews*, 170.

18. Tivnan, *Lobby*, 123.

19. Ibid., 124–125; Bard, *Water's Edge*, 41–50.

20. Bard, *Water's Edge*, 49.

21. Gruen, "The United States, Israel, and the Middle East," in *American Jewish Year Book*, vol. 80 (New York: American Jewish Committee, 1980), 87–117.

22. Feuerlicht, *Fate of the Jews*, 174; Tivnan, *Lobby*, 131.

23. Feuerlicht, *Fate of the Jews*, 175.

24. Ibid., 176.

25. Gruen, "The United States," 1980, 101; quoted in Edward Bernard Glick, *The Triangular Connection: American, Israel, and American Jews* (London: George Allen & Unwin, 1982), 142. Gruen, "The United States, Israel, and the Middle East," in *American*

Jewish Year Book, vol. 82 (New York: American Jewish Committee, 1982), 111–135; quoted in Tivnan, *Lobby*, 133.

26. Quoted in O'Brien, *Organizations*, 77.

27. Wertheimer, "Jewish Organizational Life," 74; Findley, *They Dare*, 267.

28. Brettschneider, *Cornerstone*, 69.

29. Quoted in Wertheimer, "Breaking Taboo," 412; Cynthia I. Mann, "The Rise of the New Israel Fund," *Moment* (October 1994): 35–38; Rafael Medoff, "The New Israel Fund—for Whom?" *Midstream* (May 1986): 13–16.

30. Friedman, *Zealots*, 113, 145; Julie Wiener, "UJC Is the Largest U.S. Charity," *Jewish Telegraphic Agency*, 5 November 2000.

31. Rael Jean Isaac, "New Jewish Agenda: The Jewish Wing of the anti-Israeli Lobby," in Alexander, *With Friends*, 143–190; Wertheimer, "Jewish Organizational Life," 55; Puder, "Israel Fund," 206; Ruth R. Wisse, "The Anxious American Jew," *Commentary* (September 1978): 47–58; Shmuel Katz, *Battletruth: The World and Israel* (Tel Aviv: Dvir, 1983), 100.

32. Glick, *Triangular Connection*, 138; Gruen, "The United States," 1980.

33. Feuerlicht, *Fate of the Jews*, 181; Gruen, "The United States," 1982; Avishai, *New Israel*, xii.

34. Findley, *They Dare*, 273; Tivnan, *Lobby*, 120–121; Gruen, "The United States," 1980; J.J. Goldberg, *Jewish Power*, 212–213.

35. "A Parliament of the Jewish People? A *Moment* Report on the World Jewish Congress," *Moment* (May 1981): 17–23.

36. Isaac and Isaac, "Rabbis"; Allon Gal, "Overview: Envisioning Israel—the American Jewish Tradition," in Gal, *Envisioning Israel*, 13–37. Hertzberg is quoted in Auerbach, "Are We One? Menachem Begin," 345.

37. Quoted in Feuerlicht, *Fate of the Jews*, 170; Puder, "Israel Fund"; R.J. Isaac, "Jewish Agenda," 183; Gedal, "American Jewish Community," 72.

38. R.J. Isaac, "Jewish Agenda," 183, 190; Wertheimer, "Breaking Taboo"; quoted in Toll, "American Jews," 35.

39. Tivnan, *Lobby*, 129; George Gruen, "Solidarity and Dissent in Israel-Diaspora Relations," *Forum* (spring/summer 1978).

40. Quoted in Feuerlicht, *Fate of the Jews*, 269.

41. Gruen, "The United States," 1980; Cohen, "Romantic Idealism," 177.

42. Norman Podhoretz, "Abandonment of Israel," *Commentary* (July 1976): 23–31; Gruen, "The United States," 1980, 105; Ruth Wisse, "The Delegitimation of Israel," *Commentary* (September 1978)): 47–58.

43. Quoted in Gruen, "The United States," 1980, 105; Tivnan, *Lobby*, 111, 125.

44. Quoted in Tivnan, *Lobby*, 257.

45. Albert O. Hirschman, *Exit, Voice and Loyalty: Responses to the Decline in Firms, Organizations, and State* (Cambridge: Harvard University Press, 1970); quoted in Wertheimer, "Jewish Organizational Life," 43; R.J. Isaac, "Jewish Agenda," 176.

46. Gruen, "Solidarity"; Elie Wiesel, *And the Sea is Never Full: Memoirs 1969—* (New York: Alfred A. Knopf, 1999), 134.

47. Quoted in Tivnan, *Lobby*, 119; "Interview with Jimmy Carter," *Moment* (March 1984): 13–20; Findley, *They Dare*, 269; Tivnan, *Lobby*, 124; Theodore R. Mann and Burton S. Levinson, "Should American Jewish Organizations Publicly Criticize Israel on Peace Issues," *Moment* (March 1988): 18–25.

48. Toll, "American Jews," 35.

49. Leonard Fein, "The Mideast Impasse: Skeptics, Cynics, and Rational Debate," *Commentary* (June 1978) 12–16; Harold Schulweis et al., "Our House Divided," *Moment* (April 1982): 56–63; J.J. Goldberg, *Foreign Policy*, 21; Gruen, "The United States," 1980.

50. Quoted in Wertheimer, "Jewish Organizational Life," 43.

51. J.J. Goldberg, *Jewish Power*, 38.

52. Gruen, "The United States," 1982.

53. Gilboa, *American Public Opinion*, 242; "The Cohen Report: Speaking Hawkish, Feeling Dovish," *Moment* (July-August 1982): 15–22.

54. Gilboa, *American Public Opinion*, 251; Steven Cohen, "What American Jews Believe," *Moment* (July-August 1982): 25.

55. Gilboa, *American Public Opinion*, 253.

56. Ibid.; Cohen, "What American Jews Believe."

57. Gilboa, *American Public Opinion*, 256; "Cohen Report."

58. Raab, "Jewish Split?"; Avishai, *New Israel*, 219.

59. "Cohen Report," 18; Tivnan, *Lobby*, 134.

4: THE WAR IN LEBANON: DEFENDING AN OFFENSIVE WAR

1. Quoted in Tivnan, *Lobby*, 178; J.J. Goldberg, *Jewish Power*, 214.

2. O'Brien, *Organizations*, 199; Saba, *Armageddon*, 133; J.J. Goldberg, *Jewish Power*, 215.

3. Gilboa, *American Public Opinion*, 127.

4. Quoted in Feuerlicht, *Fate of the Jews*, 271.

5. Quoted in O'Brien, *Organizations*, 97.

6. Gedal, "American Jewish Community," 108, 275.

7. Gilboa, *American Public Opinion*, 131.

8. Quoted in Gilboa, *American Public Opinion*, 134.

9. Tivnan, *Lobby*, 173.

10. Seliktar, *New Zionism*, 219–241.

11. J.J. Goldberg, *Jewish Power*, 215.

12. Viorst, *Sands*, 9; Findley, *They Dare*, 279–280; quoted in Jonathan Marcus, "Discordant Voices: The U.S. Jewish Community and Israel During the 1980s," *International Affairs* 66, no. 3 (1990): 545–558.

13. Quoted in Tivnan, *Lobby*, 174; Steven M. Cohen, *American Assimilation or Jewish Revival* (Bloomington: Indiana University Press, 1988), 99; quoted in Auerbach, "Are We One? Menachem Begin," 346; Michael Walzer, "What Kind of Triumph?" *The New Republic* (July 1982): 11.

14. O'Brien, *Organizations*, 40–1; Saba, *Armageddon*, 139–140; Norman Podhoretz, "J'Accuse," *Commentary* (September 1982): 21–31; Irving Greenberg, "American Jews and Israel: A Symposium," *Commentary* (February 1988) 37–39; Eric Isaac, "American Jews and Israel: A Symposium," *Commentary* (February 1988): 45.

15. Auerbach, "Thomas Friedman's Israel," 59; R.J. Isaac, "Jewish Agenda," 148; Hilton Kramer, "American Jews and Israel: A Symposium," *Commentary* (February 1988): 30–31; H.J. Kaplan, "American Jews and Israel: A Symposium," *Commentary* (February 1988): 47–49; Robert S. Wistrich, "The New War Against the Jews," *Com-*

mentary (May 1985): 35–40; Wisse, "Delegitimation of Israel," *Commentary* (July 1982): 29–36; Podhoretz, "J'Accuse."

16. Auerbach, "Thomas Friedman's Israel"; J.J. Goldberg, *Jewish Power*, 296; Gedal, "American Jewish Community," 134; Friedman, *Zealots*, 76; Wisse, "Blaming Israel," *Commentary* (February 1984): 29–36.

17. Quoted in Gedal, "American Jewish Community," 134–136; J.J. Goldberg, *Jewish Power*, 296.

18. Podhoretz, "Israel: Lamentation"; Edward N. Luttwack, "American Jews and Israel: A Symposium," *Commentary* (February 1988): 53–54.

19. "Israel at 37: A *Moment* Interview," *Moment* (May 1985): 13–18; Walter Reich, "The Kahane Controversy," *Moment* (January–February 1985): 15–24. Tivnan, *Lobby*, 251; Viorst, *Sands*, 25; Leon Wieseltier, "The Demons of the Jews," *The New Republic*, 11 November, 1985, 14–15.

20. S. Cohen, *American Assimilation*, 99; Tivnan, *Lobby*, 265; Avishai, *New Israel*, 132; quoted in Chomsky, *Triangle*, 12.

21. Wisse, "Delegitimation of Israel," 34; Gertrude Himmelfarb, "American Jews and Israel: A Symposium," *Commentary* (February 1988): 43–44; Wisse, "Blaming Israel": Edward Alexander, "American Jews and Israel: A Symposium," *Commentary* (February 1988): 23–24.

22. Tivnan, *Lobby*, 250; Nathan Glazer, "On Jewish Foreboding," *Commentary* (August 1985): 32–36; "American Jews and the West Bank," *Moment* (May 1982): 11–12; Alexander Schindler, "The Rabbi and the Prime Minister: A *Moment* Interview with Alexander Schindler," *Moment* (November 1982): 17–20.

23. Alexander, "American Jews and Israel," 23–24; Maier Deshell, "American Jews and Israel: A Symposium," *Commentary* (February 1988): 32–33; J.J. Goldberg, *Jewish Power*, 69; Feuerlicht, *Fate of the Jews*, 281; "The Anguish of American Jews," *Newsweek*, 4 October 1982; Hertzberg, "Illusion of Unity"; Bernard Avishai, "An Epilogue to Zionism," *Moment* (July–August 1985): 16–20.

24. Jonathon Sarna, "American Jews and Israel: A Symposium," *Commentary* (February 1988): 64–65. O'Brien, *Organizations*, 79; Steven M. Cohen, *Ties and Tension: The 1986 Survey of American Jewish Attitude toward Israel and Israelis* (New York: The American Jewish Committee, 1987); Gedal, "American Jewish Community," 140.

25. Gilboa, *American Public Opinion*, 257.

26. Cohen, "Romantic Idealism"; Gilboa, *American Public Opinion*, 243; Novik, *United States and Israel*, 76.

27. Steven M. Cohen, *The 1984 National Survey of American Jews: Political and Social Outlooks* (New York: The American Jewish Committee, 1984), 44; Gabriel Sheffer, "The Uncertain Future of American Jewry-Israeli Relations," *Jerusalem Quarterly*, no. 32 (summer 1984): 66–80; Steven M. Cohen and Calvin Goldscheider, "Jews, More or Less," *Moment* (September 1984): 41–46; Steven M. Cohen, *American Assimilation or Jewish Revival* (Bloomington: Indiana University Press, 1988), 113.

28. Schindler, "Rabbi and Prime Minister," 20; Feuerlicht, *Fate of the Jews*, 287; Glazer, *Jewish Foreboding*, 35; Leonard Fein, "American Jews and Israel: A Symposium," *Commentary* (February 1988): 34.

29. S. Cohen, "Romantic Idealism," 179, 182.

30. S. Cohen, "What American Jews Believe"; Auerbach, "Are We One? Menachem Begin," 350; Deborah Lipstadt, Charles Pruitt and Jonathan Woocher, "What They Think: The 1984 American Leadership Survey," *Moment* (June 1984): 13–17.

31. Cohen, "What We Think," *Moment* (January/February 1985): 34–42; Lipset and Raab, *Jews*, 161; Howe and Trott, *Peddlers*, 348.

32. Sharot and Zaidman, "Israel"; Auerbach, "Are We One? Menachem Begin," 351.

33. "Anguish"; Auerbach "Are We One? American Jews."

34. Gilboa, *American Public Opinion*, 150–153, 159; Mitchell Geoffrey Bard, "Israel's Standing in American Public Opinion," *Commentary* (October 1985): 58–60; Raab, "Jewish Split," 24.

35. J.J. Goldberg, *Jewish Power*, 77; Hyman Bookbinder, "American Jews and Israel after the Pollard Affair," in William Frankel, ed., *Survey of Jewish Affairs* (Rutherford N.J.: Fairleigh Dickinson University Press, 1989), 127–143.

36. Avi Weiss, "Pollard, American Jews and Dual Loyalty," *The Manhattan Jewish Sentinel*, no. 30, (June 1993); J.J. Goldberg, *Jewish Power*, 78; Bookbinder, "American Jews and Pollard"; Marcus, "Discordant Voices"; J.J. Goldberg, "Separated by a Common Cause," *Jerusalem Report* (February 1992).

37. Novik, *The United States and Israel*, 27.

38. Aaron Rosenbaum, "PACs Vobiscum," *Moment* (March 1982): 25–29; Robert Kuttner, "Unholy Alliance," *The New Republic*, 26 May 1986, 22–25; Hertzberg is quoted in Novik, *The United States and Israel*, 68.

39. Palmutter cited in Chomsky, *Triangle*, 15.

40. Friedman, *Zealots*, 145, 150.

41. Quoted in Chomsky, *Triangle*, 13; Perlmutter and Perlmutter, *Real Anti-Semitism*, 155; Prior, *Zionism*, 142.

42. Wertheimer, "Jewish Organizational Life," 46; Friedman, *Zealots*, 144, 149–150; O'Brien, *Organizations*, 86; Kuttner, "Unholy Alliance," 22–25.

43. Quoted in Lawrence Grossman, "Jewish Communal Affairs," in *American Jewish Year Book*, vol. 90 (New York: American Jewish Committee, 1990), 268; Irving Kristol, "The Political Dilemma of American Jews," *Commentary* (July 1984): 23–29. Rosenbaum, "PACs," 25–29; Kuttner, "Unholy Alliance," 23; Raab, "Are American Jews Still Liberal," *Commentary* (February 1996): 43–44.

44. Vital, *Jews' Future*, 108.

45. Quoted in Tivnan, *Lobby*, 248; O'Brien, *Organizations*, 146, 202.

46. Schindler, "Rabbi and Prime Minister"; Gedal, *American Jewish Community*, 138.

47. O'Brien, *Organizations*, 200; J.J. Goldberg, *Jewish Power*, 218.

48. Robert Spero, "Speaking for the Jews: Who Does the Conference of Major Jewish Organizations Really Represent?" *Present Tense* 17, no. 2 (January/February 1990): 7, 15–27; Sheffer, "Uncertain Future"; Tivnan, *Lobby*, 243.

49. Peter Beinart and Hanna Rosin, "AIPAC Unpacked: The Real Story of Tom Dine," *The New Republic*, 20 & 27 September 1993, 21–23; Lloyd Grove, "The Men with the Muscle: The AIPAC Leaders Battling for Israel and Among Themselves," *Washington Post*, 14 June 1991.

50. "Interview with Terry Dolan," *Moment* (March 1982): 29–32; Tivnan, *Lobby*, 126–127.

51. J.J. Goldberg, *Jewish Power*, 221; Beinart and Rosin, "AIPAC."

52. Quoted in Tivnan, *Lobby*, 214; Friedman, *Zealots*, 223; Cheryl A. Rubenberg, *Israel and the American National Interest* (Urbana: University of Illinois Press, 1986), 337; Tivnan, *Lobby*, 176.

53. J.J. Goldberg, *Jewish Power*, 219–220.

54. Medoff, "New Israel Fund"; O'Brien, *Organizations*, 198; R.J. Isaac, "Jewish Agenda."

55. Tivnan, *Lobby*, 253; Friedman, *Zealots*, 148.

56. Quoted in J.J. Goldberg, *Jewish Power*, 217.

57. Steven L. Spiegel, "American Jews and Israel: A Symposium," *Commentary* (February 1988): 70–71.

5: THE LONG SHADOW OF THE INTIFADA: AMERICAN JEWS AND THE PALESTINIAN PROBLEM

1. Kenneth Jacobson, "The United States, Israel and the Middle East," in *American Jewish Year Book*, vol. 90 (New York: American Jewish Committee, 1990), 231; Spero, "Speaking."

2. Jacobson, "United States and Israel," 1990, 233.

3. Quoted in Jacobson, "United States and Israel," 1990, 232.

4. Jacobson, "United States and Israel," 1990, 240–241, 244.

5. Quoted in Kenneth Jacobson, "The United States, Israel and the Middle East," in *American Jewish Year Book*, vol. 91 (New York: American Jewish Committee, 1991), 146.

6. Ibid., 147, 149.

7. Ibid., 151.

8. Quoted in ibid., 156.

9. David Landau, *Piety and Power: The World of Jewish Fundamentalism* (New York: Hill & Wang, 1993), xix–xx.

10. Quoted in Kenneth Jacobson, "The United States, Israel and the Middle East," in *American Jewish Year Book*, vol. 92 (New York: American Jewish Committee, 1992), 154.

11. Quoted in Jacobson, "The United States, Israel and the Peace Process," in *American Jewish Year Book*, vol. 93 (New York: American Jewish Committee, 1993), 154.

12. Gedal, "American Jewish Community," 198; Glick, *Triangular Connection*, 101.

13. Prior, *Zionism*, 246; Michael Lerner, "A Conversation with Faisal Husseini," *Tikkun* (March–April 1990): Brettschneider, *Cornerstone*, 60.

14. Wertheimer, "Jewish Organizational Life," 73; quoted in Gedal, "American Jewish Community," 155.

15. Quoted in Bernstein, "Agony"; Grossman, "Jewish Communal Affairs," 1990, 276.

16. Eizenstadt, "Loving Israel," 100; David Vital, "Power, Powerlessness & the Jews," *Commentary* (January 1990): 25; Haggai Eshed, "Yellow Wind: A Whirlwind of Controversy," *Moment* (November 1987): 32–35; Riva Silverman, "Ruthless in Gaza," *Moment* (October 1992): 36–41.

17. Quoted in Gal, "Overview," 33; Wertheimer, "Jewish Organizational Life," 73; Yosef Goell, "Is the Occupation Brutalizing Israel? No," *Moment* (April 1988): 14–19; Danny Rubenstein, "Is the Occupation Brutalizing Israel? Yes." *Moment* (April 1988): 14–19.

18. Ephraim Yuchtman-Ya'ar and Yochanan Peres, "Public Opinion and Democracy after Three Years of Intifada," *Israeli Democracy* (spring 1991): 21–31; Ian Lustick, "The West Bank: How Late is Too Late?" *Moment* (March 1985): 16–19; Friedman, *Zealots*, 77.

19. Michael Lerner, "The Occupation: Immoral and Stupid," *Tikkun* (March–April 1988): 7; Merrill McLoughlin, "American Jews: A Private Anguish Goes Public," *U.S. News and World Report*, 29 February 1988, 44; R.J. Isaac, "Jewish Agenda"; quoted in Sharot and Zaidman, "Israel," 158; Furman, "Jewish-American Imagination," 202.

20. Prior, *Zionism*, 220; Wiesel, *And the Sea*, 125–126; Elie Wiesel, "Israel Under Siege: Symposium," *Midstream* (December 1988): 21–32; Seymour Cain, "American Jews and the Palestinian Uprising," *Midstream* (May 1989): 38–40.

21. Marcus, "Discordant Voices"; D.H. Goldberg, *Foreign Policy*, 22; Robert O. Freedman, "A Talk with Arafat," *The New York Review of Books*, 13 April 1989.

22. Tivnan, *Lobby*, 207, 250; *New York Times*, 21 February 1988; "A Report from B'Tselem," *Tikkun* (September/October 1991).

23. Benny Morris, *The Birth of the Palestinian Refugee Problem, 1947–1949* (Cambridge: Cambridge University Press, 1987), 17, 24; Edward W. Said, *Orientalism* (New York: Pantheon House, 1978).

24. Michael Widlanski, "How Dangerous Would a Palestinian State Be?" *Tikkun* (July/August 1990), Podhoretz, "Israel: Lamentation," 20.

25. Podhoretz, "Israel: Lamentation"; Alexander, "Introduction," in Alexander, *With Friends*, 4; Friedman, *Zealots*, 221.

26. Edward Alexander, "Michael Lerner: The Would Be King of American Jewry," in Alexander, *With Friends*, 53; Edward Alexander, *The Jewish Wars: Reflections by one of the Belligerents* (Carbondale: Southern Illinois University Press, 1996), 145; Friedman, *Zealots*, 222; Auerbach, "Thomas Friedman's Israel," 65; Ruth R. Wisse, *If I Am Not for Myself: The Liberal Betrayal of the Jews* (New York: Free Press, 1992), 148, 153–65; Edward Alexander, "Anti-Semitism, Israeli Style, in Alexander, *With Friends*, 41.

27. Philip Hochstein, "Israel Under Siege: Symposium," *Midstream* (December 1988): 21–32; Marvin Maurer, "Israel Under Siege: Symposium," *Midstream* (December 1988): 24–26; Andrea Levin, "PBS Does It Again," *Commentary* (July 1992): 51–53; Joel Carmichael, "A Lethal Fiction," *Midstream* (February/March 1991): 6–8.

28. Podhoretz, "Israel: Lamentation," 20; Wisse, *If I Am Not*, 117; Alexander, "Anti-Semitism."

29. Bernstein, "Agony"; Gedal, "American Jewish Community," 143.

30. Albert Vorspan, "Soul-Searching," *New York Times*, 8 May 1988; Charles Fenyvesi, "US Jewry's Response to the Intifada," in William Frankel, ed., *Survey of Jewish Affairs* (Oxford: Blackwell, 1989), 109.

31. Grossman, "Jewish Communal Affairs," 1990, 259.

32. Marcus, "Discordant Voices"; Friedman, *Zealots*, 225–228, 231, 243; Tamar Jacoby, "A Family Quarrel," *Newsweek*, 3 April 1989.

33. Grossman, "Jewish Communal Affairs," 1991, 178; Jonathan D. Sarna and Jonathan J. Golden, "The Twentieth Century Through American Jewish Eyes: A History of *American Jewish Year Book*," in *American Jewish Year Book*, vol. 100 (New York: American Jewish Committee, 2000), 3–102.

34. Vorspan, "Soul-Searching."

35. Lawrence L. Barrett, "The Diaspora Discontent," *Time*, 3 April 1989; Jacoby, "Family"; Lerner is cited in Grossman, "Jewish Communal Affairs," 1991, 177–245, quote is on 180.

36. George Gruen, "Impact of the Intifada on American Jews and the Reaction of the American Public and of Israeli Jews," in Robert O. Freedman, ed., *The Intifada: Its*

Impact on Israel, the Arab World, and the Superpowers (Miami: Florida International University Press, 1991), 220–265.

37. Grossman, "Jewish Communal Affairs," 1991, 185.

38. Yosef I. Abramowitz, "Into the 21st Century—Where Do We Go from Here?" in *Israeli and American Jews: Understanding & Misunderstanding: A Study Guide* (New York: Department of Jewish Education, Hadassah, 1992), 147–162; Gruen, "Impact"; Friedman, *Zealots*, 112–113; 120.

39. Gruen, "Impact"; Gedal "American Jewish Community," 152–153; David Bar-Ilan, "Michael Lerner's Masquerade," *Jerusalem Post*, 13 July 1991.

40. Grossman, "Jewish Communal Affairs," 1991, 184; Spero, "Speaking."

41. Lawrence Grossman, "Jewish Communal Affairs," in *American Jewish Year Book*, vol. 93 (New York: American Jewish Committee, 1993), 173.

42. Goldberg, "Separated"; Grossman, "Jewish Communal Affairs," 1993, 174.

43. Lawrence Grossman, "Jewish Communal Affairs," in *American Jewish Year Book*, vol. 94 (New York: American Jewish Committee, 1994), 174; David Margolis, "Jewish Leaders Call for Freeze," *The Jewish Journal of Greater Los Angeles*, 11–17 October, 1990.

44. *New York Times*, 2 March 1992.

45. Grossman, "Jewish Communal Affairs," 1990; Marcus, "Discordant Voices"; Michael Lerner, "Who Speaks for American Jews?" *New York Times*, 24 February 1989; Robert I. Friedman, "Israel Lobby Blacklist," *Village Voice*, 4 August 1992; David Steiner, "Letter to Editor," *Village Voice*, 18 August 1992; Grossman, "Jewish Communal Affairs," in *American Jewish Year Book*, vol. 94 (New York: American Jewish Committee, 1994).

46. McLouglin, "American Jews."

47. Mark P. Cohen, "American Jewish Responses to the Palestinian Uprising," *Journal of Palestine Studies* 17, no. 4 (1988): 97–104; Richard H. Curtiss, *Stealth PACs* (Washington, D.C.: American Educational Trust, 1990), 100; Gruen, "Impact"; J.J. Goldberg, *Jewish Power*, 256; Bernstein, "Agony."

48. Podhoretz, "Israel. Lamentation"; Lerner, "Who Speaks"; Jacoby, "Family."

49. "Foreign Broadcast Information Service" (FBIS), 16 March 1988, 22 March 1988, 20 November 1989; Tivnan, *Lobby*, 243.

50. Hertzberg, "Illusion of Unity"; J.J. Goldberg, *Jewish Power*, 149; Spero, "Speaking."

51. Cohen, *Ties and Tensions*; Raab, "No Jewish Split on Israel," *Commentary* (June 1990): 45–48.

52. McLoughlin, "American Jews"; Thomas A. Sanctions, "Crisis of Conscience," *Time*, 8 February 1988; *Los Angeles Times*, 13 April 1988; Gruen, "Impact"; Grossman, "Jewish Communal Affairs," 1990, 261.

53. Steven M. Cohen, *The 1989 National Survey of American Jews* (New York: American Jewish Committee, 1989), 27–28, 35.

54. Earl Raab and Lawrence Sternberg, *The Use of Surveys By Jewish Advocacy Professionals: A Case Study: The 1990 Jewish Public Opinion Survey* (Boston: Perlmutter Institute for Jewish Advocacy, Brandeis University, 1991).

55. Steven M. Cohen, *The 1991 National Survey of American Jews* (New York: American Jewish Committee, 1991), 10; Raab, "No Split."

56. Jacob B. Ukeles, *American Jewish Leaders and Israel: A Survey of Attitudes* (New York: American Jewish Committee, 1990); S.M. Cohen, *1989 National Survey*; "Cohen

Report"; Samuel Heilman, *Jewish Unity and Diversity: A Survey of American Rabbis and Rabbinical Students* (New York: American Jewish Committee, 1991).

57. Steven M. Cohen and Seymour Martin Lipset, *Attitudes toward the Arab-Israeli Conflict and the Peace Process* (Los Angeles: The Wilstein Institute of Jewish Policy Studies, University of Judaism, 1991).

58. J.J. Goldberg, "Shamir Sandbagged," *Jerusalem Post*, 5 December 1991; Wilstein Poll Harmful, *Jewish Post & Opinion*, 4 December 1991; Lawrence Black, "Poll Didn't Represent Jewish Stance," *The Seattle Times*, 13 December 1991; "Washington Journal," *Forward*, 3 January 1992; Jonathan Tobin, "Self-serving Stunt," *The Jewish Week*, 13–19 December 1991.

59. "Foreign Broadcast Information Service", 5 December 1991; "Insult and Injury: Editorial Comment," *Jerusalem Post*, 25 November 1991.

60. Barry A. Kosmin et al., *Highlights of the CJF 1990 National Jewish Population Survey* (New York: Council of Jewish Federations, 1991); Sidney Goldstein, "Profile of American Jewry: Insights from the 1990 National Jewish Population Survey," in *American Jewish Year Book*, vol. 92 (New York: American Jewish Committee, 1992), 77–131; Edward Norden, "Counting the Jews," *Commentary* (October 1991) 36–43.

61. Ze'ev Chafets, *Members of the Tribe: On the Road in Jewish America* (New York: Bantam Books, 1988), 250; Raab, "American Jews and Israel," *Commentary* (February 1988): 60–61.

62. Steven M. Cohen, *After the Gulf War: American Jews's Attitudes Toward Israel: The 1991 National Survey of American Jews* (New York: American Jewish Committee, 1991), 6; *Los Angeles Times*, 13 April 1988; Bernard Reisman, "The Future of the American Jewish Community: Choices for its Leadership," Raab, ed., *American Jews*, 5–10; Raab, "American Jews and Israel," *Commentary* (February 1988): 60; Hertzberg, "Israel and Diaspora."

63. S.M. Cohen, "Israel in Jewish Identity," 120–121, 133; S.M. Cohen, *Ties and Tensions*, 42, 43; S.M. Cohen, *The 1989 National Survey*, 53; Louis Feldstein, "American Jewish Student of the Nineties—Implications for the Future," in *Israeli and American Jews*.

64. Feldstein, "American Jewish"; Clyde Haberman, "My Enemy Brother," *New York Times* 15 September 1989.

65. "Introduction," in *Israeli and American Jews*; Spiegel, "American Jews and Israel," 70; Furman, "Jewish-American Imagination," 178; McLoughlin, "American Jews."

66. Calvin Goldscheider, "The Contemporary American Jewish Context; Continuities, Israel and Challenges for Leadership," in Raab, *American Jews*, 11–29; Alan Tigay, "Viewing Each Other Through Space: Reflection of an American Jewish Journalist, in Israeli and American Jews"; McLoughlin, "American Jews"; Vital, "Israel and the Jewish Diaspora: Five Comments on the Political Relationship," *Israel Affairs* 1, no. 2 (1994): 171–187; "The Smith Survey: What Israelis Think," *Moment* (September 1983): 34–39.

67. Grossman, "Jewish Communal Affairs," 1990, 275–276; Jacoby, "Family"; Gedal, "American Jewish Community," 146–147; Eyal Bor, "Four Models of Relations between Israel and American Jewish Community as Defined by the Pollard Affair" (Ph.D. diss., Baltimore Hebrew University, 1996), 60; S.M. Cohen, *The 1991 National Survey*, 44–45.

68. Stuart E. Eizenstadt, "We Are Still One: An Open Letter to an Israeli Friend on the Issues that Divide Us," *Moment* (January/February 1988): 32–38; Landau, *Piety*, 293.

69. Leonard Fein, "A People's Memory is Called History: Do American Jews Have

Collective Amnesia?" *Moment*, (June 1990): 16–17; Leonard Fein, "Judaism as a Vocation—and Not Just for Professionals," in Raab, *American Jews*, 39–50; Vorspan, "Soul-Searching"; Auerbach, "Are We One? American Jews," 22; Allan C. Brownfeld, "Israel at 50: For Many Americans It Has Become a False God," *Washington Report on the Middle East* (May/June 1998): 51–2, 82; Neusner, *Israel in America*, 56, 60, 73; Cohen is quoted in Shimoni, "How Central," 24–27; Bor, "Four Models"; Prior, *Zionism*, 244.

70. Leonard Fein, "A New Zionism," *Moment* (April 1989): 48–53. Thomas F. Friedman, *From Beirut to Jerusalem* (New York: Farrar, Straus & Giroux, 1989), 487; quoted in Brownfeld, "Israel at 50," 51–52; Starr, *Kissing*, 98; Cardin, "New Agenda"; Sharot and Zaidman, "Israel," 171.

71. Goldberg, "Separated"; Asher Wallfish and Allison Kaplan, "AJC Delegation Makes Historic Saudi Visit," *Jerusalem Post*, 23 January 1992; Edward Alexander, "Jewish Critics of Israel and the Gulf War," *Midstream* (December 1991): 8–10.

72. Forman, *Israel*, 17; Bor, "Four Models," 48; Starr, *Kissing*, 151–152; Samuel Segev, "Reflections of an Israeli Journalist," in *Israeli and American Jews*, 33–42.

73. Golan, *With Friends*, 22, 183; Goldberg, "Separated."

74. Gruen, "Impact"; Organski, *Bargain*, 55; "Israel-trouble: American Jews," *Economist*, 28 March 1992; Richard H. Curtiss, *Stealth, PACs: How Israel's American Lobby Seeks to Control U.S. Middle East Policy* (Washington, D.C.: American Educational Trust, 1990), 168.

75. Gruen, "Impact," 241; Jack Wertheimer, "Zionism, American Style," in *Israeli and American Jews*, 58; Grossman, "Jewish Communal Affairs," 1990.

76. Hershel Shanks, "Leonard Fein's New Zionism: An Inspiring Vision or a Flawed Argument?" *Moment* (April 1989): 4–6; Raab, "No Split," 45–48; *Los Angeles Times*, 13 April 1988; Waxman, "Family"; Seymour M. Lipset, "Jewish Disunity is Good for Us," *Moment* (September 1988): 58–59.

77. S.M. Cohen, *Ties and Tensions*, 13; quoted in Elliott Abrams, *Faith or Fear: How Jews Can Survive in a Christian Society* (New York: Free Press, 1997), 145.

6: THE OSLO AGREEMENT: CEMENTING THE SPLIT IN THE AMERICAN JEWISH COMMUNITY

1. Quoted in Kenneth Jacobson, "The United States, Israel and the Middle East," in *American Jewish Year Book*, vol. 94 (New York: American Jewish Committee, 1994), 156.

2. Quoted in Kenneth Jacobson, "The United States, Israel and the Middle East," in *American Jewish Year Book*, vol. 95 (New York: American Jewish Committee, 1995), 146.

3. *Highlights from a Survey of American Jewish Attitudes toward Israel and the Middle East Peace Process* (Washington, D.C.: Israel Policy Forum, 1993).

4. Renae Cohen, *The Palestinian Autonomy Agreement and Israel-PLO Recognition: A Survey of American Jewish Opinion* (New York: American Jewish Committee, 1994), 4–7, 49.

5. Renae Cohen and Jennifer Golub, *The Israeli Peace Initiative and the Israel-PLO Accord: A Survey of American Jewish Opinion in 1994* (New York: American Jewish Committee, 1995), 2–9, 49–55.

6. *American Jewish Public Opinion* (Arlington, Va.: Luntz Research Companies, 1995).

7. *American Jewish Attitudes toward Israel and the Peace Process: A Public Opinion Survey* (New York: American Jewish Committee, 1995), 1–10.

8. Auerbach, "Are We One? Menachem Begin," 349; Auerbach, "Are We One? American Jews," 23.

9. R. Cohen, *Palestinian Autonomy Agreement*, 10–11; Cohen and Golub, *Israeli Peace Initiative*, 10.

10. Gedal, "American Jewish Community," 253; Freedman, *Jews vs. Jew*, 162.

11. Nathan Podhoretz, "Statement on the Peace Process," *Commentary* (April 1993): 19–24; Nathan Podhoretz, "Israel—With Grandchildren," *Commentary* (December 1995): 38–47; Real Jean Isaac, "The Real Lessons of Camp David," *Commentary* (December 1993): 34–38; Nathan Podhoretz, "Israel and the United States: A Complex History," *Commentary* (May 1998): 38; Fiamma Nirenstein, "Hallucination of Peace," *Commentary* (July 1995): 48–49; Douglas J. Feith, "The Inner Logic of Israel's Negotiations: Withdrawal Process, Not Peace Process," *Middle East Quarterly* 3, no.1 (1996); Douglas J. Feith, "A Strategy for Israel," *Commentary* (September 1997): 21–29.

12. Ian Williams, "AIPAC 1993 Convention: Scuffling on the Bridge," *Washington Report on the Middle East Affairs* (June 1993): 14; Lawrence Grossman, "Jewish Communal Affairs," in *American Jewish Year Book*, vol. 95 (New York: American Jewish Committee, 1995), 158.

13. Gedal, "American Jewish Community," 237; Michael I. Karpin and Ina Friedman, *Murder in the Name of God: The Plot to Kill Yitzhak Rabin* (New York: Henry Holt and Company, 1998), 150–151; Neve Gordon, "The Jewish Lobby," *Z Magazine* 11, no. 10 (1998).

14. Gedal, "American Jewish Community," 238–41; Karpin and Friedman, *Murder*, 133–135; Cynthia Mann, "Rhetoric Heats Up: American Jews Debate the Peace Process with Increased Fervor," *Jewish Exponent*, 22 September 1995.

15. Grossman, "Jewish Communal Affairs," 1995, 157; Karpin and Friedman, *Murder*, 135.

16. Matthew Dorf, "Is Irving Moskowitz a Hero or Just a Rogue?" *Jewish Bulletin of Northern California*, 26 September 1997; Michael S. Serrill, "The Power of Money," *Time*, 24 September 1997; Hilary Appelman, "U.S. Cuts Taxes for Israel Settlement Donors," *Detroit News*, 19 September 1997; Elli Wohlgelernter, "His Money Talks," *Jerusalem Post*, 12 January 1999; Hope Hamashige, Paul Lieberman and Mary Curtius, "Bingo King Aids Israeli Right Wing," *Los Angeles Times*, 9 May 1996; Christopher D. Cook, "The Bingo Connection," *Mother Jones* (September/October 2000): 68–73; "Interview with Rose Mattus," *Bergen Record*, 3 May 1998; Steve Feldman, "ZOA Presents Awards, Blasts Palestinian Action," *Jewish Exponent*, 9 November 2000.

17. "The Leaderships They Deserve?," *Outpost*, April 1996; Alexander, *Jewish Wars*, 173, 179; Karpin and Friedman, *Murder*, 144, 149, 156, 161, 162.

18. Lawrence Grossman, "Jewish Communal Affairs," in *American Jewish Year Book*, vol. 96 (New York: American Jewish Committee, 1996), 154, 157; *Forward*, 14 May 1994; Karpin and Friedman, *Murder*, 140–141, 157.

19. Grossman, "Jewish Communal Affairs," 1996, 144–5; Grossman, "Jewish Communal Affairs," in *American Jewish Year Book*, vol. 97 (New York: American Jewish Committee, 1997), 177; Gedal, "American Jewish Community," 69.

20. Gedal, "American Jewish Community," 243.

21. Jack Wertheimer, "The Orthodox Movement," *Commentary* (February 1999): 18–24; Gary Rosenblatt, "Today, We Stand Divided," *Jewish Exponent*, 17 March 1995.

22. Robert S. Greenberg, "Pro-Israel Lobby Sees Role Shrink as Enemies Turn into Friends and Leaders Forge Own Ties," *Wall Street Journal*, 26 April 1994; Gedal, "American Jewish Community," 249; Grossman, "Jewish Communal Affairs," 1995, 157; David Clayman, "Barak's Challenge: Reinforce Ties with American Jews," *Jewish Exponent*, 17 June 1999; Leslie Susser, "What Exactly Are We Doing Here?" *Jerusalem Report*, 25 August 1994.

23. Goldberg, "The Ties that Bind: If the Treat to Israel Fades Will its Friends Still be Generous," *MacLean's*, 20 December 1993; Gedal, "American Jewish Community," 247; Abramowitz, "Distant Relatives"; *Boston Globe*, 15 November 1995; J.J. Goldberg, *Jewish Power*, 48–49.

24. Goldberg, "Ties"; Gedal, "American Jewish Community," 245–247; Clayman, "Barak's Challenge"; R. Greenberg, "Pro-Israel"; Grossman, "American Jewish Communal Affairs," 1995, 159.

25. Steven Bayme, "Israel Diaspora Redefining their Relations," *Jewish Exponent*, 8 July 1994; Gedal, "American Jewish Community," 249; Grossman, "Jewish Communal Affairs," 1995, 157; "A Moment Interview with Ted Mann," *Moment* (December 1978): 12–19.

26. J.J. Goldberg, *Jewish Power*, 149; Shapiro, "The Ordeal of Success," 81–100; Gedal, "American Jewish Community," 249; Steven J. Zipperstein, "Zionism and the Liberal Imagination," in Steven J. Zipperstein and Ernest S. Frerichs, eds., *Zionism, Liberalism and the Future of the Jewish State: Centennial Reflections on Zionist Scholarship and Controversy* (Providence, R.I.: Dorot Foundation, 2000), 19.

27. Williams, "AIPAC Convention," 14, Gedal, "American Jewish Community," 225; Merle Thorpe Jr., "Notes of a Bit Player in the Israeli-Palestinian Conflict," *Journal of Palestine Studies* 23, no. 3 (1994): 41–52.

28. Gedal, "American Jewish Community," 256; J.J. Goldberg, *Jewish Power*, 348; J.J. Goldberg, "Ties"; Karpin and Friedman, *Murder*, 159.

29. Grossman, "Jewish Communal Affairs," 1995; *New York Jewish Week*, 4 July 1994.

30. Bernard Susser, "Top PR Firm Boosts anti-PLO Aid Drive," *Jerusalem Report*, 27 July 1995; Bertram Korn Jr., "Lipsky's Forward: The End of an Era," *Jewish Exponent*, 20 April 2000; J.J. Goldberg, *Jewish Power*, 346.

31. David Hoffman, "Rabin Criticizes Congressional Lobby for Israel," *Washington Post*, 17 August 1992; R. Greenberg, "Pro-Israel"; Beinart and Rosin, "AIPAC"; Thomas L. Friedman, "Another Top-Israeli Lobbyist Forced to Quit After Insulting Jews," *New York Times*, 2 July 1993; Wertheimer, "Jewish Organizational Life"; James D. Besser, "Rolling with the Punches: At its Annual Conference in Washington," *Baltimore Jewish Times*, 26 March 1993; Leon Hadar, "Yossi Beilin: Peres's 'Poodle' Is a Central Figure in the Peace Process," *Washington Report on Middle East Affairs* (February/March 1994): 11.

32. Thomas L. Friedman, "Jewish Lobbyist Ousted For Slurs," *New York Times*, 29 January 1993; Yossi Beilin, *His Brother's Keeper: Israel and Diaspora in the Twenty-First Century* (New York: Schocken Books, 2000), 76.

33. Landau, *Piety*, 24; Forward Staff, "Irony at AIPAC As Feud Over Dissent Widens," *Forward*, 7 July 2000; Richard H. Curtiss, "Rabin-Arafat Agreement Splits American-Jewish Leaders," *Washington Report on Middle East Affairs* (November/December 1993); J.J. Goldberg, *Jewish Power*, 225; Matthew Dorf, "AIPAC Head of 2 Years Resigns Amid Mystery Why," *Jewish Bulletin of Northern California*, 31 May

1996; Beinart and Rosin, "AIPAC"; Grossman, "Jewish Communal Affairs," 1995; Gedal, "American Jewish Community," 46; Thomas Friedman, "Top Israeli Lobbyist"; Gordon, "Jewish Lobby"; Rosenblatt, "Today."

34. Gedal, "American Jewish Community," 250; R. Greenberg, "Pro-Israel"; Williams, "AIPAC Convention"; Jonathan Broder, "What's a Lobby to Do?" *Jerusalem Post*, 10 February 1994, 29–30; Grossman, "Jewish Communal Affairs," 1993; Israel Shahak, "Relations between Israel and the Organized Jewish Community," *Middle East Policy* 2, no.1 (1993), 40–48; Matthew Dorf, "Partisan Politics of U.S., Israel Snakes through AIPAC Conference," *Jewish Bulletin of Northern California*, 3 May 1996.

35. Morton A. Klein, "Extremist in Moderate Clothing," *Jewish Bulletin*, 26 March 1993; Wertheimer, "Breaking Taboo"; Grossman, "Jewish Communal Affairs," 1995.

36. Karpin and Friedman, *Murder*, 136–137.

37. Nachum Barnea and Shimon Sheffer, "I'll Arrange It," *Yediot Aharanot*, 2 June 1995; Rowland Evans and Robert Novak, "Likud's 'Gang of Three,' " *Washington Post*, 17 November 1994.

38. Jonathan Broder, "Maverick: Solo Lobbyist," *Jerusalem Report*, 16 June 1994. Alexander, *Jewish Wars*, 174; Morton A. Klein, "Look Closely," *Washington Jewish Week*, 3 November 1994; J.J. Goldberg, "Backfire," *Jewish Exponent*, 18 June 1998.

39. Broder, "Maverick"; R. Greenberg, "Pro-Israel"; Grossman, "Jewish Communal Affairs," 1996.

40. R.J. Isaac, "Real Lessons"; Morton A. Klein, "PLO Behavior Doesn't Merit Renewed American Aid," *Jewish News*, 8 June 1995; Daniel Pipes, "Israel, America & Arab Delusion," *Commentary* (March 1991): 26–31; Douglas J. Feith, "A Mandate for Israel," *National Interest* (fall 1993): 43–58; Grossman, "Jewish Communal Affairs," 1997; Karpin and Friedman, *Murder*, 137–138.

41. Grossman, "Jewish Communal Affairs," 1996, 149, 151; J.J. Goldberg, *Jewish Power*, 54; Karpin and Friedman, *Murder*, 137–139; Matthew Dorf, "Debate Heats Up Over Whether PLO Should Get New Aid," *Jewish Bulletin of Northern California*, 9 June 1995; Gordon, "Jewish Lobby."

42. Broder, "Maverick"; Gedal, "American Jewish Community," 58, 80; J.J. Goldberg, "AIPAC is Seeking Consensus on U.S. Aid to Palestinians," *Jewish News*, 26 September 1997; Seth Gitell, "Pro-Israel Lobby Giving the Okay on Aid to Arafat," *Forward*, 26 September 1997.

43. Jonathan Broder, "Clinton Seeks a Quick Mideast Fix," *Jerusalem Report*, 12 October 1998; Michael Dorf, "AIPAC Accuses ZOA of Endangering Israel's Interests," *Jewish Bulletin of Northern California*, 13 August 1999.

44. Dore Gold, "Land for Cash?" *Commentary* (March 1995) Center for Security Policy, "U.S. Forces on the Golan Heights? A Special Report," *Commentary* (December 1994): 73–88.

45. Frank Gaffney Jr., "On Crushing the Opposition," *Outpost* (December 1995); Michael Shapiro, "U.S. Troops on the Golan? A Debate Resumes," *Washington Jewish Week*, 15 July 1999; Howe and Trott, *Peddlers*, 300; Herbert Zweibon, "Is It Premature to Save Lives?" *Outpost* (March 1995).

46. Mitchell Geoffrey Bard, "Israel Lobby Power," *Midstream* (January 1987): 6–8.

47. *Forward*, 2 October 1998; *Forward* Staff, "Netanyahu Feeling Brunt of Right-Wing Rhetoric That Echoes Attacks on Rabin," *Forward*, 6 November 1998; Letty Cottin Pogrebin, "Two Forevers and a Maybe," *Tikkun* (November/December, 1993): 72–74.

48. Grossman, "Jewish Communal Affairs," 1996.

49. Gedal, "American Jewish Community," 253; Douglas M. Bloomfield, "Lonesome Dove Flies Bibi's Coop," *Washington Jewish Week*, 15 January 1998. Novik, *United States and Israel*, 39; Elissa Gootman, "Israel-Diaspora Ties Set for Turbulence No Matter Who Wins the Next Week's Vote," *Forward*, 14 May 1999.

50. Grossman, "Jewish Communal Affairs," 1996, 150, 152; Bloomfield, "Lonesome Dove"; Ethan Bronner and Mary Curtius, "To Israel, U.S. Jews Pose Peace Hurdle," *Boston Globe*, 11 July 1993; Laerel Rosen, "Tikkun Editor, AIPAC Leader Wrestle on Israel," *Jewish Bulletin of Northern California*, 27 November 1998; Rosenblatt, "Today."

51. Quoted in Karpin and Friedman, *Murder*, 139; Barnea and Sheffer, "I'll Arrange"; Gedal, "American Jewish Community," 289.

52. J.J. Goldberg, *Jewish Power*, 57; Michael Shapiro, "Personal Note & Response to Pro-Appeasement Ad," *MacLean* (July/August 2000).

53. Matthew Dorf, "Debate."

54. Nathan Podhoretz, "Another Statement on the Peace Process," *Commentary*. (June 1993): 25–38; Podhoretz, "Statement" Jonathan Graubart, "Podhoretz's Complaint," *Tikkun* (July/August, 1993): 48, 93; Vital, "Israel and Diaspora"; Alan J. Yuter, "The Zionist Dream: Reality and the Threat of Nightmare," *Midstream* (November/December 1988): 14–15; Isi J. Leibler, "The Israel-Diaspora Identity Crisis: A Looming Disaster," *Jewish Spectator* (spring 1995): 9–18.

55. Beilin, *His Brother*, x, xii-xiii, 50.

56. E. Angler Anderson, "Beilin Keynote," *Jewish Exponent*, 10 November 1995; Barry Shrage, "Jewish Renaissance" *Journal of Jewish Community Services* 74, nos. 2/3 (1998): 98–107; Eliyahu Meir Klugman, "Politics and Divine Message," *Jewish Observer* (summer 1999): 5–9; J.J. Goldberg, "Ties"; Heilman, "Separated"; Tom Sawicki, "Windmills 1, Burg O," *Jerusalem Report*, 27 July 1995; Susser, "What Exactly"; Cynthia Mann, "Israelis Give, Get Blunt Talk," *Jewish Exponent*, 1 July 1994.

57. Grossman, "Jewish Communal Affairs," 1997, 176–181; Karpin and Friedman, *Murder*, 149.

58. Grossman, "Jewish Communal Affairs," 1997, 177; Karpin and Friedman, *Murder*, 160; Nathan Jones, "American Jews and Israel, Rabin Government Attacks Oslo II Critics," *Washington Report on Middle East Affairs* (October/November 1995): 71–72; Paul Giniewski, "The Israel-Palestinian Peace Roots Causes and Prospects," *Midstream* (August/September 1997): 6.

59. Grossman, "Jewish Communal Affairs," 1996, 154.

60. Bernard J. Shapiro, "Personal Note & Response To Pro-Appeasement Ad," *Maccabean* (July/August 2000); Karpin and Friedman, *Murder*, 134, 155; Itamar Rabinovich, "Zionism and the Arab World," in Zipperstein and Frerichs, *Zionism*, 67.

61. Alexander, *Jewish Wars*, 5; Rael Jean Isaac, "Israel's Future—As Seen By Yasser and Shimon," *Outpost* (March 1996); Irving Kett, "Is Israel Becoming Outdated?" *Midstream* (January 1996): 11; Karpin and Friedman, *Murder*, 140.

62. J.J. Goldberg, "U.S. Jewry Pins its Future on Education," *Jerusalem Post*, 6 October 1994, 26–31; Grossman, "Jewish Communal Affairs," 1996.

63. Jack Wertheimer, "Judaism without Limits," *Commentary* (July 1997): 24–77; Netty C. Gross, "Onward Christians' Rabbi," *Jerusalem Post*, 12 April 2000; Abrams is quoted in George Cantor, "Debate on 'Vanishing American Jew' Sharpens with Push for Educational Vouchers," *Detroit News*, 24 August 1997; Jonathan Rosenblum, "There Is No Continuity Without Content," *Jerusalem Post*, 20 November 1998; Michael Medved,

"What Do American Jews Believe: A Symposium," *Commentary* (August 1996), 70; J.J. Goldscheider is quoted in Goldberg, *Jewish Power*, 73; Eric H. Yoffie, "Reviving Religious Commitment," in *At the CrossRoads: Shaping Our Jewish Future* (Boston and Los Angeles, Combined Jewish Philanthrophy and Wilstein Institute of Jewish Policy Studies, 1995), 122.

64. Bayme, "Israel Diaspora"; Wall quoted in *Boston Globe*, 15 November 1995.

65. Leibler, "Israel-Diaspora," 12: Daniel J. Elazar, "New Alliances Will Form between Israel and the Diaspora," *Moment* (June 1997): 28–29; Halkin, "Ahad Ha'Am"; Henry L. Feingold, "American Zionism in Extremis?" *Midstream* (June/July 1994): 22–25.

66. R. Cohen, *Palestinians Autonomy Agreement; American Jewish Committee, The Palestinian Autonomy Agreement and Israel-PLO Recognition: A Survey of American Jewish Opinion* (New York: American Jewish Committee, 1993); Cohen and Golub, *Israeli Peace Initiative.*

67. American Jewish Committee, *American Jewish Attitudes.*

68. Ibid., 17–20.

69. Alan Mintz, "Israeli Literature and the American Reader," in *American Jewish Year Book,* vol. 97 (New York: American Jewish Committee, 1997), 93–114; Alan Mintz, "Hebrew in America," *Commentary,* July 1993, 42–46. Abramowitz, "Distant Relatives."

70. Bronfman is quoted in Larry Yudelson, "CRB Foundation Launches Major Effort to Send Every Jewish Teen to Israel," *JTA Daily News Bulletin,* 17 November 1992; Larry Yudelson, "G.A. Grapples With Survival," *Jewish Exponent,* 25 November 1994.

71. Michael Shapiro, "Backing Israel from Right: GOP to Continue 'Pressure' on Clinton Administration," *Washington Jewish Week,* 21 August 1997; David Breakstone, "Holy Land or Disneyland: A Cautious Guide to the Israeli Experience," *Moment* (December 1995): 58–61; Raab, "Changing Attitudes," 140–145.

72. Leora W. Isaacs and Devorah A. Silverman, "It's Israel, Chochem! Factors Affecting Participation of Youth in Israel Experience Programs," *Journal of Jewish Communal Service* 74, no. 4 (1998): 194–202; Mittelberg, *Israel Connection,* 17–18.

73. Michael Lerner, "The Civil War Has Begun," *Tikkun* (January/February 1996): 33–39.

74. Quoted in Grossman, "Jewish Communal Affairs," 1997, 187.

75. American Jewish Committee, *The 1996 Annual Survey of American Jewish Opinion* (New York: American Jewish Committee, 1996).

7: LURCHING TO THE RIGHT: RESPONDING TO NETANYAHU'S VISION OF THE PEACE PROCESS

1. Grossman, "Jewish Communal Affairs," 1997, 176–215; *Outpost,* June 1996; Bernard J. Shapiro, "Victory at Last—Israel Saved," *Maccabean* (June 1996).

2. Jonathan Broder, "The Right Kind of Friends," *Jerusalem Post,* 11 July 1996; "Our Money's Worth," *Coastal Post,* November 1996; Michael Kapel, "Why Joe Gutnick is Right," *The Australia/Israel Review,* 15–28 February 1997; Jonathan Broder, "Heeding the Call," *Jerusalem Report,* 29 March 1999; Lawrence Cohler-Esses, "Lauder's Rebuttal Moved Skeptics," *New York Jewish Week,* 12 February 1996; Lawrence Cohler-Esses, "Likud's Tangled Charity Web," *New York Jewish Week,* 19 February 1999; Lawrence Cohler and David Makovsky, "Lauder's Ties to Bibi Raise Questions," *New York Jewish*

Week, 29 January 1999; Julia Goldman, "Ronald Lauder is Nominated to Lead Conference of Presidents," *Jewish Telegraphic Agency*, 14 January 1999; Julia Goldman, "Report Prompts New Questions About Lauder's Bid for Top Post," *Jewish Telegraphic Agency*, 31 January 1991; Matthew Dorf, "The Road to Israel's Election," *Jewish Telegraphic Agency*, 1 February 1999; Karpin and Friedman, *Murder*, 135; Gordon, "Jewish Lobby" Hamashige, Lieberman, and Curtius, "Bingo King" Margot Dudkevitch, "Netanyahu Dismisses Reports of Apartment Purchase Probe," *Jerusalem Post*, 9 July 2000; Serril, "Power of Money;" *The Standard*, 26 July 1999; Sara Leibovich-Dar, "Things Change," *Ha'aretz*, 21 July 2000.

3. Joseph Gutnick, "Oslo's Damage: A Dead-end Process," *Jerusalem Post*, 22 July 1998; Bernard Shapiro, "Victory at Last"; Karpin and Friedman, *Murder*, 161.

4. Grossman, "Jewish Communal Affairs," 1997, 189.

5. Grossman, "Jewish Communal Affairs," in *American Jewish Year Book*, vol. 98 (New York: American Jewish Committee, 1998), 110.

6. Yari Ettinger, "Opening of the Tunnel at the Wall: Some of Netanyahu's Financial Considerations," *Kol Ha'ir*, 27 September 1996; Cook, "Bingo," 68–73; Matthew Dorf, a "Hero or a Rogue."

7. Grossman, "Jewish Communal Affairs," 1998, 110.

8. Ibid., 112.

9. David Wilder, "The Jewish Community in Hebron-Impending Disaster," *Freeman Center Broadcast*, 30 October 1996; Kapel, "Why."

10. "Jerusalem Roundtable," *Tikkun*, (May/June 1997): 33–40; Daniel Pipes, "If I Forget Thee—Does Jerusalem Really Matter to Islam?" *New Republic*, 28 April 1997, 16–18; Manfred R. Lehmann, "A Shared Jerusalem Equals a 'Judenrein' Jerusalem," Manfred and Anne Lehmann Foundation, <manfredlehmann.com>, 1997.

11. Isabel Kershner, "The Habit of Hatred," *Jerusalem Report*, 21 December 1998.

12. Michael Lerner, "Israel after the Bombing: America's Moment to Bring Peace to the Middle East," *Tikkun* (September/October 1997): 11–17; J.J. Goldberg, "AIPAC is Seeking Consensus on U.S. Aid to Palestinians," *Jewish News*, 26 September 1997; Seth Gitell, "Clinton's Moral Equivalence at Gaza Sparks Furor Among Jewry and Congress as Impeachment Looms," *Forward*, 18 December 1998.

13. The Center for Security Policy, *Publication No. 96-D 126*, 7 December 1996; J.J. Goldberg, "Backfire," *Jewish Exponent*, 18 June 1998; *Editor & Publisher*, 25 January 1997, 12.

14. Avi Weiss, "Saying What Israel Wants to Hear," *Washington Jewish Week*, 12 September 1996.

15. Lawrence Cohler-Esses, "New Climate Emerges at President's Conference," *Jewish News of Greater Philadelphia*, 31 October 1997; Mann, "Blunt Talk" Anthony Lewis, "Silencing Other Ideas" *New York Times*, 12 January 1998; *Forward*, January 9, 1999; Rachelle Marshall, "In the U.S. Even Staunchly Pro-Israel Jews Dare Not Criticize Israeli Prime Minister Binyamin Netanyahu," *Washington Report on Middle East Affairs*, March 1998, 19.

16. Hoenlein is quoted in Cynthia Mann, "Torah and Pluralism Spark Passion for Delegates to NJCRAC Gathering," *Jewish Telegraphic Agency*, 18 February 1997; National Council of Young Israel Israel Press Release, 26 September 1997; Cynthia Mann, "Israel Settlements Place U.S. Jews in Awkward Role," *Jewish Telegraphic Agency*, 23 December 1996.

17. Mann, "Israel Settlements"; ZOA, Press Release, 20 June 1997; Frank J. Gaffney. Jr., "Start Fixing What Ails U.S. Mideast Policy by Fixing Indyk's Wagon," *Intellectual Captial.com*, 18 September 1997.

18. Bloomfield, "Lonesome Dove."

19. American Jewish Committee, *1997 Annual Survey of American Jewish Opinion* (New York: American Jewish Committee, 1997), 39–41; *Survey of American Jews* (Washington, D.C.: Israel Policy Forum, 1997).

20. Jonathon Broder, "Netanyahu and American Jews," *World Policy Journal* 15, no.1 (1998): 88–98; Cohler-Esses, "New Climate"; quoted in Grossman, "Jewish Communal Affairs," 1998, 116.

21. *Moment*, December 1998, 27; Cook, "Bingo."

22. Hilary Appelman, "U.S. Cuts Tax For Israel Settlement Donors," *Detroit News*, 19 September 1997; Elli Wohlgelernter, "His Money Talks," *Jerusalem Post*, 12 January 1999; Michael Dorf, "Irving Moskowitz."

23. *1997 Survey*, 21.

24. Peter Ephross, "Mississippi Preacher Aims to Breed Red Heifer in Israel," *Jewish Exponent*, 9 September 1999; Prior, *Zionism*; Debra Nussbaum Cohen, "Evangelicals Voice Solid Support for Israel," *Washington Jewish Week*, 17 April 1997; Jonathon Broder, "Monica Lewinsky: Bibi's Queen Esther?" *Jerusalem Report*, 19 February 1998, 34–37; Broder, "Netanyahu"; Netty C. Gross, "Women in Green," *Jerusalem Report*, 16 April 1998, 22–24; Baruch Kra, "What's Wrong With Protestant Money?" *Ha'aretz*, 25 January 2000.

25. Broder, "Netanyahu"; Yoel Marcus, "Even If He Emerged Pure as Driven Snow," *Ha'aretz*, 22 September 2000; Ehud Ya'ari, "American Stewardship," *Jerusalem Post*, 23 November 1998.

26. Freedman, *Jew vs. Jew*, 17–22; Jacob Ner-David, "Riot at the Wall," *Moment* (August 1997): 23–28.

27. Jack Wertheimer, "Judaism Without Limits," 24–27; Grossman, "Jewish Communal Affairs," 1998, 122; Meryl Hyman, *Who Is A Jew: Conversation, Not Conclusion* (Woodstock, Vt.: Jewish Light Publishing, 1998), 178; 181; Samuel Heilman, "Separated," 8–15.

28. Fein, "New Zionism," 48–53; Broder, "Netanyahu"; Alexander M. Schindler, "Reform in Israel—No Deals," *Jewish Exponent*, 29 February 1996; Judith Miller, "Israel's Controversy Over Religious Donations by Jews in U.S.," *New York Times*, 17 November 1997; Ira Stoll, "Conversion Crisis Will Cause $100 Million Drop in American Giving to Israel, Reform Leaders Warn," *Forward*, 8 January 1999.

29. Grossman, "Jewish Communal Affairs," 1998, 125.

30. *Jewish Exponent*, 8 August 1996.

31. Broder, "Netanyahu"; Ramon quoted in Schindler, "Reform"; Beilin, *His Brother*, 71; Allen C. Brownfeld, "Israeli Religious Intolerance and Rejection of the Peace Process Alienating Majority of American Jews," *Jerusalem Report* (April 1998): 85–86, 93.

32. Klein is quoted in Broder, "Monica"; Mona Charen, "Readers Response," *Jewish World Review*, 16 December 1997.

33. Arthur J. Finkelstein & Associates, *Survey of Jewish Voters*, 1997; John McLaughlin & Associates, *Survey of Jewish Voters*, 1998.

34. James D. Besser, "AIPAC Veers Right," *New York Jewish Week*, 22 May 1998; *Forward*, 15 May 1998; Bloomfield, "Lonesome Dove"; Daniel Kurtzman, "Delegates to AIPAC Confab Back Israel in Peace Talks," *Jewish Bulletin of Northern California*,

22 May 1998; Matthew Dorf, "Returning the Pressure," *Jewish News of Greater Phoenix*, 15 May 1998.

35. Gordon, "Jewish Lobby"; *Israel Wire*, 4 August 1998; APN, Press Release, 13 May 1998.

36. James D. Besser, "AIPAC's Bag of Surprises," *Jewish Week*, 11 April 1997; "The Embassy Fiasco," *Forward*, 29 May 1998; M. Shapiro, "Backing Israel from Right"; Douglas M. Bloomfield, "Chairmanship of Key House Committee Will Be Up for Grabs," *Jewish Exponent*, 6 April 2000; Broder, "Monica."

37. Bloomfield, "Lonesome Dove"; Matthew Dorf, "Jewish Split Over Policies Spills Over to Public Arena," *Jewish Telegraphic Agency*, 7 April 1998.

38. Letter cited in Dorf, "Jewish Split," *Jewish Telegraphic Agency*, 7 April 1998; Dorf, "Israel's Labor Head Launches Own Lobbying Campaign in D.C." *Jewish Telegraphic Agency*, 3 March 1998.

39. American Jewish Committee, *1998 Annual Survey of American Jewish Opinion* (New York: American Jewish Committee, 1998).

40. *Los Angeles Times*, 19 April 1998.

41. *Survey of American Jews* (Washington, D.C.: Israel Policy Forum, 1998).

42. Yale Zussman, "How Much Do American Jews Support the Peace Process," *Middle East Quarterly* 5, no. 4 (1998): 3–12.

43. Howard Squadron, ed., *U.S. Middle East Policy and the Peace Process* (New York: Council on Foreign Relations, 1997).

44. Ami Eden, "Local Leaders Head New Initiative for Peace," *Jewish Exponent*, 17 September 1998; APN, Press Release, 11 September 1998; Jonathan Broder, "Clinton Seeks a Quick Middle East Fix," *Jerusalem Report*, 12 October 1998; *Jewish Exponent*, 17 September 1998.

45. American Jewish Commitee, *1998 Annual Survey*; AJPS cited in Eden, "Local."

46. *New York Post* ad cited in *Jewish Exponent*, 1 October 1997; Gutnick, "Oslo's"; *Jewish Exponent*, 29 October 1998; *Forward*, 2 October 1998; Douglas J. Feith, "Wye and the Road to War," *Commentary* (January 1999): 44.

47. *New York Post* ad cited in *Forward* Staff, "Irony at AIPAC as Feud over Dissent Widens," *Forward*, 7 July 2000.

48. Leslie Susser, "Bringing Down Bibi," *Jerusalem Report*, 21 December 1998; *Outpost*, January 1999; *Israel Wire*, 14 June 1998; Morton A. Klein, Op-Ed, ZOA Press Release, 7 December 1998; Morton A. Klein, "Wye We Can't Trust Arafat," *Jewish Exponent*, 26 November 1998; Jonathan Tobin, "Calling Things
By Their Right Names," *The Jewish Exponent*, 17 December 1998.

49. APN, Press Release, 16 November 1998; Bryen cited in Lawrence Cohler-Esses, "Wye 'Report Card' Rapped," *New York Jewish Week*, 20 November 1998.

50. Rosenblum cited in *New York Jewish Week*, 2 October 1998; Seth Gitell, "Congress, Clinton Clash Over Mideast Policies in Run-Up to Election," *Forward*, 19 March 1999.

51. ZOA Letter to APN, 4 January 1999.

52. Gitell, "Clinton's."

53. Smerling and Silverfarb quoted in Gitell, "Congress."

54. *Jewish Exponent*, 1 October 1998.

55. Jack Wertheimer, "The Disaffection of American Jews," *Commentary* (May 1998): 44–49; "Is Israel Still Important to American Jews, *Moment* (August 1988): 22–27; Daniel Siegal, "Israel and Diaspora: Limbs of a Single Body," *Tikkun* (May/June

1998): 64–65, 78; Cynthia Dettelbach, "Moving Apart: The Gap Widens between American Jews and Israel," *Jewish Spectator* (spring 1998): 40–42; Jonathan D. Sarna and Jonathan J. Golden, "The Twentieth Century," 99; Hillel Halkin, "Ahad Ha'Am," 102.

56. American Jewish Committee, *1997 Annual Survey*; American Jewish Commitee, *1998 Annual Survey*; Steven M. Cohen, "Response," in *Diaspora-Israel Contacts: Rethinking the Partnership*, (New York: World Council of Jewish Communal Services, 1998), 23–25.

57. AJC, *1997 Annual Survey*; AJC, *1998 Annual Survey*.

58. *Los Angeles Times*, 19 April 1998; "high observers" observe most religious precepts; "low observers" observe very few religious practices.

59. Charles S. Liebman, "Has the Romance Ended?," *Society* 36, no. 4 (1999), 15–21; S.M. Cohen, "Response"; Steven M. Cohen and Liebman, "Rethinking Israel/Diaspora Relations, View from Israel," *Journal of Jewish Communal Services* 74, nos. 2/3 (1998): 94–98; Gruen, "Israel and the American Jewish Community: Changing Realities Test Traditional Ties," in Robert O. Freedman, ed., *Israel's First Fifty Years* (Gainesville: University Press of Florida, 2000), 29–66.

60. Michael Lerner, "Israel's 50th Anniversary: How It Is Being Abused," *Tikkun* (May–June 1998): 8–10.

61. Brownfeld, "Israel at 50."

62. *New York Times*, 4 December 1998; Abrams, *Faith or Fear*, 133.

63. Elazar, "New Alliances," 28–29; quoted in Freedman, *Jew vs. Jew*, 338.

64. Yaron Ezrachi, "Individualism and Collectivism in Zionist Culture and the State of Israel," in Zipperstein and Frerichs, *Zionism*, 30–46.

65. Freedman, *Jew vs. Jew*, 77; *Jewish Exponent*, 7 January 1999; *Jewish Exponent*, 4 February 1999.

66. Stanley K. Sheinbaum, "The Imposition of Israel," *New Perspectives Quarterly* 15, no. 1 (1998): 60; Ze'ev Chafets, "A Two-State Solution," *Jerusalem Report*, 28 November 1996.

67. Jerold S. Auerbach, "Are We One? American Jews," 20–24; Wertheimer, "Disaffection," 44; Hertzberg and Hirt-Manheimer, *Jews*, 276; Herbert C. Kelman, "Israel in Transition from Zionism to Post-Zionism," *The Annals of the American Academy of Political and Social Science* 555 (1998): 46–62; Martin J. Raffel, "American Jewish Public Affairs and Israel: Looking Back, Looking Ahead," *The Reconstructionist* 9 (March 1999); Menachem Kellner, "Israel-Diaspora Relations After the Assassination: Can We Remain One People?" in Norman Linzer, David J. Schnall and Jerome A. Chance, eds., *A Portrait of the American Jewish Community* (Westport, Conn.: Praeger, 1998), 165–176; Forman, *Israel*, 21; *Los Angeles Times*, 19 April 1998.

68. Heilman, "Separated"; Halkin, "Ahad Ha'Am," 109; Dershowitz, *Vanishing American Jew*, 241.

69. Jonathan Rosenblum, "When Jews Cheer for the Desecration of the Sabbath," *Jewish Exponent*, 26 August 1999; Yonason Rosenblum, "The Arrogance of Israel's Elite, *Jewish Observer* (December 1999); Yoram Hazony, "The Zionist Idea and Its Enemies," *Commentary* (May 1996): 30–38; *Los Angeles Times*, 19 April 1998; Norman Rosenberg, "Israel's New School Curriculum: Teaching History Without Fear," *Washington Jewish Week*, 30 September 1999.

70. Yossi Beilin, "An Interview," *Mifgashim Matters* (spring 1998); Bar-Ilan cited in *Forward*, 14 May 1999.

71. Gary Rosenblatt, "Trading Places at the GA," *New York Jewish Week*, 20 November 1998.

8: LURCHING TO THE LEFT: RESPONDING TO BARAK'S VISION OF THE PEACE PROCESS

1. Tom Tudent, "U.S. Donors Have Given Generously to Israeli Candidates Paper Reports," *Jewish Telegraphic Agency*, 3 March 2000; "Bronfman Questioned Over NPO," *Jerusalem Post*, 10 August 2000; *Arutz 7*, 9 August 2000 (Arutz 7 is a radio station; see www.israelnationalnews.com); "In Defense of Barak," *Forward*, 11 February 2000; Lawrence Cohler—Esses, "Likud's Tangled Charity Web," *New York Jewish Week*, 19 February 1999; Matthew Dorf, "The Road to Israel's Election," *Jewish Telegraphic Agency*, 1 February 1999; Jonathan Broder, "Hostess Nets the Mostest," *Jerusalem Post*, 11 October 1999; Shlomo Shamir, "U.S. Jews Protest Donations to Israeli Campaign," *Ha'aretz* 25 January 1999; Esther Fink, "Barak Campaign Scandal: Money Trail Leads to North America & UK," *Jewish Press*, 11 February 2000; Broder, "Heeding the Call"; Douglas Davis, "Blair Admits Barak Contributor is Personal Envoy," *Jerusalem Post*, 24 February 2000; Lawrence Cohler-Esses, "Centrist Party to Use Charity for Campaign," *New York Jewish Week*, 12 March 1999; "Left-Wing Election Flights May Be Illegal," *New York Jewish Week*, 7 May 1999; Eli Wohlgelernter, "Backlash Mounts Against Avital for Comment on US Jews," *Jerusalem Post*, 7 January 2001.

2. APN Press Release, 17 May 1999, August 6, 1999, September 23, 1999; AJCongress, Press Release 6 July 1999; Elissa Gootman, "Barak's Favorite Peace Group Loses Its Founder," *Forward*, 3 March 2000; Howard Lovy, "Barak Seeks Pragmatic Approach to Peace Process," *Jewish Exponent*, 25 November 1999; *Forward*, 23 July 1999; Akiva Eldar, "The Importance of Wearing Glad Rags," *Ha'aretz*, 1 December 1999; Elaine Pasquini, "Yossi Beilin Delivers Video Address at New Israel Fund Symposium," *Washington Report on Middle East Affairs* (April/May 1999): 79–80.

3. Lawrence Grossman, "Jewish Communal Affairs," *American Jewish Year Book*, vol. 100 (New York: American Jewish Committee, 2000), 208–241; Gootman, "Israel-Diaspora"; Matthew Dorf, "AIPAC Must Again Shift Gear to Reflect Israeli Regime," *Jewish Telegraphic Agency*, 25 May 1999; David Makovsky, "Barak Letter Tries Soothing AIPAC's Ruffled Feathers," *Ha'aretz*, 24 May 1999; J.J. Goldberg, "Jockeying for Position," *The Jewish Journal*, 28 May 1999.

4. American Jewish Committee, *1999 Annual Survey of American Jewish Opinion* (New York: American Jewish Committee, 1999).

5. *Israel Security Watch* (Washington, D.C.: Israel Policy Forum, August 1999).

6. AFSI, afsi.org, 18 May 1999; Cook, "Bingo," 68–73; Jonathan Broder, "The Right's Red Lines: American's Hard Line Jews Get to Battle Barak," *Jerusalem Post* (June 21, 1999): 36–37.

7. George E. Gruen, "The United States, Israel and the Middle East," in *American Jewish Year Book*, vol. 100 (New York: American Jewish Committee, 2000), 189–207.

8. AFSI, paid advertisement, *Jewish Voice* (November 1999); Morton A. Klein, "Financing a New Arab Dictatorship," *Jewish Exponent*, December 9, 1999; ZOA, Press Release, 29 October 1999; APN, Press Release, 8 October 1999, 11 October 1999, 29 November 1999; National Unity Coalition for Israel, Press Release, 1 November 1999.

9. Michael Shapiro, "Jewish Activists Mount Full—Court Press to Lobby for Wye Aid," *Jewish Telegraphic Agency*, 4 November 1999; *Arutz 7*, 4 November 1999; Janine

Zacharia, "Senior Republicans Want Quicker Cut in U.S. Aid for Israel," *Jerusalem Post*, 3 December 1999; Douglas M. Bloomfield, "Selling Peace to American Jews May Be Harder than Barak Thinks," *Jewish Exponent*, 15 December 1999; Douglas M. Bloomfield, "A Lobby Against Wye May Hurt Israel Later," *Jewish Exponent*, 28 October 1999.

10. Michael Shapiro, "Foreign Aid Gets Trapped in U.S. Budget Battles," *Jewish Exponent*, 14 October 1999; Nitzan Horowitz, "What Will Happen to the Wye Money," *Ha'aretz*, 20 October 1999; Nitzan Horowitz, "Uncle Sam as an Automatic Teller Machine," *Ha'aretz*, 9 November 1999; Michael Shapiro, "Battle Erupts Over Wye Aid," *Jewish Exponent*, 28 October 1999; ADL, Press Release, 25 October 1999; Nitzan Horowitz, "Support Rises for Wye Aid," *Ha'aretz*, 22 October 1999; Nitzan Horowitz, "Jewish Lobby Preparing for Protracted Struggle Over Wye Funds," *Ha'aretz*, 25 October 1999; Yosi Verter, "Sharon Wants End to Anti-gov't Lobbying Abroad," *Ha'aretz*, 19 November 1999; *Forward* Staff, "Sharon Seeks Ban on Lobbying D.C.," *Forward*, 26 November 1999.

11. Yohanan Ramati, "Peace With Syria: A Kind of Suicide," *Outpost*, April 1999; "The Next U.S. Peacekeeping Boot to Drop; The Golan Heights," *Center for Security Policy*, No. 99-D 76, 6 July 1999; The National Unity Coalition for Israel, www.israel unitycoalition.com; Michael Shapiro, "U.S. Troops on the Golan? A Debate Resumes," *Washington Jewish Week*, 15 July 1999; *Arutz 7*, 22 March 2000.

12. Michael Shapiro, "No Troops No Money Declared Opponents of Israel-Syria Deal," *Jewish Telegraphic Agency*, 13 February 2000; *Arutz 7*, 11 February 2000, 22 March 2000; ZOA, Press Release, 13 July 1999; M. Shapiro, "U.S. Troops"; Frank Gaffney Jr., "Weighing Real Costs of a Golan Deal," *Washington Times*, 14 December 1999; Eli Lake, "Battle Brews over Aid to Syria Regime as AIPAC, Zionist Organization Diverge," *Forward*, 3 March 2000.

13. APN, Press Release, 3 February 2000; Lake, "Battle."

14. "Conference Call," *Forward*, 4 August 2000; "A Democratic Conference," *Forward*, 17 January 2000; Janine Zacharia, "The Unofficial Ambassador of the Jewish State," *Jerusalem Post*, 2 April 2000; Gad Nashon, "Ron Lauder: The Next Chairman of the Conference of Presidents," *Jewish Post of New York* (March 1999); Ruth King, "More on the Presidents Conference," *Outpost*, February 1999; Jonathan Tobin, "The Bibiphobia Conspiracy," *Jewish World Review*, 5 February 1999.

15. Dorf, "AIPAC Must Again Shift Gear"; Eli Lake, "Bush Backers in Uproar Over AIPAC's Tilt to Gore at Washington Meeting," *Forward*, 21 March 2000; Murray Kohl, congressional release, *Israeli & Global News*, 24 October 1999; Sharon Samber, "Lobbyist Wonders What it Means to be an Israeli Supporter These Days," *Jewish Telegraphic Agency*, 30 May 2000.

16. Matthew Dorf, "AIPAC Accuses ZOA of Endangering Israel's Interests," *Jewish Bulletin of Northern California*, 13 August 1999; "The Kohr-Klein Conundrum," *Forward*, 6 August 1999; AIPAC letter cited in James D. Besser, "ZOA Blasted for Jordan Tactics," *New York Jewish Week*, 6 August 1999; ZOA, Press Release, 18 June 1999.

17. Aluf Benn, "The Battle of Who Failed to Keep More Promises Erupts Anew," *Ha'aretz*, 17 October 2000; David Beidin, "Israelis and Palestinians Differ on Education," *Jewish Exponent*, 7 September 2000; Steve Feldman, "Getting Tough on Killers," *Jewish Exponent*, 17 June 1999; Jews for Truth Now, paid advertisement, *Jewish Exponent*, 21 December 2000.

18. Matthew Dorf, "Congress Heeds Barak's Plea to Back Peace Moves," *Jewish*

Exponent, 29 July 1999; Seth Gitell, "Moynihan, Beilin and Ganchrow Press Clinton on Move of American Embassy to Jerusalem," *Forward*, 20 August 1999; Religious Action Center of Reform Judaism, Press Release, 18 June 1999.

19. Jonathan Tobin, "Can We Still Ask, is it Good for the Jews," *Jewish Exponent*, 14 October 1999; Donna Harman, "Barak and the Rabin Legacy," *Jerusalem Post*, 8 October 1999; Gootman, "Israel-Diaspora"; Douglas M. Bloomfield, "Great Expectations: Ehud Barak Will Chart His Own Course," *Jewish Exponent*, 20 May 1999; Debora Sontag, "Sharon Cautions West Against Aid to Syria in Any Peace Deal," *New York Times*, 1 March 2000.

20. Jonathan Tobin, "All's Fair in Love, War and Jewish Politics," *Jewish Exponent*, 30 September 1999; Elissa Gootman, "Charity Hires a Gumshoe to Discover its Plan to Honor Arafat," *Forward*, 5 November 1989.

21. Jason Maoz, "Government, Media Push Assassination Scare," *Jewish Press*, 9 June 2000; Shlomo Shamir, "Ouster of *Forward*'s Editor Leaves Paper Stalled," *Ha'aretz*, 25 April 2000.

22. Morton A. Klein, "ZOA Agenda Has Broad Support," *Forward*, 29 October 1999.

23. Leonard Fein, "Israel Must End the Conflict With Palestinian Now," *Jewish Exponent*, 13 July 2000; "The Pathetic Mr. Barak," *Jewish Press*, 7 July 2000; Friends and Families of Victims of Oslo, paid advertisement, *Jewish Voice* (August 2000); FLAME, paid advertisement, *New Republic*, 6 March 2000; "Camp David Outcome—Assisted Suicide for Israel?" *Center for Security Policy*, No. 00-D 70, 24 July 2000; Margot Dudkevitch, "Settlers Raising Funds to Buy Arms," *Jerusalem Post*, 12 September 2000.

24. Daniel Pipes, "Lebanon Turns Into Israel's Vietnam," *Wall Street Journal*, 10 March 1999; Daniel Pipes, "Israel's Moment of Truth," *Commentary* (February 2000): 19–25.

25. Friends and Families of Victims of Oslo, paid advertisement, *Jewish Voice* (August 2000); Dave Boyer, "Clinton Warned on Cost of Mideast Deal," *Washington Times*, 18 July 2000; Nina Gilbert, "Kleiner: Senate Panel to Hold Hearing on Final-Status Deal," *Jerusalem Post*, 29 June 2000.

26. Michael J. Jordan, "Letter Criticizing Barak Could Affect Peace Process," *Jewish Telegraphic Agency*, 9 July 2000; *Forward* Staff, "Irony at AIPAC as Feud Over Dissent Widens," *Forward*, 7 July 2000.

27. "No Time for Mourning," *Forward*, 28 July 2000; Melvin Salberg, "American Jewish Critics of Barak Should Pipe Down," *Jewish Exponent*, 6 July 2000; Marilyn Henry, "The Battle for the Hears and Minds of US Jewry," *Jerusalem Post*, 16 July 2000.

28. Jacob Schreiber, "It's an American Right to Speak Out on Israel's Situation," *Jewish Exponent*, 13 July 2000.

29. Bloomfield, "Selling Peace"; Philip Shenon, "Another Dangerous Mission for a Veteran Israeli Warrior," *New York Times*, 18 September 2000; *Jewish Press*, 7 July 2000; Shlomo Shamir, "Siso Digs in His Heels in New York," *Ha'aretz*, 11 August 2000; Harman, "Foreign Ministry: Poor PR, Coordination at US Diplomatic Mission," *Jerusalem Post*, 8 May 2000; Aluf Benn, "NSC: Israel Must Bolster Ties with US Jews," *Ha'aretz*, 3 January 2001.

30. Mitchell G. Bard, "American Jews Cannot Dictate Policy in the Middle East," *Jewish Exponent*, 6 January 2000; Jonathan Tobin, "The 'Peace Bug' Strikes Home," *Jewish Exponent*, 6 January 2000.

31. Hoenlein, Cardin, and Foxman quoted in Larry Yudelson, "As Israel Mulls Col-

lapse of Mideast Summit, U.S. Jews Face End of Illusion on Jerusalem," *Forward*, 31 July 2000; American Jewish Committee, *2000 Annual Survey of American Jewish Opinion* (New York: American Jewish Committee, 2000); Ami Eden, "Dear Prime Minister Barak," *Jewish Exponent*, 22 June 2000.

32. Ami Eden, "Israel Puts Fundraisers 'Renaissance' on Hold," *Forward*, 17 November 2000.

33. Eli Wohlgelernter, "A Sobering Experience," *Jerusalem Post*, 30 October 2000; Jonathan Tobin, "Off the Reservation," *Jewish Exponent*, 22 June 2000.

34. Herb Keinon, "Israel Accuses PA of Violating Oslo Accord," *Jerusalem Post*, 5 January 2001; Aluf Benn, "White Paper Tiger Unleashed," *Ha'aretz*, 24 November 2000; "Barak, Opposition Square off at GA," *New York Jewish Week*, 18 November 2000; Norman Podhoretz, "Intifada II: Death of an Illusion?" *Commentary* (December 2000): 27–39; Yonason Rosenblum, "Israel on the Brink," *Jewish Observer*, November 2000, 4–11.

35. Wohlgelernter, "Sobering"; Gary Rosenblatt, "Listening, Finally to the Palestinians," *Jewish Exponent*, 28 December 2000; *Arutz 7*, 17 November 2000; Julie Wiener, "Depth of Outrage, Violence Shakes Jews Across the Spectrum," *Jewish Telegraphic Agency*, 11 October 2000; APN Website, <peacenow.org>.

36. Hillel Halkin, "Intifada II: Israel's Nightmare," *Commentary* (December 2000): 44–48; Leonard Fein, "Jews and Arabs Must Listen to Each Other's Pain," *Jewish Exponent*, 23 November 2000.

37. Gerald M. Steinberg, "The Oslo Accords Created a Terrorist State, Not Peace," *Jewish Exponent*, 11 January 2001; Daniel Pipes, "A Father's Pride and Glory," *Jerusalem Post*, 15 August 2001; Ami Eden and Julia Goldman, "Diaspora Support for Settlers Growth with Violence," *Ha'aretz*, 30 July 2001; AJC, *2000 Annual Survey*.

38. Robert O. Freedman, "Separation Means Dividing Both the Land and Jerusalem," *Jewish Exponent*, 28 December 2000; Michael J. Jordan, "Jews in U.S. Revive Division Over Peace," *Jewish Telegraphic Agency*, 29 November 2000.

39. Michael J. Jordan, "American Jews Launch Campaign to Halt Temple Mount 'Surrender,' " *Jewish Exponent*, 28 December 2000; *Arutz 7*, 22 December 2000; Akiva Eldar, "Hoenlein: U.S. Jews Must Fight Deal on Mount," *Ha'aretz*, 29 September 2000.

40. Tamar Hausman, "Sacrifice of Temple Mt. Risks Ties to U.S. Jewry," *Ha'aretz*, 5 January 2000.

41. Mallow is quoted in Barry Schweid, "Rabbis: Holy Site Can Be Shared," *Forward*, 15 December 2000; Foxman is quoted in Jordan, "American Jews Launch Campaign" to Halt Mount 'Surrender,' " Clayman is quoted in Hausman, "Sacrifice of Temple Mt." *Jerusalem Post* Staff, "U.S. Jewish Leaders Question Israel's Right to Deal on Jerusalem," *Jerusalem Post*, 21 December 2000; *Arutz 7*, 2 October 2000; Eldar, "Hoenlein," Shlomo Shamir, "Sharanky Under Fire From U.S. Jewish Leaders," *Ha'aretz*, 5 January 2001.

42. Wohlgelernter, "Avital Tells US Jews to Stay Out of Israeli Politics," *Jerusalem Post*, 5 January 2001; idem, "Backlash"; Shlomo Shamir, "Weary and Wary," *Ha'aretz*, 20 October 2000; Nina Gilbert, "Jerusalem Rally Financed by Foreigners," *Jerusalem Post*, 8 January 2000; *Jerusalem Post* Staff, "Lauder Praised, Slammed for Attending Jerusalem Rally," *Jerusalem Post*, 10 January 2001; Lauder quoted in Lisa Keys, "Jewish Group in Uproar as Their Top Spokesman Joins Jerusalem Protest," *Forward*, 12 January 2001; Lauder quoted in Nadav Shragai, "250,000 Gather to Rally for Jerusalem," *Ha'aretz*, 9 January 2001.

43. Ami Eden, "U.S. Jews Stuck Between Barak and Hard Place," *Forward*, 5 January 2001; Rachel Donadi, "Israel's Beilin Rips U.S. Jews for Undercutting PA Chief," *Forward*, 8 October 2000.

44. Melissa Radler, "US Jewish Leaders Congratulate Sharon," *Jerusalem Post*, 8 February 2001; Sharon Samber, "AIPAC Reverts to a Harder Line," *Jewish Telegraphic Agency*, March 22, 2001; Jonathan Friendly, "Calls to Unity Shouldn't Silence Dissent on Israel," *Jewish Exponent*, March 29, 2001; Schneider quoted in Melissa Radler, "US Urges Discreet Hunt for Terrorists," *Jerusalem Post*, 6 April 2001; Matthew E. Berger, "Pressure Mounts for Washington to Take Harder Line with Palestinians," *Jewish Telegraphic Agency*, 13 March 2001; Natan Gutman, "US Congress Rides the Terror Wave," *Ha'aretz*, 15 August 2001.

45. Michael J. Jordan, "Reform leader Doesn't Shy Away from Controversy," *Jewish Telegraphic Agency*, 13 June 2001; Berger, "Pressure Mounts!"

46. Menachem Z. Rosensaft, "Defending Dissenters, On all Sides," *Forward*, 9 February 2000.

47. Julie Wiener, "American Jewish Survey Wrestles with 'Who is a Jew,'" *Jewish Telegraphic Agency*, 7 February 2000; AJC, *2000 Annual Survey*.

48. Elissa Gootman, "Renaissance Commission Starts to Gain Adherents as Past Programs Falter," *Forward*, 4 December 1998; Julie Wiener, "Reform Movement Most Aggressive in Synagogue Transformation Efforts," *Jewish Telegraphic Agency*, 10 September 2000; "Funders Ruffle Rabbinic Feather at Synagogue Renewal Gathering," *Jewish Telegraphic Agency*, 10 September 2000; "Donors Discuss How to Spread Word of the Jewish Day School Alternatives," *Jewish Telegraphic Agency*, 20 September 2000.

49. AJC, *2000 Annual Survey*; Gad Nahshon, "De-Israelization of American Jewry?" *Jewish Post of New York*, 22 November 2000; *Jewish Telegraphic Agency*, 13 June 2000; Eliahu Salpeter, "US Jews Get Mixed Message from Israel," *Ha'aretz*, 23 November 2000; Lisa Keys, "Study: Conservative Youth Maintain Ties," *Forward*, 19 January 2001.

50. Yoram Hazony, *The Jewish State* (New York: Basic Books, 2000); Daniel Pipes, "The Oslo Process: An Israeli Choice," *Jerusalem Post*, 3 January 2001; Gil Troy, "What's Left of Zionism," *Moment* (April 1999): 63–66; Clayman, "Barak's Challenge"; Marc Perleman, "Scholars Clash at Israel's History Confab," *Forward*, 3 March 2001.

51. Freedman, *Jew vs. Jew*, 349–350; *Hamodia*, 10 November 2000; *Arutz 7*, 22 May 2000; Gideon Alon, "Shahs Looks to Bypass Court's Decision," *Ha'aretz*, 23 May 2000; Nina Gilbert, "Knesset Bill: Women Who Read Torah at the Wall Can Be Jailed," *Jerusalem Post*, 31 May 2000.

52. Clayman and Alpher quoted in Catherina Cohen, "Burying their Heads Deep in the Sand," *Ha'aretz*, 17 March 2000; Moshe Katsav, "Good Grief, Mr. President," *Forward*, 4 August 2000; Friends and Families of Oslo, paid advertisement, *Jewish Voice* (August 2000).

53. Yosef quoted in Dalia Shehori, Yair Sheleg and Gideon Alon, "Rabbi Yosef Storm Over Shoah," *Ha'aretz*, 7 August 2000; Gideon Samet, "Shah Unleashes a Postmodern Crisis," *Ha'aretz*, 16 June 2000; Haim Shapiro, "World Leaders of the ADL Meet with Rabbi Ovadia Yosef," *Jerusalem Post*, 20 September 2000; Matt Rees, "Miracle Campaign," *Time*, 11 September 2000; "We're Here, O Israel," *Inside Magazine* (fall 2000): 69–75; AJC, *2000 Annual Survey*.

54. Katsav quoted in Gil Hoffman, "Katsav Negates Diaspora, Calls for Mass Aliya," *Jerusalem Post*, 11 September 2000; Marilyn Henry, "Katsav Hit in US for Underrating Jewish Education," *Jerusalem Post*, 12 September 2000; Michael Arnold, "Don't Legit-

imize Diaspora, Israel's New President Warns," *Forward*, 15 September 2000; "Katsav Tirade," *Forward*, 15 September 2000; Gil Hoffman, "Shumer Clarifies Katsav's Remark on Diaspora Jews," *Jerusalem Post*, 15 September 2000; Eliahu Salpeter, "Unfortunate Utterances on the Diaspora," *Ha'aretz*, 20 September 2000.

55. Yair Sheleg, "The Diaspora as a Strategic Asset," *Ha'aretz*, 9 January 2001; Bradely Burston, "Security Chiefs Urge Closer Ties to U.S. Jewry," *Forward*, 12 January 2001; Yair Sheleg, "American Jewry High Up on Sharon's Agenda," *Ha'aretz*, 13 February 2001.

56. Jordan, "Reform Leader"; Michael Jordan, "Maccabiah Disputes Reflects Israel Angst," *Jewish Telegraphic Agency*, 5 July 2001; Julie Wiener, "Orthodox Students Still Staying in Israel," *Jewish Telegraphic Agency*, 5 August 2001; Gerald Steinberg, "No. 1 Demand of Agency: Solidarity with Israel," *Jewish Exponent*, 28 June 2001; Saul Singer, "If We're Indeed Family, Now's the Time to Show It," *Jewish Exponent*, 21 June 2001; Charlotte Halle, "Leading Politicians Call for More North American Aliyah," *Ha'aretz*, 13 April 2001.

57. "Israel Options, and Ours," *Forward*, 30 March 2001; Michelle Dardashti, "Students Intern Learn Leadership, But Clash Over Zionist Programming," *Jewish Telegraphic Agency*, 16 August 2001.

58. Steven T. Rosenthal, *Irreconcilable Differences: The Waning of the American Jewish Love Affair with Israel* (Hanover, N.H.: Brandeis University Press, 2001), 30ff.; Erick J. Greenberg, "National Rally Set for Monday," *The Jewish Week of New York*, 12 April 2002; AJC, *2001 Annual Survey of American Jewish Opinion* <ajc.org>.

59. AJC, *2001 Annual Survey*.

60. *Forward*, 9 November 2001; Uzi Benziman, "Doing Well by Powell," *Ha'aretz*, 12 April 2002; AJC, *2001 Annual Survey*; Judith Apter Klinghoffer, "The Blood Libel," *History News Network* <historynewsnetwork.org>.

61. "Kingdom Come," *Forward*, 5 April 2002, quoted in Rachel Pomerance, "American Jewish Groups Bring Mostly United Message to Israel," *Jewish Telegraphic Agency*, 19 February 2002.

9: CONCLUSION: COMPETING VISIONS OF ISRAEL IN AMERICAN JEWISH IDENTITY

1. Morris J. Amitay, "The Definition of 'Pro-Israel,' " *Jewish Exponent*, 24 February 2000; Abraham Ben-Zvi, *Partnership Under Stress: The American Jewish Community and Israel* (Tel Aviv: Jaffe Center for Strategic Studies, Tel Aviv University, 1998), 42.

2. Elazar, "The Jewish People," 241.

3. "The Color of Money," *Forward*, 10 November 2000.

4. Raab, "No Split," 45–48.

5. Gedal, "American Jewish Community," 286.

Selected Bibliography

Abrams, Elliott. *Faith or Fear: How Jews Can Survive in a Christian Society.* New York: Free Press, 1997.

Alexander, Edward, ed. *With Friends Like These: The Jewish Critics of Israel.* New York: S.P.I. Books, 1993.

———. *The Jewish Wars: Reflections by One of the Belligerents.* Carbondale: Southern Illinois University Press, 1996.

American Jewish Committee. *American Jewish Attitudes Toward Israel and the Peace: A Public Opinion Survey.* New York: American Jewish Committee, 1995.

———. *The Palestinian Autonomy Agreement and Israel-PLO Recognition: A Survey of American Jewish Opinion.* New York: American Jewish Committee, 1993.

———. *1997 Annual Survey of American Jewish Opinion.* New York: American Jewish Committee, 1997.

———. *1998 Annual Survey of American Jewish Opinion.* New York: American Jewish Committee, 1998.

At the CrossRoads: Shaping Our Jewish Future. Boston and Los Angeles: Combined Jewish Philanthropy and Wilstein Institute of Jewish Policy Studies, 1995.

Auerbach, Jerold S. *Rabbis and Lawyers.* Bloomington: Indiana University Press, 1990.

———. "Are We One? American Jews and Israel." *Midstream.* 44, no. 1 (January 1998): 20–24.

———. "Are We One? Menachem Begin and the Long Shadow of 1977." In Allon Gal, ed., *Envisioning Israel: The Changing Ideals and Images of North American Jews* (335–351). Jerusalem: The Magnes Press, 1996.

Avishai, Bernard. *A New Israel: Democracy in Crisis 1973–1988: Essays.* New York: Ticknor & Fields, 1990.

Bard, Mitchell Geoffrey. *The Water's Edge and Beyond: Defining the Limits to Domestic*

Influence on United States Middle East Policy. New Brunswick, N.J.: Transaction Publishers, 1991.

Beilin, Yossi. *His Brother's Keeper: Israel and Diaspora in the Twenty-first Century.* New York: Schocken Books, 2000.

Beinart, Peter, and Hanna Rosin. "AIPAC Unpacked: The Real Story of Tom Dine." *The New Republic,* 20 and 27 September 1993, 21–23.

Ben-Eliezer, Moshe. "Political Metaphors Used by American Jews for the State of Israel." Ph.D. diss., New York University, 1981.

Bernstein Philip. *To Dwell in Unity: The Jewish Federation Movement in America, 1960–1980.* Philadelphia: Jewish Publication Society, 1983.

Bloom, Melvyn H. "Image Israel: Then and Now." *Journal of Jewish Communal Service* 75, nos. 2/3 (1999): 145–149.

Bor, Eyal. "Four Models of Relations between Israel and American Jewish Community as Defined by the Pollard Affair." Ph.D. diss., Baltimore Hebrew University, 1996.

Borowitz, Eugene B. *The Mask Jews Wear: The Self-Deception of American Jewry.* New York: Simon and Schuster, 1973.

Brettschneider, Marla. *Cornerstones of Peace: Jewish Identity and Democratic Theory.* New Brunswick, N.J.: Rutgers University Press, 1996.

Brown, Michael. "Israel and the Diaspora: An Introduction." In Michael Brown and Bernard Lightman, eds., *Creating the Jewish Future.* Walnut Creek, Calif.: AltaMira Press, 1999.

Cardin, Shoshana. "The New Agenda for Jewish Leadership." In Earl Raab, ed., *American Jews in the 21st Century: A Leadership Challenge.* Atlanta: Scholars Press, 1991.

Chafets, Ze'ev. *Members of the Tribe: On the Road in Jewish America.* New York: Bantam Books, 1988.

Chomsky, Noam. *The Fateful Triangle: The United States, Israel & the Palestinians.* Boston: South End Press, 1983.

Claude, Inis L., Jr. *National Minorities: An International Problem.* Cambridge: Harvard University Press, 1955.

Cockburn, Andrew, and Leslie Cockburn. *Dangerous Liaison: The Inside Story of the U.S. Israeli Covert Relationship.* New York: HarperCollins, 1991.

Cohen, Mark P. "American Jewish Responses to the Palestinian Uprising." *Journal of Palestine Studies* 17, no. 4 (1988): 97–104.

Cohen, Naomi W. *American Jews and the Zionist Idea.* New York: Ktav Publishing House, 1975.

Cohen, Renae. *The Palestinian Autonomy Agreement and Israel-PLO Recognition: A Survey of American Jewish Opinion.* New York: The American Jewish Committee, 1994.

Cohen, Renae, and Jennifer Golub. *The Israeli Peace Initiative and the Israel-PLO Accord: A Survey of American Jewish Opinion in 1994.* New York: The American Jewish Committee, 1995.

Cohen, Steven M. *After the Gulf War: American Jews's Attitude toward Israel: The 1989 National Survey of American Jews.* New York: American Jewish Committee, 1989.

———. *American Assimilation or Jewish Revival.* Bloomington: Indiana University Press, 1988.

———. "Israel in the Jewish Identity of American Jews: A Study in Dualities and Contrasts." In David M. Gordis and Yoav Ben-Horin, eds., *Jewish Identity in America*. Los Angeles: University of Judaism, 1991, 119–35.

———. *Ties and Tensions: The 1986 Survey of American Jewish Attitudes toward Israel and Israelis*. New York: The American Jewish Committee, 1987.

———. "Romantic Idealism to Loving Realism: The Changing Place of Israel in the Consciousness of American Jews." In William Frankel, ed., *Survey of Jewish Affairs*. Rutherford, N.J.: Fairleigh Dickinson University Press, 1985.

———. "Response." In *Diaspora-Israel Contacts: Rethinking the Partnership*. New York: World Council of Jewish Communal Services, 1988.

———. "What American Jews Believe." *Moment* (July–August 1982): 23–27.

———. "What We Think," *Moment* (January–February 1985).

———. *The 1984 National Survey of American Jews: Political and Social Outlook*. New York: The American Jewish Committee, 1984.

———. *The 1991 National Survey of American Jews*. New York: American Jewish Committee, 1991.

———, and Calvin Goldscheider. "Jews, More or Less." *Moment* (September 1984): 41–46.

———, and Charles Liebman. "Rethinking Israel/Diaspora Relations. View from Israel." *Journal of Jewish Communal Services* 74, nos. 2/3 (1998, 1999).

———, and Seymour Martin Lipset. *Attitudes toward the Arab-Israeli Conflict and the Peace Process*. Los Angeles: The Wilstein Institute of Jewish Policy Studies, University of Judaism, 1991.

"The Cohen Report: Speaking Hawkish, Feeling Dovish." *Moment* (July–August 1982): 15–22.

Cook, Chrisopher D. "The Bingo Connection." *Mother Jones* (September/October 2000): 68–73.

Cotrell, Robert. "I.F. Stone and Israel." *South Atlantic Quarterly* 80, no. 2 (1987): 159–168.

Curtiss, Richard H. *Stealth PACs: How Israel's American Lobby Seeks to Control U.S. Middle East Policy*. Washington, D.C.: American Educational Trust, 1990.

Davis, Moshe, ed. *World Jewry and the State of Israel*. New York: Arno Press, 1977.

Dershowitz, Alan M. *The Vanishing American Jew: In Search of Jewish Identity for the Next Century*. Boston: Little, Brown, 1997.

Destler, I.M., Leslie H. Gelb, and Anthony Lake. *Our Worst Enemy: The Unmaking of American Foreign Policy*. New York: Simon and Schuster, 1984.

Dumbrell, John. *The Carter Presidency: A Re-evaluation*. Manchester: Manchester University Press, 1993.

Eizenstadt, Stuart E. "Loving Israel—Warts and All." *Foreign Policy* 81 (1990–91): 87–105.

Elazar, Daniel J. *Community and Polity: The Organizational Dynamics of American Jewry*. Philadelphia: The Jewish Publication Society, 1976.

———. "The Jewish People as the Classic Diaspora: A Political Analysis." In Gabriel Sheffer, ed., *Modern Diasporas in International Politics*. New York: St. Martin's Press, 1986.

———. "New Alliances Will Form between Israel and the Diaspora." *Moment* (June 1997): 28–29.

Fein, Leonard. "Judaism as a Vocation—and not Just for Professionals." In Earl Raab, ed., *American Jews in the 21st Century: A Leadership Challenge* (39–50). Atlanta: Scholars Press, 1991.

Fenyvesi, Charles. "US Jewry's Response to the Intifada." In William Frankel, ed., *Survey of Jewish Affairs* (108–17). Oxford: Blackwell, 1989.

Feuerlicht, Roberta Strauss. *The Fate of the Jews: A People Torn between Israeli Power and Jewish Ethics.* New York: Times Books, 1983.

Findley, Paul. *They Dare to Speak Out: People and Institutions Confronting Israel's Lobby.* Chicago: Lawrence Hill, 1989.

Forman, David J. *Israel on Broadway: America Off-Broadway: Jews in the New Millennium.* Jerusalem: Gefen, 1998.

Forster, Arnold, and Benjamin R. Epstein. *The New Anti-Semitism.* New York: McGraw-Hill, 1974.

Freedman, Samuel G. *Jew vs. Jew: The Struggle for the Soul of American Jewry.* New York: Simon and Schuster, 2000.

Friedman, Robert I. *Zealots for Zion: Inside Israel's West Bank Settlement Movement.* New York: Random House, 1992.

Furman, Andrew Scott. "Israel through the Jewish-American Imagination: A Survey of Jewish-American Literature on Israel, 1948–1993." Ph.D. diss., Pennsylvania State University, 1995.

Gal, Allon, ed. *Envisioning Israel: The Changing Ideals and Images of North American Jews.* Jerusalem: The Magnes Press, 1996.

Gedal, Zoe Danon. "The American Jewish Community and U.S.–Israeli Relations: Maintaining Influence in the Face of Increasing Pluralism." Ph.D. diss., Brandeis University, 1997.

Gilboa, Eytan. *American Public Opinion toward Israel and the Arab-Israeli Conflict.* Lexington, Mass.: Lexington Books, 1987.

Gleicher, David. *Louis Brandeis Slept Here: A Slightly Cynical History of American Jews.* Hewlett, N.Y.: Gefen Publishing, 1997.

Glick, Edward, B. *The Triangular Connection: America, Israel, and American Jews.* London: George Allen & Unwin, 1982.

Golan, Matti. *With Friends Like You: What Israelis Really Think About American Jews.* Trans. Hillel Halkin. New York: Free Press, 1992.

Goldberg, David Howard. *Foreign Policy and Ethnic Interest Groups: American and Canadian Jews Lobby for Israel.* New York: Greenwood Press, 1990.

Goldberg, Jonathan J. *Jewish Power: Inside the American Jewish Establishment.* Reading, Mass.: Addison-Wesley, 1996.

Gordis, David M., and Yoav Ben-Horin, eds. *Jewish Identity in America.* Los Angeles: University of Judaism, 1991.

Green, Stephen. *Taking Sides: America's Secret Relations with a Militant Israel.* New York: William Morrow, 1984.

Grose, Peter L. *Israel in the Mind of America.* New York: Knopf, 1983.

Gruen, George. "Impact of the Intifada on American Jews and the Reaction of the American Public and of Israeli Jews." In Robert O. Freedman, ed., *The Intifada: Its Impact on Israel, the Arab World, and the Superpowers.* Miami: Florida International University Press, 1991: 220–265.

Herberg, Will. *Protestant, Catholic, Jew: An Essay in American Religious Sociology.* Garden City, N.Y.: Doubleday, 1955.

Hertzberg, Arthur. "Israel and the Diaspora: A Relationship Reexamined." *Israel Affairs* 2 (1996): 169–83.

———. *The Jews in America: Four Centuries of an Uneasy Encounter*. New York: Simon and Schuster, 1989.

———, and Aron Hirt-Manheimer. *Jews: The Essence and Character of a People*. San Francisco: Harper Collins, 1998.

Hirshman, Albert O. *Exit, Voice and Loyalty: Responses to the Decline in Firms, Organizations, and State*. Cambridge: Harvard University Press, 1970.

Howe, Russell W., and Sarah Hays Trott. *The Power Peddlers: How Lobbyists Mold America's Foreign Policy*. Garden City, N.Y.: Doubleday, 1977.

Israel and American Jews: Understanding & Misunderstanding: A Study Guide. New York: Department of Jewish Education, Hadassah, 1992.

Jervis, Robert. *Perception and Misperception in International Politics*. Princeton: Princeton University Press, 1976.

Karpin, Michael I., and Ina Friedman. *Murder in the Name of God: The Plot to Kill Yitzhak Rabin*. New York: Henry Holt and Company, 1998.

Katz, Shmuel. *Battletruth: The World and Israel*. Tel Aviv: Dvir, 1983.

Landau, David. *Piety and Power: The World of Jewish Fundamentalism*. New York: Hill & Wang, 1993.

Liebman, Charles S. *The Ambivalent American Jews: Politics, Religion, and Family in American Jewish Life*. Philadelphia: The Jewish Publication Society of America, 1983.

———. "Diaspora Influence on Israeli Policy." In Moshe Davis ed., *World Jewry and the State of Israel* (313–28). New York: Arno Press, 1977.

———, and Steven M. Cohen. *Two Worlds of Judaism: The Israeli and American Experience*. New Haven: Yale University Press, 1990.

Lipset, Seymour M., and Earl Raab. *Jews and the New American Scene*. Cambridge: Harvard University Press, 1995.

Medding, Peter Y. "Equality and the Shrinkage of Jewish Identity." In Moshe Davis, ed., *World Jewry: and the State of Israel* (119–34). New York: Arno Press, 1977.

Mittelberg, David. *The Israel Connection and American Jews*. Westport, Conn.: Praeger, 1999.

Morris, Benny. *The Birth of the Palestinian Refugee Problem, 1947–1949*. Cambridge: Cambridge University Press, 1987.

Neusner, Jacob. *Israel in America: A Too-Comfortable Exile?* Boston: Beacon Press, 1985.

Novik, Nimrod. *The United States and Israel: Domestic Determinants of a Changing U.S. Commitment*. Boulder, Colo.: Westview, 1986.

O'Brien, Lee. *American Jewish Organizations & Israel*. Washington, D.C.: Institute for Palestine Studies, 1986.

Organski, A.F.K. *The $36 Billion Bargain: Strategies and Politics in U.S. Assistance to Israel*. New York: Columbia University Press, 1990.

Perlmutter, Nathan, and Ruth Ann Perlmutter. *The Real Anti-Semitism in America*. New York: Arbor House, 1982.

Podhoretz, Norman. *Breaking Ranks: A Political Memoir*. New York: Harper & Row, 1979.

Powell, Steven S. *Covert Cadre: Inside the Institute for Policy Studies*. Ottawa, Ill.: Green Hill Publishers, 1983.

Prior, Michael. *Zionism and the State of Israel: A Moral Inquiry*. London: Routledge, 1999.

Raab, Earl, ed. *American Jews in the 21st Century: A Leadership Challenge*. Atlanta: Scholars Press, 1991.

———. "Changing American Jewish Attitudes toward Israel." *Journal of Jewish Communal Service* 75, nos. 2/3 (1998/1999): 140–145.

Rabinovich, Itamar. "Zionism and the Arab World." In Steven J. Zipperstein and Ernest S. Frerichs, eds., *Zionism, Liberalism and the Future of the Jewish State: Centennial Reflections on Zionist Scholarship and Controversy*. Providence, R.I.: The Dorot Foundation, 2000.

Rubenberg, Cheryl A. *Israel and the American National Interest*. Urbana: University of Illinois Press, 1986.

Saba, Michael P. *The Armageddon Network*. Brattleboro, Vt.: Amana Books, 1984.

Safran, Navad. *Israel: The Embattled Ally*. Cambridge: The Belknap Press, 1978.

Said, Edward W. *Orientalism*. New York: Pantheon Books, 1978.

Sarna, Jonathan D. "A Projection of America as it Ought to Be: Zionism in the Mind's Eye of American Jews." In Allon Gal, ed., *Envisioning Israel: The Changing Ideas and Images of North American Jews* (41–59). Jerusalem: The Magnes Press, 1996.

Seliktar, Ofira. "Conceptualizing Binationalism: State of Mind, Political Reality, or Legal Entity?" In Ilan Peleg and Ofira Seliktar, eds., *The Emergence of Binational Israel: The Second Republic in the Making*. Boulder, Colo.: Westview, 1989.

———. *Failing the Crystal Ball Test: The Carter Administration and the Fundamentalist Revolution in Iran*. Westport, Conn.: Praeger, 2000.

———. *New Zionism and the Foreign Policy System of Israel*. London: Croom Helm, 1986.

Shadid, Mohammed K. *The United States and the Palestinians*. New York: St. Martin's Press, 1981.

Sharot, Stephen, and Nurit Zaidman. "Israel as Symbol and as Reality: The Perception of Israel among Reconstructionist Jews in the United States." In Allon Gal, ed., *Envisioning Israel: The Changing Ideas and Images of North American Jews* (149–172). Jerusalem: The Magnes Press, 1996.

Sheffer, Gabriel. "A New Field of Study: Modern Diaspora in International Relations." In Gabriel Sheffer, ed., *Modern Diasporas in International Politics*. New York: St. Martin's Press, 1986.

Sklare, Marshall. *Jewish Identity and the Suburban Frontier*. New York: Basic Books, 1967.

———, and Benjamin B. Ringer. "A Study of Jewish Attitudes Toward the State of Israel." In Marshall Sklar, ed., *The Jews: Social Patterns of an American Group*. Glencoe, Ill.: The Free Press, 1958.

Spero, Robert. "Speaking for the Jews: Who Does the Conference of Major Jewish Organizations Really Represent?" *Present Tense* 17, no. 2 (1990): 15–27.

Starr, Joyce R. *Kissing through Glass: The Invisible Shield Between Americans and Israelis*. Chicago: Contemporary Books, 1990.

Stevens, Richard, P. *American Zionism and U.S. Foreign Policy 1942–1947*. New York: Pageant Press, 1962.

Stoessinger, John G. *Crusaders and Pragmatists: Movers of Modern American Policy*. 2nd ed. New York: W.W. Norton, 1985.

Susser, Bernard, and Charles S. Liebman. *Choosing Survival: Stategies for a Jewish Future*. New York and Oxford: Oxford University Press, 1999.

Tivnan, Edward. *The Lobby: Jewish Political Power and American Foreign Policy*. New York: Simon and Schuster, 1987.

Toll, Carolyn. "American Jews and the Middle East Dilemma." *The Progressive* (August 1979): 28–35.

Urofsky, Melvin I. *We Are One! American Jewry and Israel*. Garden City, N.Y.: Doubleday, 1978.

Viorst, Milton. *Sands of Sorrow: Israel's Journey from Independence*. New York: Harper & Row, 1987.

Vital, David. *The Future of the Jews*. Cambridge: Harvard University Press, 1990.

Wertheimer, Jack. "Jewish Organizational Life in the United States since 1945." *American Jewish Year Book*, vol. 95 (3–98). New York: American Jewish Committee, 1995.

Wiesel, Elie. *And the Sea is Never Full: Memoirs 1969–*. New York: Alfred A. Knopf, 1999.

Wisse, Ruth R. *If I Am Not for Myself: The Liberal Betrayal of the Jews*. New York: Free Press, 1992.

Woocher, Jonathan S. *Sacred Survival: The Civil Religion of American Jews*. Bloomington: Indiana University Press, 1986.

Index

About the Author

OFIRA SELIKTAR is Professor of Political Science at Gratz College and the author of *Failing the Crystal Ball Test* (Praeger, 2000).